A TIMES BARTHOLOMEW GUIDE

TURKEY

Author: **Denis Michel** and **Dominique Renou**

Translation: **Penelope Poulton**

Editor: **Lisa Davidson-Petty**

Photo credits: **A.A.A. Photo:** B. Perousse, p. 35 – **C.E.D.R.I.:** G. Sioen, pp. 27, 101, 144-145, 213, 224-225, 228 – **Diaf:** J. Hervy, p. 23; Parra-Bordas, pp. 42, 64 – **Hoa Qui:** E. Valentin, pp. 188-189 – **La Photothèque S.D.P.:** C. Ferrand, pp. 128-129 – **Pix:** M. Erhardt, pp. 120-121 – **M.-O. Renou-Conduché:** pp. 108-109 – **Sipa:** S. Rasmussen, pp. 18, 50-51, 56, 59, 72, 113, 161, 169, 172, 196-197, 240-241 – **Stock-Image:** J. Field, p. 157.

This edition published in Great Britain by
Bartholomew, Duncan Street, Edinburgh EH9 ITA.

Bartholomew is a Division of Harper Collins Publishers.

This guide is adapted from en Turquie, published by Hachette, Paris, 1989.

© Hachette, Paris, 1990. First edition.
English translation © Hachette, Paris, 1990.
Maps © Hachette, Paris, 1990.

British Library in Cataloguing Data
Michel, Denis
Turkey. – (A Times Bartholomew guide)
1. Turkey: Visitors guides
I. Title II. En Turquie. English
915.61'0438

ISBN 0-7230-0328-9

Printed in France by Aubin Imprimeur, Ligugé.

A TIMES BARTHOLOMEW GUIDE

TURKEY

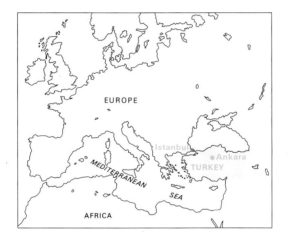

Published by Bartholomew

HOW TO USE YOUR GUIDE

• Before you leave home, read the sections 'Planning Your Trip' p. 11, 'Practical Information' p. 19, 'Turkey in the Past' p. 43 and 'Turkey Today' p. 57.

• The rest of the guide is divided into chapters discussing either **cities** (e.g., Istanbul) or **regions** (e.g., The Aegean Coast). Each of these chapters contains practical information specific to the area being discussed (accommodation, restaurants, useful information, etc.).

• There are **maps** throughout the guide. Those given for major cities (Istanbul, Ankara, etc.) should be used with the text to locate places mentioned. A **grid reference** (example: II, C3) is given for each address that is located on the map.

• At the back of the guide is a **Glossary** for helpful definitions of Turkish terms and a **Suggested Reading** list. The **Index** includes place names and monuments, and also lists practical information contained in each chapter to facilitate your search.

SYMBOLS USED

Sites, monuments, museums, points of interest
*** Exceptional
** Very interesting
* Interesting

Hotels

▲▲▲▲▲ Luxury hotel
▲▲▲▲ First-class hotel
▲▲▲ Expensive hotel
▲▲ Moderately priced hotel
▲ Inexpensive hotel

Restaurants

♦♦♦ Expensive
♦♦ Reasonable
♦ Inexpensive

MAPS

CONTENTS

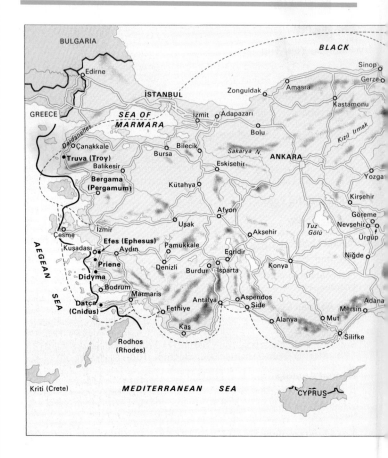

Turkey in brief

Location: Turkey is situated approximately 1984 mi/ 3200 km from London and 5580 mi/9000 km from New York. It bridges the two continents of Europe and Asia.

Neighbouring countries: Greece and Bulgaria to the north-west, the USSR to the north-east, Iran to the east and Iraq and Syria to the south-east.

Coastline: 4960 mi/8000 km, with the Black Sea to the north, the Aegean to the north-west and the Mediterranean to the south-west.

Surface area: 304,424 sq mi/780,576 sq km.

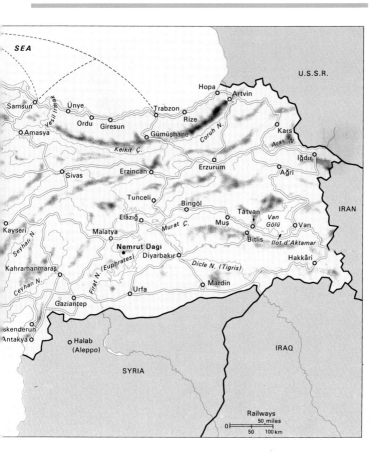

Geographical divisions: European Turkey or Rumelia – 8%, Asian Turkey or Anatolia – 92%.

Population: 52,845,000 inhabitants, with a birth rate of 2.4% per annum.

Major towns: Ankara, the administrative capital, has a population of 2,235,000. Istanbul, the cultural capital, 5,475,982.

Main religion: Islam. 99% of the Turks are Muslim, mostly Sunnite.

Official language: Turkish although some English, French and German are spoken in the larger cities.

Form of government: Secular, democratic, multiparty republic with a legislative body.

Turkey: the bridge between east and west

Officially named The Republic of Turkey, this fascinating Middle Eastern country lies partly in Asia Minor and partly in Europe. The larger area (92% of the country) is called Anatolia *(Anadolu)* and lies in Asia, while the north-west corner, Turkish Thrace *(Trakya),* lies in Europe. Because of its geographical location, Anatolia has attracted migrants and conquerors since the beginning of history. Turkey's present population includes descendants of such former conquerors as Ottomans, Hittites, Persians, Macedonians, Romans, Arabs, Cemmerians, Celts and Goths.

A rugged land, Turkey is roughly rectangular in shape, measuring about 1000 mi/1600 km from east to west and 400 mi/650 km from north to south. About half the area is covered with mountains. Two great ranges – the Taurus and the Black Sea ranges – meet in the extreme east at Mount Ararat (Turkey's highest point at 16,942 ft/5165 m) near the border of Iran and the USSR. The entire land area of the country is about five times that of Greece, while its population is larger than any of its neighbours' except the USSR.

Almost all Turks are Muslim, although there is no state religion. The only minority of notable size is the Kurdish minority, which comprises about 8% of the population.

The republic was established in 1923, by Kemal Atatürk, and since that time industry has transformed Turkey's economy from a subsistence agriculture to one in which mining and industry play important roles (see p. 60). However, agriculture still contributes about 20% to the Gross Domestic Product. The government of Turkey today owns about 47% of industry, while industrial production is divided between public and private sectors in Turkey's vigorous mixed economy.

Turkey continues to move into the modern world, but the people are rightfully proud of their rich history. During the rules of Mehmed the Conqueror and Süleyman the Magnificent, the Turkish Empire (called by the Turks themselves, The Guarded Domain of the Faith) was the most civilized and powerful on earth (see p. 49). The incredible historical treasures that remain from Turkey's illustrious past are proudly preserved.

INTRODUCTION TO TURKEY

A wonderful way to first experience Turkey is to arrive in Ankara in the early morning by train – pull back the curtains and look out over the undulating yellow steppe that fades into a landscape of modern buildings. As you leave the train station, stroll along Atatürk Boulevard, one of this capital city's most beautiful sections, amid the steel-and-glass buildings surrounded by watered lawns.

Then, continue on to the Citadel. Its centuries-old walls were tirelessly rebuilt by the Byzantines with Roman debris, including altars, stelae and stone inscriptions, and again by the various Turkish rulers who succeeded them. Inside the immense fortress walls, you'll find quiet village streets with friendly women and children in floral dresses. Some of the children are blond – testimony to a time when Turkey extended far beyond its present borders to accommodate many a now-lost land. Until the Republic of Turkey was founded in 1923, the Ottoman Empire stretched as far as Northern Africa, the Middle East and Europe, encompassing territories in the Balkans.

From the very top of the Citadel look out over the colourful clusters of small houses on the red slopes of the hill, hurriedly built to accommodate an overflow of Anatolia's rural population, mainly from the south-east. Afterward, visit the Museum of Anatolian Cultures, which takes you back over enormous stretches of time – six, seven, even eight thousand years ago, when men crowded into similar clusters of houses (which also were probably brightly coloured).

As you walk around the city, you begin to sense this country's historical continuity as well as its discontinuities: an ever-changing modern society that is firmly rooted in the past and was, in fact, one of the first places on earth settled by man.

It is impossible to understand Turkey without spending a day or two in Istanbul. This is the only city in the world that spans two continents – Europe and Asia – and the names by which it has been known throughout time – Byzantium, Constantinople and Istanbul – evoke a splendidly rich history. Along its coast, fragile wooden houses built long ago still decorate the shores of the Bosphorus. These dwellings reflect a way of life interdependent on earth and water. The simple, refined setting against the backdrop of a sea dotted with white boats lends itself to poetic contemplation. But behind the peaceful shoreline lies the noise and bustle of any Mediterranean city, which is part of the powerful charm of Istanbul.

The city is a whirlwind of impressions – dazzling Christian mosaics, sumptuous Islamic earthenware, the flowery potpourri of the spice boutiques in the Egyptian market, Topkapi treasures, and

Saint Sophia and its Ottoman counterparts. Each period of the historical architecture evokes a different feeling: compare, for instance, the Byzantine churches and Ottoman mosques. The city's architecture also meets the challenges of the site: the two bridges that span the Bosphorus are today still extremely impressive. Istanbul may be chaotic and its steep slopes disheartening, but these are inevitably softened by the extreme kindness of its people. They will surprise you by their generosity – as long as you avoid behaving or dressing in a way offensive to them. The Levantine character of Istanbul has almost entirely disappeared, but the beautiful, jostling, clamorous town is now more varied than ever.

Istanbul was Turkey's capital from the reign of Constantine the Great in 330 until that of Atatürk in 1923. Today the city has become more integrated with Anatolia, which was foreign for so long.

After Istanbul, take off to the easternmost part of the country, to the slopes of Mount Ararat, with its snowy peak that seems to float in the summer sky, and where Noah's Ark is believed to have landed. This part of the country is strongly influenced by neighbouring Caucasians: Georgians and Armenians. Nine centuries ago, through this gateway to the east and south toward the Arab and Iranian worlds, the Turks began their conquest of their present country. Whatever route you take on leaving Eastern Turkey, whether you travel toward the heart of Anatolia, which belonged to the Hittites and Seljuks, or toward the archaeological and seaside delights of the country's coasts, you'll find it paved with legends and history: the expedition of the Argonauts, the wanderings of the Amazons, the comings and goings of Assyrian merchants, the peaceful caravans along the Silk Route, the nomadic life of the Turkoman tribes, the armies of Genghis Khan's generals that were more Turk than Mongol, and the troops of Tamerlane.

In this region, the landscapes are veritable monuments. At Nemrut Daği, for instance, a Commagenean prince of Persian and Hellenic descent remodeled a mountain top for his burial site. Similarly, in order to flee from Arab invaders, the Christians in Cappadocia dug into the soft volcanic stone, called tuff, to build their incredible underground cities. They carved monasteries from eroded rock faces and covered them with intricate frescoes. Finally, along the southern coast, on the shores of the ancient kingdoms of Lycia and Caria, there are towns that are visible only from the sea. They were once humming with life but have been silently covered by sand and scrub, some for more than two thousand years and others only since the beginning of this century.

These sites are as famous as the Greek and Roman towns in the western Aegean. There are other, less famous but equally fascinating, sites such as the mountains overlooking the Dead Sea and the plateaus of ancient Phrygia. One of the very best experiences in Turkey is to be treated to the generosity of field workers during harvest time. They send their children to fetch yogurt and apricots from a hollow where they're kept cool, to share with the visitor. There are countless other pleasures: breakfast in the shade of a walnut tree, tea in a tulip-shaped glass, cherries, olives, warm bread, and exquisite Ottoman dishes. In every encounter with the Turks, you will feel the disarming kindness of a people who by tradition greet strangers as long-lost friends.

PLANNING YOUR TRIP

WHEN TO GO

The climate varies greatly according to the region.

On the **Sea of Marmara**, the **Aegean Sea**, and the **Mediterranean Sea**, the climate is typically Mediterranean with hot summers and mild winters. The best time to visit the Sea of Marmara and the north Aegean coast is from June to September. The best season for the south Aegean and Mediterranean coasts is April to October.

The climate in the **Black Sea** area is temperate with warm summers and mild wet winters. The best time to visit is from June to September.

The region of **Central and Eastern Anatolia** has a harsh continental climate with hot, dry summers and cold winters. Nights can be cool even in summer.

All in all, the most pleasant season to visit Turkey is from April to October.

Average temperatures ($^{\circ}$F/$^{\circ}$C)

	January	April	July	October
Istanbul	41/5	54/12	77/25	59/15
Izmir	45/7	59/15	81/27	64/18
Antalya	52/11	64/18	86/30	68/20
Trabzon	45/7	52/11	73/23	61/16
Ankara	36/2	46/8	68/20	57/14
Erzurum	<32/<0	39/4	68/20	48/9

Average water temperature ($^{\circ}$F/$^{\circ}$C)

	January	April	July	October
Istanbul (Sea of Marmara)	46/8	50/10	73/23	63/17
Izmir (Aegean Sea)	52/11	59/15	79/26	70/21
Antalya (Mediterranean Sea)	63/17	64/18	79/26	75/24
Trabzon (Black Sea)	50/10	50/10	75/24	66/19

GETTING THERE

By boat

There is a wide selection of car-ferries from Europe and Asia which sail to a variety of ports in Turkey.

From Cyprus

A car-ferry makes the 10-hour trip from Magosa in Cyprus to Mersin three times a week throughout the year. Between late April and September ferries leave from Mersin on Monday, Wednesday and Friday evenings and from Cyprus Tuesday, Thursday and Sunday mornings.

Two Soviet car-ferries from the **Black Sea Steamship Company,** the *Adharia* and the *Bashkyria*, take turns crossing from Cyprus (Lanarca via Piraeus to Istanbul) every 15 days from late April to late October. After stopping in Turkey they continue on to Odessa; the return trip goes on to Alexandria, Egypt.

From France (Marseille)

The **Black Sea Steamship Company** runs the *Dimitri Shostakovitch* car-ferry, which leaves Marseille every 15 days from early June to early August. It takes eight days to reach Istanbul, stopping on the way at Genoa, Naples and Piraeus. From Istanbul it continues to Odessa and Yalta. **Transtours,** 49, ave. de l'Opéra, 75002 Paris, ☎ 42 61 58 28, is the Parisian representative for the Black Sea Shipping Company.

From Greece

From Lesbos (Mytilene) to Ayvalik there's a two-hour crossing every 15 days (except on Sundays), from April 1 to September 1. From Chios (Sakiz) to Çeşme there's a daily one-hour crossing in summer, Tuesday through Sunday. From Samos (Sisam) to Kuşadasi there's a daily two-hour crossing from April 1 to October 1. A boat leaves Rhodes for Marmaris every day. The crossing takes three and a half hours.

From Italy (Venice)

The *Samsun* car-ferry, run by **Turkish Maritime Lines,** sails from Venice via Izmir to Istanbul every 15 days without stopovers, between April 4 and June 13. Then, from June 20 until the end of September, it leaves every Saturday at 9:30pm. The crossing takes three days.

Sealink British Ferries run the *Orient Express* car-ferry from Venice via Athens to Istanbul. The return journey to Venice stops in Istanbul, Kuşadasi, Patmos, Katakolon (Olympia). The Venice-Istanbul-Venice round trip takes six and a half days. There's a departure every week (from May to the end of October).

Useful addresses

Orient Express, Suite 200, Hudson's Place, Victoria Station, London SWI 1JL, ☎ (01) 928 6000; **Orient Express,** 347 Fifth Ave., New York, NY 10010, ☎ (01) 685 9690.

Turkish Maritime Lines: contact their agents, **Sunquest Holidays,** Aldine House, 9-15 Aldine St., London WI2 8AW, ☎ (01)749 9911.

For additional information about boat travel to Turkey, contact the **Turkish Culture and Tourism Office** (see p. 17).

By bus

Regular buses to Turkey leave from London, Brussels, Paris and Lyon as well as from towns in West Germany, Austria, Switzerland and Greece. From London, **National Express-Eurolines,** The Coach Travel Centre, 13 Regent St., London SWIY 4LR, ☎(01) 730 0202, runs a twice-weekly service to Munich, with connecting service to Istanbul.

By car

London-Istanbul: approximately 1860 mi/3000 km.

Leave London for Paris and then head for the south-east of France: Mâcon, Annemasse and the Mont Blanc Tunnel. Then through Italy: Milan, Venice and Trieste; through Yugoslavia: Zagreb, Belgrade and Nis. Finally, through Bulgaria (where you'll need a transit visa) via Sofia. You arrive in Turkey at Edirne, the border town, before reaching Istanbul.

If you leave from Belgium you can choose from two routes through Germany,

Austria, Hungary, and Yugoslavia: a northern itinerary: through Nuremburg, Linz, Vienna, Budapest (you need a visa for Hungary) and Belgrade – or a southern itinerary through Stuttgart, Munich, Salzburg, Ljubliana, Zagreb and Belgrade. After Belgrade you follow the itinerary suggested from London.

Useful addresses

American Automobile Association, 8111 Gatehouse Rd., Falls Church, VA 22042, ☎ (703)222 6811.

British Automobile Association, Fanum House, 5 New Coventry St., London WIV 8HT, ☎ (01)749 9911.

Bulgarian Embassy (for visa), 1621 22nd St., NW, Wash. DC 20008.

Bulgarian Legation (for visa), 186 Queen's Gate, London SW7 5HI.

By plane

Many airlines have direct links with Turkey from Europe's capitals and major airports: **THY-Turkish Airlines, Türk Hava Yollari (THY), British Airways** and **Pan American World Airways.**

These companies offer discounts on some return fares for long stays. The vacation rate, for instance, is subject to certain conditions and is applicable all year. There are also excursion rates that compete with the normal fare.

There are also special excursions for six, eight or ten days that include the flight, hotel and various tours. You should inquire at charter companies or travel agents.

From Istanbul there are flights to the international airports of Izmir and Ankara as well as to the important tourist towns in Anatolia. Turkey's national airline, THY, also runs a domestic network.

By train

From Athens

A train leaves daily for Istanbul via Thessaloniki.

From London

The Orient Express caters to wealthy passengers nostalgic for 19th-century elegance. It leaves from London twice a week with Pullman cars and arrives in Paris nine hours later. The trip from Paris to Venice (with sleeping cars)

Railway magic

The Orient Express . . . what romantic memories of past splendour are conjured up by these words! Inaugurated in 1883 to serve all the major European capitals on its route to Istanbul, it very quickly became the favourite means of transport for the rich and famous. Even today it symbolizes and epitomizes the splendour of a period known for its luxury and elegance.

The first trip began on October 4, 1883: from Paris to Istanbul in 67 hours. Several eastbound itineraries were established, some with destinations other than Istanbul – Zurich, Vienna, Warsaw, Budapest, Venice, Sofia, Belgrade – the route varied depending on the political stability of borders, and on the new tracks and tunnels that were being built to open up remote regions of Eastern Europe.

Having survived the two world wars and the Great Depression, the Orient Express buckled under the economic pressures of the latter half of the century and made its last trip in May 1977. At the end of the same year, James Sherwood, President of SEA Containers Group, in an attempt to save the legendary train, bought all 18 first-class cars and had them renovated. Great care was given to the smallest detail and the Orient Express lives again. Today the pleasure trip is possible from London or Paris to Venice, for those who can afford the fare.

takes 23 hours. It is then possible to continue the journey to Istanbul by train from Venice (see below) or by the car-and-passenger ferry, the *Orient Express,* via Athens (see page 24). Traveling this way is a pleasant but expensive way to reach Turkey.

From Munich

There are two direct *İstanbul Express* trains from Munich via Vienna and Belgrade that reach Istanbul in three days.

From Paris

Two trains a day, the *Mozart* and the *Tavern Express,* run from Paris to Munich. From there, two direct trains leave for Istanbul.

From Venice

One train a day, *The Orient Express,* leaves Venice for Istanbul via Belgrade. The journey takes three days.

Organized tours

Trips to Turkey are featured in the brochures of many travel companies. There are suggestions for every kind of vacation from the extremely organized group tour to the specially custom-made trip for the independent traveler.

For several years now, there has been a trend toward touring throughout the country rather than staying put in Istanbul or on the Aegean coast. New tourist areas are developing rapidly, such as those around the town of Antalya on the eastern Mediterranean coast, in the Cappadocia region of Central Anatolia, and in Eastern Turkey.

Contact your travel agent for further information.

▬ *ENTRY FORMALITIES*

Customs

On arrival in the country, apart from personal items, the following items may be brought in: a camera and five rolls of film as well as five blank video-cassettes; a portable radio; an amateur compass; necessary medical items; five bottles of perfume; 400 cigarettes, 50 cigars, or 1 kilo of tobacco; and five litres of liquor of which no more than three should be of the same brand.

Valuable articles should be listed in your passport which ensures that they can be taken with you when you leave.

Sharp instruments (including camping knives) or weapons are not allowed into the country without special permission.

It is strictly forbidden to possess, use, buy or sell hashish or other narcotics. Turkey enforces heavy penalties.

Antiquities in transit should be registered in your passport to avoid difficulties on departure.

Presents are allowed if they are worth no more than £150/$225 and will not be used for commercial purposes. Furthermore, presents worth no more than £100/$170 may be sent throught the post office a month before and 15 days after the following occasions: Christmas, New Year, Seker Bayrami and Kurban Bayrami.

On leaving the country, a statement or receipt from shopkeepers is required for carpets or old articles. It may sometimes be necessary to get an official certificate from a museum director stating that the article can be exported because the export of antiquities from Turkey is prohibited.

Driving and insurance

Foreign tourists may bring automobiles, minibuses, caravans (trailers), towed seacraft and motorcycles freely into Turkey once a year for a period of less than three months. These vehicles are simply registered in the owner's passport when crossing the border.

However, if you wish to drive into Turkey more than once a year or stay for more than three months, you will need a *carnet de passage* or *triptych* from the **Turkish Touring and Automobile Club** (Türk Turing ve Otomobil Kulübü, see p. 94).

Drivers need only a valid driving license from their country of origin to drive in Turkey. However, if you choose to drive through Greece, don't forget that an International Driving License is required. Ask your local automobile association for details.

For insurance, you need either an international insurance certificate, which is valid for both the Asian and European parts of Turkey, or a third-party insurance policy that you can purchase at the border. There's an insurance company at each frontier post.

Health precautions

Turkey has no vaccination requirements.

Passport

For members of the Common Market as well as for citizens of Australia, Canada, New Zealand and the United States, a visa is not required for entry into Turkey. All you need is a valid passport.

On arrival, you will be handed a receipt bearing the day's date and the Customs' stamp. Keep the paper with you because you will be asked for it on departure.

If you are planning to cross through Bulgaria, Hungary or Yugoslavia on your way to Turkey, it is advisable to check visa regulations for these countries before setting out.

Private airplanes

Visitors arriving in Turkey on private airplanes may stay for three months and should respect the International Civil Aviation regulations. Only the airports at Ankara, Antalya, Dalaman, Istanbul and Izmir have facilities for private planes.

For information, contact the **Department of Civil Aviation** of the Transport Ministry at Ankara: Ulastirma Bakanligi, Sivil Havacilik Dairesi Baskanligi, ☎ 310 9730, telex: 4220 GD-TR.

Private yachts

Foreign pleasure boats are allowed into Turkish ports and waters for a period of up to three months on presentation of the registration certificate and the title of ownership to Customs at the port of entry.

Certain ports are licensed by the Ministry of Culture and Tourism to store yachts for a period of five years.

Once in Turkish territorial waters, boats should head for the nearest of the following entry ports: Akçay, Alanya, Anamur, Antalya, Ayvalik, Bandirma, Bodrum, Çanakkale, Çeşme, Datça, Dikili, Fethiye, Finike, Güllük, Istanbul, Iskenderun, Izmir, Kas, Kemer, Kuşadasi, Marmaris, Mersin, Samsun, Tasuçu (Silifke) and Trabzon.

In these ports, information is required for the Transit Log, including details concerning the boat, owner, crew, intended route, passports, customs declarations and health clearance. The captain of any foreign yacht must, on arrival in the first port inside territorial waters, fill in the Transit Log or declaration certificate. Generally, no other formality is required until departure. On leaving, section 'V' must be filled in for Customs.

Animals

A rabies vaccination is required as well as a certificate declaring that the animal is in good health. This should be obtained 15 days before your departure.

▬ MONEY

The monetary unit in Turkey is the Turkish lira (TL). There are coins of TL5, 10, 20, 25, 50 and 100. Banknotes are as follows: TL10, 20, 50, 100, 500, 1000, 5000, and 10,000.

Currency

It is illegal to import or export Turkish currency. Foreign currency, however, is accepted in many places throughout Turkey according to the day's exchange rate. There is no black market. £1/$1.7 is worth about TL2300 (in 1990).

There is no limit to the amount of foreign currency you can bring into the country. It is advisable, however, to keep your currency exchange slips because you will be asked to show them on leaving if you wish to reconvert your Turkish money into foreign currency. They will also be needed to prove that the articles you are taking out with you were bought with money that was changed legally.

Travelers checks

Although foreign currency is widely accepted, it is a good idea to convert some of your money into travelers checks before leaving.

Credit cards

All credit cards are accepted at most international hotels and restaurants and expensive shops in major towns and popular tourist areas. Elsewhere, some cards are better known than others. Visa is the most widely accepted.

You can use cards to withdraw money from branches of the following banks: **Türkiye Is Bankasi** and **Eti Bank**. Open Mon-Fri 8:30am-12:45pm, 1:30-5pm.

Budget

Your budget will depend on your tastes, what you want to do and where you want to go. There may still be a gap between the local standard of living and that of the average tourist but it is gradually closing.

You will obviously spend more if you choose western fare over local food. A night in a hotel costs between TL14,200 (£6/$10) and TL71,300 (£31/$53). A meal in a restaurant is rarely more than TL14,200. Some hotels charge a high commission for changing money, in which case you would do better to pay directly in lira.

▬ WHAT TO TAKE

Clothes

Light, manageable clothes are best, but don't forget something warmer for the evening. For excursions and visits to archaeological sites you will need shoes with soles that grip (tennis shoes, for instance). Women should remember that shorts or revealing dresses are not recommended, especially in eastern Turkey, and that a scarf must be worn when visiting a mosque.

Luggage

There's no need to take a great deal with you. A medium-size suitcase and a smaller bag for excursions will suffice. Apart from the articles listed in the 'Health' section, you may want to bring ear plugs (in case your room overlooks a noisy street) and an eye mask (if you prefer not to be awakened by the sun).

Medicine

See 'Health Precautions' p. 28.

Small essentials

If you are going to Cappadocia or to infrequently visited areas, take a flashlight to visit poorly lit churches and an electric adapter. You will also need an English-Turkish dictionary.

Tips for photographers

If you are an avid photographer you won't be disappointed. However, film in Turkey is expensive and when you do buy it, check the expiration date. There is a wide choice of film in all large towns and tourist areas.

BEFORE YOU LEAVE: SOME USEFUL ADDRESSES

Turkish Culture and Tourism Offices

Great Britain
170-173 Piccadilly, London W1V 9DD, ☎ (01) 734 8681, 355 4207.

United States
2010 Massachusetts Ave., NW, Washington, DC 20036, ☎ (202) 429 9844, 833 8411.

Turkish embassies

Australia
60 Mugga Way, Red Hill, ACT 263, Canberra, ☎ (62) 95 02 27.

Canada
197 Wurtemburg St., Ottawa, Ontario K1N 8L9, ☎ (613) 232 1577.

Great Britain
43 Belgrave Sq., London SW1X 8PA, ☎ (01) 235 5252.

United States
1306-23 St., NW, Washington, DC 20008, ☎ (202) 387 3200.

PRACTICAL INFORMATION

ACCOMMODATION

In spite of the variety of accommodation in Turkey and the growing number of hotels, finding a place to stay in summer may be quite difficult due to the large number of visitors. The hotel industry has been developed to a greater extent in the most popular parts of the country than in the more remote areas, yet even here quite an effort has been made and you'll find modest establishments that offer basic comfort but no luxury.

Hotels, motels and vacation resorts

Some hotels are registered with the Ministry of Culture and Tourism, which means that their facilities meet certain standards and offer a guarantee of comfort and cleanliness for which they are termed 'touristic'. There are also other establishments registered with local authorities that respect standards controlling facilities and services. At the seaside resorts and tourist centres on the Mediterranean and Aegean coasts, there are a number of motels that generally have satisfactory facilities (restaurants, private beaches and automobile facilities) and there are also some large vacation resorts.

Small guesthouses

Some are very comfortable. Ask at a Tourist Information Office for a list of these guesthouses.

Youth hostels

There are very few youth hostels, given the number of inexpensive hotels and *pansiyons*. There are, however, university residence halls (Istanbul), student camps (Bursa and Çanakkale) and hostels in Ankara. Most of these places are open only in July and August.

Campgrounds

The few campgrounds registered with the Ministry of Culture and Tourism are all on major routes near towns and tourist centres. The campsites run by the **Mocamp Kervanseray** chain, modern equivalents of the old caravanserais, are very comfortable and often have restaurants and occasionally chalets with rooms. Some even have private beaches. The following is a selection of towns and sites with campgrounds: Adana, Ankara, Antalya, Aydın, Belikeşir, Bodrum, Edirne, Fethiye, Istanbul, Izmir, Marmaris, Mersin, Muğla, Ortahisar and Üçhisar.

Rooms in private houses

Rooms in family homes are very rarely rented as the Turks are traditionally extremely hospitable and would find it difficult to think of actually asking a guest to pay.

Istanbul's Grand Bazar, with 4000 shops, is easily one of the city's most fascinating places.

BUSINESS HOURS

Government offices: *Open Mon-Fri 8:30am-noon, 1:30-5:30pm.*
Banks: *Open Mon-Fri 8:30am-noon, 1:30-5pm.*
Shops: *Open Mon-Sat 9am-1pm, 2-7pm.*
Museums: Open *Tues-Sun* with some exceptions. The Topkapi Harem, for instance, is open every day except Tuesday.

Small shops often stay open later and may not close during lunch hours.

In the Aegean and Mediterranean regions of Turkey, government offices and many other establishments are closed in the afternoon during the summer months. These summer hours are set each year by the province governors.

COURTESY

Turkish hospitality is renowned for good reason, and is so much a part of everyday life that you are bound to have some experience of it. In Turkey you are never just another tourist but a *misafir*, a guest, who deserves great consideration and will be welcomed in the best possible manner even in the smallest village. The difficulty for the foreigner is knowing how to refuse what has been so kindly offered (coffee, tea, fruit) without hurting the host's feelings.

One of the things to remember is, if you are invited into a Turk's home, do not be surprised when you are presented with a bottle of cologne. It is for refreshing the face and hands. You should also take off your shoes and do whatever is asked of you by the hostess. She is very definitely the 'queen' of the house and is to be treated with the utmost respect. In the countryside, it is not considered polite for single men to engage her in conversation.

Religion

Remember to remove your shoes when visiting a mosque. In all places of prayer you are expected to be silent. If you have to speak, do so quietly, and try not to disturb others by walking near them. In most mosques women are required to cover head and shoulders. During Ramadan it is better to eat and drink in public as discreetly as possible, especially in small villages.

Photography

Be sensitive about photographing the Turks and don't insist if they refuse. Don't inflict on them what you wouldn't particularly appreciate yourself.

EMERGENCIES

Emergency Medical Help, ☎ 055. This is the only valid number for use throughout Turkey.

FESTIVALS

The 20th century may well have brought about a rupture with the long Ottoman past in Turkey but it has not wiped out ancient customs that are reverently upheld by a largely rural population. All family events, whether religious or secular, are good pretexts for dancing, feasting, and celebrating.

Calendar of fairs and festivals (by place and region)

The dates given are approximate. For further information contact the local Tourist Information Office.

January
15-16: Camel wrestling in Selçuk, near Izmir in the Aegean region.
March
21-24: Festival of 'Mesir' in Manisa in the Aegean region during the spring equinox. *Mesir macunu*, also known as 'powergum', is a sweet remedy

---

As strong as a Turk

Greased wrestling *(yağli güreş)* is a very popular traditional event in Turkey. It's a national sport for which Turkey's athletes, or *pehlivan*, have won gold medals at the Olympic Games in wrestling competitions on several occasions. The annual championships are held at Kirklareli near Edirne. According to legend, while the troops of Orhan Gazi were encamped here in 1356, Selime and Ali, two of his soldiers, died of exhaustion after a long day of wrestling with 40 competitors. The two soldiers were buried under a fig tree; a short time afterward a spring of clear water appeared which earned the site the name Kirkpinar or 'spring of the 40'.

Apart from the special technical skill of the wrestling (see Kirkpinar p. 130) – which originated in the steppes of central Asia – spectators also enjoy the chivalrous aspect of the sport and the accompanying music. This is evident throughout the different phases of the match: greeting the opponent and the appeal to Heaven before the tournament begins, gestures of submission by the loser who, at the end, kisses the hand of the winner, then bows to touch it with his forehead, and lastly when both men, arms around each other's neck, walk toward the officials for the final congratulations.

Equally interesting is the unchanging ceremony that precedes the match, including the service at the mosque, the street procession of musicians in traditional costume, the sacrifice of a bull and the arrival of the Janissary corps to the accompaniment of drums and clarinets.

Some 400 regional finalists compete at Kirkpinar, divided into different categories according to age, weight and experience. Apart from the traditional cups, medals and 'master fighter' title, the winner of each category receives household appliances donated by local merchants.

---

made with 41 different spices said to rejuvenate and restore health. On March 21 tablets of *mesir macunu* are thrown from the top of minarets.

April
15-17: Sultan Hissar Art and Culture Festival in Aydin in the Aegean region held among Greek and Roman ruins. There are international folklore events, concerts and exhibitions.

May
May-October: Sound and light shows at the Blue Mosque in Istanbul (see p. 102).
6-10: Yunus Emre Week in Eskişehir, Central Anatolia. Yunus Emre was a 13th-century mystic poet. The festival holds poetry and painting competitions.
20-26: Music and folklore festival in Silifke, near Mersin on the Turquoise coast.
21-29: International Festival of Art, Culture and Tourism in Ephesus, near Izmir, Aegean region.
25-27: Pamukkale Festival in Denizli, Aegean region.
28-30: International Marmaris Festival in Kadiköy, Istanbul.
May 30-June 2: International Fair in Bergama, near Izmir, Aegean region.

June
Sea Festival throughout the month in Çeşme, Aegean region.
June-October: *Cirit* or javelin competitions and riding events in Erzurum, Eastern Anatolia.
2-7: 'Bird Paradise Festival' in a magnificent bird sanctuary in Bandirma, Marmara region, with ballets and concerts as well as exhibitions and symposia on ornithological themes.

3-5: Cherry Festival in Tekirdağ, Thrace.

June 10-July 11: International Mediterranean Art and Culture Festival in Izmir, Aegean region.

12-15: Handicraft, folklore fair with concerts and sports events in Bursa, Marmara region.

June 21-July 15: International Music and Arts Festival in Istanbul.

24-27: Music, Folklore and Water Sports Festival in Foça, Aegean region.

26-27: Tea Festival, dances, concerts, exhibits in Rize on the Black Sea.

July

2-6: Ihlara Festival in Aksaray, Central Anatolia.

4-10: Traditional greased wrestling competition in Edirne, Thrace.

5-10: Nasreddin Hoca celebrations in Akşehir, Central Anatolia. Turkey's national caricaturist and story-teller is honoured in international competitions.

7-31: International Festival of Art and Culture in Bursa, Marmara region. Folk-dancing competitions and performances by the Karagöz shadow theatre.

7: Rose Festival in Konya, Central Anatolia.

16-31: International Folk-Dancing Festival in Samsun on the Black Sea.

19-23: Hittite Festival in Çorum, Central Anatolia.

23-29: Mount Kafkasör Bullfights in Artvin in the Black Sea region. This is an ancient tradition with popular songs and dances.

August

2-4: Festival of Gastronomy in Bolu, near Mengen in the Black Sea region.

10-14: Troy Festival, with music and dance in Çanakkale, Marmara region.

24-28: International Song and Dance Festival in Alanya on the Turquoise Coast.

September

1st week of September: Art and Culture Festival in Bodrum near Muğla, Aegean region. Concerts, art exhibitions and water sports.

1-7: International Photography Competition in Eğridir near Isparta, Southwest Anatolia.

2-5: Art and Culture Festival in Sivas, Central Anatolia. Commemoration of Atatürk's first National Congress.

8-10: Feast of Ahi Evren, patron of craftsmen in Kirşehir, Central Anatolia. Cottage industry displays.

8-11: *Cirit* or javelin competitions and riding events in Bilecik near Bursa, Marmara region.

19-22: Hazelnut Festival in Ordu, on the Black Sea. Music and exhibitions.

September 22-October 12: International Textile and Fashion Fair in Mersin, on the Turquoise Coast.

October

International Mediterranean Song Festival, throughout the month in Antalya on the Turquoise Coast.

24-27: Tourism Festival in Nevşehir, Central Anatolia.

December

4-8: St Nicholas Festival in Demre and Myra near Antalya, on the Turquoise Coast. Symposium.

12-17: Mevlâna ('our master') Festival in Konya, Central Anatolia, in honour of Celâleddin Rumi, a Sufi mystic poet who founded the order of the Whirling Dervishes in the 13th century. *Sema* ceremony, dance of the dervishes, symposium.

The traditional Turkish sport of camel wrestling, in Selçuk.

Dances

Dancing is the most popular expression of joy in Turkey. Some dances are specific to certain regions.

The Spoon Dance *(Kaşik Oyunu)* is performed in the area around Konya. Costumed men and women keep time to the rhythm with a pair of wooden spoons held in each hand.

The Sword and Shield Dance *(Kiliç Kalkan)* of Bursa is danced by men in battle dress to celebrate the Ottoman conquest of the city. The dancers themselves 'play' the music by clashing swords against shields.

The Horon Dance from the Black Sea region is a spectacular performance by men in black who leap and genuflect to a wild rhythm.

The Karsilama in Eastern Turkey is a dance in which lines of young girls and boys face each other and sing a dialogue in alternate chorus as they dance.

Karagöz

Shadow theatre, known in Turkey as *karagöz,* originated in the Ottoman Empire during the reign of Orhan, between 1326 and 1359. Legend has it that the two main protagonists, Karagöz and Hacivat, lived during this period in Bursa.

One was a mason and the other a blacksmith and they both worked on a mosque that was being built by order of the sultan. Unfortunately the two exuberant friends never stopped chattering and kept the other workers from their jobs. Attracted by their endless banter, the other workers would lay down their tools and form a circle around the two to listen. This happened every day and brought the work on the mosque to a complete standstill. When the sultan heard about this he ordered that the two culprits be put to death immediately. The deaths of the jolly fellows were all the more tragic because their lives had been spent joking and making merry. Afterward, Orhan was filled with remorse and sincerely regretted his fatal act. To console his master, Şeyh Küsteri had a large screen installed in a corner of the palace and recreated the joking conversations of the two victims for the sultan with the help of shadows.

The Dagger Dance is from Elâziğ in Eastern Turkey. A young girl sits on the edge of a drum while men try to attract her attention by performing daring acrobatic feats.

Religious festivals

The veneer of progress and westernization imposed by Atatürk has not affected the age-old tradition of religious festivals, which are as important to the Turks as secular occasions and are enjoyed just as much.

Ramazan, known as Ramadan in other Muslim countries, is more strictly observed in the country than in the city but does not interfere with the normal course of life. You will notice however that nights are livelier, as eating is permitted, and devout Muslims rise just before dawn to take some nourishment. During the 29 or 30 days of Ramazan (which takes place in the ninth month of the hegiran, the Muslim lunar calendar) Muslims may not eat, drink or smoke between sunrise and sunset but may, on the other hand, have two meals a night. Sick persons, travelers, pregnant women and young children are not expected to fast. In 1991 Ramazan begins on March 18 and ends on April 18 (March 8-April 8 in 1992).

The **Sugar Festival** or **Seker Bayrami** takes place at the end of the ninth lunar month to celebrate the end of Ramazan. Shops and offices are closed for three days of festivities that are similar to Christmas in Christian countries. Families get together and give presents. Tables are covered with delicacies and sweetmeats. According to tradition at least 40 varieties of these foods should be displayed. The second day is devoted to friends and the third to diverse entertainment: concerts, walks, and outings to the main square of any town or village where a fair is held.

The Feast of the Holy Sacrifice or **Kurban Bayrami** is celebrated ten weeks after Seker Bayrami and lasts four days (July 3-6 in 1990, June 23-26 in 1991, June 13-16 in 1992). It is held in memory of the dead but mainly commemorates the sacrifice Abraham was required to make of his son Ishmael. Flocks of sheep are driven into towns to be sacrificed in preparation for the feast. After the event their skins are laid out on terraces to dry.

On the first day of the festival a sheep is slaughtered by the head of the household. The family then gathers for a banquet after first giving some of the meat to the poor. This is in keeping with one of the five duties of Islam – giving alms to the needy. After the religious ritual the rest of the holiday is spent in the same festive spirit as for Seker Bayrami, with family outings and visits to friends and relatives.

Seasonal festivals

In addition to religious festivals there are secular celebrations in the country to honour the changing seasons. They follow ancient traditions that, as in most civilizations, recall nature's cycles and the fertility of the earth. The most popular include:

Nevruz (March 21) and **Hidirellez** (May 6), both of which celebrate the return of spring. Young girls dance farandoles, their arms festooned with flowers. Other dances are performed late into the night around huge bonfires.

Koy Katimi in late October celebrates the joining of ewes with rams.

Throughout the summer, there are harvest festivals and feasts during grape picking.

▬▬ FOOD AND DRINK

Afiyet olsum (Bon appétit!). Turkish cuisine is considered one of the best in the world. This is not surprising given the quality and variety of the ingredients and cooking techniques which preserve the natural flavors. There's a distinction between home cooking, which often requires a whole morning's preparation, and restaurant food, which is mainly *kebaps* (roast meat on a spit). Each region has its own kebap specialities and in the south-east they are especially spicy.

Turkish coffee

Turkish coffee is more than a drink, it's a ritual. When you are offered some it is impossible to refuse without offending your host. On the other hand, when a second cup is suggested, this could well be the sign that your host has something else to do and he is ready for you to leave.

It's easy to drink between 10 and 15 cups a day of this unusually thick, strong brew, although this isn't as excessive as it sounds since the cups are always tiny.

The Turks use an extremely fine grind of coffee mixed with water in a small, traditional coffee pot. Sugar is added according to taste and the pot is set on a bed of charcoal where it is allowed to boil very gently three times. If you like your coffee with a little sugar, you ask for *az şekerli* or, with no sugar, *sade*. Coffee is drunk in small sips after you've rinsed your mouth with a little water. A single cup, according to a Turkish proverb, guarantees 40 years of friendship.

Restaurants

There is a large selection of eating places in Turkey ranging from extremely smart international-type restaurants in the larger cities to the street corner where food is sold from pushcarts. You will find *locanta* or *restoran* throughout the country where you are perfectly welcome to venture into the kitchen and choose your dish if you have trouble understanding the menu. There are small snack stands *(büfes)*, or places that specialize in *kebaps* and *köfte*, others that sell delicious pita *(pide)* bread with various fillings. There are stalls for *börekci* (pastries), *işkembeci* (sweetbreads and tripe), *muhallebici* (chicken soup and milk puddings) and still other stalls for nuts and dried fruit. You'll never be at a loss to find something good to eat at a very reasonable price.

Drinks

Bottled spring water *(menba suyu)* is available everywhere. So is mineral water from Afyon. As a general rule, you should make sure that the bottle you've ordered is unopened.

There is a wide range of white *(beyaz)* and red *(kirmizi)* wines. The best known are *Doluca, Kavaklidere, Çankaya, Dikmen* and *Buzbağ*.

Apart from the *raki*, a strong alcohol distilled from grapes and flavoured with anise (see p. 89), and excellent fruit juices, there is also good quality beer *(bira)* and the traditional Turkish *aryan*, which is a refreshing tangy drink of yogurt and water whipped together.

The most common beverages are tea *(çay)* and coffee *(kahve)* drunk in tiny cups or glasses at any time of day.

Appetizers *(meze)*

One of the greatest delights in Turkey is savouring the more than 40 different types of hot and cold hors d'œuvres. Turks enjoy them while drinking *raki*, served as an aperitif or drunk with a meal. Here is a selection of the most delectable appetizers:

arnavut ciğeri	lamb's liver fried with onions
balik yumurtas	a spicy relish made with mullet roe
begyn salatasi	sheep's brain salad
börek	flaky pastry filled with white cheese, eggs, herbs or minced meat, then deep-fried
cacik	cucumber yogurt salad seasoned with garlic and olive oil
çerkes tavuğu	cold chicken in walnut sauce with garlic
çiğ köfte	spicy raw meatballs

dolma	stuffed vegetables, usually grape leaves, peppers, aubergines (eggplant) or tomatoes filled with minced meat, pine nuts and raisins
hiyar	cucumbers
lakerda	succulent slices of marinated fish
midye dolmasi	stuffed mussels
midye tavasi	Bosphorus mussels in batter, delicious with a twist of lemon
pilâki	green beans, herbs and onions lightly browned in olive oil with a little tomato
tarama	fish roe mixed into a creamy paste with garlic, olive oil and lemon juice
tchiroz	small spring mackerel, salted and dried
yaprak dolmasi	stuffed grape leaves

Soups *(çorbalar)*

düğün çorbasi	lamb or beef broth thickened with beaten egg yolks, flavoured with lemon
işkembe çorbasi	tripe soup
mercimek çorbasi	red lentil soup
yayla çorbasi	yogurt, rice and beaten egg yolks in broth

Salads *(salatalar)*

çoban salatasi	mixed salad of tomatoes, cucumbers, peppers and onions
patlican salatasi	puréed aubergines (eggplant) with olive oil and lemon juice (or yogurt)
piyaz	green-bean salad

Vegetables

Vegetables, which are nearly always served with or cooked in olive oil *(zeytinyağlilar),* are abundant: aubergines (eggplant), peppers, courgettes (zucchini), cucumbers, and beans are only a few. Plain rice *(pilav)* or rice with pine nuts, raisins and onions *(iç pilav)* are often served with vegetables.

imam bayildi	literally 'the Imam fainted'. Legend has it that an Imam or Turkish priest fainted with pleasure when presented with a dish of aubergines stuffed with onions, tomatoes and garlic in olive oil
kabak kizartmasi	fried courgettes (zucchini) served with yogurt
patlican kizartmasi	fried aubergine (eggplant) served with yogurt
zeytinyağli fasulye	green beans in tomato sauce

Fish and seafood

There is an abundant variety of good fish and seafood in Turkey. Here is a selection:

barbunya	red mullet
böcek	crayfish
dil	sole
istakoz	lobster
istiridye	oyster
kalkan	turbot
karides	shrimp
kerevit	prawn
kiliç	swordfish

An aluminium merchant displays his vast selection of wares.

levrek	sea bass
lüfer	bluefish
palamut	tunny or bonito
yengeç	crab
pisi	plaice
uskumru	mackerel

A gourmet recipe
Kalamar dolmasi (stuffed squid)

This is one of the many typically Mediterranean specialities that can be enjoyed in Turkey. Spices make this cold dish an ideal starter in any season. The squid are served on a bed of rice.

Ingredients:

14 squid (1 $\frac{1}{2}$ lbs/750 gr), one large onion, one small green pepper, one large ripe tomato, $\frac{1}{2}$ sprig of dill, 7 tablespoons of olive oil, $\frac{1}{4}$ lb/125 gr of rice, 1 c/$\frac{1}{4}$ l of water, a tsp of bicarbonate of soda, salt and pepper.

Preparation:

The evening before, cut the heads off the squid, remove the small hard part and put the heads to one side. Remove the purple membrane from the squid and then empty them, pulling out the cartilage inside. Dilute the bicarbonate of soda in a bowl with water and add the squid. They should be just covered. Soak overnight.

In a saucepan, fry the chopped onion lightly in olive oil, then add the rice and cook for 5 minutes, stirring constantly. Mix in the tomato, the chopped green pepper, salt and pepper, then pour in $\frac{1}{2}$ c/$\frac{1}{8}$ l of the water. Cover and cook until the liquid has been partly absorbed (about 7 minutes), then mix in the chopped dill. Stuff the squid with the rice mixture, sealing each one with its head.

Arrange the squid in a saucepan and add the remaining $\frac{1}{2}$ c/$\frac{1}{8}$ l of water. Cover and cook over slow heat for about 30 minutes, adding a little water if necessary. Serve cold.

Recipe by Beyhan Gence-Ünsal.

Grilled meat *(izgaralar)*

The main course in Turkey is often kebaps or meatballs of lamb, mutton or beef. Here are some dishes:

bonfile	fillet steak
döner kebap	lamb grilled on a revolving spit served with onions and tomatoes
köfte	grilled meatballs with a spicy sauce
kokoreç	barbecued tripe
kuzu dolmasi	lamb stuffed with rice pilaf
pirzola	charcoal grilled lamb chops
şiş kebap	spicy lamb and tomatoes on a skewer
şiş köfte	grilled meatballs on a skewer

Cheese

Cheeses in Turkey are few but interesting, and are made from cow's, sheep's or goat's milk:

beyaz peynir	soft white salted cheese made with sheep's milk
kaşar peynir	a mild yellow cheese
tulum peynir	strong goat's milk cheese made in a skin

Desserts *(tatlilar)*

Puddings and pastries are a delight:

baklava	flaky pastry stuffed with almond paste, walnuts or pistachio nuts in honey or syrup
dilber dudaği	'lips of the beloved'–a delicacy made with walnuts, almonds, honey and rose syrup
dondurma	ice-cream
hanim göbeği	'lady's navel'–sweet cream *(kaymak)* in batter
lokum	'Turkish delight'–cubes of jelly flavoured with flower essences and coated with powdered sugar
revani	a sort of baba cake with *kaymak* cream
sütlaç	rice pudding
tel kadayif	shredded wheat with almonds and sesame cooked in honey

Fruit

Turkish fruit is superb, varied and abundant:

erik	plum
incir	fig
karpuz	watermelon
kavun	melon
kayisi	apricot
kiraz	cherry
şeftali	peach
üzüm	grape

▬ HEALTH

Turkey is a safe country as far as health is concerned. Most doctors and dentists speak one or two foreign languages and can be recommended to you by tourist offices and hotels. There are several foreign hospitals in Istanbul (see 'Useful addresses' p. 93) and Ankara has equally good medical care.

Precautions

Because of the change of climate and food, visitors to Turkey frequently suffer from digestive difficulties. Ask your pharmacist for suitable medicine to take with you. Once there, avoid eating raw vegetables and drink bottled spring water or mineral water rather than tap water. Bottled water is available everywhere: in restaurants, bars and tourist centres. It is even sold in the street.

Protect yourself from sunstroke. Bring a hat and sunglasses, especially if you are going to the coast.

It's a good idea to bring a basic first-aid kit, which should include: aspirin, bandages, antiseptic cream, mercurochrome, vitamins B and C, treatment for stomach upsets and a cream for insect bites.

Medicines

Although most prescription medicines are available in pharmacies *(eczane)*, it is advisable to bring your own supply to save time.

LANGUAGE

The Turkish language is neither Indo-European nor Semitic, but belongs to the Ural-Altaic family of languages and is distantly related to Finnish and Hungarian. Turkish is written with Latin characters and is spoken by approximately 150 million people throughout the world.

German is becoming the best-known foreign language in Turkey, followed closely by English and then French.

For useful words and phrases, consult the section 'Useful Vocabulary' p. 246; the 'Glossary' p. 251, defines Turkish historical, religious and architectural terms.

METRIC SYSTEM AND ELECTRICITY

The metric system is used in Turkey. Some useful conversions: $15°C = 59°F$, $25°C = 77°F$, $40°C = 104°F$; 100 km = 62 mi; 1 l = approximately 1 US quart or 1.8 British pint and 1 kg = approx. 2.2 lb.

Electricity is mainly 220 volts but some places operate on 110 volts, so bring adapters for such small appliances as hair dryers or irons.

MUSEUMS

Museums are generally open Tuesday to Sunday, 10am-5pm. Admission fees vary but you can expect to pay around US 50¢ or UK 35p. Because there are exceptions, however, it is advisable to check opening times and costs before a visit. If you wish to photograph or film museums or ruins, an extra fee is charged at the entrance. You will need special permission from the General Directorate of Antiquities and Museums in Ankara if, for publication purposes, you wish to photograph or film as yet unpublished objects that are copyrighted.

ORGANIZING YOUR TIME

There is so much to see in Turkey that it is impossible to take in everything on a single visit and it is sometimes difficult to decide on an itinerary. Turkish Tourist Information Offices as well as most travel agents can help you organize your trip.

Istanbul

Istanbul has the greatest concentration of historic sites in Turkey. You need at least three days to visit its monuments and museums, but if you don't have much time, it is possible to get a general idea of the city in a day.

One-day tour

Morning: Board the boat at the Sirkeci maritime station (near Galata Bridge) and sail along the Bosphorus (Istanbul Boğazi) to Sariyer. You will pass the Dolmabahçe Palace, the Rumeli Fortress and old wooden villas along the shores.

Afternoon: Starting from Sultanahmet Square, visit the Hippodrome, Sultanahmet Mosque (the Blue Mosque), Yerebatan Sarayi, Saint Sophia and the Topkapi Palace; then in the evening go to the Grand Bazaar.

Three-day tour

Ist Day: Topkapi Museum, Saint Sophia, the Blue Mosque, the Hippodrome and the Grand Bazaar.

2nd Day: Boat trip on the Bosphorus.

3rd Day: Süleymaniye Mosque, Aqueduct of Valens, Fatih Mehmet Camii Mosque, Fethiye Camii Mosque, Kariye Museum and the Eyüp Sultan Mosque.

Mavi Yolculuk (Blue Cruise)

A seven-day cruise costs approximately TL874,000 (£380/$650) per person (1990). This sum includes the hiring of the yacht and crew, food, fuel, port fees, water and ice. These cruises run from April to October on an itinerary from Çeşme (Aegean Coast) through Kuşadasi, Bodrum, Datça, Marmaris, Fethiye, Kaş, Kemer to Antalya (Mediterranean). Blue Cruises can be organized by travel agents as well as by individual groups of 8-12 persons.

Istanbul, Central Anatolia and the Mediterranean: 12 days

Spend the first two days in Istanbul, the third in Ankara and the fourth in Konya. The fifth and sixth days could be spent visiting Cappadocia. On the seventh day go down to Mersin on the Mediterranean coast and spend the eighth and ninth days heading west toward Alanya. On the 10th day leave for Antalya via Side, Aspendos and Perge. Keep the 11th day for Antalya, returning to Istanbul on the 12th.

Aegean Coast: 15 days

Spend the first three days in Istanbul; then on the fourth take a ferry to Yalova and continue by road to Bursa. On the fifth day visit Troy, Bergama (Pergamum) and Çanakkale. Go to Izmir on the sixth and on the seventh, visit the ruins at Ephesus and Aphrodisias. The eighth days could be spent at Pamukkale and the 9th, 10th and 11th in Bodrum on the coast. Spend the 12th, 13th and 14th days in Marmaris, then return to Izmir and on to Istanbul.

Central Anatolia, Aegean and Mediterranean regions: 15 days

Leave Istanbul for Ankara on the first day, spend the second day in Konya, the third at Göreme (near Nevşehir and Ürgüp) and the fourth visiting Kaymakli and Derinkuyu before driving down to Mersin on the Mediterranean coast. Leave Mersin on the fifth day for Alanya, visiting Anamur on the way. Spend the sixth in Alanya, the seventh seeing Side, Aspendos and Perge, and the eighth in Antalya. Turn inland, going north-west to Pamukkale on the ninth day, and spend the 10th in and around Izmir visiting Pergamum and Troy. Spend the 11th day in Çanakkale, the 12th in Bursa and the last three days in Istanbul.

The Black Sea and Eastern and Central Anatolia: 19 days

On the first day, leave Istanbul by plane for Samsun on the Black Sea and then continue by road to Trabzon. Here, on the second day, visit the Sumela Monastery. Spend the third day at Erzurum, the fourth visiting the border town of Kars and then Ağri at the foot of Mount Ararat (Ağri Daği). Drive to Doğubeyazit on the fifth day to visit Işak Paşa Sarayi's palace and mosque. Spend the sixth, seventh and eighth days in and around Van, not forgetting the Island of Akdamar. On the ninth day see Diyarbakir and Mardin, on the

10th Şanliurfa. From Adiyaman on the 11th day, leave at 3pm for the excursion to Nemrut Daği (the sunset here is splendid). Visit Malatya and Kayseri on the 12th day, Göreme and environs on the 13th and 14th. Leave for Ankara by plane on the 15th day and then return to Istanbul by plane or road for the remaining four days.

PARKS

Turkey has many National Parks where you can generally camp, picnic and go for long pleasant walks. The following parks are the easiest to reach:

Uludağ, ancient Mount Olympus in the Roman province of Mysia, is 22 mi/35 km south of Bursa at a height of 6562-8202 ft/2000-2500 m. The landscape varies between mountains, forests, lakes and rivers. Walks and picnics are possible in summer, from June to September.

Kuş Cenneti (Bird Paradise) is a natural ornithological reserve on the shores of Lake Manyas, 12 mi/20 km south of Bandirma. There are about 200 different bird species and the best time to see them is between March and October.

Sipyldaği (ancient Mount Sipylus) is near Manisa on the E-23 road. The best season for the fauna, flora and hot springs is from April to November.

Dilek Yarimadasi, in the province of Aydin on the E-24, has interesting flora and fauna (you can see lynx and birds of prey) as well as a beautiful coastline (impressive beaches, bays and cliffs). The best time to visit is from April to December.

Kovada Gölü (Lake Kovada) is to the south-east of Isparta. From May to September, the lake, flora and fauna are at their best.

Düzler Cami, 19 mi/30 km west of Antalya, is the site of the ancient city of Termessos, situated in a magnificent mountain setting. Best from April to October.

Olympos-Bey Dağlari is on the coast to the south-west of Antalya. Here are the ancient sites of Phaselis and Olympos in a setting of forested mountain slopes that drop to a beautiful shore. Visit from April to December.

Köprülü Kanyon is near Beşkonak to the north-east of Antalya. In this forested canyon there is a Roman bridge near the ancient city of Selge.

Finally, certain areas have been developed by the Ministry of Agriculture and Forests so that camping is possible on the Aegean and Mediterranean coasts, mainly around Fethiye and Antalya.

POST OFFICE

Turkish post offices are easily recognizable by their yellow PTT signs. Main post offices are open Monday to Saturday 8am-midnight, Sunday 9am-7pm. Small post offices have the same opening hours as government offices (see 'Business hours' p. 20).

Postal charges for Europe vary from TL50 for a letter under .35 oz./10 gr, to TL35 for a postcard. Stamps can be bought only at post offices.

Have your general delivery letters addressed *postrestant* to the central post office, *merkez postanesi*, in the town of your choice. When collecting mail you will be required to show an identity card.

PRESS

Foreign newspapers are available in the larger towns a day after publication.

An English-language paper, the *Turkish Daily News,* reports the main world events as published by the foreign press. It is for sale in most tourist towns throughout the country.

If you are lucky enough to read Turkish, you have a choice of five dailies – *Hürriyet, Milliyet, Cumhuriyet, Güneş* and *Tercüman* – as well as two weeklies, *Nokta* and *Xeni Gündem.*

PUBLIC HOLIDAYS

Certain public holidays in the Gregorian (Western) calendar imposed by Atatürk commemorate major events that have marked the Turkish Republic.

January 1: New Year's Day.

April 23: National Independence Day, in honour of the first Grand National Assembly, which met in 1920; and also Children's Day, when school-children in uniform or regional dress parade through the streets. Some of them fill administrative posts just for the day.

May 1: Spring festival.

May 19: Youth and Sports Day, commemorating the arrival of Atatürk in Samsun, home of the Turkish War of Independence.

May 27: Commemoration of the Constitution.

August 30: Victory Day, celebrating the Turks' victory over the Greeks in 1922.

October 29: Republic Day (anniversary of the declaration of the Turkish Republic). The biggest public holiday, with military parades and processions throughout the country.

RADIO AND TELEVISION

Turkish television is run by the private company TRT (Turkish-Radio-Television). It was formed in 1967 and has developed rapidly. It began to broadcast American programs in 1970; today it produces its own series (often historical in content) and sells certain programs to other Middle-Eastern countries.

Station 1 (the oldest) broadcasts the most varied selection of programs and it is rare to see subtitled movies; most are now dubbed in Turkish. The second channel, started in 1987, mainly broadcasts musical programs. However, the evening news is given in English.

Today in Turkey, as elsewhere throughout the world, television plays an important role in daily life. Almost every household in the cities has a television set; in the villages, the cafés are a popular meeting place for an evening of television.

Turkish radio broadcasts news in English, French and German at 9am, noon, 5pm, 7pm and 10pm on several stations in the frequency range between 88MHz and 99.2MHz.

SAFETY PRECAUTIONS

Turkey's tourist boom these past few years is due in part to the peace and security that visitors enjoy there. At the moment the whole country is safe to visit, with the exception of the south-east, near the border with Iraq. If you have any difficulties, contact the nearest police station *(karakol)*.

SHOPPING

There are a thousand and one reasons for you to spend your Turkish pounds or use your credit card. There is a wide variety of items to choose from, including ancient or modern carpets, jewelry, suede or leather clothes, and local arts and crafts (pottery, ceramics, meerschaum pipes, onyx, copper-ware, fabrics and wooden items inlaid with ivory).

Although it is possible to buy all these items in most Turkish towns, remember that the farther east you go, the cheaper they become.

Useful tips

Bargaining

In Turkey a price can always be discussed but you should never begin to bargain unless you are really interested. You can certainly suggest a price that may be considered reasonable, but don't show your impatience if you want to stick firmly to your offer. Bargaining can be done in bazaars and certain tourist shops but not in luxury shops.

Antiques

Turkey forbids the export of anything that can be considered part of the country's cultural heritage such as antiquities, carpets and rugs more than a century old. Be particularly careful, and if you have any doubts ask at the local Tourist Information Office. As far as antiquities are concerned (coins, jewelry, weapons and porcelain) watch out for skillful imitations and get a statement of value from the General Directorate of Antiquities and Museums (Ankara).

Where to shop

In large towns it's advisable to go to the bazaars first in order to get an idea of prices before going into the other shopping areas. The Turkish Ministry of Tourism runs shops in Istanbul, Ankara and Izmir that offer an interesting selection of items from all over Turkey. The quality is usually good and the prices, although fixed, are moderate. See the 'Useful addresses' section for each town for additional shopping suggestions.

Addresses of shops run by the Ministry of Tourism:

Istanbul: Topkapi Museum.
Ankara: Gazi Mustafa Kemal Bulv. n° 33, Demirtepe, ☎ 29 2930; Mesrutiyet Caddesi n° 11B, Kizilay, ☎ 33 9881.
Izmir: Cumhuriyet Bulv. n° 115, Alsancak, ☎ 25 9244.

Carpets

In Turkey, there are *halis* (carpets) and *kilim* (rugs), which, as you will immediately see, are very different. A halis is fabricated on a loom, nut knotted, and has a thick pile. If you turn the *halis* over you will see whether the weave is tight by the number of knots per sq cm. The tighter the weave, the higher the quality of the carpet. *Kilims* are also made on looms, but are woven. Unlike the *halis*, they are pileless and flat, like a tapestry-woven rug, with a light, cotton-like texture.

Seven out of ten tourists come home from Turkey with a carpet! Don't forget, though, that acquiring a carpet is far more involved than just buying it. All the slow bargaining preliminaries that may seem unorthodox in your eyes are an essential part of an enjoyable negotiation. You can go into a shop and stay there for hours. You will not feel for a moment that you are bothering the shopkeeper, who will be delighted to show you a vast number of carpets and explain where they come from, how they are made and what their colours and patterns mean. Moreover, he won't forget to offer you a traditional cup of tea and will be willing to discuss different forms of payment with you.

In spite of the ritual welcome, don't be taken in by the charm of the shopkeeper. Turkish hospitality may well be renowned, but there is no reason to buy a carpet simply because you have been shown such overwhelming kindness. It is up to you to stand back and take your time before making your final decision.

If you would like to have the carpet sent home, you would do well to buy it in a large shop in Cappadocia or Istanbul. The best-quality carpets are knotted by hand and take considerable time to make. They are generally woven by women and children at home. Depending on the region and the type of carpet, the material, whether wool, pure silk, rayon or cotton, is carefully chosen. Pure silk threads are gathered from cocoons in the Bursa region whereas wool is produced from sheep reared on the plateau. The two distinct types of knot involved in carpet making are tied onto the threads of the woof that are stretched taut along the length of the loom. The strands of these knots are cut in such a way as to obtain an even, velvet-like surface. The carpet pattern is formed by the many thousands of knots tied together along the length or width. The denser the knots and the more even they are, the stronger the carpet—and the higher the price.

The different colours used indicate where the carpet or rug comes from. Traditionally, colours are extracted from vegetable dyes, but today chemical dyes are increasingly used.

The main colour in Turkish carpets is red, which symbolizes wealth and happiness. Blue is for nobility; green for paradise. Yellow and black protect against misfortune.

Where to buy carpets

You can find carpets in department stores such as the Bazaar 54 chain, mainly in Istanbul, Izmir, Antalya or Kuşadasi, or in Konya, near the Mevlăna Museum and in Ürgüp.

Leather and suede goods

They are inexpensive and of good quality. You can have a variety of clothes (coats, jackets, dresses, skirts and trousers) tailor-made in the larger towns. Sheepskin-lined coats and jackets have been popular with tourists for many years.

Jewelry

First and foremost, you will find antique shops offering silver and gold jewelry, sometimes decorated with precious stones. In general, prices are fairly high. The bazaar in Istanbul is renowned for bargains, but there are more and more stalls springing up which tend to lower the overall quality of the goods displayed. You may be better off trying the shops in the area around Taksim Square.

Copper and onyx

The choice is vast and the price range broad for copper trays, pots, braziers and samovars. The same holds true for ashtrays, coasters, vases and other objects made of onyx. Don't be afraid to ask about the colour or the veining, which obviously affect both quality and price.

Pottery

Pottery from the little town of Avanos in Cappadocia is famous and is sold throughout Turkey (see p. 191).

Ceramics

Ceramic plates, vases and jugs are patterned with traditional designs and will no doubt remind you of the beautiful mosaics in the Topkapi Palace and some of the mosques in Istanbul.

Meerschaum pipes

The name derives from the white 'seafoam' colour of the magnesium silicate stone that can be found near Eskişehir, 149 mi/240 km west of Ankara. A meerschaum pipe is certainly one of the best souvenirs for smokers to bring home from Turkey.

Narghile (water pipe)

Water pipes are bought mainly for their decorative value. It's rare to find someone actually using one back home.

▬ SPORTS

Turkey has a beautiful coastline with numerous bays and inlets that make it ideal for yachting as well as for such water sports as deep-sea diving, water skiing, wind surfing and fishing.

Deep-sea diving and harpoon fishing

Deep-sea diving with scuba equipment for sport and photography is allowed

Hand- and machine-made carpets are popular, although often expensive, purchases in Turkey.

in Turkey except in military zones and in other restricted areas determined by the Ministry of Culture and Tourism.

You can dive in the following areas:
— the entire Black Sea coast
— the Sea of Marmara, except in shipwreck zones
— the northern coast of the Straits of Dardanelles, from where they meet the Aegean Sea
— Bozcaada and the region south of Babakale
— the Bay of Izmir from Foça to the Karaburum lighthouse, except for the area around Urla
— the coastal strip between the western entrance to the port of Doğanbey and the Sisam pass
— the coast between Didim and Tekağaç and the Bay of Sisam
— in the south, the region from Bodrum to Akyarlar Kocaburun
— the port of Marmaris, the Bay of Fethiye and the region of Ölüdeniz, Yoganburnu, Fethiye, Yediburun and Kötüburun
— Kaş, Kalkan, Demre, Finike and the Bay of Antalya and its coastal strip except between latitudes 36°16′14″N and 36°32′05″N and longitudes 30°22′16″E and 30°33′58″E
— the whole coast from Antalya to Iskenderun, except between latitudes 36°47′15″N and 36°45′28″N and longitudes 31°22′33″E and 31°24′48″E, and also between latitudes 36°38′42″N and 36°35′38″N and longitudes 31°41′22″E and 31°49′04″E

Divers must have a certificate from the World Centre for Underwater Activities or a diving card from an international organization. You must also be accompanied by a qualified Turkish diver. It's advisable to get in touch with the local diving club.

A word of warning: don't dive for objects of archaeological interest.

Diving is not allowed at night.

Harpoon fishing with a speargun (catapult spring or compressed air) is allowed only if scuba equipment (oxygen tank) is not used, and it is done for sporting purposes only.

Fishing

You can fish in the sea and rivers without any special permission. Fish is abundant in Turkey: bonito, or tuna; red and grey mullet; bluefish; mackerel; and gilt-head, or dorado, as well as crayfish, crab and king-size prawns.

Hunting

You can hunt wild boar, wolves, bears and jackals all year round provided that you are on one of the expeditions organized by a Turkish travel agent authorized by the Ministry of Agriculture, Forestry and Rural Affairs. The Tourist Information Office can give you all the information you need.

Mountain climbing

You don't need any special permission unless you wish to climb Mount Ararat (Ağri Daği) – 16,942 ft/5165 m – in eastern Turkey.

Other interesting climbs are: Erciyes Dağı (12,847 ft/3916 m) near Kayseri, the Aladağlari Mountains (12,250 ft/3734 m) south-west of Niğde, Mount Süphan (14,547 ft/4434 m) near Lake Van, the Munzur Mountains (11,482 ft/3500 m), which are also in the east, and Hasandaği (10,663 ft/3250 m) near Aksaray in Cappadocia.

Skiing

The winter sports resorts in mountain ranges are easily accessible by road or by Turkish Airlines domestic flights. You can rent ski equipment at all the following resorts:

Bursa-Uludağ: The ski centre (6562-8202 ft/2000-2500 m) is 22 mi/36 km south of Bursa. You can reach it either by taking the good asphalt road or the cable car which leaves from behind the Emir Sultan Mosque and takes 30 minutes. The season for slopes at an altitude of 6561-7546 ft/2000-2300 m lasts from mid-January through the end of April.

Antalya-Saklikent: This centre is north-east of Bakirli Dağı in the Beydağı mountains, 31 mi/50 km north-east of Antalya at an altitude of 8353 ft/2546 m. The resort's main attraction is that in March and April you can both ski and take advantage of Antalya's beaches to swim, all in the same day.

Ankara-Elma Dağı: 14 mi/23 km from Ankara's noise and pollution, there's a small centre where you can relax and breathe pure fresh air.

Bolu-Köroğlu: The resort is 31 mi/50 km from Bolu (on the road to Kibrisçik) in a forested mountain area. The slopes are at a height of 6233-7218 ft/1900-2200 m.

Erzurum-Palandöken: The centre is on a good asphalt road 3.7 mi/6 km south of Erzurum at an altitude of 7218-10,170 ft/2200-3100 m. Here the slopes are long and steep with excellent snow conditions throughout the winter.

Kars-Sarikamiş: This resort is not far from Kars (where it is convenient to stay), at a height of 7382 ft/2250 m. Snow conditions are ideal from January to April.

Kayseri-Erciyes: On the Tekir Yaylasi plateau 15.5 mi/25 km south of Kayseri, there is a ski centre at an altitude of 7054 ft/2150 m right on the eastern face of Mount Erciyes. The season lasts from November to May.

Spas/thermal resorts

There are about 1000 thermal springs in Turkey. Some have been used since Roman times but most have not yet been developed. The spas are wonderfully relaxing and some, such as Pamukkale, are in exceptional settings. The most well known is in Bursa.

Bursa: Most of the historic or modern springs are in the district of Çekirge. The waters (102°-172°F/39°-78°C) contain bicarbonate, sulphate, sodium, calcium and magnesium. They are suitable for both drinking and bathing cures. They are also good for the metabolism and beneficial for rheumatic, and skin disorders.

Yalova: The thermal springs are located 7 mi/11 km south-west of Yalova and can accommodate 600-800 people. The waters (132°-140°F/56°-60°C) contain sulphate, sodium, chloride and calcium and are suitable for drinking and bathing cures. They are beneficial for rheumatic, urinary and nervous disorders.

Gönen: Located in the Provence of Balikeşir, Gönen has a treatment centre with a 150-bed capacity. The thermal waters (172°-179°C/78°-82°C) contain sulphate, chloride, sodium, hydrocarbonate and carbon dioxide. Suitable for both drinking and bathing cures, the waters are beneficial for dermatological, urinary and nervous disorders.

Çeşme: The centre is in the Bay of Ilica and Şifne (4 mi/7 km east of Çeşme), where there is accommodation of every category with a total capacity of 4000 beds. The waters (107°-131°F/42°-55°C) contain chloride, sodium, magnesium, and fluoride. Suitable for drinking and bathing cures, the waters also benefit the metabolism and help those with urinary and skin disorders.

Pamukkale and Karahayit: Located 12 mi/20 km north-west of Denizli, this centre has accommodation for 500 but still no medically supervised treatments. The waters (96°-134°F/36°-57°C) contain sulphate, hydrocarbonate, calcium, carbon dioxide and ferrous sulphate. For both drinking and bathing, they remedy heart and circulatory complaints as well as digestive, rheumatic and kidney diseases.

Hüdayi: There is a small treatment centre with a 100-bed capacity 6 mi/10 km south-west of Sandikli in Afyon Province. The waters (140°-158°F/60°-70°C) contain sulphate, hydrocarbonate, sodium, calcium, carbon dioxyde, bromide and fluoride and are good for drinking and bathing. They are beneficial for rheumatic and dermatological diseases as well as circulatory, digestive and metabolic disorders.

Herlek: This centre, 17 mi/27 km from Kütahya on the Eskişehir road, has very good treatment facilities. The waters (77°-109°F/25°-43°C) are good for drinking and bathing and have traces of hydrocarbonate, sulphate, calcium and magnesium. They help rheumatic, urinary, nervous and metabolic disorders.

Ilgin: This excellent treatment centre in the Province of Konya on the road to Afyon has only basic accommodation. The waters (107°F/42°C) contain hydrocarbonate, calcium, sodium and carbon dioxide and are beneficial for rheumatic, dermatological, urinary, circulatory and heart diseases as well as for glandular and digestive disorders.

Yachting

The best season for sailing along the Aegean and Mediterranean coasts is from May to October. After that, in winter, the winds are often gusty. For about twenty days in July and August, however, there is a north-easterly wind called the *meltem* that predominates in the sunny, cloudless afternoons, making the sea choppy.

A meteorological bulletin is broadcast every day in several foreign languages on the shortwave band from 7:30 to 8am and again at 10am, noon, 2pm and 7pm.

The ports of entry in Turkey (see page 15) remain open all year round. The best-equipped marinas are at Kuşadasi, Bodrum, Antalya, Kemer and Çeşme.

When sailing in Turkish waters, all international navigation regulations should be respected. Avoid zigzagging between Greek and Turkish waters. The Turkish courtesy flag should be flown from 8am to sunset. Furthermore, refrain from collecting any archaeological souvenirs from the water and taking them on board. The penalty can include confiscation of the yacht.

▬ *STUDENTS*

Accommodation

Students with an International Student Identity Card (ISIC) or International Youth Hostel Federation Card (IYHFC), issued by various international organizations including Inter-Rail, may benefit from reduced rates at youth hostels operated by the Ministry of Youth Affairs and Sports. You can budget approximately $2/£1.25 per person for a bed and $5/£3.15 per person for full board. Contact the Tourist Information Office for further information (see 'Useful addresses' in each town or region).

Transportation

Some organizations offer reductions to holders of the ISIC or ISTC (International Student Travel Conference) cards.

Turkish Airlines offers a 60% discount on international flights and 10% on domestic flights.

Turkish Maritime Lines offers a 15% reduction for a one-way ticket and 25% for a round-trip fare on international lines, and 50% on domestic routes.

Turkish State Railways offers a 10% discount.

Miscellaneous

Students have a 50% reduction for cinemas and concerts. Admittance to some museums and archaeological sites is free for holders of the ISIC.

▬ *TELEPHONE*

You will find telephone booths in the street or outside the post office in towns.

Local calls are made with TL40 tokens bought from the post office.

Intercity calls are requested at the post office, where you will be asked to wait until the operator can put you through. There are three different rates: ordinary *(normal)*, fast *(acele)* and urgent *(yildirim)*. There are also automatic direct-dial phones for calls between major cities and most tourist centres.

Direct dial for England: (99)44; Australia: (99)61; Canada and the United States: (99)1.

▬ *TIME*

Turkish time (for the whole country) is Greenwich Mean Time (GMT) plus 2 hours in winter, and plus 3 hours in summer. When it is 6am in London, it is 8am in Istanbul in winter and 9am in summer.

▬ *TIPPING*

Service is included on the bill in hotels and restaurants but a small tip is always appreciated (TL200 to TL500 minimum). For taxis, the Turks usually just round off the amount shown on the meter.

▬ *TOILETS* (Tuvalet)

As there are very few public conveniences in Turkey, you would do well to ask at a café, restaurant or hotel. Turkish lavatories do not supply toilet paper (instead, there is a tap for washing), so it is advisable to bring your own. However, most tourist hotels as well as large stations and airports have western-style facilities.

▬ *TOURIST INFORMATION*

There is a Tourist Information Office in each main town, run by the Ministry of

Culture and Tourism. At the end of 1989 they numbered at least 55. Very often English, German and/or French are spoken by the personnel, who are generally very welcoming and helpful. The offices are open every day in summer and can provide interpreter-guides. See the 'Useful addresses' section for each town.

TRANSPORTATION

Boat

Turkish Maritime Lines provides coastal services along the Black Sea, the Sea of Marmara, the Aegean and the Mediterranean and also give the visitor an ideal opportunity for seeing the country. All departures are from the Eminönü or Karaköy sides of the Galata Bridge in Istanbul. It is advisable to book early for cruises.

Istanbul services

Boğaziçi (Bosphorus) car ferry: Boats leave Kabataş, on the European side, and Üsküdar, on the Asian side, every 15 minutes. The crossing takes 15 minutes.

Boğaziçi tour: Boats depart from Eminönü and zigzag up the Bosphorus to Beykoz.

Princes' Islands service: From Eminönü to Büyükada (largest of the islands), the crossing takes 1 hour and 30 minutes.

Marmara car ferries

From Kartal (12 mi/20 km outside Istanbul on the Asian side) to Yalova (on the southern coast of the Sea of Marmara), ferries cross every hour from both sides and take 1 hour 40 minutes.

The Istanbul - Mundanya - Gemlik and the Istanbul - Bandirma crossings take place once a week.

Car ferries in the Dardanelles and the Aegean Sea

There is a crossing every two hours from each side between Gelibolu and Lâpseki.

The 30-minute crossing from Eceabat to Çanakkale takes place every two hours.

There is an Istanbul - Izmir - Istanbul service all year round.

Car ferries for the Black Sea and the Mediterranean

Black Sea line: These boats operate between Istanbul and Trabzon year round, departing from Istanbul every Monday at 5:30pm.

Mediterranean line: This service operates only in summer from May 27 to September 16. Its route is: Istanbul, Izmir, Datça, Marmaris, Alanya, Antalya, Fethiye, Bodrum, Kuşadasi, Izmir and Istanbul. There are departures from Istanbul every other Wednesday at 2pm.

Buses

Many private companies provide frequent day and night services between all Turkish cities. Prices vary according to the company and the route. In large towns buses leave from an *otogar* or *garajlar* (bus station). In smaller towns, they leave from the town centre.

Bus travel is the most reliable and the cheapest means of transport in Turkey.

Cars

The 31,000 mi/50,000 km of asphalt highways are well maintained and easy to drive on. The other roads, with a gravel surface, are not always in good condition. The Bosphorus crossing into the Middle East is now swift and easy thanks to the Istanbul bypass and toll bridge leading to the Istanbul-Izmit express road. The three major roads crossing Turkey are those into Syria, Lebanon and Jordan (E5), Iraq (E24) and Iran (E23). Drive with caution – Turkish drivers tend to ignore speed limits and traffic regulations.

Car rental

There are car rental agencies in Ankara, Istanbul and all major tourist towns (Antalya, Kuşadasi, Marmaris, etc.). Information is available at Tourist Information Offices. Renting a chauffeur-driven car is expensive in Turkey.

Road maps

Road maps are provided free of charge by Tourist Information Offices but are not always up-to-date. It is always best to check with them or inquire at a travel agency before venturing off main roads.

Road signs conform to international protocol. Historical and archaeological sites are indicated by yellow signposts, although often at the last minute. Some common road signs include:

Yavas:	Slow
Dur:	Stop
Tamirat:	Roadworks
Paric Yapilmaz:	No Parking
Sehir Merkesi:	Town Centre

Traffic

You drive on the right in Turkey, and Turkish driving laws are similar to those of European countries. Traffic moves freely outside cities with the exception of the Istanbul-Ankara highway, where traffic is heavy. Drive cautiously at all times. There is a 30 mph/50 kph speed limit in urban centres and a 55 mph/90 kph limit elsewhere. Although there tends to be less tooting of horns in Turkey, there are still many cars without rear lights or signals.

Gasoline

Gas is cheaper than in Europe: Regular: TL380; Super: TL400 and Diesel: TL300 per litre (as of 1990). Filling stations are frequent on main roads and are usually open day and night. Drivers have a choice of gasoline: Petrol Ofisi, Türkpetrol, BP, Mobil and Shell. Super can be bought throughout the country except in some remote areas, mainly in the east.

Repairs

In the west, there are numerous repair garages along main roads and in towns, grouped along special streets.They are often well-equipped and staffed by experienced Turkish mechanics. Larger towns have official agents for foreign cars.

In case of accident

Regardless of whether anyone is hurt or not, you must make a police report.

If you have an assistance card from the Association of International Tourism (AIT) or from the Federation of International Automobilists (FIA), the Touring and Automobile Club of Turkey (TTOK, or Türkiye Turing ve Otomobil Kulübü) will help you if you have an accident or break down. They can also arrange for your car to be sent home.

If you have to leave the vehicle in Turkey, temporarily or permanently, it must be left at a customs office where the listing of your vehicle in your passport will be cancelled. This is essential to enable you to leave the country freely.

If your car is stolen, you will need to show a police statement when leaving the country.

Road rescue services (between Edirne and Ankara on the E80):

Edirne, ☎ 1170/5240
Babaeski, 35 mi/57 km east of Edirne, ☎ 1140
Corlu, 46 mi/75 km east of Babaeski, ☎ 35 3351
Silivri, 26 mi/42 km east of Corlu, ☎ 2582
Büyükçekmece, 25 mi/40 km east of Silivri, ☎ 579 2160
Istanbul, 29 mi/47 km east of Büyükçekmece, ☎ 353 8537
Izmit, 69 mi/111 m east of Istanbul, ☎ 2330
Sakarya, 28 mi/46 km east of Izmit, ☎ 1394
Boludaği, 57 mi/92 km east of Sakarya, ☎ 1154/1244

Esentepe, 43 mi/70 km east of Boludaği, ☎ 1154/1372
Çamlidere, 17 mi/28 km east of Esentepe
Pinar, 25 mi/41 km south of Çamlidere
Ankara, ☎ 345 7151/52

Hitch-hiking

Hitching is not really advisable in Turkey. There are more efficient and other inexpensive means of transport.

Plane

THY (Turkish Airlines) runs a network of domestic flights from Istanbul, Ankara and Izmir to major towns: Adana, Dalaman near Bodrum, Diyarbakir, Elâziğ, Erzurum, Gaziantep, Kayseri, Malatya, Samsun, Trabzon and Van.

Compared to the rest of Europe, domestic flights are reasonably cheap. THY provides a bus service from the airport to the town centre.

Certain discounts are offered for flights: 5% on round-trip tickets, 10% for married couples with or without children, 50% for sports groups of five or more, 90% for children under two years old and 50% for children between 2 and 12 years old.

For further information, on arrival in Turkey ask at the THY offices in Ankara, Istanbul or Izmir (see the 'Useful addresses' section under each town).

Taxis and dolmuş

Taxis are numerous in all Turkish cities and are recognizable by their black and yellow checkered bands. They usually have a meter, but you should always ask the driver for the official price and agree on an amount before setting out.

The *dolmuş* (which may have a yellow band) is a collective taxi that follows specific routes. Each passenger pays according to the distance traveled and can get off wherever he likes. The relatively cheap fares are determined by the municipality. The *dolmuş* provides services within large cities, to suburbs, to the airport and often to neighbouring towns. It is a very practical means of transport and much cheaper than a taxi.

Train

The **Turkish State Railways (TCDD)** network connects most major towns. The trains have first- or second-class service for sleeping cars and restaurant cars. Prices vary according to the distance and the category of wagon. Students have a discount on round trip fares.

Traveling by train in Turkey gives you an ideal opportunity to see the beautiful landscapes and is reliable – but very slow. If there's a choice between train or bus, take the bus.

In Istanbul, the station you use for Europe is Sirkeci near the Galata Bridge and that for the Middle East is Haydarpaşa. There is a ferry link between the two stations.

TURKEY IN THE PAST

A natolia, migratory corridor and crossroads of two continents,
has been inhabited since the dawn of mankind.

EARLY TRACES

Stone implements and various household objects were found
in the Karain Cave, near Antalya, together with human skeleton
remains that date from early Palaeolithic times (20,000 BC).

Near Konya, at Catal Höyük, archaeologists excavated a
Neolithic site considered to be the first known urban settlement,
which revealed artifacts dating from 6500-5500 BC: weapons,
tools and statuettes of a fertility goddess.

On the site at Hacilar, jar-shaped tombs were excavated that
contained weapons, ornaments and pottery from the Chalcolithic
period (5500-3500 BC).

Bronze Age (2600-1900 BC) articles – figurines, bronze and
silver sun discs – were found in Anatolia, mainly in royal tombs
from Alaça Höyük and Horoztepe. Thanks to thousands of
cuneiform tablets found in ancient commercial centres set up by
Assyrian merchants, mainly in Kanesh (today's Kültepe), we know
that Hatti peoples (or Proto-Hittites) lived in Anatolia at the
beginning of the second millennium BC.

THE HITTITES

As early as 1600 BC, Central Anatolia was overrun by a people
from the Caucasus Mountains who spoke an Indo-European
language. They were the Hittites, led by Labarnas, whose power
soon spread through a network of city-states. During the next
century his successors fortified and expanded the empire. At the
beginning of the 15th century BC, King Telipinus built his capital
at Hattuşaş, present-day Boğazkale, to the north-east of Ankara.
Toward the end of the century, however, invaders from Asia
brought the first period of Hittite domination to an end.

Ruins of the Greek theatre in Side.

A second kingdom was established through the brilliant expeditions of its king, Suppiluliumas I (1375-1335 BC), who restored Hittite sovereignty throughout Anatolia. The Hittites prospered and developed a rich culture. Hattuşaş was surrounded by strong walls and a temple was built in the lower court. It housed an impressive library of cuneiform tablets containing valuable information on religious practices of the time.

In about 1286 BC, in the famous battle of Kadesh (in which control of Phoenicia was at stake), the Hittite troops of King Muwatallis opposed those of Ramses II. Though outwitted, Ramses II refused to admit defeat. However, the Hittite victory ensured total superiority for the Anatolians throughout the Syrian states.

The empire crumbled in 1200 BC with the arrival of the Phrygians or 'Sea Peoples', who attacked fortresses and destroyed Hattuşaş. The Hittites who managed to escape took refuge in mountains to the south and south-east of Anatolia. The Phrygians ruled the vast plains of Western Anatolia from the towns of Gordium (Yassi Höyük) and Midas until they too were overcome by Cimmerians from the Ukraine.

THE URARTIANS

Another kingdom was established around the year 1000 BC in the mountains of Eastern Anatolia and on the shores of Lake Van. It was founded by the Urartians, an Asian people whose influence in the area grew as Hittite influence declined. The Urartians built their fortresses and palaces on mountaintops and dedicated temples to their god, Haldi.

In the ninth and eighth centuries BC they controlled the north of Syria, Mesopotamia and almost the whole of Anatolia. They were then at the height of their power but were to disappear a century later at the hands of the Assyrians under Sargon II. Their major sites are at Altintepe, Cuvustepe and Toprakkale.

THE HELLENISTIC PERIOD

In the 11th century BC, the Greeks controlled the western coast of Anatolia with Aeolians in the north, Ionians in the centre and Dorians in the south. Further inland was a powerful domain called Lydia, which ruled over its colonies from Sardis, the capital. A series of powerful Lydian kings – Gyges, Alyattes and especially Croesus (who standardized the shape and weight of coins) – strengthened their kingdom politically and encouraged expansion. But in 546 BC, King Croesus was defeated and captured by Cyrus the Great, King of Persia, who took control of the whole of western Asia.

Greek towns in Asia revolted against the Persian tyrant but to no avail. They were mercilessly suppressed. It wasn't until Alexander the Great that the Persians were overthrown (in 334 BC) and all of Asia Minor was reconquered. The Hellenistic age had begun.

TURKEY AT THE START OF CHRISTENDOM

Ancient name	Modern name	Ancient name	Modern name
1 Ancyra	Ankara	14 Laodikeia	Eskihisar
2 Antiocha Pisidiae	Yalvac	15 Lystra	
3 Antioch	Anta'kya	16 Miletus	Balat
4 Broussa	Bursa	17 Neapolis	Kuçadasi
5 Caesarea	Kayseri	18 Nicaea	Iznik
6 Chalcedon	Kadiköy	19 Patara	Gelemis
7 Cnidus	Datça/Knido	20 Pergamum	Bargama
8 Colossae	Hönaz	21 Perge	Murtuna
9 Didyma	Didim	22 Philadelphia	Alesehir
10 Ephesus	Efes	23 Sardis	Sart
11 Hierapolis	Pamukkale	24 Smyrna	Izmir
12 Iconium	Konya	25 Tarsus	Tarsus
13 Byzantium	Istanbul	26 Thyatira	Akhisar
13 Constantinople	Istanbul	27 Troy	Truva

In twelve years Alexander managed to conquer an empire that stretched from his homeland, Macedonia, to India. Although at the time of his death in 323 BC this immense territory was divided between quarreling generals, the Greeks had had time to leave their mark on it: they had imposed their language, which became the medium for culture, business and government.

Meanwhile two powers were preparing to fight for the territory: a growing power from the west, that of the Roman conquerors, and another from Syria, whose Seleucid kings had set themselves up in Anatolia.

THE ROMAN EMPIRE

At the battle of Magnesia (Manisa) near Izmir, in 190 BC,

Roman legions defeated the king of Seleucia, Antiochos III, and thus took control of Anatolia. This victory marked the beginning of three centuries of Roman rule. In 129 BC, the Romans established the Province of Asia, with Ephesus as its capital.

For two centuries, from 31 BC to AD 180, the country enjoyed a peaceful period of stability known as the Pax Romana. The Roman Empire was at its height and the Anatolian provinces prospered accordingly. Christianity emerged and St Paul traveled throughout Anatolia, spreading the gospel and founding communities that are mentioned in the Bible, such as the seven churches of Asia Minor: Ephesus, Laodicea, Pergamum, Philadelphia, Sardis, Smyrna and Thyatira.

By AD 250, Roman rule had grown insecure: Christianity was gaining strength and Emperor Decius responded by decreeing a general persecution of Christians; the Goths attacked the Aegean cities and invaded Anatolia; and the Persian Empire threatened from the East. Emperor Diocletian (AD 284-305) managed to help restore the empire to some degree but maintained the persecution. It was his successor, Constantine, who truly united the empire; he declared equal rights for worshippers of all religions, called the first Ecumenical Council and set about building his magnificent new capital city – New Rome (later known as Constantinople) – in Hellenic Byzantium. In AD 313 Constantine declared Christianity legal throughout the empire and was himself converted to the religion, on his deathbed, in AD 337.

THE BYZANTINES

New Rome (Constantinople) was expanded, fortified and enriched by a succession of rulers. After the fall of Rome in AD 476, the eastern half of the empire (renamed the Byzantine Empire by 18th-century historians) remained powerful for another thousand years. Christian subjects were even called *Rumi* (Romans) up until the dissolution of the Turkish Empire.

Emperor Justinian (AD 527-65) brought the Byzantine Empire to its greatest glory. Under his rule, Constantinople grew in wealth and strength; the superb Saint Sophia (the Church of the Holy Wisdom) was constructed; Italy, the Balkans, Egypt and North Africa were all reconquered.

Sultans and caliphs

Sultan: In Arabic, *sultan* means an authority, or domain. The word was originally used in a moral or spiritual sense, but later came to express political or governmental power. Beginning in the 11th century Muslim sovereigns began to use it as a title. Under the Seljuks of Anatolia and Iran, the title became normal practice and was frequently bestowed on sovereigns by the *caliph*. Eventually it was adopted by princes throughout the Islamic world.

Caliph: The title given to the iman, the titular head of the Muslim community, caliph was first used after the death of Mohammed in 632. It was used by heads of the Umayyad and Abbasid dynasties and also by the Ottoman sultans; as such, it meant 'supreme leader'. The title was abolished by the Turkish Republic.

Justinian's successors did not manage to maintain his spirit of successful conquest, however, and the 'jewel of the Christian world' (Constantinople) was invaded many times over the following centuries. Having held out against a series of enemies, the city was sacked and pillaged by fellow Christians in 1204, during the Fourth Crusade. The Byzantine army regained control, however, resisting further invasions by the Turks, until the middle of the 15th century. (See p. 78.)

THE MUSLIMS

Mohammed was born in Mecca five years after the death of Justinian. He was later forced to flee (his celebrated *hejira,* or flight) by those who objected to his preaching, and he organized a religious commonwealth in Medina. In 10 short years this group had grown strong enough to conquer Mecca (624-30). And before Mohammed's death two years later, militant Muslims had begun to conquer other Arab tribes as well – including Persians and Egyptians. In 669-78 they attacked Constantinople.

Mohammed's rule was succeeded by *caliphs* – deputies responsible for maintaining the welfare of the Muslim community. His friends and son-in-law were succeeded in this role by the Umayyads (661-750), whose empire was in Damascus, and by the Abbasids (750-1100) of Baghdad. Both these dynasties continually challenged and weakened the power of Byzantium.

THE SELJUKS

Toward the end of the 10th century, Seljuk, leader of a nomadic tribe from the steppes of Central Asia, adopted Islam. His grandson, Toghrol-Beg, led the Seljuk Turks on what was to become an incredible invasion of Mesopotamia in the early 11th century. They captured the Caliphate of Baghdad and continued their advance. Toghril-Beg was succeeded by his nephew, Alp Arslan, who took control of the whole area between the Caspian Sea, the Taurus Mountains and the Black Sea. Still heading west, the Seljuks had their first decisive victory against the Byzantine army in 1071 at Manzikert, where they took the Byzantine emperor prisoner. At the end of the 11th century, they controlled most of Anatolia and reached the shores of the Bosphorus without actually crossing into Constantinople. Instead, they modified their nomadic life-style to settle in Central Anatolia and made Konya their capital, thus becoming the first Turkish state to rule Anatolia. Their territories included modern Turkey, Iran and Iraq. The Seljuk Sultanate of Rum (Roman Asia), based in Anatolia, produced great artists and thinkers, including Celaleddin Rumi, or Mevlana, founder of the Whirling Dervish order (see p. 202).

But the Great Seljuk Turkish Empire was short-lived. It declined in the middle of the 13th century, weakened by internal quarrels among the various generals and overrun in 1243 by Genghis Khan's Mongol hordes.

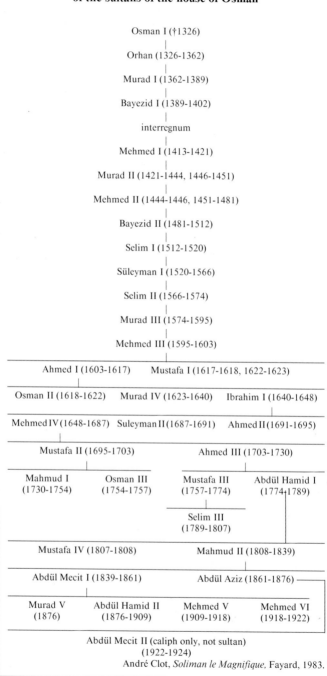

Genealogy
of the sultans of the house of Osman

Osman I (†1326)

Orhan (1326-1362)

Murad I (1362-1389)

Bayezid I (1389-1402)

interregnum

Mehmed I (1413-1421)

Murad II (1421-1444, 1446-1451)

Mehmed II (1444-1446, 1451-1481)

Bayezid II (1481-1512)

Selim I (1512-1520)

Süleyman I (1520-1566)

Selim II (1566-1574)

Murad III (1574-1595)

Mehmed III (1595-1603)

Ahmed I (1603-1617)   Mustafa I (1617-1618, 1622-1623)

Osman II (1618-1622)   Murad IV (1623-1640)   Ibrahim I (1640-1648)

Mehmed IV (1648-1687)   Suleyman II (1687-1691)   Ahmed II (1691-1695)

Mustafa II (1695-1703)   Ahmed III (1703-1730)

| Mahmud I (1730-1754) | Osman III (1754-1757) | Mustafa III (1757-1774) | Abdül Hamid I (1774-1789) |

Selim III
(1789-1807)

Mustafa IV (1807-1808)   Mahmud II (1808-1839)

Abdül Mecit I (1839-1861)   Abdül Aziz (1861-1876)

| Murad V (1876) | Abdül Hamid II (1876-1909) | Mehmed V (1909-1918) | Mehmed VI (1918-1922) |

Abdül Mecit II (caliph only, not sultan)
(1922-1924)

André Clot, *Soliman le Magnifique,* Fayard, 1983.

THE OTTOMAN EMPIRE

In the 1200s another Turkish tribe was engaged in local combat on the Anatolian peninsula. This time it was led by a young Turk named Osman who, at the end of the 13th century, freed his people from Seljuk rule by defeating Alaëddin Keykubad II. In about 1288, he founded a principality which grew into the Ottoman *(Osmanli)* empire.

Osman's son (Orhan) and later his grandson (Süleyman) continued the conquest by first taking Bursa (which they made their capital), Nicaea and Nicomedia and then Gallipoli, the first 'European' territory. A later victory by Sultan Murad I against Christian armies allowed Turkey to spread further west. In 1362 the capital was moved from Bursa to Adrianople (today's Edirne), as the latter was a better site from which to control their Balkan territories. Constantinople was still ruled by the Byzantines. Murad's son Bejazit conquered Serbia, laid siege to Constantinople without success, invaded Bulgaria, and at Nicopolis in 1396 defeated a European alliance led by Sigismund, King of Hungary. By 1452, the Ottomans were strong enough to consider attacking Constantinople. Under the leadership of Mehmed the Conqueror, the Ottomans took the capital of Christendom in 1453. The reign of Mehmed (1451-81) initiated the outstanding period of Ottoman dominion.

THE FALL OF CONSTANTINOPLE

Having pushed back the Byzantine Empire to the shores of the Bosphorus, the Ottomans prepared for the coup de grâce. At the end of 1452 the new sultan, Mehmed II, built a fortress on the

---

The all-powerful Grand Vizir

When the empire was at its height, up to the end of the 16th century (1574), even the poorest child could aspire to the highest and most respected post in the land, that of Grand Vizir.

The Grand Vizir (or *sadrazam*), can be compared to a prime minister of today. He held the imperial seal of the sultan (who alone represented the Ottoman Empire) and had full authority to command the army, run the administration and enforce law and order. Other vizirs, the 'Vizirs of the Divan' (or *vezirazam*), whose titles corresponded to the number of horse tails (one, two, or three) that were conferred upon them, assisted the Grand Vizir, although only he was entirely responsible for the government.

In the 14th century, recruiters bought or kidnapped children from the western territories of the empire (Serbia, Greece, Bulgaria, Albania, Russia) and brought them from the Balkans to Istanbul. Although almost all of them were Christians, the most gifted of these children, called *içoğlan,* were educated according to Islamic and Ottoman tradition. They were sent to a special school in the sultan's palace where they began the *enderun,* the intellectual training to become vizirs. Those who were not eligible for the *enderun* were sent to the Janissaries or became *sipahi* (horsemen). In this way, Ottoman society recruited its leaders solely on merit without any ethnic, social or religious discrimination. For more than a century, from 1453 to 1574, 23 out of 25 vizirs were originally Christians.

Necmi Gürmen

Completed in 1548, Saint Sophia was the greatest church in Christendom for close to 1000 years.

European side of the straits. Byzantium knew that a siege was coming but the empire was weak and drained, Christianity indifferent and the Ottomans all-powerful.

On April 5, 1453, the Turkish army set up at the gates for a siege that lasted until May 29. At dawn that day the sultan's Janissary (Yeni-Ceri) troops attacked the ramparts for the last time. Resistance weakened, the gates opened and Turkish soldiers invaded the city. That very evening Constantinople fell and with it the last Byzantine emperor, Constantine XI, sword in hand. Mehmed II paraded triumphantly through the streets to Saint Sophia which was transformed into a mosque under his orders. He became known as Fatih (the Conqueror) and made Constantinople his capital. The name was later changed to Istanbul.

Mehmed II continued a policy of expansion until his empire (apart from Anatolia) included the southern Balkans and most of Greece. His troops were driven back however, from Rhodes, where a Christian fortress was guarded by the crusaders of St John of Jerusalem. His reign ended on his death in 1481.

THE GOLDEN AGE OF THE OTTOMAN EMPIRE

One of Mehmed II's successors was Selim I, known as 'The Cruel', who considered himself first and foremost a soldier of God. He quashed the Persians at Azerbaijan and launched an Egyptian campaign that brought him to Cairo in 1517. It was here that he appointed himself caliph and took the title Commander of Believers.

Under his successor, Süleyman the Magnificent, the empire reached the height of its glory, from 1520 to 1566. Süleyman took the title of Emperor *(padisha)* and, though he wasn't a born warlord, he fought in Asia and in Europe, expanding the Ottoman Empire until it extended from the gates of Vienna to the Red Sea and from the Persian Gulf to Algeria. The Ottoman fleet appeared invincible. He also instigated legal reforms – so much so that his people called him 'The Lawgiver'. He rebuilt Jerusalem and beautified Istanbul, building splendid mosques with the help of his famous architect, Sinan. His Süleymaniye mosque is the largest and one of the most beautiful in the city.

TURKEY'S DECLINE

The decline of Turkey had set in by 1585 – almost immediately after the rule of Süleyman, credited to the fact that neither his eldest son, Selim II, not Murad III, who reigned later, had acquired his genius. In terms not only of scientific and social progress, but also of military might, the country was slowing down and beginning to stagnate.

Turkey suffered its worst naval defeat at Lepanto in 1571, in a struggle against a new European coalition formed by Pope Pius V. For about another century there were minor victories, but the general trend was toward the relinquishing of former territories.

By the end of the 18th century, Austria and Russia had pushed the Turkish frontiers in Europe back to the Danube River and had seized their lands on the northern Black Sea coasts.

Despite attempts to introduce reforms that would bridge the gap between Turkey and the West, the sultans' power continued to dwindle. Internal crises increased, often of a religious or ethnic origin. Misrule bred internal revolt, and in 1830, the Greeks gained their independence. Serbs, Bulgarians, Romanians, Albanians and Arabs all sought their independence soon after. The empire was breaking up and the European powers waited eagerly to annex the pieces.

The Russian emperors pressured the Turks to grant them religious power over all Ottoman Orthodox subjects, resulting in the Crimean War (1853-56). Supported by the British and the French, the Turks took a firm stand against the Russians, who occupied the Danubian principalities on the Russo-Turkish border in July of 1853. By March 1854, the French and British had also declared war on Russia. In 1856, with Austria's threat to join the allies, Russia finally accepted preliminary peace terms.

The situation worsened with nationalist insurrections in Crete, Armenia, Bulgaria and Macedonia.

In 1908, the Young Turk Revolution, led by a group of Europeanized intellectuals, tried to revitalize the empire. Supported by the army, they deposed Abdul Hamid – the last strong sultan – and demanded a new constitution (1908) and the summoning of a national parliament.

Although still officially a sultanate, in its final years the Ottoman Empire was ruled by three members of the Young Turks' Committee of Union and Progress: Talat, Enver and Jamal. They were energetic, but misguided, and when World War I started, they chose to side with the Germans and the Central Powers. The Central Powers were defeated and with them, the Ottoman Empire. After the war, Turkey lost its Arab provinces and part of Asia Minor.

In 1923, Mustafa Kemal (Kemal Atatürk) created the Republic of Turkey and obtained the abolition of the sultanate. Under his presidency (1923-38) the Turkish Republic fostered Turkish nationalism and secularism and imposed a firm control over the country's economy. Turkey, under the direction of its great reformer Kemal, began its journey into the industrialized 20th century.

MUSTAFA KEMAL: FATHER OF MODERN TURKEY

Mustafa Kemal was born in Salonika to a family of modest means in 1881. His father was a government clerk and his mother a robust and religious countrywoman.

As a child he was reserved and silent, but he had tremendous vitality and very little taste for school. He decided early on that he wanted a military career and at 15 entered the cadet school in Salonika. There he demonstrated a gift for foreign languages and proved especially competent in mathematics, which earned him the name Kemal (excellence).

At 17, he was sent to the military school at Monastir, where he was noted for his brilliance and his revolutionary ideas. He studied Voltaire, Montesquieu and Rousseau while the writings of Hobbes and John Stuart Mill gave him a background in political economy. When he was 21 he moved to Constantinople where he studied at the War Academy and refined his principles on the country's badly needed reform: the sultanate should be abolished; the legal system should be freed from the restrictions of Islam; Turkey should free itself from foreign supervision. He shared his ideals with other young officers he met in the capital. With them he joined secret societies that were hostile to foreign interference and the sultanate. He was arrested during one of these meetings and spent several weeks in prison.

In 1907, he was back in Salonica, where his ideas were favourably received as the town had become an active centre of political agitation.

Aware of the demands made by young army officers, Sultan Abdül Hamid tried to champion the cause for reform by instituting the 'Young Turk' government. But Mustafa Kemal, because of his extreme views, was held at a distance.

In 1909, Abdül Hamid was succeeded by his ineffectual brother, Mehmed V. A former military companion to Mustafa Kemal and member of the Young Turks, Enver, was named head of state, but he was unable to stop the country's decline. Turkey's size and power continued to shrink. In 1914, the country was ruled by a triumvirate (Enver and two other Young Turks) who signed a treaty of alliance with Germany on August 2, thus bringing Turkey into World War I.

In 1915, during the Gallipoli Campaign, Mustafa Kemal staged a militarily brilliant defense of the Dardanelles. The Allies were driven back, their expedition a failure. Meanwhile the Russian offensive in eastern Anatolia during the winter of 1914-15 was largely supported by Armenians who suffered terrible repression during the Turkish counterattack in the spring of 1915. Many of them died as they were deported en masse to south-east Turkey.

In 1918, the Allied Forces invaded Turkey. The British, the French, the Italians and especially the Greeks (long-time enemies of the Turks) were to have a share of the Ottoman Empire.

From this moment on, Mustafa Kemal fought against the partition of his country, leading his soldiers tirelessly against the Greeks until he had chased them out of Izmir and part of Asia Minor. The success of this war of independence won Mustafa Kemal the title of Ghazi the 'Victorious'.

On November 1, 1922, the sultanate was abolished, bringing an end to 643 years of rule by the Osman dynasty. Mehmed VI, the last sultan, appealed to Britain for refuge and quietly left his palace to board a British warship.

In 1923, when the Treaty of Lausanne defined Turkey's modern borders, Mustafa Kemal at last secured independence for his country. The Greeks retreated, evacuating Thrace and all the islands they had occupied near Anatolia. The Allies also withdrew, leaving Istanbul on October 2, 1923. The Turkish Republic was declared on October 29, 1923, with Mustafa Kemal as president. To symbolize the country's break with Ottoman tradition, the capital was transferred to Ankara.

The new president immediately undertook a radical modernization of both nation and state. The reforms he initiated guaranteed that Turkey would look resolutely to progress and the West. The caliphate was abolished on March 3, 1924. Religious leaders were stripped of most of their former power and freedom of worship was proclaimed. The fez was banned. Polygamy was forbidden, and the emancipation of women begun. The Arabic alphabet was replaced by a modified Latin one. Islamic law was replaced by the Swiss legal code and the international Gregorian calendar was adopted. Roads were built, agriculture was modernized and industry developed. Mustafa Kemal decreed that all Turks from then on should have a surname. In 1934, the Turkish parliament gave him the name Atatürk, 'Father of the Turks'.

Four years later, on November 10, 1938, the great reformer died in Istanbul after having appointed Ismet Inönü as his successor. The constitution he had given his country on April 30, 1924, remained in effect until 1961.

FROM 1939 TO MODERN TIMES

When World War II broke out, Turkey declared itself neutral. The country already had treaties with France and Great Britain and then signed non-aggression agreements with the USSR (in March 1941) and Germany (in June of that same year). However, after a meeting in December 1943 between Churchill, Roosevelt and Inönü, the Turkish government stopped delivering goods to the Axis countries and a few days before the hostilities ended declared war on them. This development in foreign affairs led to a spectacular rapprochement with the United States during the 1950s. Toward the end of 1945, threats from Stalin's Russia increased, with Russia demanding the right to have military bases along the Bosphorus and the Dardanelles. Turkey refused, the USSR reacted strongly and the United States jumped at the opportunity to officially support Turkey. Turkey put aside the principle of neutrality in foreign affairs and opted for a Western democratic ideology by joining NATO in 1951.

In 1950 the Democratic Party, led by Adnan Menderes, came to power. By the end of the 1950s however, the country's economy had worsened to such a degree that the Army intervened and took over in May 1960. A new constitution was agreed to by referendum and elections were held in 1961. In 1965, Turkey was governed by the True Path Party, with Süleyman Demirel at its head. His policies were ultra-liberal and ultra-nationalistic, giving special support to Turkish Cypriots. But by 1970, the social and economic situation had deteriorated once more, causing the Army to step in until the end of 1973. The following year, Bülent Ecevit came to power and governed alternately with Demirel until September 1980.

In July 1974, the Cyprus crisis erupted. Turkish soldiers disembarked on the north of the island, which created grave tension with Greece. Political instability and inflation paralyzed the country, and in 1980 General Evren took power, backed by the military. In 1988, however, with the election of Vassiliou as president of the Cypriot Republic, negotiations to reunify the island began again.

Chronology of historical events

2200-1200 BC	Hittites rule Anatolia.
546 BC	Anatolia under Persian domination.
334 BC	Alexander the Great defeats Persians, takes control of Anatolia.
129 BC	Becomes a Roman province of Asia Minor.
AD 284-305	Roman Empire divided into the East and the West.
AD 330	Christianity declared official religion of the Roman Empire; Constantine transfers the Byzantine capital to Constantinople (where it remains until 1453, when it is conquered by the Ottomans).
1037	Seljuk Empire (Muslim) founded.
1300?	Osman I establishes the Ottoman Empire.
1300-1520	Expansion of the Empire to include present-day Greece, Yugoslavia, Albania, Bulgaria, Hungary, Egypt, Syria, Tunisia and Iraq.
1520-1560	Rule of Sulëyman the Magnificent; apogee of Ottoman power.
1566-1792	Stagnation and decline of the Empire; loss of Persia, Crete, Tunisia and Hungary.
1798	Napoleon invades the Sultan's province of Egypt.
1830	Greece gains independence.
1887-1878	Russo-Turkish War; Turkey sues for peace and the Congress of Berlin declares Serbia and Romania independent, Cyprus is given to Britain, Bulgaria declared a self-governing principality.
1908	Young Turks movement leads a revolt in Macedonia; Abdülhamid grants new constitution.
1914	Turkey is allied with Germany in World War I; British, French and Russian Alliance declare war on Turkey.
1923	Turkish Republic proclaimed with Mustafa Kemal (Atatürk) as first president.
1928	Turkey becomes a secular state.
1932	Admission to the League of Nations.
1938	Atatürk dies, Ismet Inönü becomes the Republic's second president.
1945	Turkey declares war on Germany and Japan.
1952	Joins the North Atlantic Treaty Organization (NATO).
1961	First free elections held.
1980	Military coup suspends all political parties, arrests major party leaders.
1983	Turgut Özal becomes prime minister following legislative elections.
1989	Yildirim Akbulut replaces Özal as prime minister.

TURKEY TODAY

Turkey is as large as Texas, or as Great Britain and France put together. To the west it is surrounded by the Aegean Sea and the Sea of Marmara, to the north by the Black Sea and to the south by the Mediterranean.

Because the country is larger than its neighbours and because it controls the Straits of Bosphorus and the Dardanelles, which link the Black Sea to the Mediterranean, Turkey has been able to maintain a strategic position between the West, Eastern Europe and the Middle East since the end of World War II.

GEOGRAPHY

The country is outlined by mountain ranges along the coast – the Black Sea (Pontic) range to the north and the Taurus range to the south. The two ranges meet in the east, forming Turkey's eastern mountain range where there are high volcanoes: Mount Ararat (16,942 ft/5165 m), Erciyes Daği (12,851 ft/3917 m) and Süphan Daği (14,547 ft/4434 m). Between the two mountain ranges there is a vast plateau with an average altitude of 3281 ft/1000 m.

The coastline is generally very uneven, with beaches interrupted here and there by mountains descending to the sea. On the other hand, the country's only plains are found on the coastal strip.

Turkey has many unnavigable rivers. In Thrace, the Mariça River with its tributary, the Ergene, flows along the border with Greece. In Asian Turkey, the Menderes, the Gediz Nehri and the Bakir Cayi flow into the Aegean Sea while the Ceyhan and the Göksu run into the Mediterranean. Much farther north, the Çoruh River, which crosses into the USSR, ends up in the Black Sea along with the Sakarya and the Kizilirmak (758 mi/1220 km), Turkey's longest river. Two of the Near East's major rivers begin in Eastern Anatolia: the Tigris (1212 mi/1950 km, of which 280 mi/450 km are in Turkey) and the Euphrates (1731 mi/2785 km, of which about 621 mi/1000 km flow through Turkey).

The two mountain ranges determine the climate of the country. In the north between the Black Sea coast and the mountains, the climate is temperate and humid with high rainfall in winter. The Anatolian plateau in the middle of the country has

A corbeled wooden house in Üsküdar, on the Asian shore of the Bosphorus.

temperature differences ranging from 37°F/3°C in January to 86°F/30°C in summer. In the south beyond the Taurus Mountains, the climate resembles that of the western coast with mild winters and hot summers. Finally, in the east, winters are harsh and summers very hot, scorching hot sometimes in the daytime. Nights are generally very cool.

The diversity in terrain and climate give Turkey a great variety of landscapes. Northern Turkey is covered with fruit-tree orchards of all kinds. There are also forests of oak, beech, hazel, chestnut, walnut, maple, fir and birch. In the centre there are rolling stretches of wheat fields and pastures. The south has pine, cedar and sycamore trees in abundance as well as palm and fig trees and vineyards, while cotton plantations and market gardens typify the Aegean and Mediterranean coasts.

ECONOMY

Turkey's economy is developing rapidly. The country has had the best performance of the members of the OECD (Organization for European Cooperation and Development) with an average growth rate of 4.8% between 1980 and 1989. Furthermore, improvements in the standard of living means that Turkey is catching up with other OECD members and is now ranked 19th. These results have been brought about by a change in priorities, aimed toward greater access to outside markets and a more liberal economy. This policy, decided at the beginning of the 1980s, is still in force today. This growth is also evident in the modernization of the energy sector and in important projects affecting the industry's infrastructure. Highways and airports have been built, as well as dams and bridges such as those over the Bosphorus. The telecommunications network has been developed and there are ambitious urbanization programs.

The problem of the national debt, however, which was about one billion dollars in 1988, counterbalances the impact of the new policy and its undeniable success. Inflation and unemployment are also pressing problems. The rate of inflation may well have decreased (120% in 1980, 70% in 1989) but not enough, and unemployment is estimated at three million – an estimated 10.4% of the working population.

Tourism

Tourism has become an important source of foreign currency. In 1988 revenue from tourism in Turkey amounted to US$ 2,355 million compared with US$ 358 million Turks spent on tourism abroad.

The number of foreign tourists, about four million in 1988, should increase as a result of governmental efforts to open up tourist areas in Eastern Turkey and to continue developing the hotel infrastructure. This aspect of the country's economy has been a priority for a number of years.

The areas visited most by tourists apart from Istanbul, Ankara and Izmir, are the surrounding areas of Istanbul on the shores of the Sea of Marmara, Bursa, the entire Aegean coast, the Mediterranean (around Antalya, Side and Alanya) and such sites as Cappadocia.

Lake Van and the island of Akhtamar.

Agriculture

Agricultural output is growing, although slowly. The farming potential of the country is restricted by a lack of capital and technical equipment. Even so, 49% of the working population is employed in agriculture and 36% of the country is cultivated – approximately 77,220 sq mi/200,000 sq km.

The Anatolian plateau is basically used to farm crops, fruit and vegetables and to raise livestock. In the coastal regions there is a great deal of arable land but its potential is not fully exploited: grain crops still account for 45-60% of the land. Each region, from the Black Sea to the Sea of Marmara and from the Aegean to the Mediterranean, has its own grain production.

In 1988, wheat was the most widely grown crop with a yield of 19 million tons, making Turkey eighth in world production. The other crops are barley, rice (in the Adana region), potatoes and maize. Cotton production reached two million tons in 1988. This is an important Turkish product and the country rates sixth in the world market. Other flourishing commodities include sugar beets, fruit (apples, oranges, figs, apricots, etc.), tea, which is grown around Rize, and grapes, which produce Turkey's famous raisins, of which three million tons are exported each year.

The climate and terrain of Turkey are also favourable for breeding livestock. The country's livestock consists of 40 million sheep, 17 million head of cattle and 13 million goats. Turkey is the world's fifth-largest producer of sheep and goats.

Energy and industry

Although Turkey's soil is rich, there is little mineral exploitation apart from lignite. Oil, coal, iron and chrome ore are extracted on a small scale. On the other hand, the manufacturing capacity for export products such as cement, fertilizers, steel ingots and cast iron is growing.

To meet industrial needs and consumer demand, Turkey requires a large amount of fossil fuel. Yet, because there is little oil and natural gas, 50% of the country's energy has to be imported. Until 1986, the high price of oil made it difficult for the country to build much-needed power stations. Faced with an energy shortage, the government has set up a long-term plan to meet the future needs of the country. Production of electricity is to double, due to the construction of two dams on the Euphrates: the Atatürk, which is the fifth largest in the world, and the Karakaya.

Foreign trade

In 1988 the trade deficit reached $3.7 billion and has remained relatively stable since. Turkey's exports are mainly industrial, manufactured, and chemical products and agricultural and meat products. More than 50% of exported goods are destined for the EEC (European Economic Community). The main countries importing from Turkey are West Germany (20%), Italy (8%), the United States (8%), Saudi Arabia (5%), the United Kingdom (5%) and France (4%). The financial difficulties and decrease in development projects in the Middle East have resulted in more exports to countries in the OECD. This fits in with one of Turkey's major priorities: joining the EEC.

Turkey imports mainly industrial and mineral products (machinery, chemical products, oil and iron). The EEC, once again, supplies 41% of Turkey's imports. The major exporters to Turkey are West Germany (16%), the US (11%), Italy (8%), Iraq (7%), Japan (6%), France (5%) and the UK (5%).

Transportation

Internal transportation is not yet fully developed and remains a weak point in the Turkish economy.

The railway network of more than 5095 mi/8200 km is popular but slow. The advantage of the train is that it reaches some areas in the east that are less accessible by other means.

Roads and highways are being improved all the time. Of the 186,420 mi/300,000 km of good, uncrowded roads, more than half are asphalt. Bus and minibus *(dolmuş)* are the most widely used means of transport in Turkey.

The merchant navy has a fleet of 830 ships. There are also ferryboats and cruise ships, but river traffic is almost non-existent.

As for air transport, the national airline, THY, has regular flights to 15 domestic airports.

Major political figures in Turkey today

Turgut Özal, born in the east of Turkey in 1927, is President of the Republic and the only real newcomer to the political scene. He is an electrical engineer who studied economics in the US. After working on several dam projects, he became technical adviser to the former prime minister, Süleyman Demirel, from 1965 to 1967, then was responsible for the State Planning Organization for four years. Reappointed as Under-Secretary of State in charge of Planning in the fourth Demirel Cabinet, he kept this post until the coup d'état in 1980.

He was then nominated Deputy Prime Minister of Economic Affairs but left the government in 1982 to form the Motherland Party. He won the general election in 1983 and again in 1987. He is pragmatic, a practicing Muslim, and has a moderate attitude toward integrationist policies.

Kenan Evren was born in 1918. He is a general whose military career won him recognition in the Korean War (1950-1953). He was appointed Army Chief of Staff in 1978. On September 12, 1980, when the country was in a state of economic turmoil and terrorism was rife, he overthrew the civil government with the help of four military officers. As a result of a referendum in November 1982, he was elected president by 92% of the votes for a seven-year term. In 1983 he decided on a return to civilian rule and organized a general election.

Süleyman Demirel was born in 1924 in Eastern Anatolia. He studied engineering first at Istanbul University and later in the US. At 31, he was appointed State Director of Hydraulic Works and had a start to his career similar to that of Turgut Özal. In 1964, he became president of the Justice Party and was elected prime minister a year later when he was 41 years old. He held that position until 1971, when he retired from the political scene, although he still wielded considerable influence. He returned to power in 1975 and remained in office until 1980, during which time he alternated as head of government with his contemporary, Bülent Ecevit. He specializes in coalitions and is popular in campaigns, presenting a serious challenge to Turgut Özal.

Bülent Ecevit was born in 1924. He studied literature then worked at the Turkish Embassy in London before beginning a career in journalism. During the 1950s he moved to the US to study at Harvard. On his return to Turkey, he caught the attention of Ismet Pasa Inönü, Mustafa Kemal's successor, and became Minister of Labour. In 1972 he took over the presidency of Atatürk's Republican People's Party (PRP). He became prime minister in 1973 and thereafter shared power with Demirel. Ecevit gave the order for the military occupation of Cyprus in 1974. Like his contemporary Demirel, Ecevit has often worked with coalition governments, and although he announced his intention to retire from political life after the general election in 1987, his decision does not seem to be final.

Erdal Inönü, Ismet Pasa Inönü's son, is an unassuming academic who created the Social Democratic Populist Party (SDHP) in 1985 and became its president in May 1986. His party has 99 deputies.

Deniz Baykal, a former minister in Bülent Ecevit's government, was elected head of the SDHP in June 1988.

Ismail Cem is a journalist for *Günes,* an important Turkish daily. He is a brilliant and popular intellectual and, as one of the officials in the SDHP party, could replace Erdal Inönü.

POLITICAL REVIVAL OF THE 1980s

Since the inception of the Turkish Republic under Kemal Atatürk on October 29, 1923, Turkey has become a secular democracy with a powerful executive branch. The president of the republic is decided by open election and holds office for a non-renewable seven-year term. He has the power to dissolve the Assembly and the right to veto laws and amendments to the constitution as well as to nominate civil servants and government officials, including members of the Supreme Court. General Kenan Evren was elected president in 1982; Turgut Özal succeeded him as president in 1989. The Parliament is made up of the Senate and the Chamber of Deputies headed by a prime minister.

The first general election since the military coup d'état in 1980 was held in November 1983. It brought the new centre-right party, the Motherland Party led by Turgut Özal, to power. Ever since his nomination to the post of prime minister, Turgut Özal has favoured a return to stable political life. The former leaders who were considered responsible for the political and economic decline of the country were not allowed to take part in the 1983 elections. Thus neither Süleyman Demirel, leader of the True Path Party, nor Bülent Ecevit, leader of the Democratic Left, were officially able to lead their parties or run for election.

In 1987 Turgut Özal organized a referendum to repeal political bans levied before 1980. It won by a small margin (50.16% for, 49.84% against), showing that most voters wanted to see the process of democratization continue, but a significant minority still supported the former political leaders. After the prime minister called early elections in November 1987, his party won a comfortable majority in Parliament, and Turgut Özal continued his regular duties as prime minister until 1989, when he was replaced by Yildirim Akbulut. Turkey's political history has recently been marked by upheaval, but the country is striving to become an industrialized Western nation.

THE TURKISH PEOPLE

The diversity of Turkey's ancient inhabitants and successive waves of immigrants make the population an extremely complex one. Turks, Greeks, Sumerians, Kurds, Albanians, Georgians, Italians and Jews have long lived together to form such a varied population that it is impossible to describe a typical Turk. Although the dark Mediterranean type is often encountered, there are also fair Turks with blue or green eyes and blond hair.

In the year 2000, with an estimated 73 million inhabitants, Turkey will have the largest population in Europe. Fifty-three percent of the country's present population is urban; the remaining 47% rural. Half the population is less than 25 years old and half a million jobs must be created every year. More than 15% of the population is unemployed. The problem of urban unemployment is worsened by the constant influx of people from rural areas looking for work.

Alevis

Although the majority of Turkish Muslims are Sunnis, there is an important minority of Alevis who are associated with the Shiites and represent between 15 and 20% of the population.

Alevis recognize Ali, the cousin and son-in-law to Mohammed, as the rightful successor. They differ from other Shiites. Indeed, the differences that distinguish them from Iranian or Lebanese Shiites are as deep and numerous as those that separate them from orthodox Anatolian Sunnis who consider them heretics.

They believe in a gnostic doctrine based on a God-Reality – a sort of Holy Trinity comprising Allah, Mohammed and Ali. To adhere to this doctrine one must go through a period of initiation. Alevis also differ through language and liturgy; they use only Turkish as opposed to Arabic, although the latter was the language used to pass on the Word of Allah. Instead of going to mosques they prefer belonging to secret prayer communities where they make use of allegorical techniques, the science of letters and numbers. They also partake of alcohol – wine or raki – during a kind of communion service and in general prohibit the eating of certain animals like hares.

They stand out socially as well, by their sense of solidarity and their attitude to women, whom they regard as equals.

They were victims of Sunni persecution for centuries and their refusal to convert caused them to approve of and welcome Atatürk's militant secularism. Islamites today still bring the old accusation of heresy against them and because they're a minority they make an easy scapegoat. They are, however, essential to Turkey's national equilibrium through their concern for secularity and pluralism.

ISLAM IN TURKEY

Ninety-nine percent of the population is Muslim. There is, however, freedom of worship for non-Muslims, tolerance of other religions having been the norm for some time. Furthermore, the State is secular rather than religious. Atatürk believed that Islam slowed the country's progress, and consequently launched a policy of secularization which separated Church and State. He replaced traditional Koranic law with new civil, penal and commercial codes. He replaced Arab characters with the Latin alphabet and adopted Western numerals. He also encouraged women not to wear the veil and outlawed the Ottoman fez.

Yet, it is not easy to subjugate a deeply rooted faith and despite reforms, religious feeling has remained strong in Turkey. Daily life follows the pattern of the five calls to prayer from the tops of minarets, and fasting during Ramadan is always observed. For the 28 days of the ninth month of the Muslim lunar year, a practicing Muslim does not smoke, drink (water or alcohol), or eat from dawn until sunset. Not only have the Turks remained religious but there is an Islamic revival throughout the land. Mosques are being built everywhere and women who used to dress in the Western style are beginning to wear veils again. All Muslim schoolchildren have a mandatory Islamic religious education. Nevertheless, the religious parties are not dominant; they attract less than 1.0% of the vote.

ART AND CULTURE

A natolia has a rich past encompassing several great civilizations that flowered over a period of eight thousand years and left behind a multitude of artistic traditions. From the bronze work of Alaça Höyük to Hittite ceramics, Greek temples, Roman theatres, Byzantine mosaics and Islamic mosques, the diversity and wealth of the country's heritage is overwhelming.

The oldest known city in the West dates from 6750 BC and was discovered in Çatal Höyük, south of Konya. Excavations uncovered tools, obsidian weapons, jewels, Mother-Goddess statuettes and wall paintings. Examples of these are on display in Ankara's Museum of Anatolian Cultures where you can also see the replica of a religious sepulchre from the same era (see p. 180).

The Bronze Age began in the third millennium BC. Objects from this period have been found in royal tombs at Alaça Höyük and Horoztepe in Central Anatolia. There are bronze figurines inlaid with silver and gold, sun discs, stylized human statuettes, sculptures of bull-like creatures with threatening horns, and deer-like animals with giant antlers, all of which seem to have been used in burial ceremonies.

FROM THE HITTITES TO THE LYCIANS

Some of the best-known art in Anatolia was created by the Hittites. They were an intelligent, industrious people who conquered their enemies with ease and set up their capital in Hattuşaş near present-day Boğazköy (or Boğazkale), north-east of Ankara.

At both Hattuşaş and another centre called Karkemiş, their buildings were monumental, especially the temples. They used neither columns nor capitals but supported their buildings on immense stone pillars, decorated with reliefs. The sculptures are simple and sometimes quite refined, hewn in regular lines that repeat an identically shaped face or outline of eyes, mouth and ears. Human figures are usually represented in long lines, series of men in exactly the same position with one arm bent against the body and the other slightly extended. They are shown in profile wearing conical hats that have slightly rounded points. In the Hittite section of the Museum of Anatolian Cultures in Ankara, there are several

One of the many marvelous mosaics in Saint Sophia.

impressive reliefs on freestanding blocks, such as those of the *Gateway of the Sphinxes.* There are also displays of later works with animal or sacrificial motifs. Some of the most remarkable pieces are the libation vases (or *rhyta*) in the shape of bulls' heads.

Traces of Phrygian art were discovered in Gordium, capital of the ancient kingdom of Phrygia. These are mainly ceramic pieces but there are also rock monuments such as the famous tomb of King Midas, which is decorated with geometric designs and crowned by a triangular pediment.

In Sardis, capital of Lydia, a vast necropolis was found, housing painted terracotta pieces and precious stones, as well as coins and gold plates bearing the image of King Croesus.

The Lycians, like the Phrygians, also excavated rock to build their tombs. Their tombs in Xanthos are shaped like their wooden dwellings.

GRECO-ROMAN INFLUENCES

The Phrygian, Lydian and Lycian kingdoms soon came under a new influence, that of Greek settlers. Between the eighth and fifth centuries BC, Anatolia became the second cultural centre of the ancient Greek world, known as Ionia. Cities of Ionia at that time had an acropolis, a citadel, wide porticoed avenues, public buildings and vast theatres. Ephesus and Miletus were the major urban centres of the day, followed a few centuries later by Priene and Pergamum. Here a new art form was born, known as eastern Greek or Ionic art. For monumental buildings the architects were initially inspired by Doric art, then they lightened the style, making it softer, more slender and decorative. This development can be seen in the Temple of Artemis at Ephesus (see p. 158) and in the Temple of Athena at Assos. In spite of the Persian invasion of 534, the Hellenic tradition persisted and Ionic art flourished on Anatolian soil for a long time to come. Two of its masterpieces are the tomb of King Mausolus at Bodrum (see p. 168) and the Temple of Athena at Priene (see p. 165).

With the arrival of Alexander the Great in 334 BC, the Hellenistic era truly began. Colossal edifices were built to adorn older cities. Among these monuments are the Temple of Apollo at Didyma (see p. 166), the theatre at Priene (see p. 165) and the altar in Bergama (see p. 146), dedicated to Zeus, with its remarkable bas-relief.

The period following Alexander's conquest produced beautiful sculptures. Two of the finest pieces are exhibited in the Archaeological Museum in Istanbul (see p. 114). They are the marble sarcophagi of Alexander and the *Pleureuses* (weeping women).

The Greeks continued producing magnificent works in Anatolia up until the arrival of the Romans. The Romans invented the design for the dome and were the first to use cement. They brought their engineering expertise to Anatolia for the building of bridges, roads, aqueducts and theatres. The Aqueduct of Valens, remains of which can still be seen in Istanbul, the Stadium in Aphrodisias, which is one of their best-preserved constructions, and the theatre in Aspendos, are fine examples of their work. Roman architecture was imposing and majestic. Arches and vaults were widely used until the Corinthian order replaced the Ionic.

Roman architecture in Anatolia provided the basis for the Byzantine genius that was to bloom so magnificently in Constantinople.

BYZANTIUM THE MAGNIFICENT

Byzantine history stretches over 11 centuries from the Roman Empire to the Renaissance. In AD 330, the Roman emperor Constantine I transferred his seat of power to a new town which he named 'Constantinople'. He was a tireless builder determined to rival all the cities of the ancient world by making his empire a 'new Rome,' a dazzling capital worthy of the name. This was achieved through the endeavours of numerous workers under the supervision of the architect Euphrates.

The Byzantine city

In order to protect his new Christian city, Constantine had vast, 12 mi–/20 km–long ramparts built around it and a chain strung across the harbour, the Golden Horn. A single defensive wall was built along the shores of the Sea of Marmara and of the Golden Horn, but to protect against land attacks that might have weakened the city, a triple wall was built. A large ditch about 50 ft/15 m wide and 20 ft/6 m deep would put the first advance of any enemy in check. It was normally dry but special canals stood ready to fill it if necessary. Behind the moat was one low wall guarded by archers, then a second of about 26 ft/8 m high, followed by a third fortified by towers of about 66 ft/20 m high.

Inside the walls, city life revolved around the Augusteion, the main public square. This was colonnaded and paved with black marble. Three buildings surrounded it.

The first was the Hippodrome, where people went for entertainment. It was a vast stadium 1279 ft/390 m long, adorned with columns and modeled after others from antiquity.

The second was the Imperial Palace (located under today's Blue Mosque) decorated inside with luxury and refinement. The floors and walls were covered in red-, blue- and emerald-coloured marble and onyx. Extensive use was made of gold as well as glass panels that shimmered with bright colours. The furniture was just as sumptuous: gilded or natural wood inlaid with ivory or mother-of-pearl. Unfortunately none of these splendours nor the palaces belonging to wealthy patrons of the arts have survived.

Finally there was Saint Sophia, closing off the city's main square.

These three monuments symbolize the three forces of the Byzantine world: the people, the emperor and Christ.

The outer gate of the Imperial Palace opened onto a strip of land and then onto a colonnaded main street. This was lined with arcades of luxurious workshops, interspersed here and there by majestic squares erected to honour emperors and empresses. The triumphal arch no longer exists. It disappeared along with the residences facing it; these were usually wooden houses with two corbeled storeys, allowing the inhabitants to see what was going on in the street below.

With each new emperor the city grew bigger. Theodosius inaugurated his forum in 393 and Arcadius his in 403. In the fifth century Theodosius II moved Constantine's wall farther back, although surprisingly this did not mean that a new population immediately occupied the extra space.

The city's main plan featured wide avenues that were to be lined with monuments. Later changes were brought about by churches being built, which meant the destruction of former public buildings. Baths, fountains and theatres, for example, were abandoned and gradually fell to ruin. Among the few remaining civil and military monuments are Constantinople's triple walls, the Golden Gate and a large triumphal arch that dates to Theodosius I (380). Churches, on the other hand, were well kept, redesigned and embellished right up until the fall of the empire. Then they were often used as models by Ottoman architects.

In the sixth century, after five days of a devastating fire, Emperor Justinian (527-565) rebuilt the town with slight modifications. With Saint Sophia he laid the basis for Byzantine architecture in its purest form.

Roman law and Hellenistic cultural traditions were maintained in the Byzantine Empire and a number of Greek and Roman works of art were preserved. But in general, Byzantine taste tended toward ornamental profusion rather than sober classical aesthetics. Later, Seljuk art brought new inspiration to the empire and was in turn modified by Byzantine tradition.

Religious architecture

The teachings of Christianity originated in Asia Minor (Ephesus, Nicaea, Chalcedonia), which meant that its active nucleus was in the East. Evangelist monks set out from there to convert the West to the new religion. The New Christians, gripped by a kind of mysticism, believed they had been chosen by God, and the emperors inherited 'divine right'. They glorified Christian spirituality through art.

The different influences from the East, plus those of classic antiquity and its own history, combined to make Byzantine art vibrantly original.

The importance of Constantinople as a religious centre could be measured by the extraordinary number of crosses, reliquaries, oratories and chapels dedicated to the Virgin Mary. In the middle of the sixth century, there were more than 80 monasteries and places of worship. Christian architecture was characterized by churches shaped like the Greek cross (with four equal parts), featuring arches, cupolas with pendentive (square) bases, and superimposed capitals resembling inverted pyramids. Marble and mosaics were the rule inside, with brick and stone used outside. Design ideas for these churches were borrowed from palaces and monuments dating from the fourth and fifth centuries BC in Ephesus, Miletus and Pergamum, as well as from other Greek cities on the Aegean coast of Anatolia. Vaults and domes became widespread, as did the technique of a compact floor plan (in the shape of the Greek cross) inspired by the layout of Greek and Roman tombs.

There were three phases in the development of religious architecture in the Byzantine Empire:

The first lasted from the sixth to the middle of the ninth century. During this phase the basilica of Saint Sophia was built and became a major reference point for other churches. Its conception was simple, its decoration complex and refined.

During the second phase, from the ninth to the middle of the 13th century, Byzantine churches became smaller. The number of window arches doubled or even tripled and the interiors were filled with elaborate sculptures. From then on, domes had high square bases and roofs were tiered. In the centre of Anatolia, in Cappadocia, religious groups dug tiny churches into the rocks with the same characteristics as larger ones built in the open air.

During the last phase, from the 13th century to the fall of the empire in 1453, columns, pillars and buttresses reached extraordinary heights. From then on the central dome was flanked by four smaller lateral ones. A new exuberance appeared in the decoration of chapel fronts and outside walls. This was expressed by moulded or indented surfaces and by intertwined patterns on brickwork.

Wall decoration

In the interiors of Istanbul's rich churches, the art of polychromy was meticulously applied to produce the most subtle colour gradations. Whether to capture light or create a mirror effect, mosaic pieces were arranged in tight lines, loose circles or free undulations. Mosaics can be made in a number of ways, usually with small squares of marble or glass. Paste, coloured with metal oxides, can also be used or even clear glass covered by a thin layer of gold or silver, which is then protected by another sheet of transparent glass. This was a well-known technique throughout Mesopotamia and the Mediterranean basin and was used exclusively for ornamental tiling. In the middle of the 14th century, a hundred years before the fall of Constantinople, mosaic art died out because it was too costly.

Another technique, which was less expensive but equally dazzling, came into being in Cappadocia's sanctuaries. This was the fresco for which the artist applied his watercolours directly onto wet plaster. Whereas the mosaic was an urban art of harmony, balance and refinement, the fresco was a provincial art that portrayed human feeling and expression and was associated with the lower clergy. It prospered between the 10th and 14th centuries.

Byzantine artists were directed to express Christian faith in their work and to help spread the word of God. Because these concepts are essentially mystical, they used symbolic images, rather than naturalistic ones.

Mosaic art makes no use of perspective; it is flat and one-dimensional. Its strength is in outline and the controlled use of colour. Because the scenes are simple with immediately identifiable figures, the effect on the onlooker is intensified. Prophets and apostles are always shown from the front, frozen in hieratic poses. Their faces are stylized with huge eyes and there is a distinct absence of personalized features, although outlines are always pronounced. A portrait has its code and the code its characteristics. The emperor, for example, has a halo; kindly St Peter a soft white beard, St John the Baptist an unruly one; St Paul is bald and St Demetrius has a coat of chain mail.

Like religious architecture, there are three periods in the history of wall decoration. Unfortunately, apart from large black crosses with gold backgrounds, most of the religious works from the first period have not survived, as the result of the disputes over iconoclastic images that shook the empire between AD 726 and 843. Those in favour of icons managed to put an end to the debate and restored the use of divine representation that had hitherto been forbidden. From then on, no portrayal of God and his saints was erased on the orders of an emperor. On the other hand, church decoration had to be arranged in a precise way according to a prescribed hierarchy. Thus Christ, surrounded by prophets and apostles, figured in a central position in the main dome overlooking the whole church. The four evangelists were placed on the pendentives supporting the dome. Theotokos, or Mother of God and protectress of the Church, was enthroned in the apse accompanied by archangels Michael and Gabriel. The 12 feasts of the liturgical orthodox year were featured in the nave and transept. Finally, the central panel of the tympanum in the nave was devoted either to the Last Judgment or to St Peter.

During the intermediary medieval period, from the ninth to the 12th century, icons became more descriptive. They began to illustrate religious narratives or scenes from the Gospels, such as the life of the Virgin, the infant Jesus, and the ministry and Passion of Christ. Ceremonial portraits began to adorn Saint Sophia.

The third and last period was characterized by a far more realistic expression. In this new realism proportions were strictly respected. A person's body, for instance, had to be nine times the size of his head and the thickness of his hair had to be equivalent to the length of his nose.

From its beginnings right up to the artistic revival during the Palaeologos dynasty (1259-1282), figurative mosaic art developed slowly, gradually giving more life-like and subtle qualities to human attitudes and feelings while always maintaining its preoccupation with religion.

Water networks

During the Byzantine era and then again under the Seljuks and Ottomans up to the present day, the country's hydraulic systems have never ceased to expand and improve. *Bendes* or dykes built near towns collect water that is taken by aqueduct, then stone or clay supply pipes to various reservoirs, baths, fountains and even to the tanks of rich landlords. These latter in fact obtain a lifelong right to water which guarantees them a permanent supply.

Islam, through its mandatory custom of ablutions, requires a vast number of water outlets: in mosques, streets and also in large residences. These fountains are often built with great imagination and are sometimes hidden, in windows for instance. A fountain can usually be found in a courtyard but also in a main room where a Baroque sculptor may well have chosen to transform it into a kind of water sideboard from which water zigzags down into a series of overhangs, making a refreshing murmur as it flows.

SELJUK INFLUENCES

In the 11th century, Seljuk rule extended from Baghdad to Persia, and from Syria to Samarkand. When the empire became too vast and unwieldy, it was divided into Asia Minor (Anadolu), Syria and Persia.

In the first two states, architecture developed along different lines from that in Persia, but at the same time was closely tied to the traditions of the Sassanid dynasty (AD 226 to 641). Asia Minor, stretching from the Black Sea to Adana, was in the hands of Seljuks of Rum (part of the Seljuk empire), who made Konya (Iconium) their capital. Konya became a major centre of learning for both the arts and sciences.

Because of their location on the trade route between East and West, the Seljuks built vast fortified caravanserais (inns), where merchants could conduct their bargaining. This proved lucrative for the Seljuks, who, apart from building caravanserais, strengthened the fortifications of conquered towns, opened large *medreses* (free theological universities) and built mosques.

A typical feature of Seljuk architecture is the use of stone for walls, such as sandstone or limestone as in former Byzantine structures. The Seljuks were at their most innovative, however, when designing main entrances for their buildings. These grand portals were set deeply into high walls and decorated with stalactite patterns, often surrounded by columns of all shapes and sizes, some spiral, others fluted or hourglass shaped. The doorways were sometimes framed by a series of identical miniature niches. The arch itself was usually flattened, decorated with an elaborate lattice of alternating light and dark stone. In addition to zigzag patterns, curves, stalactites and arabesques, Seljuk art specialized in flowers and leaves. Animal and human figures were also included, in spite of the fact that portrayal of these is forbidden by the Muslim religion. Portals were richly adorned with sculptures of angels, lions, rams' heads, eagles and dragons.

Medreses and caravanserais were laid out in the shape of a cross around a central courtyard. Their rectangular, columned mosques bring to mind both Arab mosques and ancient Greek monuments. Tombs *(türbe)* are funeral towers and resemble decorated tents, similar to the *Tekke* (dervish convent) of Mevlâna in Konya (see p. 199).

The Persians and Turkomans revived architectural techniques. The use of brick enabled them to build corbeled cornices on outside walls. Interior decoration consisted of ornate geometric patterns and Kufic script on finely chiseled pieces of marble, interwoven with earthenware tiles.

But at the beginning of the 14th century, Seljuk domination began to crumble. Osman, the head of a Turkish clan, conquered the land and formed what was to become the Ottoman Empire (see p. 49).

OTTOMAN ARCHITECTURE

Further refinement came with the Ottomans, who first

developed their architecture in Bursa (Prusa), then in Edirne, and finally in Constantinople after the conquest by Mehmed II in 1453. Traces of Ottoman art can be found today in Bulgaria, Romania, Serbia and Greece, as these were all Turkish provinces for centuries. Its influence spread even farther afield through architects who traveled to Syria, Egypt and even to India where they immortalized the splendour of Mogul emperors.

After conquering Constantinople, the Ottomans added Byzantine features to the Seljuk heritage. The main characteristics of their architecture were the central dome and, like Seljuk *medreses*, a cruciform layout in their buildings.

The profusion of Ottoman buildings can be explained by the duties of the leaders, each sovereign required to endow his town, and usually others as well, with a mosque. It was never simply a single religious building, but an entire social centre comprising reservoirs, baths, fountains, schools, hospices, hospitals and bazaars. Similarly, a rich man could atone for his sins by building a mosque or a fountain in his quarter or in his home town.

Istanbul's mosques, with their slender minarets, are impressive from afar and, seen together, create a grandiose effect. They are positioned harmoniously throughout the city at regular intervals. Inside, rich mosaics are interspersed with decorative arabesques and inscriptions in plaster stucco. This is a background for works of art, sculptures of marble or wood embellished with inlaid ivory, mother-of-pearl, silver and gold. Human beings are almost never portrayed. Only the sun and plants (flowers and cypress trees) are depicted in this highly stylized art form.

In the 16th century, during the reign of Süleyman el Kanuni (the Magnificent), Istanbul was blessed with a real town planner. This was the architect Sinan to whom more than 300 buildings are attributed.

Two centuries later, the effects of the Renaissance in Europe emerged in Ottoman art, detectable in the tulip style at the beginning of the 18th century under Ahmed III. Baroque was introduced in 1730 under Mahmud I and was developed under Selim III.

The Ottomans perfected all the arts including carpet weaving, calligraphy, manuscript illumination, miniatures, book binding and leather work.

MUSIC

More than in any other Muslim country, traditional music in Turkey has been influenced by Europe, attesting to the country's openness to the West. However, Turkish music is based on a scale of 24 notes per octave whereas Western ears are accustomed to 12. As a result, Westerners sometimes think they hear 'false notes' – an impression reinforced by the nasal tones of certain instruments.

Apart from percussion instruments, which differ very little from those of a Western classical orchestra – kettledrums, cymbals, drums and tambourines – Turkey has many typical instruments; the most common are:

The Blue Mosque, completed in 1616, is considered to be the most beautiful in Istanbul.

– *kemençe:* a kind of violin with three strings which is held upright on the knees. To achieve maximum harmony the base string is plucked with a fingernail;
– *keman:* a type of violin;
– *kanun:* a 72-stringed instrument that is played with a plectrum;
– *saz:* a stringed instrument with a long neck and movable frets;
– *ney* and *nisfiyye:* reed flutes with horn mouthpieces.

The most common music in Turkey is folk music, which is coloured by strong regional variations and plays an important role in daily life. Everyday themes and events are celebrated in songs and dances.

Modern popular music is what is usually heard on the radio. Although it derives its rhythms from folk music, it is heavily influenced by Western music brought back by the many emigrant workers on their return home or imported by foreign tourists.

Classical music was developed toward the middle of the 19th century, influenced by Western musicians, despite strong resistance from traditionalists. This led to the emergence of a new genre of Turkish music at the beginning of the 20th century, which drew to a large extent on the European repertoire of classical music but which integrated Ottoman rhythms and traditional themes from Turkey's literary heritage. Thus, in the repertoires of early 20th-century musicians such as Cemal Reşid Rey, Adnan Saygun and Ulvi Cemal Erkin, there are operas, operettas, symphonies, and chamber music.

Since 1923, with the opening of conservatories in Istanbul and then in Ankara in 1936, Turkey's music has developed considerably.

LITERATURE

Classical Ottoman literature, known as Divan literature, is inaccessible to Turks today unless they are specialists. (*Divan* in Turkish means 'gathering together' and can mean both the imperial council during the days of the sultanate and a collection of poems.) The middle of the 18th century marked the beginning of its decline, and it disappeared entirely in the second half of the 19th century.

At the beginning of this century, the first Turkish novels were written by writers steeped in Western culture and literature. Until then, this was an unknown genre even in well-read circles. The writers broke with the Ottoman language, which was mixed with Persian and Arabic, to use a more homogeneous medium. This was a more popular, less erudite form of Turkish that also conformed to the language spoken by cultivated Turks. The authors attempted to more clearly understand the realities of everyday life in their country by treating different aspects of social life. Of these writers, the most outstanding are Halide Edipe Adivar, the precursor of women's literature in Turkey, and Yakup Kadri Karaosmanoğlu and Sabattin Ali, spokesmen for critical realism.

Over the last four decades, pastoral novels have emerged in rural Anatolia in which the strong national character of the people comes to the fore to denounce the harshness of life in the country and the problems of those who depend on the land. Of this genre, the most representative are Fakir Baykurt, Orhan Kemal, Mahmut

Makal and Yaşar Kemal. The last is a self-taught farmer who became a journalist and novelist. His work has been translated into several languages and he is considered one of the best contemporary Turkish authors. He won the French Del Duca literature prize in 1982. Another person who has influenced modern Turkish prose is Sait Faik, a short-story writer.

One of the most important names in literature with social themes is that of a major innovator, the communist poet Nazim Hikmet (1902-1963). He militated for combatant poetry in free verse and was a friend of both Aragon and Maïakovski. Other voices that deserve a mention include those of Yahya Kemal, Beyatli (1884-1958), Ahmed Hachim (1885-1933) and Haşim Orhan Veli (1914-1959) from the Garip school of poetry.

A film-maker's Turkey

The following is a selection of well-known films made between 1978 and 1988, chosen for their common theme: a journey. They are representative of the relatively large output of Turkish films (approximately 150 a year).

The Herd (Zeki Ökten and Yilmaz Güney, 1978). In eastern Turkey, an entire family is taking a train journey. The father is shown as an authoritarian patriarch with a vague hint of despair. His is the severe face of the nomad with worn features and a proud moustache. With him are his gentle yet rebellious sons and a daughter-in-law who has been ill and silent for some time. They are traveling with their flock of sheep. Their destination is Ankara, 20th-century Turkey and its conflicts. During the journey in a confined world of second-class carriages, where different paths cross and secret meetings take place, the spectator is impressed by the rich drama of human nature set against a background of Asia Minor's steppes and mountains.

Yol (Şerif Görem and Yilmaz Güney, 1982). In Turkish, *yol* means route, road or path. This film, which won the Palme d'Or at the Cannes Film Festival, tells the story of a group of prisoners who are given a short parole to visit their families. After traveling by bus and train, these reunions bring them face to face with their alienation in its most insidious form: social pressure, religious morality, taboos and constraints dictated by tradition.

A Season in Hakkâri (Erden Kiral, 1982). A young intellectual from Istanbul spends a brief period as a teacher in the extreme south-east of the country. Lost in the mountains, in an isolated village, he observes the life of the peasants.

Three films by veteran director Atif Yilmaz provide revealing insights into Turkish life, particularly in Istanbul.

A Drop of Love (1984) is set in the working-class neighbourhoods of Istanbul, where we see people, particularly women, struggling to take control of their destinies. *Aaahh, Belinda* (1986) explores the personal fulfilment of someone from a modest background, handicapped by the rigidity of social taboos and hierarchy. In the third film, set in Old Istanbul with its Levantine backdrops, *My Dreams, My Love, and You* (1988), the hero allows himself to be seduced by a beautiful, unfathomable woman.

Finally, to conclude the retrospective, we have *Night Journey* (Omer Kavur, 1988). A film-maker sets up his home in the ruins of an Ionian church. In the midst of a creative crisis he takes stock of his life as an artist by writing a scenario. He does this in a setting that is so out of touch with reality that the weight of history seems light and liberating.

Film-lovers have the privilege of constantly traveling. The wonderful adventures depicted in these films make you want to live some real ones!

Mehmet Basutçu
Film critic for the daily *Cumhuriyet* newspaper.

ISTANBUL

I stanbul was destined to play an important role in history because of its unique position as a world crossroads bridging two continents. It is the guardian of the Bosphorus and the strategic channel between the Black Sea and the Mediterranean.

As Constantinople, the city reigned over the Christian part of the Roman Empire for more than a thousand years. With equal splendour it later became the capital of the immense Ottoman Empire and remained so for five centuries. More recently, in 1923, the capital was transferred to Ankara but Istanbul is still the largest Turkish city and the most important economic, cultural and tourist centre.

In the beginning the town covered only the upper part of the peninsula where there are seven hills. Today this part of the city is known as Stamboul and stretches from the Sea of Marmara to the Golden Horn. This is the old quarter, the heart of the city with traces of Byzantine splendour that have marked the town throughout history. Opposite, on the northern shores of the Golden Horn, is Beyoğlu, an ancient commercial centre inhabited mainly by ethnic minorities. Finally, on the other side of the Bosphorus in the middle of an island of greenery, lies Üsküdar, gateway to Asia.

There seem to be two cities in Istanbul: the first recalls the past; it is solemn, grand and dignified. The second is modern, teeming, noisy, dirty and polluted. Five times a day from minarets all over the city, this background hum of human bustle is drowned out by the insistent cry of the Muezzin. Istanbul had one million people in 1950. In 1988 there were six million, 32% of whom live on the Asian side. By 1990 the population was estimated to be 8.5 million.

The significant population growth has meant that considerable efforts have been made to improve traffic – every day one and a half million people cross to the historic peninsula with its magnificent Topkapi Palace – as well as to build new housing and fight against water pollution. Pockets of decaying Levantine dwellings from the 19th century have been replaced by expressways through the city centre to alleviate some of the worst traffic jams in the world. Inhabitants have bitterly criticized this policy and reproach the authorites for demolishing some of their oldest houses and changing the face of picturesque old quarters, all in the name of progress. Unhealthy slums, workshops and warehouses on the shores of the Golden Horn have also been replaced by green spaces and luxury hotels to accommodate the ever-increasing visitors.

In 1973, to celebrate 50 years of Mustafa Kemal's Republic, the first suspension bridge was completed over the Bosphorus, followed by a second (the Fatih) in 1988 and a third is now being planned. These bridges not only link the two halves of Istanbul, but also draw together two different worlds and cultures.

HISTORY

In the middle of the seventh century BC, a Greek named Byzas decided to leave Megara, his homeland, and consult the Oracle at Delphi to find out where he should build his colony. He was told to 'sail to the city of the blind and found a town opposite'. Encouraged by this reply, Byzas set sail. After a few weeks' navigation, he reached the Dardanelles, crossed the Sea of Marmara and entered the Bosphorus. There he came upon a magnificent gulf overlooked by a city founded by Greeks, called Chalcedon. The Oracle's words came to mind. Chalcedon was certainly the city of the blind, of people who hadn't noticed that just opposite, less than a kilometre away, the hills on the triangular peninsula, the very point of the European continent, formed a unique site that was undoubtedly destined to have a wonderful future. Thus Byzas settled at a place called Lygos, opposite the 'city of the blind' and gave the town his name. And so Byzantium was born.

The colony grew and prospered rapidly due to fishing and shipping tariffs paid by vessels passing through the straits. It wasn't long, however, before other nations were attracted to Byzantium's wealth. At the end of 600 BC it was attacked by Persians, whereupon Sparta came to the rescue; from then on the city was under Athenian domination. This situation ended only when the city rebelled against Philip of Macedon.

Later, Byzantium looked to Rome and was given the title Civitas Libera. By AD 200, it had grown into a commercial outpost for Rome and became the subject of rivalry between Pescennius Niger and Septimius Severus. The latter won, decapitated his opponent and seized the city. Resentful of the city's initial support of his enemy, he punished the inhabitants by massacring the garrison and destroying monuments. His son Caracalla, however, resolved to rebuild the city and endowed it with temples and edifices of all kinds.

More than a century after Caracalla's death, another Roman emperor, Constantine, decided to move his capital to the centre of his empire and chose Byzantium, located about 1240 mi/2000 km from Rome. On September 18, 324, Constantine entered *Nova Roma* (New Rome) and later renamed it Constantinopolis after himself.

Back to the roots

Stamboul, today's Istanbul, was the Turkish name for the former Constantinople. In ancient times when the Greeks of the Lower Empire went to the metropolis, they would say: *Eis tên polin,* which meant 'I'm going to the city'. The Turks who heard this thought that it was the name of their city which they translated as *Is-tam-bol.* Hence the three names: Stambol, Stamboul and Istanbul.

The emperor hoped to transform the new capital into such a splendid and luxurious city that it would eclipse Rome. He built monuments modeled after those in Rome and transferred all the statues and works of art he could from Rome to embellish the new capital. Among them were the column of Porphyrogenetus, known as *Constantine's Column* and a bronze spiral column he had brought from Delphi depicting three entwined serpents, known as the *Serpentine Column.*

Tens of thousands of workers toiled over the city for six years. The result was a resplendent Constantinople gleaming with sumptuous churches and magnificent monuments. There were theatres, baths, aqueducts, cisterns, palaces and patrician mansions. Finally, in great pomp, the city was inaugurated on May 11, AD 300.

Constantine's successors continued to adorn the city that had by then become a centre for philosophers and scholars. Valens endowed it with an aqueduct, and Theodosius with an obelisk from Heliopolis which he placed in the Hippodrome.

As the stronghold of Christianity in the East, Constantinople was surrounded by ramparts during the fifth century. In the sixth century, Justinian the Great once again changed the face of the city by ordering the building of some of the masterpieces of Byzantine architecture, among them the basilica of Saint Sophia. His successors tried to perfect his works by enlarging the imperial palace, building new churches, embellishing the forum and opening public gardens.

For almost a century afterward, the Byzantine Empire weakened, but from 867 to 1056, during the rule of the great Macedonian dynasty, it regained its strength and unity to reach the height of its glory.

Meanwhile the Seljuk Turks, nomadic shepherds from the high plateaus in Asia, were moving west. They were valiant warriors who, in 1071, overcame the troops of the Christian emperor at Manzikert. Little by little the Byzantine Empire lost its stability and began its slow decline. During this time, the Turks, toward the end of the 11th century, marched westward to establish their capital in Konya.

As the Seljuks began taking the Holy Land from the Arabs, Christians in the West vowed to free Palestine's holy sites. This was the beginning of the Crusades. Unfortunately, during the Fourth Crusade, the crusaders concentrated their efforts on Constantinople instead of waging war with Egypt. They disembarked there in 1203, to support the Byzantine emperor Isaac II, who had been driven off the throne by his brother Alexius. This led to violent clashes between the Byzantines and the Latins (sent from Venice) who mindlessly pillaged, burned, raped and stole, destroying most of the treasures the city had acquired over the last nine centuries. Having taken the capital by force, they were determined to stay and ruled for nearly 50 years.

With the help of the Genovese, the Byzantine emperor Michael Palaeologus, reclaimed the city from the crusaders in 1261. Although the Palaeologus dynasty had the longest reign in Constantinople (1261-1453), it only partially restored Byzantine strength. In reality the empire was crumbling while its enemies were gaining ground. Ottoman troops pushed their way to the very ramparts of the city. In the middle of the 15th century the young Ottoman sultan Mehmed II prepared the coup de grâce. In record time (just a few months) he built a fortified castle overlooking the straits and set an army of 500,000 men at the city gates to begin a siege on April 5, 1453, that was to last seven weeks. On May 29, a break appeared in the walls and the sultan's troops entered the city. Mehmed II allowed his soldiers the customary three days' pillage, then called them to order and named Constantinople the new capital of the Ottoman Empire.

Mehmed II and his son Bayezid II built up the city, now called Istanbul, that became the capital of the Islamic world. The city's finest hours were those of the empire's, under Süleyman I the Magnificent (1520-1566). He was conqueror, administrator and lawgiver. Through Sinan, his inspired architect, he gave the city some of its most beautiful buildings. Selim II continued work on the city, bedecking it with domes and minarets.

Through the centuries thereafter, each sultan tried to leave his stamp on the city, but none of them could bring back the golden age of the first centuries after the conquest (see p. 51).

By the end of World War I, the capital was occupied by the Allies and it wasn't until the emergence of Mustafa Kemal that the country's destiny changed. He incarnated the burst of Turkish nationalism after the war and was elected president of the new Turkish Republic. On October 29, 1923, he transferred the capital to Ankara, in the heart of Anatolia.

Eternal city

You have always existed, Istanbul, living in time without a before or an after. Constantinople was once your name. You were capital of a great empire with your three rows of crenellated walls, your towers, banners, palaces, stone edifices set high above the sea, your devout population, your churches and your monasteries with their miraculous fountains, icons, monks and cherubs. Constantinople was once your name. The most famous cupola in history, visible even from Mount Olympus, crowned the basilica of Saint Sophia like a starry sky, like an upturned chasm. Mosaics, majestic columns of green porphyry, gold crucifixes and silver candelabra gleamed in the light that filtered through arched windows. It lit up the walls, the wide nave that could hold all the inhabitants of the city, and reached right down to the dark underground galleries that only the monks could fathom. In those days, storks flew overhead as they still do now. That was before the pointed minarets pierced the sky, but the storks fleeing toward Mecca, like the coppery mauve clouds, the seagulls and the cormorants have always circled above you. The shadow of Galata Tower has long fallen over the roofs of the houses and across the alleys lined with Genovese taverns. Your shoals of fish that drift down from the Euxine to Propontis, like your gentle breezes and north winds, have known no equal. You have always existed, Istanbul!

Nedim Gürsel
The First Woman
(*La Première Femme,* le Seuil, 1986).

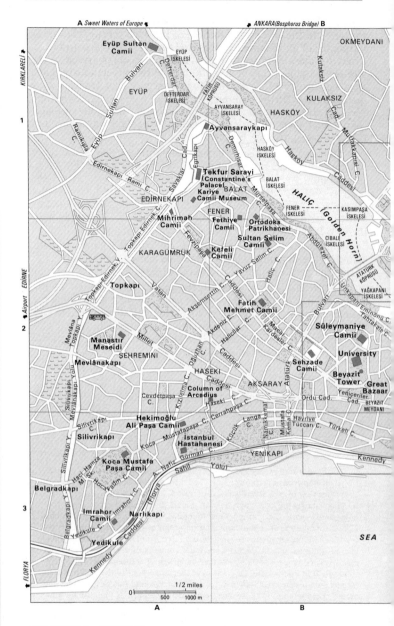

ISTANBUL I – GENERAL

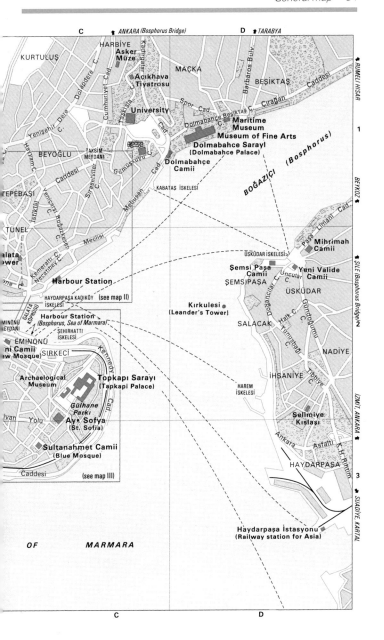

C ↑ *ANKARA (Bosphorus Bridge)*   D ↑ *TARABYA*

KURTULUŞ

HARBİYE **Asker Müze**

MAÇKA

Açıkhava Tiyatrosu

BEŞİKTAŞ

University

Spor Cad.

Çırağan Caddesi

↑ *RUMELİ HİSAR*

Dolmabahçe Beşiktaş C.

Maritime Museum
Museum of Fine Arts
Dolmabahçe Sarayı
(Dolmabahçe Palace)

BEYOĞLU

TAKSİM MEYDANI

Dolmabahçe Camii

(Bosphorus)

TEPEBAŞI

İstiklal Caddesi

KABATAŞ İSKELESİ

BOĞAZİÇİ

↑ *BEYKOZ*

TÜNEL

Meclisi

alata; wer

Kemeraltı C.

Necatibey C.

ÜSKÜDAR İSKELESİ

Mihrimah Camii

Paşa Limanı Cad.

↑ *ŞİLE (Bosphorus Bridge)*

Harbour Station

HAYDARPAŞA KADIKÖY (see map II)
İSKELESİ

Şemsi Paşa Camii
ŞEMSİPAŞA

Yeni Valide Camii

Uncular C.

ÜSKÜDAR

MİNÖNÜ
EYDANI

Harbour Station
(Bosphorus, Sea of Marmara)
ŞEHİRHATTI
İSKELESİ

Kırkulesi
(Leander's Tower)

SALACAK

Doğancılar C.

Halk C.

Gündoğumu C.

Tunusbağı

NADİYE

İZMİT, ANKARA ↑

EMİNÖNÜ
ni **Camii**
ew Mosque) SİRKECİ

Archaelogical Museum

Topkapı Sarayı
(Tapkapi Palace)

Gülhane Parkı

İHSANİYE

Tibaiye C.

HAREM
İSKELESİ

Selimiye Kışlası

ivan Yolu

Aya Sofya
(St. Sofia)

Ankara

Asfaltı

A.H.Rıhtım

HAYDARPAŞA

Sultanahmet Camii
(Blue Mosque)

Caddesi (see map III)

3

↑ *SUADİYE, KARTAL*

OF   *MARMARA*

Haydarpaşa İstasyonu
(Railway station for Asia)

C   D

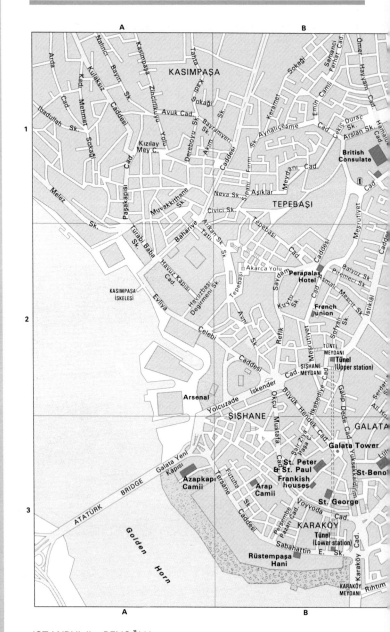

ISTANBUL II – BEYOĞLU

C

TAKSIM

Sakızağacı

Karakurum Sk.

Caddesi

French
Consulate

TAKSIM
MEYDANI

Taksim
Parkı

D

Kültür
Sarayı

Taki Zafer C.

Cad.

Tarlabaşı

Caddesi

Caddesi

Mesafelik Sk.

Church of the Holy
Trinity

Gümüşsuyu

Kazancıbaşı Yokusu

Ağa Çırağı Sk.

Hatun Camii

Sk.

ost Office

İstiklal

Turnacıbaşı

Çeşme Billurcu
Sk.

Sormagir

Selime

Mebusan

 ASARAY
YDANI

Ahududu Sk.

Mat Sk.

Cd Arslan
Yatağı

Somuncu

Cihangir
Sokağı

Akyol

Sk.

Yok.

Caddesi

urch
of
Anthony

Galatasaray
School

Liva Sk.

Sirasevilen

riziya Sk.

Çarşı Cad.

Bostancıbaşı C.

Bostancıcuma Cad.

Güneşli

Kumrulu Yok.

Cad.

Palace of
rance

BEYOĞLU

Çukurcuma Cad.

Yeni Yuva Sk.

Akarsu Yokuşu

Sk.

CİHANGİR

ntom Kaptan Sk.

Palace
of Venice

Kadiriler

Güçü

Türk

Defterdar Yokuşu Cad.

Kumrulu
Sk.

Sk.

Mebusan

Cama
F Ornelit Sk.

Boğazkesen

İlyas
Çelebi

Meclisi

mbaracı Yokuşu

BOĞAZKESEN

Caddesi

Sanatkarlar Cad.

Nusretiye
Camii

Tophane
Fountain

Kılıçalipaşa Camii

dek Cad.

Caddesi

Cad.

TOPHANE

emeraltı

Necatibey

Caddesi

Mumhanesi

Caddesi

Galata

Cad.

Harbour
Station

BOSPHORUS

iya

emankeş

YDARPAŞA KADIKÖY
SKELESİ

0   200   400 m

yds

C

D

1

2

3

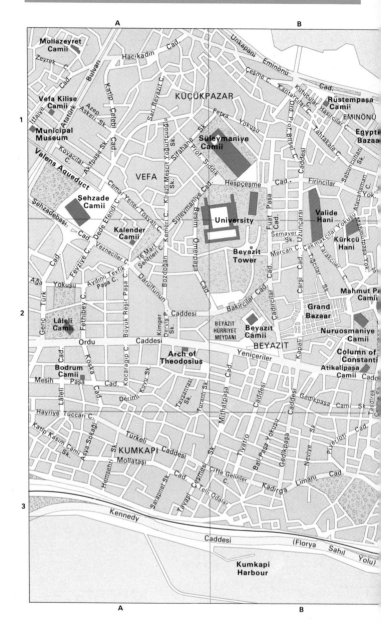

ISTANBUL III – EAST STAMBOUL

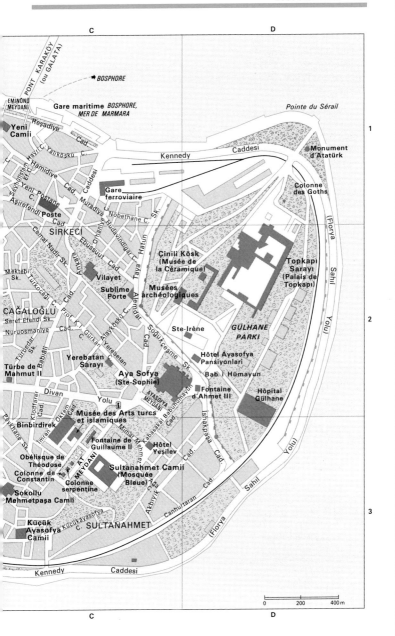

C

D

PONT KARAKÖY
(ou GALATA)

→ *BOSPHORE*

EMINÖNÜ
MEYDANI

Gare maritime *BOSPHORE,
MER DE MARMARA*

Pointe du Sérail

Yeni
Camii

Reşadiye

Cad.

Kennedy   Caddesi

Monument
d'Atatürk

C. Hamidie

Yeni Postane

Gare
ferroviaire

Colonne
des Goths

Cad.

Muradiye

Nöbethane C.

Aşirefendi Poste
Cad.

SIRKECİ

Cemal Nadir Sk.

Ankara

Ebussuut Cad.

Hatun

Çinili Kösk
(Musée de
la Céramique)

Topkapı
Sarayı
(Palais de
Topkapı)

(Florya)

Mektebi
Sk.

Turocağı

Vilayet

Musées
archéologiques

CAĞALOĞLU

Şeref Efendi Sk.

Sublime
Porte

Alemdar

Soğukçeşme Sk.

Sahil

Nuruosmaniye Cad.

Ste-Irène

GÜLHANE
PARKI

Türbe de
Mahmut II

Türbetar Sk.

Babıali

Yerebatan
Sarayı

Yerebatan C.

Aya Sofya
(Ste-Sophie)

Hôtel Ayasofya
Pansiyonları

Bab i Hümayun

Yolu)

Divan

Yolu

AYASOFYA
MEYDANI

Fontaine
d'Ahmet III

Hôpital
Gülhane

Klodfarer Cad.

Pierre Loti Cad.

Binbirdirek

İmran Öktem

Musée des Arts turcs
et islamiques

Mimar Mehmet

Babunhayun Cad.

Fontaine de
Guillaume II

Hôtel
Yeşilev

İshakpaşa

Obélisque de
Théodose

AT
MEYDANI

Sultanahmet Camii
(Mosquée
Bleue)

Cad.

Colonne de
Constantin

Colonne
serpentine

Akbıyık

Sahil

Sokollu
Mehmetpaşa Camii

Canhurtaran Cad.

Küçük
Ayasofya
Camii

Küçükayasofya

C. SULTANAHMET

(Florya)

Yolu)

Kennedy   Caddesi

0   200   400 m

C

D

PRACTICAL INFORMATION

Telephone area code: 1

Istanbul is 285 mi/459 km north-west of Ankara, 392 mi/631 km north of Izmir and 458 mi/737 km north of Antalya.

When to go

Istanbul is delightful all year round, but the ideal time to visit is from April to November. In summer the heat is often cooled by the north wind off the Bosphorus. In winter, it can snow unexpectedly so it is advisable to bring warm clothes.

Access

The **Atatürk Airport** is 14 mi/23 km from the town centre. You can either take one of Istanbul's many taxis into town or use the THY (Turkish Airlines) bus (one leaves every half hour).

If you arrive by train, you come into **Sirkeci Station**, III, C1, at the foot of Topkapi Palace overlooking the Bosphorus. The station is on the corner of Ankara Caddesi and Kennedy Caddesi.

Accommodation

Map coordinates refer to maps I, II and III, pp. 80-81, 82-83, 84-85. There are so many hotels in the city that, depending on your budget, you'll have no difficulty finding one, except perhaps in July and August. See p. 4 for an explanation of hotel classifications.

Hotels

▲▲▲▲▲ **Ayasofya Pansiyonlari**, Soğukçeşme, III, C2, ☎ 512 5732. 75 rooms. This is the latest of Istanbul's grand hotels, located near the main gate of the Topkapi Palace. Nine old wooden mansions that were residences of court dignitaries in the 19th century have been faithfully restored according to Ottoman tradition. Each house has between 5 and 10 bedrooms, decorated differently but in keeping with the style of the time.

▲▲▲▲▲ **Büyük Surmeli**, Saateibayir Sok. G. Tepe, I, D1, off map, ☎ 172 0515. 224 rooms. This is a recent (1985) luxury hotel in the residential area of the city.

▲▲▲▲▲ **Etap Marmara**, Taksim Square, II, D1, ☎ 151 4696. 432 air-conditioned rooms. This is one of Istanbul's most beautiful hotels. Because of its vantage point on one of the city's hills, it has magnificent views (especially from the 20th floor) of the Bosphorus, the Sea of Marmara and Topkapi Palace. It's conveniently situated for a seminar or conference and gives special rates to groups.

▲▲▲▲▲ **Hidiv Kasri**, in Çubuklu on the Asian shore of the Bosphorus (off map), ☎ 146 7090. 16 rooms. This is the former residence of the khedive of Egypt and dates from the early 1900s. It has been perfectly restored and is now a luxurious hotel.

▲▲▲▲▲ **Hilton**, Cumhuriyet Cad., Harbiye, I, C1, ☎ 131 4646/ 148 7752. 410 rooms. Luxury hotel with a beautiful view over the Bosphorus and the Sea of Marmara.

▲▲▲▲▲ **Sheraton**, Taksim Parki, Taksim, I, C1, ☎ 131 2121. 459 rooms. The hotel offers the same service as the others in the Sheraton group. There is an impressive view from the upper floors.

▲▲▲▲▲ **Yeşil Ev**, between Saint Sophia and the Blue Mosque, III, C3, ☎ 148 4744. 21 rooms. This is another wooden Ottoman residence that has been restored with great taste. It is expensive and nearly always full, so you should reserve well in advance.

▲▲▲▲ **Dedeman**, Yildiz Posta Cad. 50 Esentepe, I, D1, off map, ☎ 172 8800. 261 rooms. This is a quiet, recently built hotel in the residential area of Esentepe about 10 minutes from the new town.

▲▲▲▲ **Divan,** Cumhuriyet Cad., I, C1, ☎ 131 4100. 96 rooms. This is a very good hotel, with excellent service and a restaurant.

▲▲▲▲ **Etap Istanbul,** Meşrutiyet Cad., Tepebaşi, II, B2, ☎ 151 4646. 200 air-conditioned rooms. Located in the centre of the city in the lively Pera quarter near the old Pera Palas Hotel. The bar on the 22nd floor gives you a panoramic view of the Bosphorus, the Golden Horn and old Istanbul.

▲▲▲▲ **Fuar,** Namik Kernal Cad., I, B2-3, ☎ 525 9732. 61 rooms. This is a recently built hotel right in the middle of the old town (Aksaray area).

▲▲▲▲ **Maçka,** Eytem Cad., 35 Teşvikiye, I, CD1, ☎ 140 1053. 184 rooms. This quiet hotel with a panoramic view is located in a residential area on a little hill below Taksim Square.

▲▲▲▲ **Pera Palas,** Meşrutiyet Cad., 98/100, Tepebaşi, II, B2, ☎ 151 4560. 116 rooms. Built in 1892 and recently renovated. The hotel has a 19th-century atmosphere and is as well-known as the Orient Express. Heads of state including Atatürk (whose room is now a museum) have stayed here, as has Agatha Christie.

▲▲▲ **Klas,** Harikzedeler Sok. 48, Aleli, III, A2, ☎ 511 7874. 60 rooms. A very comfortable hotel in the old part of Istanbul.

▲▲▲ **Ons,** Kocaragip Cad., III, B2, ☎ 512 1683. 39 rooms. This is a quiet, modest but comfortable hotel not far from the Grand Bazaar.

▲▲▲ **Ramada,** Ordu Cad. 226, III, A2, ☎ 519 6390. 275 rooms. In the heart of the old town within easy reach of Topkapi Palace and the Grand Bazaar. Four buildings of four storeys each, connected by glass walkways.

▲▲▲ **Tamsa,** Namik Kernal Cad., I, B2-3, ☎ 523 8616. 125 rooms. A modern hotel in the Grand Bazaar quarter.

▲▲ **Barin Oteli,** Fevziye Cad. 7, III, A2, ☎ 522 8428. A well-situated hotel with 65 rooms.

▲▲ **Cidde Oteli,** Aksaray Cad. 10, I, B2-3, ☎ 522 4211. 84 rooms.

▲▲ **Eyfel,** Kurultay Sok. 19, Beyazit, III, A2, ☎ 520 9788. 85 rooms. This hotel is very pleasant and you get good value for the price.

▲▲ **Sokullu Pasa,** Mekmetpaşa Sok. 10, III, C3, ☎ 512 3753. 36 rooms. A newly restored hotel behind the Blue Mosque near Küçük Aya Sofya.

▲ **Optimist Guesthouse,** on the Hippodrome square near the Islamic Arts Museum, III, C3, ☎ 519 2091. 15 rooms. You should reserve ahead of time. Good value.

There are many other hotels near Sirkeci Station, on the Hippodrome and in Askaray.

Outside the city

▲▲▲▲ **Büyük Tarabya,** in Tarabya, ☎ 162 1000. 262 rooms. Located 11 mi/18 km from Istanbul on the shores of the Bosphorus in Tarabya Bay, overlooking a little fishing village. Highly recommended if you would prefer peace and quiet to the bustle of Istanbul.

▲▲▲▲ **Turban Kilyos Moteli,** Kilyos, ☎ 142 0208. 136 rooms. Situated 22 mi/35 km from the centre of Istanbul and 6 mi/10 km from the Bosphorus. It is set in a lovely garden facing an enormous beach. The swimming season begins in May and ends in October.

There are other hotel possibilities in the following towns outside Istanbul: Beykoz (10.5 mi/17 km), Bükuk Ada (15 mi/24 km), Kartal (15 mi/24 km), Kemerburgaz (31 mi/50 km), Küçükçekmece (15 mi/24 km), Pendik (16 mi/26 km), Silivri (45 mi/72 km), Şile (43 mi/70 km) and Yalova (43 mi/70 km).

Student accommodation

Atatürk University Halls of Residence, in Topkapi, Londra Asfalti, Cevizlibag Duragi, ☎ 582 0455/582 0461.

Kadirga Students' Hostel, Cömertler Sok. 6, 81, Kumkapi, III, A3, ☎ 528 2480.

Ortaköy Students' Hostel, Palanga Cad. 20, Ortaköy, I, D1, off map, ☎ 161 7376.

Campgrounds

Ataköy Mokamp, in Sahil Yolu on the airport road, ☎ 572 4961. *Open Apr 1-Oct 31.*

Kervansaray BP Mocamp, on the E5 near the airport, 7 mi/12 km from Istanbul, ☎ 575 4721. Clean, shady and well planned. *Open Apr 1-Oct 15.*

Yeşilyurt Kamping, near the airport, ☎ 573 8408. Quite expensive. Swimming is possible. *Open all year round.*

Entertainment

Festival

The **Istanbul International Festival** takes place in June and July. Both Turkish and foreign companies give excellent performances in historic buildings throughout the town. These include traditional, classical and contemporary productions of music, dance, opera and theatre. For program and price information, contact the **Tourist Information Office,** Meşrutiyet Cad. 57, Galatasaray, II, B1, ☎ 145 6593.

Cinemas

Istanbul's cinemas are in the area around Taksim, I, D1.

Beaches

The Sea of Marmara has good beaches for swimming; so does the Black Sea, especially at Kilyos. Be careful, however, when swimming in the Bosphorus away from organized bathing areas because there are swift currents that can be dangerous.

Food and drink

Map coordinates refer to maps I, II and III, pp. 80-81, 82-83, 84-85. Turks are proud of their cuisine, considered to be one of the finest in the world. To foreigners meal times appear far less formal than in Europe and you can have quickly prepared dishes at any time in many of Istanbul's restaurants.

The very best restaurant food is served in large hotels or restaurants in the Taksim quarter. Restaurants tend to be concentrated in tourist areas – old Istanbul, near Galata Bridge, Taksim Square, Üsküdar (on a more modest scale) and in Tarabya's small port 11 mi/18 km from Istanbul.

By European standards, prices are relatively low except in large hotels where the higher price is often compensated for by the magnificent view of the Bosphorus.

See p. 4 for an explanation of restaurant price classifications.

Old Istanbul

◆◆◆ **Pandelis,** in the middle of the Egyptian Spice Bazaar, opposite the Galata Bridge, III, B1, ☎ 527 3909. *Open 11:30am-3:30pm. Closed evenings and Sunday.* Striking Oriental decor with excellent Turkish cuisine. Frequented by tourists and businessmen.

◆◆ **Konyali,** in the Topkapi Palace, III, D2, ☎ 526 2727. *Closed evenings.* Pleasant view of the Bosphorus, mainly frequented by tourists.

◆◆ **Konyali Kafeterya,** Ankara Cad. 233, III, C1, ☎ 527 0202. Near Sirkeci Station. Quick service and good Turkish food.

◆ **Hacibozanoğullari,** Ordu Cad. 214, opposite Laleli mosque, III, A2, ☎ 528 4492. *Open daily, 11am-9pm.*

On **Beyazit Square** many small restaurants serve *kebaps*..

The art of Raki

The Turkish poet, Orhan Veli, wrote this well-known verse:
> 'In a Raki bottle
> I turn into a fish.'

Beware! A 45° proof aniseed-flavoured alcohol shouldn't be taken lightly – drinking this beverage requires some initiation, and should be done according to the rules of the art.

Wine, vodka, whisky, tequila: each alcoholic beverage has its own special effect, but *raki* produces a state of exaltation unlike any other. You begin to soar far above the contingencies of everyday life after only a second little glass. *Raki* is *raki* only in Turkey, especially in Istanbul – in a bar with 'its feet in the water', or at least in an establishment overlooking the sea. The sea, any sea – the Black Sea of the Marmara, even the waters of the Bosphorus – will do. It doesn't matter which, just as long as you have an undulating salt-water surface to keep you company.

Once inside the bar, be it simple or luxurious (in a little while it won't make any difference), order a bottle of *Altin Bas* (Golden Head) for a start. Its taste is unquestionably superior to any other, and when it arrives, take your time and consider the following options:

1. Drink it neat, straight up (the most dangerous method).

2. Add a little water and some ice (the traditional method).

3. Follow the aesthetic method (Istanbul old-school style), which means taking a sip of *raki* and holding it in your mouth then sipping a little water. Let the two combine slowly in your mouth before raising your eyes heavenward and swallowing. But be careful – this delicious technique will put you under the table in no time. You can, of course, approach the matter more cautiously by ordering an ordinary *bir doubl* (a small double raki) instead of a whole bottle, just to get the feel of it first.

Another important point: although it's possible to drink wine or whisky without eating, *raki,* like vodka, requires some sort of food and the best accompaniment is *meze* (appetizers). The success of an establishment depends to a large extent on the variety of its *meze.* Indeed, the list can be very long, confronting you with several choices including what order to eat them in? The following suggestion may help: start with the simplest and work toward the more elaborate then go back and begin again! Alternate, that's the secret. So, after a *çiroz* (deep-sea mackerel) proceed to some *patlican kizartmasi* (fried eggplant, country style). Alternate hot with cold, cooked with raw, seafood with meat and so on. Remember, it's not a question of having a meal but simply of providing a culinary counterpoint to the principal theme. *Raki* proudly reigns over the *meze* like a sultan over his subjects!

Finally, not only does *raki* stimulate analytical discussion but it may serve as a catalyst for extreme emotions as well. You only have to look at the expressions on the faces of the customers of the Turkish cafés to realize that for them this is no joking matter. *Raki* stimulates metaphysical reflection; nothing escapes debate or question – the destiny of man, the nature of God. . . .

Raki seems to transport you to a state of grace, like an astronaut floating blissfully through space, where you abandon yourself to a delightful feeling of 'weightlessness'.

And now *serefe,* 'to your good health!'

Inside the **Grand Bazaar** are convenient cafés and restaurants open Monday to Saturday for lunch only.

Below the Blue Mosque along the European shore of the Bosphorus there are many restaurants with terraces, like the **Kalyon**, III, C3, ☎ 511 4400. *Open daily, noon-2:30pm, 7pm-midnight.* Continuing on along the road that borders the Sea of Marmara, there is a wide choice of small modest eating places.

In the port under **Galata Bridge,** there are unusual inexpensive restaurants on the waterfront that serve fresh fish. *They are open all day and well into the night.*

Galata-Taksim

♦♦♦ **Liman Lokantasi,** Riktmi Cad., II, BC3, ☎ 144 0133. *Closed evenings.* Near the harbour station next to Galata Bridge with a beautiful view of the port.

♦♦ **Haci Baba,** Istiklâl Cad. 49, II, CD1, ☎ 144 1886. *Open daily, 11am-11pm.* It's extremely pleasant in summer on the terrace overlooking the garden of the Aya Triyada (Greek Orthodox church). Good Turkish dishes.

♦♦ **Pera Palas,** Meşrutiyet Cad. 98/100, II, B2, ☎ 151 4560. The decor recalls the 19th-century atmosphere of the Orient Express. It may well be pleasant to have a drink here but eating is disappointingly expensive.

♦ **Etap Coffee Shop,** opposite Pera Palas, II, B2. Convenient, quick service.

♦ **Galata Tower,** II, B3, ☎ 145 1160. *Open daily.* Evening shows with Turkish dances accompanied by traditional music. Good view of the town. It is advisable to reserve a table in advance.

In **Çiçek Pasaji,** (literally 'Flower Passage') near the Balikpazari market, Istiklâl Cad., Galatasaray, II, C1, there are unusual little restaurants serving quality dishes. Very lively tavernas in the evening.

Near Taksim Square the restaurants of the **Etap Marmara, Divan** and **Hilton** hotels, *open mostly until 11pm,* serve good food although it is more international than Turkish. The restaurant at the Etap Marmara has a wonderful view of the Bosphorus.

Üsküdar

There are lots of small restaurants near the ferry port, but for top quality food you should go to old Istanbul or the area around Galata Tower.

Outside Istanbul

In Emirgân

♦♦♦ **Abdullah,** on the Bosphorus, 6 mi/10 km from Istanbul, ☎ 163 6406. *Open daily, 9am-3pm, 7pm-midnight.* Wonderful terrace.

In Tarabya

♦♦♦ **Façyo Elliz.** This is an excellent fish restaurant.

♦♦♦ **Palet 2** and **Palet 3.** *Open late.* Both these restaurants serve delicious fish specialities.

This small port is becoming a popular tourist site and you can find other less expensive restaurants.

In **Rumeli Kavaği**

Lots of moderately priced fish restaurants in this town located 6 mi/10 km beyond Tarabya.

On the **Asian coast**

There are restaurants in **Kanlica** to the north and **Bostanci** to the south, opposite Princes' Islands.

Getting around Istanbul

By boat

This way of seeing the city is both unusual for a tourist and practical. It is unusual in the sense that it is mainly used by Istanbul residents (Stamboullus); morning and evening during rush hour, you'll see crowds of people on the wharves. Because the town is composed of three distinct areas each separated by the sea, it was absolutely essential to develop water transport. Ferryboats carry passengers between the areas along the Golden Horn and the Bosphorus including Üsküdar, Kadiköy, Haydarpaşa (station), Princes' Islands and Yalova. See p. 39 for ferry information.

By bus

This is a convenient, inexpensive means of transport but you do need to have a good idea of the town in order to pick out the right bus, because there are so many of them going in different directions all the time. The name of the route is usually indicated on the front left-hand side of the bus. Itineraries of the main bus routes are available from **Tourist Information Offices.** There are stations at Taksim, Eminönü and Beyazit (near the Bazaar) on the European side of Istanbul, and at Üsküdar and Kadiköy on the Asian side.

By car

Traffic has improved over the past few years after a one-way system was set up through the city. The two bridges crossing the Golden Horn are both one-way: traffic flows over Galata Bridge in the Eminönü-Karköy direction and over Atatürk Bridge in the opposite direction. Driving is not recommended around old Istanbul or near Galata Tower in the Beyoğlu quarter. It is much easier to drive along the shores of the Bosphorus. Wherever you go, take late-afternoon traffic jams into account, especially on weekdays.

Car rental

Avis: Divan Hotel, Cumhuriyet Cad., I, C1, ☎ 146 2020; Hilton Hotel, Cumhuriyet Cad., Harbiye, I, C1, ☎ 148 7752/131 4646.
Europcar: Cumhuriyet Cad., 472/2, Taksim, I, C1, ☎ 150 8888; and Atatürk Airport.
Hertz: Cumhuriyet Cad., 295, I, C1, ☎ 141 2336.
Sheraton Hotel, Taksim Parki, Taksim, I, C1, ☎ 148 9000.

Garages and parking lots

These are near the entrance to Topkapi Palace, opposite the docks and on Taksim Square behind Pera Palas.

By taxi and dolmuş

This can be a practical and inexpensive way to get around. Most taxis now have a meter; just make sure that it's working when you set off. There may not always be a taxi stand nearby if, for instance, you are not in a tourist area, so don't hesitate to wave down a taxi in the street.

The dolmuş are taxis that you share on set routes. They are worthwhile not only inside towns but on longer distances between towns. The main departure points are from Taksim, Eminönü, Sirkeci, Üsküdar and Kadiköy.

By underground

Don't count on Istanbul's charming little underground train, the Tünel, to get you very far around the city. French engineers began building it before World War I but stopped after barely 1.2 mi/2 km. There are only two stations covering the area between Galatasaray and Karaköy. It is built on a slope and functions by traction, going up and down the hill like a funicular railway or lift. *Open Mon-Sat 7am-9pm, Sun 7:30am-9pm.*

On foot

This is certainly the best way to see old Istanbul because many of the famous monuments are so close together (Saint Sophia, the Blue Mosque and the Topkapi Palace). There's no sense in using a car or taxi and wasting time in traffic jams especially in the late afternoon. Furthermore, on foot you'll be able to explore old streets – you'll come across quarters that have not yet been restored and get an idea of what the city is really like.

Nightlife

Nightlife in Istanbul may not be as varied as in many large cities, but there are a number of interesting possibilities. The **Sound and Light Show** at the Blue Mosque, which takes place every evening (ask your hotel for the times), provides a fascinating view of this splendid mosque. Restaurant nightclubs put on shows that are often very good, although they cater mainly to a tourist audience. The most well-known night spots are the **Kervansaray** (Cumhuriyet Cad. 30, near the Hilton, I, C1, ☎ 147 1630), the **Galata Tower** (see

p. 90), the **Maksim** (Taksim Square, I, C1, ☎ 144 3134), and the **Parisiennes** (Cumhuriyet Cad. 16, Elmadaği, I, C1).

There are also discos either in big hotels like the **Etap Istanbul** and the **Sheraton** (see p. 86), or outside Istanbul at the **Çinar** in Yesilköy, 11 mi/18 km west of Istanbul (☎ 73 2910), at the **Tarabya,** on the Bosphorus 11 mi/18 km east of Istanbul (☎ 62 0710), or at **Saray Disco** (☎ 572 4945) in Ataköy near the airport.

Organizing your time
See p. 30.

Shopping
See the section 'Shopping' p. 32 for the many articles you can find in Turkey. Istanbul's best shopping areas are in the old town, in and around the Grand Bazaar, III, B2 (see p. 120), and along Istiklâl Cad., which begins behind Galata Tower and ends at Taksim Square I, C1. Quality shops have recently sprung up on Cumhuriyet Cad., I, C2, near the major hotels. There are also modern shops in Bahariye Cad., II, AB1-2, and Bağdat Cad. in the Asian part of the city, I, D3 (off map).

Alabaster and copperware: Grand Bazaar, III, B2.

Antiques: In the Grand Bazaar, III, B2, and in the Nişantaş area, I, D1.

Books: Sahaflar Cad. Çarşisi, not far from the Grand Bazaar, III, B2, and Beyazit Mosque, III, B1, where there is an interesting display of old books.

Carpets: Bazaar 54 Nuruosmaniye Cad. and 54 ve Sengor on the same street, not far from the Grand Bazaar, III, B2. You will also find many carpet dealers in the Grand Bazaar itself.

Clothes: There are shops in the Grand Bazaar, III, B1, which specialize in custom-tailored garments.

Jewelry: Again, the Grand Bazaar is the place to go, but be forewarned – the export of antiques is strictly regulated.

Spices: Egyptian Spice Bazaar, III, B1 (Misir Çarşisi), provides a staggering selection of common and exotic spices.

Useful addresses
Map coordinates refer to maps I, II and III, pp. 80-81, 82-83, 84-85.

Airline offices
Air France, Cumhuriyet Cad. 1, Taksim, I, C1, ☎ 156 4356 *(open Mon-Fri 9am-6pm);* and at the airport.

British Airways, Cumhuriyet Cad. 10, Elmadağ, I, C1, ☎ 148 4235.

Lufthansa, Cumhuriyet Cad. 179, Elmadağ, I, C1, ☎ 146 5130.

Sabena, Talirmhana Topçu Cad. 1/2, Taksim, I, C1, ☎ 150 6026/27, 150 6762 *(open Mon-Fri 9am-1pm).*

THY (Turkish Airlines): Main office, Abide 1 Hurriyet Cad. Vakis Ishana Kat. 2 154/156 Harbiye, I, C1, ☎ 146 4017/147 1338; **Information and reservations,** Cumhuriyet Cad. 131, Elmadağ, I, C1, ☎ 146 2050 (domestic flights), 146 2061 (international flights); **Taksim office,** Cumhuriyet Cad. Gezi Dükkanlan, Taksim, I, C1, ☎ 145 2454/82; and at the airport.

Airport
The Atatürk Airport is at Yesilköy, 14 mi/23 km west of Istanbul on the road to Edirne, ☎ 573 7360.

Banks
You will always find a bank open at Sirkeci Station, III, C1, below the Topkapi Palace. *Banks are open Mon-Fri 8:30am-noon, 1:30-5pm.*

American Express, Hilton Hotel, Cumhuriyet Cad, Harbiye, I, C1

Iktisat Bankasi Türk A.S. (International Bank of Commerce), Büyükdere Cad. 165, Esentepe, ☎ 174 1111/to 30. Currency exchange, near the Grand Bazaar, Nuruosmaniye Cad., Benice Han, Çağaloğlu, III, B2, ☎ 526 9773.

The hamam party

Despite restrictions felt everywhere now, the sultana decided that her *haman* (bathing) parties should have all the luxury of former days. The guests are welcomed into the large hall by all the female staff of the palace, about 30 *kalfa*, who greet them with a shower of rose petals. Their *tcharchaf* are removed and they are shown into boudoirs adjoining the hamam, hung with mirrors and flowers. Here, a servant first plaits their hair with long gold and silver ribbons and ties it up around their heads, then wraps them in a *peştemal* (a long, finely embroidered bath towel) and finally gives them each a pair of thick-soled slippers inlaid with mother-of-pearl.

Thus adorned, the women enter the circular salon, where the sultana awaits them. They are served cardamom-flavoured coffee, like that drunk by the Arabs, to revive them during the hottest months: while they sip, they exchange compliments on the various beauty cases of silver and gold that each of them has brought. These bath parties are the ideal occasion to bring out the ewers, perfume flasks and precious ointment caskets that every young bride receives at her wedding.

The guests then proceed into the hot rooms. Each is attended by two servants who bathe and massage them, remove body hair and perfume them from head to toe. There are three successive rooms of white marble with gushing fountains. The last is an opaque cloud, so thick is the steam. Here the women stay for hours before moving into the resting room with its sofas, green plants and pool of cool water. Here, lounging voluptuously, eating rose- and violet-flavoured sherbets served by silent young *kalfa*, they listen to the soft music of an orchestra playing behind a screen.

This is the time for intimate secrets and all manner of indiscretions. By some strange license, the strict rules of the perfect upbringing given to all Ottoman girls of good family are completely forgotten in the *hamam*.

Kenizé Mourad
'On Behalf of the Dead Princess'
(De la part de la princesse morte), Robert Laffont, 1987.

Ottoman Bank, Voyvoda Cad. 35-37, Karaköy, II, B3, ☎ 143 8260.

Türkiye İş Bankasi, İstiklâl Cad., Beyoğlu.

Türkiye Emlak Bankasi (and **Change**) İstanbul Subesi, ☎ 527 5611.

Consulates

Canada, Honorary Consul Mr. Yavuz Kireç, Büyükdere Cad. 107/3, Gayrettepe, ☎ 172 5174.

Great Britain, Meşrutiyet Cad. 34, Tepebaşi, II, B1-2, ☎ 144 7540.

United States of America, Meşrutiyet Cad. 104, Tepebaşi, B1-2, ☎ 151 3602.

Hamams, or Turkish baths

Cağaloğlu, Hilali Ahmer Cad. 334, III, C2, ☎ 522 2424. *Open 7am-9pm.*

Galatasaray, Turnacibaşi, Sok.24, Beyoğlu, II, C1, ☎ 1441412. *Open 6:30am-10pm men's section, 8am-7pm (women's section).*

Hospitals

Amerikan Hastanesi (American), Güzelbahçe Sok, Nişantaş, I, B2, ☎ 131 4050.

Pasteur Hastanesi (French), Taskisla Cad., Elmadağ, I, C1, ☎ 148 4756.

Alman Hastanesi (German), Siraselviler Cad. Taksim, I, C1, ☎ 143 8100.

Balikli Hastanesi (Greek), Hastaneler Yolu Cad., Yedikule, I, A3, ☎ 528 7330.

Topkapi Hastanesi, Vakif Guraba Cad., Bexm-i Alem, Sok. 22, Gapa, I, A2, ☎ 542 1919.

Places of worship

Sunday services are shown in brackets.

Most places of worship are in the Beyoğlu area.

Catholic churches

Cathedral of the Holy Spirit, Cumhuriyet Cad. 205, Beyoğlu, I, C1 *(9am and 7pm).*

Saint Anthony, Istiklâl Cad. 327 Beyoğlu, II, C2 *(10am, 11am and 7pm).*

Saint Louis des Français, Nuri Zıya Sok. Beyoğlu, II, C2 *(11am).*

Saint Mary-Draperis, Istiklâl Cad. 429, Beyoğlu, II, B2 *(9am and 11:30am).*

Saint Peter and Paul, near Galata Tower, Beyoğlu, II, B3 *(11am).*

Greek Orthodox churches

Aya Triyada (Holy Trinity), Meselik Sok. 13, Taksim, Beyoğlu, II, D1 *(9am).*

Panaghia Service, Emim Nevruz Sok. 20, Galatasaray, II, B1 *(9am).*

Patriarchate, Sadrazan Ali Paşa Cad. 3513, Tarlabaşi, Beyoğlu, I, B1 *(8am):*

Protestant churches

Church of England, near the Consulate, Meşrutiyet Cad., Tepebaşi, II, B1-2 *(10am).*

German Church, Emin Camii Sok., Tebebaşi, II, B1 *(10:30am).*

Synagogues

Beth Israël, Efe Sok. 4, Şişli, I, C1 (off map).

Neve Shalom, Büyük Hendek Cad., II, B2-3 *(Sat 8am).*

Post office

Central Post Office, Yeni Postahane Cad., near the Yeni mosque, III, C1. **Other offices:** one near Taksim Square on Cumhuriyet Cad., I, C1, another opposite the British Consulate, Meşrutiyet Cad., II, B1.

Tourist information

Tourist Information Office, Meşrutiyet Cad. 57, Galatasaray, near Pera Palas, II, B2, ☎ 145 6593. Other offices: **Karaköy,** Karaköy Limani Yolcu Salony (port), II, B3, ☎ 149 5776; **Harbiye,** Hilton Hotel, I, C1, ☎ 133 0592; **Sultanahmet,** Divan Yolu Cad. 3, III, C2, ☎ 522 4903; **Yeşilköy,** Atatürk Airport, ☎ 573 7399.

Tourist police

Turizm Polisi, Alemdar Karakolu, Sultanahmet, III, C2, ☎ 528 5369.

Turkish Maritime Lines (agency)

Rihtim Cad., Karaköy, II, BC3, ☎ 144 0207/149 9222.

Turkish Railways (TCDD)

Trains to Istanbul's suburbs leave from both of the city's main stations: **Sirkeci,** III, C1, for European destinations and **Haydarpaşa,** I, D3, for towns in Anatolia.

Daily departures from Sirkeci Station (☎ 527 0050): trains for Edirne leave at 3:40pm; for Europe at 8:50pm; and for Athens at 8:40pm.

Daily departures from Haydarpaşa Station (☎ 336 2063): trains for Adapazari leave throughout the day about every two hours starting at 5:30am; for Ankara, the *Bosphorus Express* at 9:15am and the *Anatolia Express* at 8:55pm; trains for Denizli (Pamukkale) leave at 6pm; and trains for Lake Van leave on Mondays, Thursdays and Saturdays at 7:15pm.

Turkish Touring and Automobile Club

Türkiye Turing ve Otomobil Kulübü, Halaskargazi Cad. 364, Şişli. ☎ 131 4631/37.

GETTING TO KNOW ISTANBUL

The topography of Istanbul is quite complex but you should be able to get around on your own if you have a good map. The town is built on seven gentle hills and is bordered by the Bosphorus and the Golden Horn, which meet in the Sea of Marmara. The Bosphorus separates Europe from Asia.

The European part of Istanbul is divided by the Golden Horn, which is an extension of the Sea of Marmara. On one side there is **Eminönü,** Istanbul's old quarter with most of the famous mosques, Topkapi Palace and the Grand Bazaar. **Beyoğlu,** on the other side, is the modern part of town with Taksim Square, new hotels and the main shops.

The Asian part of Istanbul, known as **Üsküdar,** has a few reminders of Istanbul's past but is more a new town with many modern buildings, especially around Haydarpaşa station.

The shores of the Bosphorus are lined with villages that are gradually becoming suburbs of Istanbul.

Several bridges now cross the Golden Horn and the Bosphorus, but by far the most pleasant way to explore Istanbul is to take one of the many boats that leave regularly from Galata Bridge (see p. 39).

What to see

Each of these sites is described fully and map references are given in the following pages.

Hippodrome Square: This is the heart of old Istanbul. Starting from the square, begin with a visit to the Blue Mosque, then on to Saint Sophia at the far end of the square, followed by the Yerebatan Saray cistern. End this tour with the Turkish and Islamic Arts Museum in a former private residence (the entrance is in front of the Obelisk of Theodosius).

Topkapi enclosure: There is an entire city quarter inside this enclosure, including the Topkapi Palace and Harem, the Archaeological Museum, the Museum of the Ancient Orient and the Museum of Turkish Ceramics (Tiled Pavilion).

Around the Grand Bazaar: This area includes the Grand Bazaar, with its thousands of stalls, the old Book Market (Sahaflar Carşisi), which leads to to Beyazit Mosque and Beyazit Tower in the middle of the university. You can also see the remains of the Burnt Column (Çemberlitas) on the other side of the Grand Bazaar, Divan Yolu (Istanbul's main street), and finally the Nuruosmaniye and Mehmet Paşa mosques.

Around Süleymaniye Camii (the mosque of Süleyman the Magnificent): Visit the mosque and its numerous buildings, including the tombs of Süleyman and Roxelana, the Valens Aqueduct with the Municipal Museum below and finally, Şehzade Mosque.

Galata Bridge area: Here you will find the Yeni Mosque, the Egyptian Spice Market, a shopping district, Rüstem Paşa Mosque, and the lively quays on each side of the bridge.

Fatih Camii (mosque) and Kariye Camii Museum: From Fatih Mosque, take Darutşşafaka Cad up to Fethiye Mosque, then follow Draman Cad. to the museum at Kariye Camii in the former Church of Saint Saviour in Chora.

Şişhane and Tünel districts: Take a look at the Galata Tower and the main shopping streets such as Istiklâl Cad., which leads to Taksim Square. Continue along this street via Pera Palas and the Etap Istanbul Hotel (beautiful view from the top of the hotel).

Dolmabahçe district: Be sure to see Dolmabahçe Palace and Mosque, the aviary and art gallery, the Maritime Museum beyond the palace and finally, the hilltop gardens of the Yildiz Palace.

Eyüp district: It is best to get here by bus, car or boat. The area around the Eyüp Mosque, which contains the tomb of the prophet's friend and standard bearer, is extremely lively. There is a large cemetery between the mosque and the Pierre Loti Café on the top of a hill. On the way home, stop to look at the city walls.

Üsküdar district: Located on the Asian shore of the Bosphorus with three mosques: Şemşi Paşa, Yeni Valide, and Mihrimah; and the pretty Üsküdar fountain.

Environs of Istanbul: Visit the Bosphorus by boat (see p. 125); Princes' Islands (see p. 128); Edirne (143 m/230 km west of Istanbul, see p. 130); and Bursa (149 m/240 km south-east of Istanbul, see p. 131).

Palaces

Dolmabahçe Palace*** I, D1

Dolmabahçe Cad, on the European shore of the Bosphorus. Access: take a bus or ferry from Galata Bridge. Get off at Dolmabahçe Saraye for a full view of the immense palace façade.

Open 9am-3:30pm, closed Mon, Thurs. Check with the Tourist Information Office as hours sometimes change. The palace is owned by the Ministry of Defense and is closed to the public when foreign dignitaries come to stay. TL1000 admission charge.

Sultan Ahmed I chose an area of reclaimed land on the European shore of the Bosphorus to build a new palace in the early 18th century. From then on it was successively enlarged, transformed and embellished by all the monarchs of the Ottoman throne who succeeded him. After several fires in the first half of the 19th century, however, the imperial dwelling was no longer fit for its occupants or its guests. Sultan Abdül Mecit had it destroyed and constructed the current monumental building in the middle of gardens and fountains. The palace design was heavily influenced by 19th-century Renaissance-Baroque style. With the exception of Abdül Hamit II, all the sultans from 1853 lived there, and it became inextricably linked with the country's history. On March 19, 1877, the first meeting of the Ottoman Chamber of Deputies was held in the throne room. After World War I, the imperial palace became a presidential residence; Kemal Atatürk died there at the age of 57 on November 10, 1938. Since the transfer of Turkey's capital to Ankara in 1923, the palace has been used by foreign guests on official visits to Istanbul.

Once you've climbed the grand double staircase, you come to a series of rooms, each more sumptuously furnished and decorated than the last. The reception rooms, antechambers, offices, bedrooms and bathrooms are exuberantly adorned with crystal, bronze, ceramics, rare ornaments, precious stones and fabrics.

The **Blue Room** for the women of the harem has relief work on the painted walls and ceilings. The chandeliers and candelabra are crystal. On the floor is an enormous 1184 sq ft/110 sq m *hereke* carpet (a rare type from Anatolia). There is a marble bathroom and a beautiful glass-ceilinged room with an extraordinary transparent piano with crystal legs. The furniture in the **Ambassadors' Room** was specially made in France. The four fireplaces are decorated in green, blue and purple ceramics topped by a glittering panel of cut crystal. The furniture and carpets in the **Pink Room** are all unique. This room features a huge oriental vase of bronze flowers with gold plating. The **reception room of the Valide Sultan** (sultan's mother) has a rococo fireplace and a richly decorated door with golden sculptures. The adjoining bedroom was where Empress Eugenia slept on her visit to Istanbul. In **Atatürk's bedroom** the clock has been stopped at 9:05am, commemorating the time of his death on November 10, 1938. His office is next door. You can also visit the room belonging to the concubines' guard and the **bedroom of Abdül Mecid.**

The most impressive room in the palace, however, is the grand reception room or **Throne Room** because of its sheer size (more than 21,528 sq ft/2000 sq m) and also because of the famous chandelier sent by Queen Victoria that weighs 4.5 tons and has 750 light bulbs. It is suspended from the middle of a *trompe l'œil* ceiling.

There are two masterpieces of Baroque architecture in the square at the entrance to the palace: the **Clock Tower** and **Dolmabahçe Mosque.** The

The sultan's titles

The Ottoman administration created impressive titles for the sultans, handed down from the Iranian and Arabian courts.

What we know as *sultan* is, in fact, *padişah*, the equivalent of the Persian word meaning 'king of kings'. The *padişah* can add various titles to his name, such as *sultan*, which is used by all members of the imperial family be they male or female: *şah* (king); *han* or *khan* (lord), a Turko-Mongolian title; *gazi* (conqueror of infidels); and *daïmer muzaffer* (ever victorious). He is addressed as *hünkar* (sovereign); *hümayun* (august); or *hazretleri* (your majesties, in the plural form).

After the conquest of Egypt and the addition of the holy Muslim sites of Medina and Mecca to the empire at the beginning of the 16th century, the *Padişah* decided to increase the importance and dignity of the position of caliph. *Halife* in Turkish means 'lieutenant,' that is to say 'lieutenant of the prophet', the spiritual leader of the Muslim community.

The title of *padişah* is followed by a series of praises and blessings. He is the 'sanctuary of the world' *(âlem-penah);* 'shadow of God over the world' *(zell üllah fi'l-älem),* or 'on earth' *(fi'l-arz),* 'Lord of both worlds' *(iki cihanda devlet);* 'holder of fortune' *(sahib-u devlet);* or simply 'blessed' *(saädetlü)* and 'fortunate' *(devletlü).* He lives in the 'house of bliss' *(dar üs-saädet).*

The vocabulary and syntax in these expressions are most often Arabic (as in religious and political texts), sometimes Persian (the language of culture and poetry), but rarely Turkish.

Each sultan had a personal emblem, or *tuğra,* a calligraphic arrangement of the letters of his name and titles. These *tuğra* are featured at the top of imperial decrees *(firmans),* and you can see them everywhere on buildings (gates, fountains, mosques, palaces), especially at Topkapi. Here are two examples:

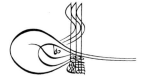

Süleyman the Magnificent
(1520-1566)
'Sovereign Süleyman, Son of Lord Selim, Ever Victorious'.

Abdül Hamid II
(1876-1909)
'Lord Abdül Hamid, Son of Abdül Mecid, Ever Victorious, Conqueror'.

Necmi Gürmen

latter's *mihrab* (prayer niche) and *mimber* (pulpit) of red marble match the ornamental style of the palace.

Topkapi Palace*** III, D2

Sogukçesme Sok., in old Istanbul. Access: bus or taxi.

Open daily, 9:30am-5pm, except the harem, open Wed-Mon 10am-4pm. The guided tour of the harem lasts 30 minutes and there are long lines in summer. TL1000 admission charge for the palace, TL500 for the harem.

A Roman acropolis stood on the tip of the Stamboul peninsula 1500 years before Mehmed the Conqueror decided to build a residence there for Ottoman sultans. This was the Topkapi Palace, home of the sultans from 1478 until 1853, when Abdül Mecit transferred his court to Dolmabahçe Palace on the shores of the Bosphorus. In 1924, Topkapi was converted into a museum and opened to the public. The site is like a separate town with its own fortifications. Inside, among courtyards, gardens, pools and fountains,

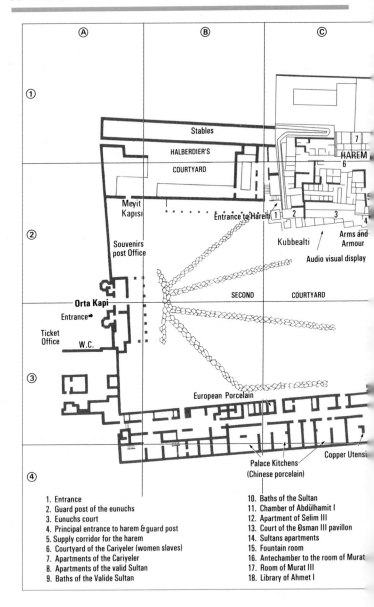

1. Entrance
2. Guard post of the eunuchs
3. Eunuchs court
4. Principal entrance to harem & guard post
5. Supply corridor for the harem
6. Courtyard of the Cariyeler (women slaves)
7. Apartments of the Cariyeler
8. Apartments of the valid Sultan
9. Baths of the Valide Sultan
10. Baths of the Sultan
11. Chamber of Abdülhamit I
12. Apartment of Selim III
13. Court of the Osman III pavillon
14. Sultans apartments
15. Fountain room
16. Antechamber to the room of Murat
17. Room of Murat III
18. Library of Ahmet I

there are both public and private buildings, audience chambers, kiosks and pavilions.

You enter the First Courtyard, which is now a parking lot, through the Imperial Gate, Gate of Majesty (Bab-i Hümayun). There you'll notice **Saint Irene,** one of the first Christian churches built by the Byzantines and later transformed into an arsenal by the Ottomans.

At the end of the First Courtyard, the Orta Kapi (Middle Gate) opens onto the *Court of the Divan,* where affairs of state were discussed. This Second Courtyard encloses some extremely interesting buildings:

The **palace kitchens** stretch along the eastern wall of the courtyard. They

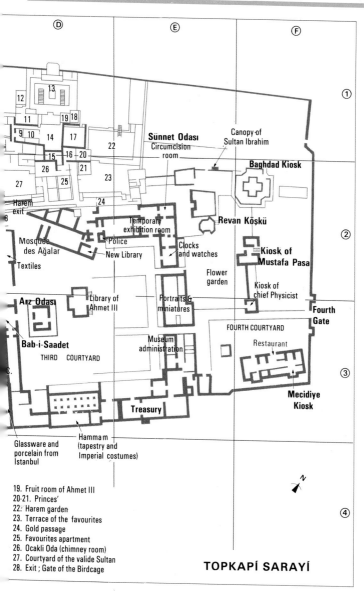

Sünnet Odası
Circumcision room

Canopy of
Sultan Ibrahim

Baghdad Kiosk

Revan Köskü

Temporary
exhibition room

Police

**Mosquée
des Ağalar**

New Library

Clocks
and watches

**Kiosk of
Mustafa Pasa**

Textiles

Flower
garden

Kiosk of
chief Physicist

Arz Odası

Library of
Ahmet III

Portraits &
miniatures

**Fourth
Gate**

Bab-i-Saadet

THIRD   COURTYARD

FOURTH COURTYARD

Restaurant

Museum
administration

Harem
exit

Treasury

**Mecidiye
Kiosk**

Glassware and
porcelain from
Istanbul

Hammam
(tapestry and
Imperial costumes)

19. Fruit room of Ahmet III
20-21. Princes'
22. Harem garden
23. Terrace of the favourites
24. Gold passage
25. Favourites apartment
26. Ocakli Oda (chimney room)
27. Courtyard of the valide Sultan
28. Exit ; Gate of the Birdcage

TOPKAPI SARAYI

were built by Mehmed the Conqueror and were later enlarged and restored
by Sinan, who added 10 cylindrical chimneys. Apart from the kitchens
themselves, the buildings included a mosque and dormitories for the cooks.
They now house one of the most beautiful **porcelain collections** in the world,
featuring pieces brought from China and Japan several centuries ago. On no
account should you miss this exquisite display, especially the green celadon
ware[*] from the Song and Yuan dynasties. In a neighbouring room, there's a
collection of kitchen utensils used at the time of the Ottoman empire. Some
of these are enormous, because the kitchens had to produce vast meals for
the normal palace residents as well as for the sultan's guests. It was not
unusual for 200 sheep, 100 lambs, 40 calves, 80 chickens, 60 geese and

The laws of the harem

By its size alone, the imperial harem formed a state within a state. It had administrative regulations that had authority over His Highness himself, whose private life was rarely a succession of debaucheries with his wives. These rules, or what one hears of them, were sometimes rather surprising: virgins, for instance, were never available to their master except on special occasions, such as official holidays or upon the arrival of good news.

The number of women in the harem varied from sultan to sultan and changed according to the eye of the beholder – there were sometimes 40, 400 or 4000. Apart from the anonymous multitude of female slaves, there were the concubines, or *cariye,* who often married someone close to the palace. Among them were the *gözde,* those who had been honoured with attention from His Highness. The *ikbal* were those who had had the most recent favours, and the *kadin,* the women who had borne the sultan a child. The sultan never took a legal wife – her potential power would have been too daunting – but that didn't prevent several *kadin* from having considerable influence over the sultan through their beauty and intelligence. A period of Ottoman history in the 17th century is called the Reign of the Sultanas, because of the formidable authority held by the sultan's mother, the *Valide Sultan..*

The imperial harem was not located in some inner sanctuary at the end of a series of courtyards; it was next to the men's quarters and even encroached on the public courtyard. The gallery that hid the sultan from view during his ministers' deliberations was built as part of the harem, which meant that its residents could also be present at the proceedings. The sultan alone was master of this area – not even the black eunuchs dared approach the sultanas – and his familiarity with this feminine world gave him a subtly androgynous quality.

A. M. Moulin and P. Chuvin
Islam at the Peril of Women
(*Letters from Turkey* by Lady Montagu,
1717-18, La Découverte, 1981.)
L'Islam au péril des femmes

various accompanying dishes to figure on the daily menu. Two adjoining rooms hold an assortment of silver, gold, and glassware, made in imperial workshops.

The **Divan or Imperial Council Chamber**[*] faces the kitchens. This is where the grand vizir met his ministers. The sultan himself had a room known as the 'eye of the sultan', which was hidden behind a screen so that he could listen to these meetings secretly.

The entrance to the **Harem**[***] is right next door to the Divan Chamber. In imperial days the harem was reached from the sultan's apartments in the Third Courtyard. During the 16th century, about 1200 women lived and intrigued in this strange world of passageways, private apartments, boudoirs, closets, baths and courtyards. The sections open to the public, where you see lavish mosaics, marble, carved wood, murals and sumptuous fabrics, give an idea of the wealth with which the palace was adorned.

At the far end of the Second Courtyard, the Bab-i-Saadet (Gate of Felicity) leads into the Third Courtyard to the sultan's private apartments and his official chambers.

The **Arz Odasi,** or audience chamber, at the entrance to the courtyard is decorated with a distinctive tiled façade and a fountain. This is where foreign ambassadors accredited to the Sublime Porte (a metaphor for the Ottoman government) were received with great pomp and ceremony. The sound of running water prevented conversations from being overheard from outside.

The **Library of Ahmed III,** just behind the audience chamber, is in a white marble pavilion with a domed roof. Some of the doors are inlaid with mother-of-pearl. The red stone building nearby that holds another library was once a mosque for the palace pages and Ağas (a title given to the

The Blue Mosque.

commanding officers of the militia or the Ottoman army). The doors are beautifully inlaid with ivory.

The **Treasury**[**] is in a series of halls around the courtyard that house not only imperial treasures but also holy relics and sacred objects. The first door on the right opens onto a room of imperial costumes. The next room houses the actual treasures, the richest collection of jewels in the world.

The first room displays drinking vessels, vases, and bowls embellished with precious stones, pearls and gold. You can also see Murad IV's ebony throne inlaid with ivory and mother-of-pearl as well as the sultan's armour set with precious stones.

In the second room is a beautiful collection of emeralds including the Kandjar, a famous 14 in-/35 cm-long Topkapi dagger. This has a gold sheath set with diamonds and an emerald-studded hilt. There is also a golden cradle and Ahmed I's throne of precious wood adorned with gems and gold leaf.

Don't miss a fabulous 86-carat diamond in the third room, known as the spoonmaker's diamond, surrounded by 49 smaller stones.

One of the loveliest pieces in the fourth room is the Indian throne of enameled wood decorated with emeralds and rubies.

Opposite the Treasury, the room containing the **Holy Relics** and the **Pavilion of the Sacred Cloak** are both superbly decorated with mosaics. The Prophet's belongings have been reverently kept here since the time of the Ottoman sultans. Among the relics are a tooth, a hair from the Prophet's beard, two battle swords, a cast of his footprint, a standard and finally, his goat-hair cloak in a golden chest.

Two passageways lead into the fourth and final palace courtyard where the most magnificent pavilions are scattered about terraced gardens among fountains and pools. Both the **Baghdad Pavilion**[*], built to commemorate the peace with Baghdad in 1638, and the **Revan Pavilion,** built to celebrate the taking of Erivan in 1635, are remarkably decorated with blue Iznik tiles.

Between the two pavilions, the spectacular view from the marble terrace encompasses the Bosphorus and the Golden Horn.

Yildiz Palace* (off map)

On a hillside in the Beşiktaş area overlooking the European shore of the Bosphorus.

Open daily, 9am-6pm. The restoration of the palace should be completed in 1990. Concerts are given in the park from mid-June to the end of July.

In the 19th century, Abdül Hamid II planted a beautiful, walled hillside with copses of exotic trees and banks of flowers. He added kiosks, pavilions, summer houses and chalets, scattered among cascades and pools in the park. It was here that Murad V was kept prisoner for more than 30 years by his brother Abdül Hamid.

On entering the main gate, you'll see a pavilion to the left, which is where the sultan's guests were welcomed. Opposite the gate and farther up the hill is the main building that was once the harem and the sultan's library. To the left of this building is a large porch, behind which, to the right, is the palace containing the sultan's private apartments.

The lake in the park has been converted by landscape gardeners into the shape of Abdül Hamid's seal.

Mosques

No admission fee. All visitors are required to take off their shoes and to be properly dressed: scarves for women and trousers (not shorts) for men.

The Blue Mosque*** (Sultan Ahmet Camii) III, C3

On the Hippodrome Square in old Istanbul.

Every evening there's a free Sound and Light show at the Blue Mosque in either Turkish, German, English or French depending on the day (check with your hotel or at the Tourist Information Office, p. 94).

This elegant mosque was built like a tiara on the top of one of the city's hills opposite Saint Sophia, on the site of the ancient imperial palace of Byzantium. Its grace and beautiful proportions were intended to reflect the splendour of Islam. One of Sinan's disciples, Mehmed Ağa, built it in 1609 at the request of Sultan Ahmed I who wanted it to be 'very light, and inside, as blue as the azure of a clear sky'. To make it stand out from all the other holy places in the city, he endowed it with six minarets. Hitherto only the Kaaba Mosque in Mecca had been allowed as many and in order to appease the imams (religious leaders), Mehmed Ağa was sent to Mecca to add a seventh.

From the outside, the Blue Mosque is a finer achievement than its illustrious neighbour, Saint Sophia, with its remarkable cascade of domes framed by the delicate points of its six minarets. However, its real charm becomes apparent once inside. The famous blue and green tiles of the walls and arches are bathed in glorious light that is filtered through 260 windows. The central dome, 142 ft/43 m high and 73 ft/22 m in diameter, rests on four massive pillars each with a 53 ft/16 m circumference. Notice also the *mihrab* (prayer niche) and *mimber* (pulpit) of finely worked marble, the carpets of wool and silk and the chandeliers decorated with precious stones.

The sultan added a series of public buildings to his mosque, including a refectory, *medrese* (theological school) and *imaret* (refuge for the poor).

Mosque of Süleyman the Magnificent*** (Süleymaniye Camii) III, B1

Süleymaniye Cad., on a hill next to the university overlooking the port, Galata Bridge and the shores of the Golden Horn.

In 1550, when the all-powerful padishah Süleyman the Magnificent was at the height of his power, he asked his great architect, Sinan, to build a monument. Not only did it have to be worthy of his reign but it also had to outdo proud Saint Sophia, the magnificent work of Justinian the Christian. Sinan supervised thousands of builders, who worked for seven years to complete the work.

Courtyard: Enter the mosque through the wide courtyard with domed porticoes. The 24 columns and arches are made of white marble, porphyry and pink granite. In the middle of the courtyard is a *sardivan* (a fountain for ritual ablutions).

The **prayer room** itself is an enormous square of nearly 37,674 sq ft/3500 sq m. The central dome, 174 ft/53 m high, rests on a square base with an 87 ft/26.5 m diameter and has 32 windows. The pendentives and arches holding it are themselves supported by four quadrangular pillars with sides measuring 25 ft/7.5 m. The whole structure is completed by two semidomes with windows. In all, there are about 150 windows and flower-patterned stained-glass panels that give the mosque its incomparable radiance and luminosity. Note the fine workmanship of the white marble *mihrab*, the *mimber*, the imperial loge and the choir gallery.

Adjoining buildings: Because Süleyman wanted the mosque to be an important religious centre, Sinan surrounded it with a complex of buildings around the courtyard. Among them are schools for Koranic teaching, a caravanserai, baths, shops, a hospital for the poor and a medical school.

Mausoleums: Süleyman's mausoleum stands out among the white stelae of the cemetery. It is an octagonal-domed monument surrounded by an open gallery. The sultan's cenotaph is in the middle together with others of his family. His wife Hürrem Sultan, known as Roxelana, is buried nearby. Sinan, Süleyman's great builder, who died in 1588, is buried in a far more modest enclosure behind the mosque.

Beyazit Camii** III, B2

Darülfunun Cad., near the university entrance and not far from the Grand Bazaar.

Built between 1501 and 1505, this is one of the oldest mosques of the city and the first to be inspired by Byzantine architecture through the use of a single cupola flanked by two semidomes. The prayer room is a vast square of 12,917 sq ft/1200 sq m surmounted by a central dome. The *mihrab*, *mimber* and choir gallery are all made of white marble. The courtyard is lined with a portico of 20 columns with an elegant ablutions fountain in the

---

Sinan's late genius

Sinan was born in 1498 in Djülavuk, modern day Sinan-Köy, and died when he was over 90. After finishing his studies he began a military career in the Janissary corps until the advanced age, for those days, of 50. Then, through his work as foreman on both civil and military constructions such as bridges, aqueducts and barracks, he caught Süleyman the Magnificent's attention and became the sultan's court architect.

His fame, however, is due to the mosques that he built, particularly his two masterpieces that mark the height of Ottoman architecture. These are the Süleymaniye (1550-1557) or mosque of Süleyman the Magnificent in Istanbul, known as the 'splendour and glory' by Turkish poets, and the Selimiye (1569-1575) in Edirne.

Sinan took Saint Sophia as his supreme reference and was also inspired by Seljuk models in Anatolia. With these in mind he would build a central dome resting on two or four half-domes over the main prayer room. Preceding the prayer-room would be a vast courtyard surrounded by a portico. The slender minarets would contrast gracefully with the majestic body of the domes, both parts reflecting the same purity and nobility of line.

Although Sinan's talent revealed itself rather late in life, he nonetheless left more than 300 edifices; among them 81 *djami* (mosque-cathedrals), 50 *masdjid* (sanctuaries), 55 *medrese*, 33 palaces, 32 hamams, 26 *türbe* (including that of Süleyman in Istanbul), 17 caravanserais, 14 minarets, 8 bridges, 5 viaducts and 3 hospitals.

middle. Slightly apart from the main body of the mosque, two minarets shoot skyward.

Fatih Mehmet Camii** I, B2

In the Fatih district on a hill behind the Valens Aqueduct at the extreme west end of Karaman Sok.

The mosque was built between 1463 and 1471 by Mehmed the Conqueror on the ruins of the Church of the Holy Apostles, which was destroyed during the siege of Constantinople. An earthquake brought it down, however, and it was rebuilt in the second half of the 18th century according to the original design. Today the only features dating from the time of Mehmed the Conqueror are the Crown gate and the courtyard that is decorated above the windows with mosaics. Inside it is a traditional ablutions fountain.

The main feature of the mosque is the enormous complex of buildings surrounding it. The sultan wanted to develop a religious, social and cultural nucleus for his people and what you can see today reflects his wish. The whole area spreads over 25 ac/10 ha and includes baths, a school, caravanserai, library, market, soup kitchen, *imaret* (refuge for the poor), *medrese* and funerary monuments.

Mehmed Fatih's mausoleum lies to the east of the mosque.

Rüstem Paşa Camii** III, B1

Located on Hasirlcilar Cad., in the heart of the Spice Bazaar, near the shores of the Golden Horn. It is not far from Galata Bridge, three steps up from street level and quite easy to miss.

This little masterpiece, hidden in the Spice Bazaar, was built by Sinan for Rüstem Paşa, son-in-law and grand vizir to Süleyman the Magnificent. From the outside it is a simple, seemingly modest, building on the same level as the first floors of the neighbouring houses. The interior, however, is a treasure chest of glistening tiles. The walls and columns above the red carpet are covered in superbly coloured tiles of different blues and greens mottled with red. The variety and richness of the patterns leave us in no doubt as to the imagination and ability of artists at that time.

Yeni Camii** III, C1

In Eminönü between Hamidiye and Reşadiye Cad., in front of Galata Bridge.

The mosque, called the New Mosque, was begun at the insistence of the valide sultan (mother) of Mehmed III in 1597; work continued until 1663, when it was finished under Mehmed IV's mother.

It is like the mosque of Süleyman the Magnificent (Süleymaniye) with a large courtyard in front, where there is a wonderful octagonal ablutions fountain with a cupola. The interior of the mosque is decorated with tiles on the lower part of the pillars and on the walls up to the base of the gallery. Restoration work currently under way partially obstructs the interior.

Eyüp Sultan Camii* I, A1

Eyüp Sultan Bulvari, in Eyüp outside the old city, on the shores of the Golden Horn. Access: bus, taxi or boat. We recommend you go at least one way by boat (there's a departure from both Eyüp and Galata Bridge every half hour, see p. 39).

The mosque was built in 1458 in memory of Prophet Mohammed's revered standard bearer, Eyüp, who died fighting for the cause of Islam on the ramparts of Constantinople in 670. The building suffered earthquakes and underwent a number of transformations before becoming in 1800 what it is today.

There is a **porticoed courtyard** in front of the mosque with an ablutions fountain. The nearby mausoleum, with its rich mosaic-decorated interior, houses the silver shrine of Eyüp. On entering the mosque itself, you come into a vast, light **prayer room**, where the main dome is supported by eight smaller ones.

The whole area around the mosque is a **cemetery***where tombstones and funerary stelae with traditional turban points rise above the wild grass. Unlike most Christian cemeteries, Turkish ones are not arranged in neat rows or kept up. Instead, they're overgrown, left to be invaded and covered by natural vegetation, which to the Muslims is a symbol of life.

A little path leads up the hill behind the mosque to the **Pierre Loti Café**, namesake of the French writer who frequented it during one of his stays in Turkey at the end of the 19th century. From the terrace, you have a wonderful view of the Golden Horn, although this is now slightly spoiled by factories and warehouses.

Fethiye Camii* I, B 1-2

Fethiye Cad., just outside the old city centre, on the shores of the Golden Horn, near Sultan Selim Camii.

Originally intended as a convent when it was built at the end of the 13th century, the building was converted into a mosque in 1591 and given the name 'Fethiye' to celebrate the conquest of Georgia and Azerbaijan. In spite of this change of function, the interior was not modified and the mosque has kept the basic shape of a Greek cross. On the other hand the icons and most of the mosaics have disappeared. Only two admirable mosaics can still be seen today: *Christ at the Last Judgment* and *Christ Pantocrator with Twelve Prophets*.

Travelers to Turkey

In 1402, Gilles le Bouvier left the court of King Charles VII of France to 'delight in seeing and traveling the world.' On his way, the explorer met the Turks: 'These people are straightforward, especially when they put their minds to something; they are the most honest of all the Saracens, the bravest warriors . . . and they are the strongest men of all nations.'

A few years later, in 1418, another traveler, Bertrand de la Broquière, official carver to the court of French king Philip the Good, went to Anatolia, where he spent time with the Turks and observed how they lived. They were, he said, 'very charitable with one another, and people of good faith.'

About a century later, the mother of Francis I asked Süleyman the Magnificent to rescue her son, then held prisoner by Charles V. Süleyman sent his fleet to Toulon under the command of an Admiral Barbarossa; in the face of this threat, Charles V immediately released the French king. To thank Süleyman, the king of France sent a delegation to Constantinople. Among them was the Reverend of Antibes, who wrote a glowing account of the trip, praising the Turks for their honesty. One could, he wrote, walk around Constantinople 'with an outstretched hand full of gold' without anyone stealing it from you.

Turks and the landscapes of Istanbul seem to have affected every writer who has visited the country. Chateaubriand wrote in his memoirs: 'Just as we were approaching the point of the Palace, a north wind rose and in just a few minutes dispersed the mist that had hidden the view. Suddenly, like a stroke of magic, I was in the middle of the Palace of the Commander of Believers. Before me, the Black Sea canal wound its way between bright hillsides like a superb river . . . It is no exaggeration to say that Constantinople has the most beautiful view in the universe.'

Several generations of Orientalist painters, from Antoine Favray to Decamps, did, in fact, dedicate themselves to this very task. A sort of descriptive rivalry developed between painters and writers. Flaubert visited Istanbul in 1850 and was intrigued by the city, by its people, and particularly its women – at least those he was able to meet. 'Within a hundred years the harem will be abolished in the Orient,' he lamented. 'The example of the European woman is contagious. One of these days the women here will begin reading novels and then it will be good-bye to Turkish peace and quiet!' Flaubert was not entirely wrong. Not only would Turkish women read novels, but better still, they would one day write very beautiful ones.

Guzine Dine

Nuruosmaniye Camii* III, B2

Nuruosmaniye Cad., near the entrance to the Grand Bazaar, behind the Çemberlitaş (Burnt Column).

Nuruosmaniye Camii, or Light of Osman Mosque, built between 1745 and 1756, is one of the first examples of the influence of European Baroque on religious Ottoman architecture. The mosque has a lovely many-sided courtyard with porticoes. Its other features are a vast prayer room, a large *mihrab* with a semidome, an imperial loge, a choir gallery, and a second gallery for high-ranking government officials.

Küçük Ayasofya Camii (Little Saint Sophia Mosque) III, C3

Küçük Ayasofya Cad., behind the Blue Mosque on the shores of the Sea of Marmara.

This was the former Church of Saints Sergius and Bacchus built in 536 and later converted into a mosque under the Ottomans.

Mihrimah Camii I, A 1

Fevzi Paşa Cad., in old Istanbul near the Edirne Gate.

Sinan built the mosque on the request of Mihrimah, Süleyman's daughter, who was also the wife of Grand Vizir Rüstem Paşa. Earthquakes destroyed part of the building at the end of the 19th century but it was restored at the beginning of the 20th.

Şehzade Camii III, A 1

Not far from the Valens Aqueduct on Şehzade Cad., near the intersection with Atatürk Bulvari.

Şehzade Camii, the Mosque of the Prince, was built by Sinan on Süleyman's request as a memorial to the sultan's son Mehmed who died in 1543. It's the first of the famous architect's major works. The interior plan of the prayer room is similar to that of the Blue Mosque. In the nearby cemetery Prince Mehmed's *türbe* (tomb) is particularly noteworthy with stone mosaics on the outside walls. Inside, tiles with a yellow background cover the walls right up to the base of the dome.

Sokullu Mehmet Paşa Camii III, C3

Iman Cad., near the Blue Mosque.

Sinan built this mosque in 1571. The mosaics are particularly striking around the *mihrab* and on the conical capital of the *mimber*, which is unlike any other in Istanbul.

Sultan Selim Camii I, B2

In Yavuzselim Cad., on a hill overlooking the Golden Horn on the way to the Valens Aqueduct and the city walls.

Süleyman's great architect Sinan was once again asked to build a mosque, this time in memory of the sultan's father, Selim I. Both the *mihrab* and the *mimber* are of finely worked wood. The vast courtyard with its ablutions fountain extends into a garden where you'll find the mausoleum of Selim I. There's a beautiful view of the Golden Horn.

Museums

Kariye Camii Museum*** (former Church of St Saviour in Chora) I, A 1

Ulubati Hasan Sok., near Edirne Gate (Edirne Kapi) and the city walls. Access: by bus; get off at Edirne Kapi.
Open Wed-Mon 9:30am-5pm.

This rather insignificant looking red brick building with its white minaret is in fact an outstanding tribute to the height of Byzantine glory with the finest collection of frescoes and mosaics produced by Byzantine artists.

A small church was probably built here in the early fifth century. It was then restored by Justinian in the sixth century and then gradually forgotten.

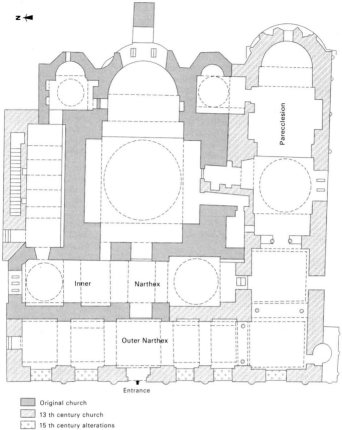

KARIYE CAMII

However, when the Comnenian rulers (11th century) moved into the Blachernae Palace nearby, the little church was completely restored and embellished. During the Fourth Crusade, the church was pillaged and abandoned once again. It wasn't until the beginning of the 14th century that a private donor and patron of the arts, Theodore Metochites, came to its rescue. He renovated the double narthex, added the parecclesion (side chapel) and endowed the church with frescoes and mosaics of breathtaking beauty.

Between 1495 and 1511, St Saviour was converted into a mosque and called Kariye Camii. The frescoes and mosaics were plastered over but luckily preserved. The Ottoman government restored the building in the 17th century and it remained a mosque until after World War II, when it became the Kariye Camii Museum.

Mosaics

The double narthex is covered with an orderly series of mosaics retracing the lives of Christ and the Virgin Mary. They were created between 1310 and 1320, when the unknown artist began a special phase in Byzantine art. He reinterpreted the well-known story imaginatively, ignoring the traditional rules that controlled not only what was represented but how and with what means. In order to give an impression of movement and life, he used smaller tiles, picturesque details, and new colour effects such as the use of pink for faces.

Superb tiles line the walls and columns of Rüstem Paşa Camii, built by Sinan.

Outer narthex

The first mosaic shows Joseph dreaming. An angel appears to tell him to take Mary as his wife, that she has been visited by the Holy Ghost and is 'with child'. The middle scene depicts Mary meeting Elizabeth, Zacharias's wife, in her house in the mountains of Judah. To the right, Mary and Joseph leave Nazareth for the census in Bethlehem. At the census, in the presence of Quirinius, the governor, Mary is wearing a loose dress and Joseph is barefoot. Quirinius is seated on his throne with an armed guard to his right and, in the middle of the mosaic, a high-ranking official is assisted by a scribe who is filling in the register.

On the vault above are medallions of saints: Mandaea, Auxentius, Eustathius, Eugenia and Orestes. The Holy Family (Jesus, Mary and Joseph) return to Nazareth after Passover in Jerusalem. On the vault above them are busts of saints. The central mosaic is barely visible but could be of Jesus at the age of 12 having a discussion with Doctors of Law in the Temple.

On the narthex side of the arch is a mosaic of St Andronicus and on the façade side, one of St Tarachus. This latter was an army veteran who willingly sided with a group of Christians martyred during the rule of the Roman emperor Diocletian. Andronicus from Ephesus is portrayed as an adolescent with long curly hair. Under his portrait you can just make out a faint mosaic of St Anne carrying Mary as a baby.

In the centre of the mosaic depicting the Saviour's birth, you can see Mary in the stable. Above her is the infant lying in the manger while a ray of light descends from heaven to denote the divine nature of the birth. To the left, above the cradle, angels glorify God and announce peace on earth while to the right, above the cradle, an angel brings the good news to the shepherds. Below, to the right, Joseph has his head slightly turned, meditating on the mystery of Christ's birth. Below, to the left, servants wash the infant after the birth. There are medallions of saints on the arch above.

In the flight from Egypt, the left-hand side of the mosaic shows an angel appearing to Joseph in a dream. On the right, the Holy Family is on its way home. Mary is wearing a dark blue dress and Joseph, barefoot, is carrying Jesus on his shoulders. The town of Nazareth is in the background. On the arch above there are medallions of St Demetrius of Salonica and St George of Palestine. In the middle of the vault, Jesus is being baptized in the River Jordan by St John the Baptist.

Beside this mosaic is another of the Temptation of Jesus in the desert. St George appears on the narthex side of the arch and below him is a very faint mosaic of Mary. The façade side of the arch has a portrait of St Demetrius.

Above the door into the narthex Christ Pantocrator holds the Gospel against his chest with his left hand while his right hand is raised in blessing. To the side you can see the initials of Jesus Christ together with the inscription 'Land of the Living'. The Virgin Mary is depicted twice, once with a medallion of Christ and then again in prayer. There are adoring angels on either side.

When you reach the central crossing, look above the door to the left, where you'll see the *Wedding Feast of Canaa.* Here the artist shows servants carrying water which by the time the organizer of the feast tastes it, has changed into wine. To the right is the Miracle of the Loaves and Fishes and to the left a mosaic of Mary. The background of this last mosaic depicts on the left the *Miracle of the Loaves at Passover,* and on the right a bull being sacrificed. There are two anonymous saints at the ends of the arch.

Another mosaic portrays the Magi asking Herod about the new king who has just been born. Herod is shown seated on his throne with the Wise Men before him. Medallions of saints are on the arch above. There is also a scene of Elizabeth trying to rescue baby St John the Baptist from Herod's swords. In the arch above, there are more medallions of saints. In another picture, Herod sends the Wise Men to Bethlehem (this mosaic is partly missing). On the arch above, there are anonymous saints (also damaged). Weeping Mothers of Bethlehem are shown with their massacred children in their arms. The mosaics on the vault have disappeared.

In the extension of the outer narthex, on the side-chapel side, there is a series of mosaics depicting the healing of the palsied man. He is lying on his bed holding out his hands to Jesus, who is surrounded by disciples and Pharisees. The cured man then carries his bed away on his back. The next mosaic has completely disappeared. The one following that is of Jesus and the Good Samaritan near Jacob's well (partly damaged).

In the bay, facing the opening into the side-chapel, you can see Herod to the left, sitting on a throne ordering the Massacre of the Innocents. To the right is a very realistic interpretation of the massacre itself showing the distress of the mothers whose children have been killed. The mosaic on the vault has disappeared.

Inner narthex
On the edge of the alcove a mosaic depicts the healing of a leper who is shown imploring Jesus. This is followed by another healing, of a paralyzed man.

In the centre of the southern cupola is Christ Pantocrator explaining the Gospel. Between the ribs of the dome, Christ's ancestors can be seen, beginning with Adam and including the 12 sons of Jacob: Reuben, Simeon, Levi, Judah, Dan, Naphtali, Gad, Asher, Issachar, Zebulun, Joseph and Benjamin. There is another healing of a sick woman and, under the vault to the left, on the nave side, the healing of St Peter's mother-in-law. St Peter is standing to her right while Jesus takes her hand and the disciple behind him explains the scene to onlookers.

The outer narthex side of the southern dome features the healing of two blind men. The panel on the nave side has Christ and the Virgin Mary. To Mary's right on the lower part of the picture is a portrait of Isaac Comneni and to the right of Christ is a nun. Another mosaic in this section show Jesus in Capernaum healing the sick. There is also a scene of Mary taking bread offered by the Archangel Gabriel (the mosaic opposite has been erased). St Paul is portrayed with his epistles and St Peter is holding the Keys.

Above the door leading into the nave, Christ Pantocrator sits enthroned. Theodore Metochites, who rebuilt the church and the convent, lies prostrate before him.

The mosaics that follow portray scenes from the life of Mary. Joachim, her father, takes her to the Temple, where Temple virgins are shown with flaming torches in their hands. Mary is given wool to weave into veils. She is pictured taking her first steps with a servant behind her ready to catch her in case she should fall. In another scene the high priest lies prostrate before 12 virgins representing the 12 tribes of Israel.

In the picture of the birth of Mary, her mother, Anne, is shown resting on a bed in the middle of the mosaic, surrounded by servants who wash the baby and lay it in a cradle, while Joachim stands at the doorway attentively observing the scene. Another mosaic shows the high priest giving Joseph the rod that has flowered as a result of his prayers and that appoints him to be Mary's husband. Other mosaics show Anne telling her husband Joachim about the Annunciation; Joseph taking Mary into his house; Mary surrounded by her family (Mary, the infant Jesus, St Anne and Joachim); Mary being healed by three priests; the Annunciation of St Anne by the Archangel Gabriel near the fountain, and finally, another mosaic of Joseph.

To the left, on the northern end of the cupola, a bearded high priest is portrayed on a throne supported by columns and surmounted by domes. Mary's father, Joachim, is depicted in another scene. In the centre of the cupola, at the far left of the inner narthex, are the Virgin and Child. Finally, between the ribs of the cupola, there are portraits of 19 patriarchs.

Nave

Above the portal you've just come through, on the inside of the nave, you'll see the Dormition of the Virgin. In the middle of this scene, Mary is shown on her deathbed while behind her, Christ, clad in gold, holds a baby in his arms. It is Mary's soul. Apostles and the faithful gather around the bed and there are cherubs in the sky above Jesus.

To the left of the apse is a mosaic of Christ standing with the Gospel in his hand.

Above, in a marble frame, Christ is surrounded by acanthus leaves. In the four corners of the frame, portraits of the four Evangelists can be made out.

Frescoes

The side chapel is a mortuary chapel that runs the entire length of the church building. Its walls and central dome are covered with frescoes. Although the artist is unknown, these are considered the last masterpieces of the Byzantine Renaissance.

There is a striking scene of the Harrowing of Hell in the semidome of the apse. The Devil lies defeated at Christ's feet. The Gates of Hell have been thrown asunder, and their locks and keys lie scattered on the ground. In a dramatic portrayal of redemption and resurrection, Christ pulls Adam (with his right hand) and Eve (with his left) out of their tombs. To the left, you can see the 'righteous' from the Old Testament: John the Baptist, David, Solomon, Moses and the prophets; to the left the first martyr, St Stephen, and the Apostles, all witnesses to the resurrection. On the lower part of the apse there are six Fathers of the Church. There are three on the right, St Basil, St Gregory the Theologian and St Cyril, but only two on the left, St John Chrysostom and St Athanasius, because the third patriarch has practically disappeared.

In the middle of the arch supporting the vault is a medallion portrait of Archangel Michael. You can also see the return of Christ. The end of the world is depicted by an angel unrolling a parchment of the canopy of Heaven. Below this is a scene of Christ enthroned, with Mary on his right and John the Baptist on his left. On either side, six apostles sit in judgment. Behind them is a choir of angels. The Book of Life is on an altar below Christ, surrounded by cherubs. Farther down is a pair of scales representing the Last Judgment, followed by a scene depicting the weighing of souls. Condemned souls are directed to the left, to Hell, while the Chosen Ones go to the right to join Abraham in Paradise. There are other scenes in this section such as the miraculous resurrection of Jairo's daughter, the resurrection of Lazarus, and below, the Virgin and Child.

On the funerary alcove to the right, on the choir side, there are four figures, most likely representing the four people buried there. On the arch Christ is portrayed in a medallion flanked by two angels. Above Christ are two medallions, one to the left showing St Flora and the other to the right, St Mark. Other figures represented here are St George, standing without his horse, and Demetrius and Theodore shown as both saints and martyrs.

On the funerary alcove to the right, on the narthex side, you can see Michael Mouskos (also known as Makarios) and his wife Eugenia, together with a nun. On the vault above, Christ is in the centre with an angel on either side. Above them the epigram of Makarios (Tornikes) and his wife is engraved on a finely chiseled stone edge. St Theodore is shown to the left of the alcove and St Mercury to the right. Three saints are portrayed on a side panel: Protes, Saba and a third who is anonymous.

On the choir side above the funerary alcove, to the left, is a medallion of St Bacchus.

On the narthex side of the vault above the alcove, to the left, is a picture of Christ with the Archangel Raphael on his left and the Archangel Gabriel on his right.

There are saints on either side of the alcove but their names are illegible. St Samson is shown a little farther to the left and St Mugratha is in the angle.

The Virgin and Child (holding his arms up to Heaven) are shown in the centre of the side-chapel dome. There are 12 angels between the ribs of the dome representing the 12 biblical choirs of angels.

The pendentives of the dome feature St John Damascene on the choir side to the left; the poet and hymn writer St Cosmo to the right, and at the back on the left, the hymn writer St Heophanus.

On the choir side of the right tympanum, David is shown dancing in front of the Ark of the Covenant and in the background the Ark of the Covenant is being carried up Mount Zion while two people carry religious objects.

On the choir side of the left tympanum, God appears to Moses in the Burning Bush and Moses is instructed to lead the people of Israel out of Egypt. In the background Jacob is wrestling with the angel. You can also see Jacob's Dream and his Ladder. The top of the ladder disappears into Heaven, where there is a picture of the Virgin and Child.

Saint Sophia Museum*** III, C2

Located in old Istanbul near the Hippodrome, you can reach it by bus; get off at the Aya Sofya stop.
Open Tues-Sun 9am-5pm. You need two separate tickets to see the entire museum.

The first church on this site was built under Constantine the Great in 325. Destroyed by fire in 404, the Church of Holy Wisdom (Hagia Sofia) was rebuilt by Theodosius II in 415. A fire broke out yet again, this time during the Nike Revolt of 532, reducing the church and most of the city to ashes. Emperor Justinian then ordered two architects, Anthemius of Tralles and Isidorus of Miletus, to build 'the greatest church ever, and the most beautiful'. Ten thousand workers and vast fortunes from the imperial coffers were required to construct the basilica which was inaugurated by Justinian on December 27, 537.

After the Ottoman conquest of the city in 1453, Mehmed II converted the church into a mosque and added minarets, an ablutions fountain and a *mihrab* (prayer niche). Later, because Islam forbids any representation of the human figure in artwork, the holy pictures and mosaics that adorned both the inside and the outside of the building were covered over in plaster and verses from the Koran were engraved around the dome. Finally, in 1935, Atatürk decided to make Aya Sofya a secular museum.

The central dome of Saint Sophia, flanked by two semidomes, rises 164 ft/50 m above the floor.

The former elegance and finesse of the exterior has been greatly diminished by the addition of minarets, buttresses and outlying buildings that give the church a heavy, cluttered effect. However, the minute you go inside you cannot help being awed by the magnificent proportions, the muted atmosphere and the blue and gold mosaics that have managed to survive through the ages.

The immense rectangle is 253 ft/77 m long and 233 ft/71 m wide. If you take away the courtyard and the outer and inner narthexes, you are left with a square space, the main part of the edifice, with 107 columns. In the corners there are enormous pillars supporting a huge dome 102 ft/31 m in diameter that looks as if it is suspended 164 ft/50 m above the ground. This is where the architects performed a masterstroke of genius, for the impression of lightness is due to the fact that the customary square base (or drum) has been done away with and the vault rests instead on spherical triangles known as pendentives. Procopius, a Byzantine historian, wrote that Saint Sophia's dome looked as though it just 'hung from the sky'. The immense central dome is flanked to the east and west by semidomes of the same diameter, which in turn are flanked by smaller semicircular vaults.

Although most of the mosaics have disappeared, the mastery and delicacy of Byzantine mosaicists can still be admired through those that remain.

Above the tympanum of the Imperial Door, Christ, sits on a bejeweled throne, lifting his hand in blessing – the image of divine wisdom. The book in his left hand bears an inscription in Greek that reads, 'Peace be with you, I am the Light of the World'. At his feet kneels Emperor Leo VI, humbly imploring Christ to forgive him his many marriages. There are also two fine mosaics of the Madonna and Child, the first on the apse and the second above the tympanum of the southern portal. These show the Virgin Mother being offered the city of Constantinople by Constantine the Great and the basilica by Justinian. Both emperors are thus portrayed fulfilling their duties toward the state and the church.

A work that is considered to be the triumph of Byzantine mosaic art, dating most likely from the 13th century, can be seen in the middle of the South Gallery. It shows Jesus with a blue halo holding his right hand in blessing while his left is on the Gospel. On either side, Mary and John the Baptist lean toward him interceding on behalf of humanity. Other mosaics of saints (dating from the 10th century) can be seen in the galleries. Two of the most celebrated are at the end of the South Gallery – one of Christ between Constantine IX Monomachus and Empress Zoë, and the other of the Virgin with John II Comnenus and Empress Irene (11th and 12th centuries, respectively).

Saint Sofia's two marble ablutions fountains were added by Murad III. Behind the one in the north-west part of the museum is a marble column known as the Weeping Column, which in the days of the Byzantines, was believed to have curative powers. A soothing feeling certainly emanates from the entire building, largely due to the gentle light that falls from the crown of windows in the cupola and the crescent-shaped openings in the semidomes.

When you leave Saint Sophia, walk out behind it for a pleasant stroll along Soğukçeşme Sok. In 1985 and 1986, the Turkish Touring and Automobile Club under Celik Gülersoy restored parts of this area including nine former Ottoman residences which are now a hotel.

Archaeological Museum** III, CD2

Soğukçeşme Sok., in the Topkapi enclosure. Three museums are conveniently grouped here: the Museum of the Ancient Orient, the Archaeological Museum and the Museum of Turkish Ceramics (Tiled Pavilion).

Open Tues-Sun 9:30am-5pm.

The museum was founded at the end of the last century to house archaeological treasures from the ancient Greek, Roman and Byzantine empires. Unfortunately the presentation is somewhat haphazard with items grouped together instead of clearly displayed. Because the main entrance is

SAINT SOPHIA

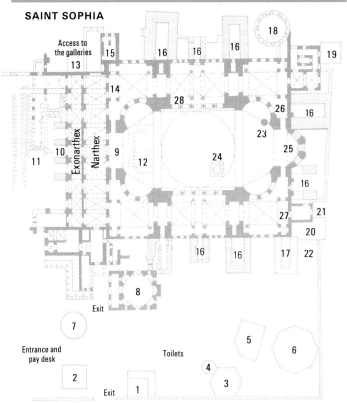

1. Clock-House
2. Mektep of Mahmut I
3. Tomb of Murat III
4. Tomb of the Princes
5. Tomb of Selim II
6. Tomb of Mehmet III
7. Ablution fountain
8. Baptistry ; tombs of Mustafa I and Ibrahim I
9. Imperial Gate
10. Remains of latin steeple
11. Entrance to the church of Theodosius II
12. Remains of the church of Constantine (excavation)
13. Minarets of Sultan Selim

14. Sweating column
15. Stairs to the galleries
16. Byzantine buttresses
17. Turkish buttresses
18. Treasure (Skevophylakion)
19. Minaret of Beyazit II
20. Minaret of Mehmet II Fatih
21. Eastern door
22. Sacred well
23. Sultan's loge
24. Cantor 's gallery
25. Apse and Mirhab
26. Ceramics
27. Ceramics (of the Kaaba of Mecca)
28. Portrait of Alexander (gallery)

between rooms eight and nine, the easiest way to begin your visit is with room eight, to your left.

Room 8 is known as the **Alexander sarcophagus** room. The sarcophagus most likely belonged to a Phoenician nobleman and was found in 1887, in Sidon, when Lebanon was still a province of the Ottoman Empire. The white marble decoration depicts scenes from Alexander the Great's life. There's a battle scene between Greeks and Persians on one side of the sarcophagus, where Alexander, on the far left, is astride his horse with a lion skin (a reference to Hercules) on his head. On the other side he's shown at full gallop during a lion and deer hunt. Here he's wearing a royal headband, a symbol of power. On one end of the sarcophagus is a battle scene and on the other, a hunting scene. Originally all these sculptures were painted and you can still see traces of blue and ochre.

At the end of the room there's another work that was found in Sidon, known as the **Sarcophagus of the Pleureuses** (weeping women). Here, on 18 panels separated by columns and pilasters, the artist has worked with great mastery and delicacy to represent 18 women in different clothes and postures, all expressing grief and sorrow. They are said to be the wives of Strato I, King of Sidon, who died in 360 BC.

Room 7 contains lead coffins and sarcophagi from Phoenicia and Syria.

Rooms 4, 5 and 6 have displays of Greek and Italian sarcophagi.

Room 3 is known as the room of the **Sidamara sarcophagus.** This is a large sarcophagus with pilasters that dates from the third century AD and was found in Konya province on the site of the ancient city of Sidamara. Against the wall, to the right of the window, you can see the door of a funeral vault with two monolithic panels. On the other side, you will see the display of bronze ornaments taken from the door of a hypogaeum (underground tomb) in Langaza.

Room 2 primarily contains mosaics, bas-reliefs and friezes. In the middle of the room there is a mosaic of Hercules killing the Nemean lion. There are also architectural items of note from the Temple of Artemis Leucophryene in Magnesia and from the Temple of Hecate in Lagina.

Room 1 displays texts and inscriptions of laws, imperial edicts and municipal decrees, dating from the third and fifth centuries BC. You can also see statues, tombstones and stelae.

To continue the visit, retrace your steps to the main entrance and enter the right wing of the museum. Begin with room nine.

Room 9 is also called the **Tabnit sarcophagus** room. Sarcophagi from Sidon are displayed here, of which three are particularly remarkable. Opposite the entrance is the sarcophagus of a satrap (a Persian province governor) taken from Sidon's royal necropolis. It is considered a masterpiece of Ionian art and dates from the mid-fifth century BC. On its sides are scenes from the satrap's life. In one of these he's seated, crowned, with his sceptre in hand; in another he's celebrating with his wife and courtiers; in the third he's getting ready to go hunting; and in the last he is out hunting and has just fatally wounded a doe that is collapsing behind him.

The second outstanding exhibit is the **Lycian sarcophagus** in the centre of the room. It dates from the end of the fifth century BC and is thought to be one of the most beautiful examples of Greek sculpture. It is so named because of the shape of its pointed cover, a characteristic of sarcophagi from Lycia, an ancient province of south-west Anatolia. The sides are decorated with hunting scenes and a fight between a lion, boar, and centaur.

Continue to the back of the room to the third sarcophagus, of **Tabnit,** King of Sidon. The cover depicts an Egyptian mummy swathed in a winding sheet and the mummy it contained is exhibited alongside. Hieroglyphic inscriptions indicate that the sarcophagus first belonged to an Egyptian general. Tabnit's epitaph was engraved later.

In **room 10** are displayed early Greco-Roman sarcophagi together with Phoenician inscriptions from Sidon on the walls.

Room 11 is called the **ancient sculptures** room. As you enter you'll notice the remains of a relief showing a chariot drawn by galloping horses, followed by a relief from Thasos of Hercules as an archer (sixth century BC). To the left is a funerary tablet from Daskyleion (fifth century BC). Among the sculptures on the left-hand side of the room is a torso of Apollo (sixth century BC) and a statue of an enthroned Cybele. The right-hand side contains relief pieces and funerary stelae. In the middle of the room there is a portrait of a man (sixth century BC) with statues from Kuros on either side.

On the walls of **room 12** you'll see metopes (slabs between the tablets in Doric friezes) together with fragments of the architrave from the Temple of Assos in the Troad (sixth century BC) and also ancient reliefs from Xanthus.

To the left, by the wall next to a large painted sarcophagus, is a colossal statue of the god Bes from Amathus (in Cyprus).

Room 13 is known as the **Attic reliefs** room. To the left is a lioness from the mausoleum of Halicarnassus, and in the middle a far more recent caryatid, together with a collection of funerary reliefs. To the right is a marble vase, a head of Dionysius and a fragment from an Attic relief that dates from the 4th century BC.

Room 14 features statues of the muses found at Miletus. There is an enormous head in the middle of the room, the Roman copy of a fifth-century BC statue believed to be of Sappho.

Don't miss the beautiful statue in the centre of **room 15. Ephebos of Tralles** (first century BC) comes no doubt from one of antiquity's gymnasiums. Other fine works include a huge statue of Apollo also from Tralles (third century BC), another of Alexander the Great (second century BC) and, on a circular altar, a head of Zeus that was found in Troy (third century BC).

Some of the finer pieces in **room 16** are a Roman caryatid with a Phrygian top, a stele from Ariston and a bust of a naked nymph.

Room 17 displays statues of Tyche, Aphrodite and Cleopatra.

Room 18 is called the **Roman room,** with portraits of emperors, gods and mythological figures: Athena, Hadrian, Valentinian, Augustus, Tiberius, Marcus Aurelius, Agrippina, Nero and a colossal statue of Zeus.

Room 19 is the room of **Christian antiquities.** Among the items displayed are grave-slabs that once belonged to Latin families in Constantinople taken from the former Church of St Paul in Galata, a marble sarcophagus, and a statue of the Virgin at prayer.

Room 20, the last room, is devoted to **Byzantine works of art.** The collection includes fragments of frescoes and mosaics, as well as reliefs and sculptures. The main piece here is the base of a statue of Porphyrius, a famous chariot driver, which came from the Hippodrome in Byzantium; an effigy of the emperor watching the race from his loge, and the names of the victorious horses, are visible.

Museum of the Ancient Orient** III, CD2

Soğukçeşme Sok., located in the Topkapi enclosure.

Open Tues-Sun 9:30am-noon, 1-5pm.

Eight well-organized rooms exhibit artifacts from territories of the former Ottoman Empire found in excavations from the 19th century to the beginning of World War I.

Rooms 1 and 2 contain works from **pre-Islamic Arabia** and **Persia.** Among them are two large red-clay sculptures that guarded the temple of Al Ula in Northern Arabia, bas-reliefs, funerary objects and statuettes. There are Phoenician inscriptions on the walls. The Egyptian antiques section features temple fragments, stelae, funerary statuettes and sarcophagi from the necropolis at Thebes.

Rooms 3 to 5 display work from **Mesopotamia.**

Room 3 contains the admirable **obelisk of Adad-nirâri III** (810-783 BC), with cuneiform inscriptions. There are also enameled brick reliefs with animal motifs that once adorned the monumental Gate at Ishtar and Babylon's triumphal way. In display cases you can see weapons, jewels, various utensils and coloured pottery from Tell Halaf (near the Turkish-Syrian border) which was inhabited in the fourth millennium BC.

Displayed in **room 4** are two statues from Sumer (in southern Iraq), one, of Lugal Dalu, king of Adab, which dates from 2500 BC and the other of Gudea (2141-2122 BC) who reigned from the ancient city of Lagash. Terra-cotta statuettes and reliefs from the third and second millennia BC can be seen in display cases. The **Assyrian section** has stelae, fragments of monuments and bas-reliefs as well as a colossal head of Shalmaneser III (858-824 BC) found at Assur in Iraq.

Room 5 contains objects from **Babylon** dating from the sixth century BC, together with cuneiform tablets from a number of different places.

In **room 6** are metal objects from **Urartu.**

Rooms 7 and 8 specialize in the **Hittite Empire,** displaying items discovered in Anatolia.

The items in **room 7** from Boğazköy include a tablet of the Treaty of Kadesh (1269 BC) between the Egyptians and the Hittites after the battle of the same name.

Room 8 contains items from a site in Zinjirli. There's a selection of palace reliefs and an enormous statue of a neo-Hittite king dating from the ninth century BC.

Museum of Turkish and Islamic Art** III, C3

On the Hippodrome opposite the Blue Mosque.

Open Tues-Sun 10am-5pm.

The museum has been housed since 1983 in the palace built by Süleyman the Magnificent in 1524 for his grand vizir, Ibrāhim Paşa. Restorations were carried out between 1965 and 1983 on what was the largest private palace built under the Ottomans. It is a magnificent example of Ottoman architecture and should not be missed. Not only is the richness of the collection impressive, so is the care with which it has been displayed.

Walking through the rooms, you will discover beautiful examples of different kinds of carpets (prayer carpets, others with animal motifs from the 15th century, still others from Usak, Iran and the Caucasus). The Korans come from all over the Islamic world, as do the masterful works of calligraphy featuring imperial signatures and *firmans* (decrees). Admirable 9th- and 10th-century craftsmanship is evident in chairs and Koran cases inlaid with pearls, ivory and tortoiseshell. There are collections of glassware, earthenware and utilitarian objects such as oil lamps, incense burners, lanterns, lecterns, vases and chandeliers of copper and gold. The ethnographic section has exhibits explaining the everyday life of nomads as well as that of the inhabitants, Istanbullus, in the 19th century.

Tiled Pavilion* (Çinili Köşkü) III, D2

Soğukçeşme Sok., opposite the Archaeological Museum.

Opening hours vary.

Ceramic tiles

Persian and Chinese ceramics were a major source of inspiration for the mosaics that have covered Turkish buildings for centuries. These ceramics were carried west into Turkey along the Silk Route by trading caravans.

During the Seljuk era in the 12th century, hexagonal tiles were mainly produced in Sivas, and later in Konya. They were usually monochrome: blue, turquoise, blue-green, black, and white and were sometimes shaped into letters (examples can be seen at the Karatay *medrese*, constructed in 1252; the Alaeddin Mosque in Konya, built in 1220; and on various *türbe* in Bursa).

In the 14th century, ceramic production was centered in Iznik (ancient Nicaea), a former Byzantine town, where the raw materials, kaolin and feldspar, were of exceptionally good quality. The adaptation of new techniques enriched the range of colours by adding mauve, violet, yellow, and later, tomato red.

Drawings were finally made possible and a special style of ornamentation developed in the 15th century known as the 'four flowers' pattern. These stylized hyacinths, tulips, carnations and sweet-briars became an integral part of Turkish art.

An earthquake in the 16th century completely disrupted the work of Turkish craftsmen and ancient Nicaea's famous production declined. A new centre developed in Kütahya, but it never equaled that of Iznik.

This is one of the oldest-surviving Turkish buildings in Istanbul as is borne out by the inscription that mentions 1466 as the year it was finished under Mehmed II. It was first restored in 1590 under Murad III, then again in the 18th century under Mahmud I and once more in this century when it was converted into a museum. As its name suggests, it is a tiled monument with beautifully decorated walls both inside and out, of blue, green and turquoise tiles. The collection has lovely examples of Seljuk and Ottoman ceramics.

Municipal Museum* III, A 1

Between Niyazi Sok. and Atatürk Bulv., at the foot of the Valens Aqueduct.
Open Mon-Fri 9-11:45am, 1-5:30pm; closed the 5th day of the month.

The museum is housed in a former *medrese* (religious school) that was built in the 16th century by one of Sinan's students for Gazanfer Ağa, head of the white eunuchs of the Serai (harem) under Mehmed III.

The collection is a dusty assortment of interesting memorabilia. You can see drawings, maps, engravings and photos, souvenirs of old Istanbul through the changing faces of Byzantium and Constantinople. There are Karagöz (shadow theatre) puppets, household utensils, bronzeware, ceramics, fabrics and imperial *firmans* (decrees), signatures and seals.

Maritime Museum I, D 1

Beşiktaş Cad., in Beşiktaş behind Dolmabahçe Palace.
Open Wed-Sun 9:30am-5pm.

Imperial *caïques* (small, light Turkish boats) that used to transport the sultans across the Bosphorus are on display here together with an exhibition of Ottoman naval history.

Military Museum I, C 1

Near Cumhuriyet Cad. and the Hilton Hotel, beyond Taksim Square.
Open Wed-Sun 9am-noon, 1:30-5pm.

The museum features an exhibition of Ottoman uniforms and weapons. In the afternoon there is usually a lively concert given by the Janissary Corps (see p. 122).

Museum of Fine Arts I, D 1

Dolmabahçe Cad., an extension of Dolmabahçe Palace.
Open Wed-Sun 9am-5pm.

Here you can see the development of Turkish paintings and sculptures from the late 19th century to the present.

Other places of interest

Galata Tower** II, B 3

Opposite old Istanbul on the other side of the Golden Horn, in the Galata district.
Open daily.

As capital of the empire, Constantinople rivaled its illustrious model, Rome, in every aspect. Therefore, because one of Rome's 14 districts was founded on the right bank of the Tiber, one of Constantinople's districts had to be founded on the other side of the Golden Horn, in Pera. Genoese merchants subsequently moved here, establishing two distinct areas, the first in the hills of Pera and the second in Galata overlooking the Golden Horn. To protect themselves from invaders they fortified the entire area and built a massive cylindrical tower at the highest point in the walls.

After the conquest of Constantinople, Mehmed II demolished the upper part of the tower and converted the building into a prison. From the beginning of the 18th century onward, it was used as a watchtower for the city's fires. Also, because of its height, 198 ft/60 m, and altitude, a total of 396 ft/120 m above sea level, it became an ideal observation post for the ships that hurried up and down the Golden Horn.

The sumptuous Dolmabahçe Palace on the European shores of the Bosphorus was constructed by Sultan Ahmed I in the 18th century.

The tower was restored on a number of occasions and a conical top was added in 1824, replaced 50 years later with the roof you can see today. In 1967, new restorations were carried out and the building now includes a panoramic restaurant, a café and a nightclub (see p. 90). From here you can see all of Istanbul between land and sea.

Grand Bazaar** III, B2

In the heart of the old town.

Open Mon-Sat 8:30am-7pm. The most convenient of the many entrances is on Yeniceriler Cad.

The first bazaar was wooden, built over a former market in 1461 under Fatih Mehmed II. In those days the only transactions that went on were the buying and selling of silk and wool. Little by little all kinds of trades began to flourish until the bazaar grew into an entire city district. It was destroyed by an earthquake at the end of the 19th century, rebuilt along the same lines, restored again in 1958 after a fire and finally completely refurbished, cleaned and modernized a few years ago.

You enter through one of the 18 doorways into a bustling world of commerce where 4000 stalls and shops spread over a fascinating network of alleys and streets. In the past, each trade had its own well-defined area but now modernism and efficiency have overtaken tradition. Some shop-keepers, though, are still grouped together, such as carpet dealers, jewelers and those selling clothes and leather goods.

The **Old Bedesten,** or covered market, in the centre of the bazaar is where you can find older items such as crockery, silverware, coins, watches and Persian miniatures. These may not always be antiques but they have the advantage of being inexpensive, especially if you have time to practice *pazarlik,* the famous Oriental bargaining without which each purchase loses its relish for both buyer and seller.

Yerebatan Saray: the Cistern Basilica or Sunken Palace** III, C2

Yerebatan Cad., near Saint Sophia.

Open Wed-Mon 9am-5pm.

From the sixth century onward, thanks to Justinian, the problem of Constantinople's water supply was more or less resolved. Water from surrounding hills was brought into the city by aqueducts and stored in covered cisterns or open tanks. It was then distributed to the populace through fountains on street corners or in public gardens. Built under Constantine and enlarged by Justinian, Yerebatan supplied the imperial palace near the Hippodrome.

It is the only underground cistern open to the public. More the size of a cathedral than a cistern, 459 ft/140 m long by 230 ft/70 m wide, it was known to the Ottomans as the Sunken Palace. The vaults, like those of a church, are made of brick and the supporting 336 columns have Corinthian capitals adorned with sculptures.

Two years of restoration work, during which tons of mud and stone were excavated, have revealed still more sculptures at ground level around the columns.

Beyazit Tower* III, B2

Near Beyazit Mosque on the University grounds.

Access is permitted only at certain times (available from a Tourist Information Office).

Mehmed II had the tower built in 1823 as a lookout post for fires. These were frequent because most of the city's inhabitants lived in wooden houses. A climb to the top (279 ft/85 m) gives you a beautiful view of Istanbul, the Sea of Marmara and the Bosphorus.

The Janissaries

Orhan, son of Osman, founder of the Ottoman dynasty, formed the Janissary Corps in the 14th century. It was a professional army, created to replace the undisciplined Yaya troops. To create this army, Christian soldiers who agreed to convert to Islam were trained and accepted as salaried soldiers in the sultan's personal guard. The name 'Janissary' comes from the Turkish *yeni çerî*, meaning new army. Later, under Murad II (1421-1451), Christian boys were forcibly inducted into specialized military training and were made to convert to Islam. They then entered the Janissary corps. These soliders were considered slaves of the sultan and were forbidden to marry and have children, therefore ensuring undivided loyalty to their leader.

One day, accompanied by a hundred of his Janissaries, Orhan went to seek the blessing of an old dervish who was known for his piety. The holy man asked one of the younger soldiers to step out of the ranks so that he could bless him and, through him, all the troops. As he lay his arm on the head of the soldier, who was visibly moved, the wide sleeve of his robe fell onto the young man's shoulder. This event was recorded by Lamartine in his *History of Turkey:* 'Orhan and his soldiers, with a superstition natural to primitive peoples, saw this gesture and interpreted the strange sight of the dervish's sleeve draped over their comrade's shoulder as a good omen and a supernatural sign indicating the kind of headdress they should wear into battle. Consequently, they cut a piece of cloth into the shape of a sleeve and added it to their white felt caps. This hung at the back of their heads and they secured a wooden spoon between it and the turban instead of the customary feather. In this way they showed their pride in the fact that they, unlike the voluntary troops, were financed and fed by the emir.'

Hippodrome* III, C3

In old Istanbul.

In front of Saint Sophia, Sultan Ahmed Square extends into a long avenue with three obelisks. The former Roman Hippodrome was built by Septimius Severus at the beginning of the third century AD and enlarged by Constantine a little more than a century later. More than 60,000 spectators could watch events in the vast space that once measured 1280 ft/390 m long by 482 ft/147 m wide. The *spina,* a kind of central axis marked by a low stone wall, divided the square in two. At either end, three pylons indicated where the runners or chariots had to turn. The *spina* itself was bristling with statues and works of art that have all disappeared, except for the following three:

The Obelisk of Theodosius was taken from Heliopolis in Egypt and erected in the Hippodrome in AD 390. It is a porphyry monolith 85 ft/26 m high, decorated with well-preserved hieroglyphics. The marble base is engraved with bas-reliefs showing the emperor and his family enjoying the games from the imperial box and Theodosius either crowning the winners or accepting homage from the losers.

The Serpentine Column was taken by Constantine from the Temple of Apollo in Delphi, where it had been erected to commemorate a Greek victory over the Persians in Plataea. The column's original shape was of three intertwined snakes with their heads together holding a golden tripod, but the column was knocked down and the heads broken. Of its 25.6 ft/7.8 m only about 17.4 ft/5.3 m can be seen today.

The Column of Constantine VII Porphyrogenitus (912-959) is made of different blocks and measures about 98 ft/30 m. It was once covered with bronze plates but these were stolen during the Fourth Crusade, leaving behind a bare stone monument, which explains why it is sometimes referred to as the black obelisk.

The Hippodrome was the centre of the city. Apart from games that were played there, crowds came for grand celebrations or used it as a political arena to protest against iniquitous laws or heavy taxes. The famous Nike

Cemeteries

Some of the most remarkable features of Istanbul are its Muslim cemeteries. They greatly impressed 19th-century travelers, who devoted pages of inspired writing to them. The many *hazire* inside the city are encircled by walls, punctuated here and there by large windows decorated with ornamental ironwork. Immense graveyards lie at the foot of the Byzantine walls outside the city gates and others cover entire hillsides overlooking the Golden Horn and the Bosphorus.

The vast sweeps of sculpted marble stelae, often as tall as a man, seem to have made a great impression on the 19th-century traveler. They were brightly painted so that the gilded epitaphs would stand out clearly. Atop many of them were different kinds of decorative headgear: the *kavuk* of the high Ottoman dignitaries; various turbans indicating either the role in society of the deceased (always specified in the epitaph) or marking membership in some mystic order; the Janissaries' *üsküf;* women's bonnets draped with garlands of small coins; and the *fez* from the Reform period.

There is no sadness in the shady lanes of these cemeteries, none of the monotony of plots arranged in perfectly straight lines that we know in the West. Everything here seems permeated by a serene resignation, emphasized by the epitaphs: *'Dear visitor, I ask only a prayer of you. If today it is my turn, yours will come tomorrow.' 'He left the world of the perishable for that of the perpetual.' 'That God in His Justice make of this tomb a Garden of Paradise.'* Or: *'Here lies X, who never smiled in this world, and who found no remedy for his pain.'* There are also some regrets: *'I didn't have my fill of this world, I had yet to begin accomplishing my aspirations.'* And of course expressions of unbearable outrage when the dead were young people: *'A rose wilted before she had time to bud; even the nightingale sobs with tears.' 'She was on odalisque of Sultan Abdül Mecid. Her youthful soul had but begun to unfold its wings. The garden of life here on earth is full of sadness because of that evil called consumption.' 'My oh-so-young one has sailed off towards the Garden of Paradise, the pain of separation remains forever in the heart of his mother.'*

Unfortunately, these messages are rarely noticed; visitors today do not read or understand the Ottoman Turkish that was banned from official use more than 50 years ago. Despite a few noteworthy efforts to preserve the cemeteries, these rich reminders of a former civilization have been largely left to deteriorate. Urban planning has gnawed away at them or leveled them completely. What has replaced them on the outskirts of the city is not unlike what we have in the West.

Jean-Louis Bacque-Grammont
Director of the French Institute of Anatolian Studies in Istanbul

Revolt broke out here in 532, which caused the deaths of more than 30,000 people.

Üsküdar: the Asian Shore[*] I, D2

Access: by private car, taxi or dolmuş (from Taksim) over one of the Bosphorus bridges, or by ferry.

Üsküdar is the largest suburb of Istanbul on the Anatolian shore of the Bosphorus. Drivers can take the suspension bridge between Ortaköy (European side) and Beylerbeyi (Asian side) while foot-passengers can catch a ferry from Kabatas near Dolmabahçe Palace or from Eminönü Square near Galata Bridge. If you arrive at Üsküdar by ferry, don't miss the enormous fountain in the middle of the square in front of the ferry landing.

Near the landing stage, among trees hundreds of years old is **Mihrima Camii**, a mosque built by Sinan in 1548 on the orders of Mihrimah Sultane, one of Süleyman the Magnificent's daughters. The main cupola rests on four window-studded walls that are flanked by semidomes. Before reaching the mosque itself , you pass under a canopy then through a peristyle (columned court) with five cupolas.

Şemşi Paşa Camii on Şemşi Paşa Cad., on higher ground to the west of the landing square, is another of Sinan's mosques. It is built of freestone and has a single dome.

Rumi Mehmed Paşa Camii is a brick mosque not far from the ferry landing on a cliff overlooking the sea. It is one of the oldest mosques of the town, dating from the 15th century.

Atik Valide Camii was built in 1553 on the request of Selim II's wife, the mother of Murad III. The mosque has a vast courtyard surrounded by porticoes and columns. It also has a hospital and *medrese* (religious school).

From Üsküdar Square it is pleasant to drive up into the Çamlica hills where, over a glass of tea or cup of coffee, you can enjoy the splendid panorama of the Bosphorus, the Sea of Marmara and Princes' Islands.

Walls of Constantinople* I, A 1-3

While there's practically nothing left of the coast wall built by Septimius Severus to defend the city's Golden Horn shore, the wall that stretches inland across the peninsula from the Sea of Marmara to the Golden Horn has managed to withstand earthquakes and enemy attacks better than most. Although it has been restored, modified and reinforced by every single Byzantine emperor and Ottoman sultan since it was built, the wall should really be considered the work of Theodosius the Great (mid-fifth century).

If you begin your visit from the south (Sea of Marmara) and take the road that runs alongside the walls, you first come to **Debaghane Kapi** or Gate of Christ, which was the first military gate. Several hundred feet from here the **Mermer Kule,** or Marble Tower, used as a prison by the Byzantines, rises from the shoreline. Heading north, between the eighth and 11th towers you come to the **Golden Gate,** a triumphal arch with three openings that was built outside the city by Theodosius I in the year 380 to welcome home the empire's victorious armies. Continuing on beyond the 11th tower you will see **Yedikule,** the Fortress of Seven Towers, which lines the ramparts. Mehmed the Conqueror added three towers to the existing four to make a fortress where the imperial treasure could be kept. It was later used as a state prison.

Farther on among the impressive line of bastions, ditches, and gates that lead to Istanbul's outer suburbs, you come to Belgrad Kapi (Belgrade Gate), and Siliviri Kapi (Silver Gate) with its two octagonal towers.

Between the fourth and fifth towers you can see the third military gate which was known as Kalagros Gate in the Middle Ages. A little more than half a mile farther around is Mevlevihane Kapi with two square towers, and less than a mile beyond that you reach **Top Kapi,** or Canon Gate, known in the past as St Roman Gate. This is where Mehmed II set up camp and fired his largest canon during the attack that led to the fall of Constantinople. In fact, the entire stretch of the wall from this point to **Edirne Kapi,** including all 23 towers that once strengthened it, is more or less in ruins as it was here that Mehmed the Conqueror chose to concentrate his army. Edirne Kapi is historically the most significant point in the wall, as it was through this gate that the Conqueror rode triumphant on May 29, 1453, to claim the city. The walls stretch on in a muddle of ruined embankments and wasteland all the way to **Tekpur Sarayi,** the palace of Constantine Porphyrogenitus, with its interior façade of red brick and variegated marble.

Valens Aqueduct III, A 1

The aqueduct arches over Atatürk Bulv.

Confronted with Constantinople's drinking-water problem in 368, Emperor Valens decided to rebuild and extend an immense aqueduct between two hills. This double-storeyed, 2953 ft/900 m—long structure was damaged by invading barbarians in the seventh century and then repaired. It wasn't fully restored, however, until much later under Süleyman the Magnificent.

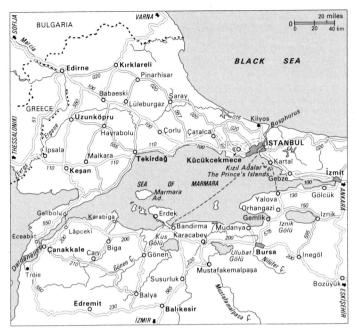

ENVIRONS OF ISTANBUL

ENVIRONS OF ISTANBUL

The Bosphorus (Boğaziçi)***

A visit to Istanbul would be unthinkable without a boat trip along Boğaziçi, the deep 18 mi-/30 km–long Bosphorus strait that winds between the hilly shores of Europe and Asia. The simplest and most pleasant way to see it is to take one of the many boats from Galata Bridge that zigzag from shore to shore up and down the strait.

Access

Boats leave from Galata Bridge (see p. 39). Make sure 'Boğaziçi' is marked on the boat.

You can also visit the strait by car, taking the roads that run along it on either side. To cross from Istanbul, take the Bosphorus Bridge a couple of miles north of the city.

European Shore

Distances are given from Istanbul.

Yıldız Palace (1.6 mi/2.5 km). See p. 102.

Ortaköy (2.8 mi/4.5 km). A small residential area of beautiful villas dotted about a hillside.

Arnavutköy (3.7 mi/6 km). A pretty fishing port.

Bebek (5 mi/8 km). A residential area and yacht harbour.

Rumeli Hisar* (6 mi/10 km). Mehmed the Conqueror built the **fortress** in barely six months in preparation for the attack against Constantinople. He chose the narrowest stretch of the Bosphorus, opposite another fortress, Anadolu Hisar (Fortress of Asia), so that he could control access to the Black Sea. There are three main dungeons and six smaller towers. From the

---

The origin of the Bosphorus

In ancient Greek, bosphorus means 'cow's crossing'. This strange name has its origins in Greek mythology and refers to an episode in the tumultuous love life of Zeus.

One day, the god fell in love with Io, his wife Hera's young priestess from Argos. In a dream, the young girl heard Zeus ordering her to come to him on the banks of Lake Lerna (Peloponnesus). Overjoyed, but worried, Io explained her dream to her father, who consulted the oracles of Delphi and Dodona. Their answer was definite: Io was to go to Zeus.

So she did, but Hera, who didn't trust her husband, caught wind of the lovers' adventure and Zeus had to transform the gentle Io into a white heifer. He vowed to Hera that he could never love such an animal, but Hera, still doubting her husband's sincerity, demanded that he hand the heifer over to her. She then entrusted it to Argus, the giant with a hundred eyes.

On Zeus' urgent request, Hermes, the Olympian messenger, killed Argus. This provoked Hera's wrath; she flew into a rage and decided to punish the heifer by sending a ferocious fly to harass it. In an attempt to flee the unrelenting bites of the insect, the young cow set off at a gallop along the west coast of Greece, giving her name to the Ionian Sea as she passed. She headed north, then east, and finally crossed over into Asia Minor by leaping the strait, which became known as the Bosphorus.

---

highest tower on the east side (75 ft/23 m), you have one of the best panoramas of the Bosphorus.

Emirgân (6.5 mi/10.5 km). A wealthy suburb known as the cypress village.

Yeniköy (9 mi/15 km). A lovely village surrounded by vineyards.

Tarabya★ (11 mi/18 km). A summer resort for well-heeled Istanbullus. It is developing rapidly; there is a beautiful yacht harbour and a wide choice of restaurants and hotels.

Büyükdere (13 mi/21 km). A village in the middle of Tarabya Bay, which gives you access to Belgrade Forest.

Sariyer (13.6 mi/22 km). A pretty little village where you can catch a bus or dolmuş to Kilyos, a summer resort on the Black Sea.

Asian Shore

Beylerbeyi Palace★★. Now in the shadow of a large suspension bridge over the Bosphorus, the white marble Beylerbeyi Palace was built in 1865 by Sultan Abdülaziz on the site of a former imperial domain. It became the sultans' summer residence and was frequented by foreign dignitaries, including Empress Eugénie of France in 1869. Its architecture and interior decor are reminiscent of Dolmabahçe Palace (see p. 96).

Çengelköy (3 mi/4.5 km). A small fishing village.

Vaniköy (4 mi/6 km). Beautiful summer homes.

Kandilli (4.3 mi/7 km). A small palace called Göksu or Küçüksu. *Open Tues, Wed, Fri-Sun, 9:30am-4:30pm, public holidays 9:30am-3pm. Admission charge.* It was built during the reign of Ahmed III and restored in 1751 by Mahmud I.

The Sweet Waters of Asia (5.5 mi/9 km). A fertile, shady plain watered by the Göksu River. The Ottoman upper classes loved coming here for picnics in the 18th and 19th centuries.

Anadolu Hisar★ (6 mi/10 km). Beyazit I built this fortress in 1395 to prevent Black Sea trade from making its way to Constantinople. It was reinforced by Mehmed II when he was preparing his siege of the city. He already held Rumeli fortress on the opposite shore of the Bosphorus and with these two strongholds, he could keep an eye on ships in the strait. Anadolu Hisar, with

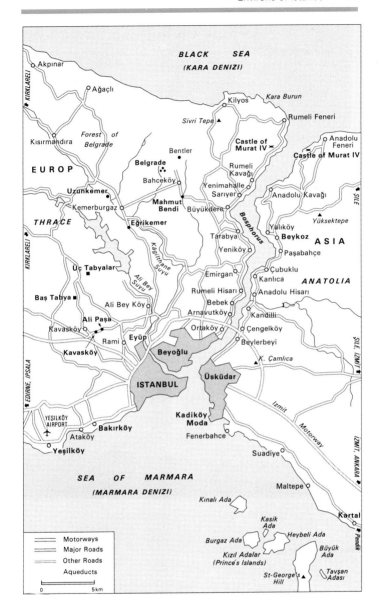

its inner walls, square dungeon and three towers on its outer walls, is the oldest Turkish building on the outskirts of Istanbul.

Kanlıca* (7 mi/12 km). The 18th-century *yalı* (residence) of Amcazade Hüssein Paşa is one of the oldest wooden houses on the Bosphorus. Its distinctive red façade hangs directly over the water.

Beykoz (12 mi/19 km). From this fishing village, a road leads to the sandy beaches of Sile on the Black Sea.

Anadolu Kavağı (17 mi/27 km). Here you can see traces of the ramparts, from a 14th-century Genovese fortress.

An Ottoman yali, *or villa, in Kandilli, on the Asian side of the Bosphorus.*

Princes' Islands*

This is a group of nine islands in the Sea of Marmara, about 12 mi/20 km south-east of Istanbul, beyond the southern entrance to the Bosphorus.

The islands were formerly known as Panadanisia ('Priests' Islands'). They were used as retreats for hermits or members of monastic communities who needed to escape the turbulent city life and find a peaceful place to meditate. Later, they became a kind of golden prison for undesirable princes or elderly statesmen banned from the Byzantine court. Hence the name Princes' Islands, or *Kizil Adalar* in Turkish. At the end of the 19th century they became a vacation resort area, where Istanbul's wealthier citizens came to relax. In 1928, a regular steamship service was set up between Istanbul and the islands.

The scenery is picturesque and the beaches sandy throughout the islands. The air is pleasantly cool, even on hot summer days. The police and public services have the only vehicles on the islands; therefore, even on the largest

and most popular island, Büyük Ada, your transport along shaded roads of umbrella pines will be by horse-drawn carriage or donkey. Several beautiful wooden villas on this large island are now being restored.

Access

It takes about an hour to reach the islands from Istanbul. You pay only for the trip from Istanbul (Galata Bridge); the return journey is free (see p. 39).

Accommodation

Splendid Oteli, 23 Nisan Cad., 71, on Büyük Ada Island, ☎ 351 6775. *Open from June 1 to September 30.* 70 rooms. It has lost its former splendour but still has an old-fashioned, turn-of-the-century charm.

Food

You can find pleasant, small restaurants on the waterfront in Büyük Ada.

Edirne[*]

Telephone code: 1811.
143 mi/230 km west of Istanbul.

Edirne was founded in AD 125 by Hadrian, who named it Hadrianopolis. This later became Adrianople and remained so for centuries until the Turks changed it to its current name.

Strategically located on the border between east and west, Edirne withstood numerous attacks until it finally succumbed to the Ottomans in the second half of the 14th century. It became a wealthy trading centre in 1362 when Murad I moved his capital from Prusa (Bursa) to Adrianople. However, in 1458, five years after the fall of Constantinople, the sultans decided to move their capital there (to Constantinople). As a result, Edirne lost its prestige and economic power and dwindled into a mere garrison town.

Today, Edirne is a provincial centre of 60,000 people whose interests are more agricultural than commercial. The town seems to be living in the wake of its past splendour. Yet the E5 motorway, which connects Asia and Europe, is a reminder that Edirne can still participate in a modern Turkey, eager to enter the EEC.

What to see

Selimiye Camii[**], Talat Pasa Cad. The mosque is flanked by four tall minarets and has numerous outbuildings. Constructed between 1569 and 1575 under Sultan Selim II, the monument is one of architect Sinan's masterpieces. It is modeled on the Süleymaniye in Istanbul, and opens onto a rectangular courtyard where the portico of antique columns is embellished with floral paintings. You enter the prayer room through a richly decorated 14th-century portal. The magnificent dome, like that of Saint Sophia, is 102 ft/31 m in diameter. Brightly coloured stained-glass windows light up the tiles on the walls. The cone-shaped capital of the white marble *mimber* (pulpit) is covered in beautiful tiles.

Üçşerefeli Camii[*] or the 'mosque with three galleries', Hürriyet Meydani. The name refers to one of the minarets that has three balconies. The mosque was finished in 1447 and is unique in that all four minarets are decorated differently. Üçşerefeli Camii is an example of the transition period in mosque architecture between classic Ottoman style and the inverted T shape typical of mosques in Bursa.

The **Roman walls** have almost disappeared, except for the large **Clock Tower** that was partly rebuilt in the 12th century and restored in the 19th. Near the tower is the **covered bazaar** with a barrel-vaulted roof. Like most Oriental markets, it's a feast of colours, sounds and smells.

The **Mosque of Beyazit II** was built at the end of the 15th century and, like the Yeşil Cami in Bursa, is shaped like an inverted T.

Sarayiçi Island is located in the middle of the Tunca River; you can get there by first taking Saraçilar Cad., then crossing the Kanuni Bridge. Every year the Greased Wrestling Championships (Turkey's national sport) take place on the island at Kirkpinar stadium. Wrestlers are covered in olive oil and they compete wearing only black leather breeches. The aim of the game is to force the opponent down until his shoulders touch the ground. It is not only a test of strength but also of intelligence and cunning, as oily bodies are difficult to catch hold of, slipping ludicrously between the arms and hands of even the most solid grip. The tournament takes place in June and attracts huge crowds.

Access

The E5 highway links Edirne to Europe and Istanbul. There are also regular daily train and bus services (see p. 39).

Accommodation

▲▲ **Balta Oteli,** Talatpaşa Asfalti, ☎ 5210. 80 rooms.
▲▲ **Park Oteli,** Maarif Cad., ☎ 4610. 35 rooms.

Festivals

The **Greased Wrestling Championships** take place in June on Sarayiçi Island.

Food

♦♦ **Fifi Lokantasi,** Demirkapi Mekvii, ☎ 1354.

There's a selection of restaurants in the eastern part of the town along Hadrian's Wall.

Useful Address

Tourist Information Office, Hurriyet Meydani, Londra Asfalti 48, ☎ 1490.

Bursa**

Telephone code: 241.

149 mi/240 km south of Istanbul via Izmit, 239 mi/385 km west of Ankara and 242 mi/391 km north-east of Izmir.

Bursa is a lovely town spread over the wooded foothills of ancient Mount Olympus of Mysia, known today as Uludağ or the 'great mountain'. Yew, plane and cypress trees stand above red rooftops, fountains and squares. The town's princely mausoleums, pale mosque domes and slender minarets are silhouetted against an azure sky. The sun sparkles on the enameled tiles of the *türbe* and the mosques are adorned with the most subtle variations of green, the colour of Islam, hence the name of the town, Yeşil Bursa, or 'Green Bursa'.

Prusias I, king of Bithynia, founded the town toward the end of the second century BC. Under the Romans, it was governed by Pliny the Younger and was later converted to Christianity by St Andrew. Byzantine emperors built a fortress and came to enjoy the warm, sulphurous waters of the baths. After an 11-year siege, Bursa was conquered in 1326 by Sultan Orhan, who made it the first Ottoman capital. It remained so until 1413 when the capital was moved to Adrianople (Edirne).

The town adapted to this change of fortune and began to develop a silkworm industry, including weaving of precious fabrics. Although it has since become the centre for sponge toweling (sold by the metre, as towels, bathrobes etc.), the silk brocades in shop windows and in the bazaar still look particularly soft and shimmering.

The most pleasant time to visit Bursa is in the spring, fall or even winter (the latter are generally mild). If possible, it is best to avoid traveling during the hottest months of summer.

What to see

The sumptuous monuments in Bursa are among the best examples of Turkish Muslim art in the country. At the same time, the town has managed to preserve a gentle way of life that you can feel while walking around the alleys of the old town, on Bursa Hill, in the area around Ulu Cami or in the fragrant gardens surrounding the mausoleums of the first sultans.

Yesil Türbe*, D2. The famous Green Mausoleum, considered to be the jewel of the city, stands in a garden on the hillside to the east of the town centre. This octagonal, domed edifice, covered with turquoise tiles, is the final resting place of Sultan Mehmed I. His imposing sarcophagus lies in the main room under a stately vault of green tiles, while members of his family are in a smaller room.

Yesil Cami, D2. Just opposite the Green Mausoleum is the Green Mosque, with its superb decoration of marble and enameled tiles. It was built under Sultan Mehmed I Çelebi in 1424, in the inverted T shape characteristic of early Ottoman mosques. Inside the building, just above the main entrance, you can see the tiled galleries reserved for the sultan and his harem. Two small tiled rooms lead off from each side of the central hall. They contained a library and were used for government business or as a private corner where visitors could rest.

BURSA

The *medrese* (theological school) nearby, also part of the mosque complex, now houses a museum of traditional Turkish and Islamic artifacts. You can see various utensils, costumes, a room where boys stayed before circumcision, and puppets made of cardboard or camel leather, used in shadow theatre plays. The most well-known puppets, Karagöz and his mate Hacivat (equivalent of Punch and Judy), come from Bursa and have amused young Turks for generations.

Caravanserai*, C2. This is an attractive old caravanserai near the covered bazaar that is now used for an office and workshops, but also serves the silk trade during the annual cocoon sales.

Muradiye Camii*, A1. To reach the mosque from the town centre, take Çekirge Cad. to your left (there's a sign) just before you get to the Çelik Palas Hotel. Sultan Murad II's mosque was constructed between 1424 and 1427 and decorated inside with floral and geometric patterns of turquoise tiles. The sultan himself is buried in the shade of ancient plane and cypress trees in a garden full of roses and magnolias. He is surrounded by princes and princesses from the imperial Ottoman family. Each of the mausoleums was built according to a hexagonal floor plan similar to the shape of the big tents used by the family's nomadic Seljuk ancestors. Inside, beautiful enameled tiles testify to the mastery of Ottoman craftsmen. Murad II's mausoleum, with its awning of sculpted wood, was built according to his

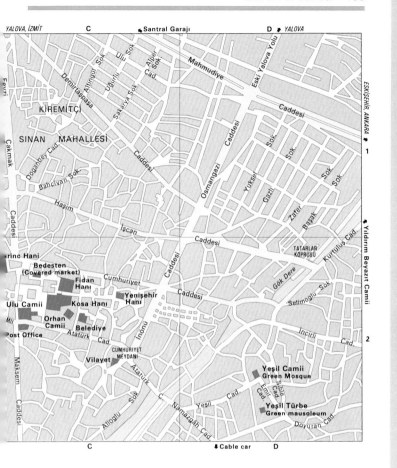

own design; he wanted his tomb to be open to the sky so that he could be blessed by rain from Heaven.

Ulu Cami*, C2. The mosque rises up toward Mount Olympus from the main street, Atatürk Cad. (near the bazaar). The 20 domes are supported by 12 main columns organized in three rows. The interior decoration of enormous red and black Ottoman calligraphy was added later, but the major architectural innovation was the large ablutions fountain, built right in the middle of the prayer room.

Ottoman House (museum), A1. When you leave the Muradiye Cemetery, cross the road to visit the 18th-century residence of a wealthy Ottoman. The furniture and decor have been faithfully restored to recreate the atmosphere of the time.

Thermal Baths, A1 (off map). These baths are mainly concentrated in the Çekirge area. Among the best-known are the New Baths, the Boiling Baths, the Eskipaphea Hamam and the **Grand Çelik Palas Hotel Baths***.

Access

By boat: There are daily crossings from Istanbul (Galata Bridge) to Yalova. From there you take a connecting bus to the city.

By bus: Regular service from Istanbul and Izmir.

By car: You can either take the ferry or the E5 highway as far as Izmit where you turn off for the road to Bursa (a total of 149 mi/240 km from Istanbul).

By ferry: There are departures from Kartal (12 mi/20 km south-east of Istanbul) for Yalova; continue by road to Bursa (51 mi/82 km from Yalova).

By plane: There are regular flights to Bursa from Istanbul, Ankara and Izmir. Contact a THY (Turkish Airlines) office for flight information (see p. 92).

Accommodation

Bursa

▲▲▲▲ **Çelik Palas,** Çekirge Cad. 79, A1, ☎ 6 1900. 173 rooms. A very comfortable, charming old hotel famous for its baths.

▲▲▲ **Akdoğan,** Murad Cad. 5, A1 (off map) ☎ 2 4755. 120 rooms. Comfortable, but located some distance from the town centre (2.5 m/4 km from Çekirge Cad.).

▲▲▲ **Dilmen,** Hamamlar Cad., ☎ 6 6114. 88 rooms. With thermal pool and Turkish bath.

▲▲▲ **Diyar,** Çekiye Cad. 47, A1, ☎ 6 5130. 35 rooms. Pleasant location.

▲▲ **Artiç Oteli,** Fevzi Çakmak, 123, C1, ☎ 1 9500. 63 rooms. Not far fom Ulu Cami.

▲ **Yat Oteli,** Hamamlar Cad. 31, ☎ 6 3112. 47 rooms.

Hasanağa Youth and Scout vacation camp, outside Bursa, Küçük-kumla, Gemlik, Kumla, ☎ 289. For students.

Uludağ *(22 mi/36 km south of Bursa)*

▲▲▲▲ **Grand Hotel Yazici,** ☎ 1050. 155 rooms.

▲▲ **Büyük Panorama Oteli,** ☎ 1237. 98 rooms.

▲▲ **Turistik Uludağ Oteli,** ☎ 1187. 126 rooms.

Food

Wherever there's a good view, there's often a café or restaurant. It's extremely pleasant to sit out on one of the terraces in the town or in Kültür Park, A1.

Useful addresses

Banks

International Bank of Commerce (Iktisat Bankasi Türk A.Ş), for currency exchange. Fevzi Çakmak Cad. 67, C1, ☎ 15 7080-85.

Ottoman Bank, Atatürk Cad. 75, C2, ☎ 12 4435.

Türkiye Emlak Bankasi, for currency exchange, Bursa Subesi, ☎ 21 8895.

Other

Post Office, Atatürk Cad., C2.

Tourist Information Office, A Hamdi Tanpinar Cad., Saydam Iş Merkezi 21 Kat. 5, ☎ 22 8005.

THE AEGEAN COAST

This is probably the most popular tourist destination in Turkey. No one can remain indifferent to the beauty of the jagged coast that in ancient times was the subject of numerous battles between Greeks and Persians.

The coastline is a series of rocky bays and wooded peninsulas, deep creeks and golden beaches, dotted with ancient sites rich in history. Among them are Troy, described in *The Iliad,* where excavations have uncovered ruins dating from several millennia BC; Pergamum, where parchment was first used, with an Asclepion and a 2000-year-old theatre; and Sardis, on the Pactolus River which provided golf for famous King Croesus. The remains of one of the Seven Wonders of the Ancient World, the Temple of Artemis, can be seen at the ancient port of Ephesus. Priene was a centre for the League of Ionian Cities which, with nearby Miletus, rebelled against Darius. There is also Didyma with its incredible Temple of Apollo; Bodrum, ancient Halicarnassus, where the dazzling funerary monument to King Mausoleus once stood; Izmir, Foça, and many other places with civilizations stretching back over thousands of years.

The Cradle of Civilization

Ancient Ionia was located in the north-west of Asia Minor, covering the central part of the Aegean Coast. It stretched between Phocaea to the north and Miletus to the south and included the neighbouring islands of Chios and Samos. Twelve of its famous cities united to form the *Dodecapolis:* Chios, Clazomenae, Colophon, Ephesus, Erythrae, Miletus, Myonte, Lebedos, Phocaea, Priene, Samos and Teos.

This highly prosperous region of Ionia, halfway between the Oriental and Hellenistic worlds, made a significant contribution to Greek culture. The foundations of scientific and philosophical thought were laid down in the school at Miletus, well-known for Thales, Anaximander and Anaximenes. Among Ionia's famous scholars were such learned men as Heraclitus (from Ephesus), Leucippus, Democritus and the sophist Protagoras (all three from Abdera on the Thracian coast), Pythagoras (from Samos), Xenophanes (from Colophon) and Anaxagoras (from Clazomenae). Ionia's literature included Homer's epics and Mimnermus' elegy (both men were from Izmir). The father of history, Herodotus, was from Halicarnassus (now Bodrum) and medicine's Hippocrates from Cos. Ephesus and Colophon also produced many well-known artists.

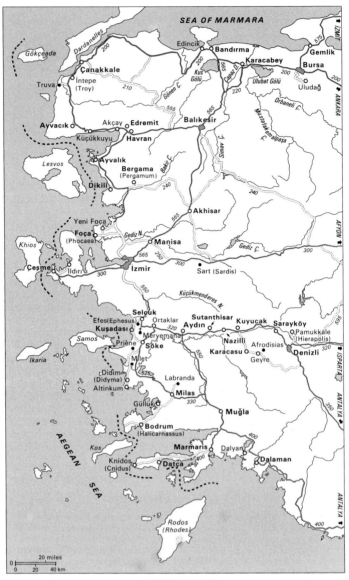

AEGEAN COAST

IZMIR

Telephone code: 51.

370 mi/596 km west of Ankara, 391 mi/631 km south of Istanbul (via Izmit) and 164 mi/264 km north of Bodrum.

Almost two million people live in Izmir and it is the third largest city in Turkey. It is the second largest port after Istanbul and is the most important commercial centre.

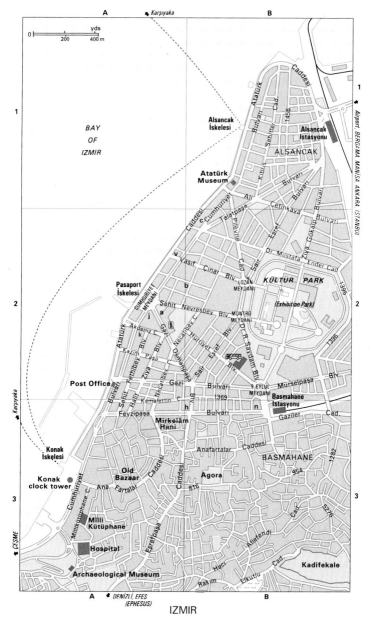

IZMIR

Smyrna, as it was formerly known, was founded in the 11th century BC and was attacked and destroyed on a number of occasions. It was rebuilt by Lysimachus, one of Alexander the Great's generals, after which it gradually grew to become one of the major cities in Asia Minor. The Romans later constructed fine monuments that have now disappeared, except for a few remains. Under Constantine it became a diocese for the church and a brilliant Byzantine centre. Thereafter, it was oppressed by a series of rulers until it was integrated into the Ottoman Empire in 1415. Many years later, as a result of the Mudros Armistice signed between Turkey and the Allies in

1918, Greek troops occupied Smyrna. In 1921, when the victorious Mustafa Kemal drove the Greeks from the town, a great fire broke out, which destroyed entire sections of the city.

Today, however, Izmir is a prosperous modern city set attractively in a deep bay surrounded by mountains. Every year, between August 20 and September 20, the town hosts the largest industry and amusement fair of the Mediterranean, the International Fair. The city's efficiency and dynamism is evident around the port, around the docks, and on the seafront along Atatürk Bulvari, where you will see modern buildings, grand hotels, restaurants and luxury shops.

The best time to visit Izmir is between April and October, when the climate is good.

What to see

Kadifekale*, B3, or Velvet Fortress, on top of Mount Pagus. Built in the sixth century BC, the fortress was restored by the Byzantines and later, walls were added by the Ottomans. Ancient water cisterns can be seen inside. There is a spectacular view of the bay and town.

Agora, B3, in the Namazğah district. *Open daily, 9am-noon, 1-6pm; admission charge*. This Roman marketplace was rebuilt in the second century by Emperor Marcus Aurelius – it had been partly destroyed in an earthquake shortly after it was constructed under Alexander. There is now little left to see: a few columns, the remains of a basilica and some damaged statues such as those of Poseidon and Demeter.

Archaeological Museum, A3, not far from Konak Square, between Turgut Reis Park and Cici Park. *Open 7:30am-5:30pm in summer and 9am-5:30pm in winter; admission charge*. Here you can see collections from Western Anatolian civilizations: statues, pottery, tombstones, sarcophagi and coins.

Bazaar, A3, located on both sides of Anafartalar Cad. Although the bazaar has been modernized considerably since the fire in 1921, it has kept the colourful bustle typical of Oriental markets.

Clock Tower, A3 This tower stands 15.5 ft/25 m high on Konak Square and was a gift from Emperor Wilhelm II of Prussia.

Kültür Park, B2. The International Fair is held in this huge park every year. There are botanical gardens, a zoo and an amusement park.

Access

By boat: Izmir has sea links with Italy, Greece, Istanbul (a 15-hour crossing) and several Aegean and Mediterranean ports (see pp. 11, 39).

By bus: The bus station is located on Hürriyet Bulvari, B2. From here, several bus companies run services to all the big towns throughout the country.

By car: Good asphalt roads link Izmir to Istanbul, Ankara and the south coast.

By plane: Izmir's international airport is north of the town, at Çiğli. Daily domestic flights connect Istanbul, Ankara and other Turkish towns. (A new airport has just been built 16 m/26 km south of the city.)

By train: There are two stations: the Alsancak Istasyonu near the stadium, B1, for trains to Ankara, Denizli and Ephesus; and the Basmahane Istasyonu near the bus station, B2-3, for services to Istanbul and Ankara via Balikesir.

Accommodation

Hotels

Izmir has a wide selection of hotels, from the luxurious Büyük Efes Oteli (Grand Ephesus Hotel) to inexpensive boarding houses. Reserve early as rooms fill up quickly during the International Fair, between August 20 and September 20.

▲▲▲▲▲ **Büyük Efes,** Gazi Osman Paşa Bulv. 1, A2a, ☎ 14 4300. 296 rooms. This hotel has private gardens, a swimming pool and a long list of amenities including a post office, Tourist Information Office and a travel agency. It's near the sea and Izmir's main shops.

▲▲▲▲ **Etap Izmir,** Cumhuriyet Bulv. 138, A2j, ☎ 14 4290. 128 rooms. Centrally located near the Büyük Efes.

▲▲▲ **Anba,** Cumhuriyet Bulv. 124, A2k, ☎ 14 4380. 53 rooms. Located in the fashionable neighbourhood.

▲▲ **Billur,** Basmane Meydani 783, B2n, ☎ 13 6250. 60 rooms. Located opposite the Basmahane railway station.

▲▲ **Kismet,** 1377 Sokak 9, AB2, ☎ 21 7050. 68 rooms. Comfortable; good value.

▲ **Babadan,** Gazi Osman Paşa Bulv. 50, AB3, ☎ 13 9640. 37 rooms. Three blocks from the waterfront.

Izmir's inexpensive hotels are centred mainly around the train stations and the bazaar.

Student accommodation

Atatürk Student Hostel, Inciralti 1888 Sok. 24. Inciralti, A3, off map (17.5 mi/12 km south of Izmir on the Çeşme road), ☎ 15 2856/2980.

Campgrounds

Denizati, in Gümüldür on the coast, 28 mi/45 km south of Izmir, ☎ 1 9366. 100 sites. *Open June 1-September 15.*

Inciralti Mokamp, on the road to Çeşme, just outside Izmir, ☎ 15 4760. 400 sites. *Open May 1-October 15.*

Festivals

International Mediterranean Art and Culture Festival (both Turkish and foreign folklore groups). The festival takes place in June.

Izmir International Fair, August 20-September 20.

Contact the Tourist Information Office for complete schedule and information (see Useful addresses).

Food

Izmir is often a stopover town for tourists, who rarely stay more than a night, so don't expect to find the same atmosphere as in Istanbul or a Mediterranean port. Apart from restaurants in large hotels, there is a good selection on the waterfront, particularly on Atatürk Cad., B1, to the right of Cumhuriyet Meydani, looking toward the sea. There are other good restaurants near the bazaar, especially lively at lunch time. Here are some suggestions:

◆◆ **Beyama,** Atatürk Cad. 190, A2v.

◆◆ **Yosun,** Atatürk Cad. 194, A2, ☎ 14 2626.

There are other restaurants inside Culture Park (Kültür Parki), B2.

Shopping

For arts and crafts, carpets and clothes, walk along the seafront on Atatürk Cad., AB1-2, on Cumhuriyet Bulv., AB1-2, or around the bazaar, A3. The Turkish Ministry of Tourism runs a shop which sells arts and crafts from all over Turkey. It is located on Cumhuriyet Bulv. 115, A2, ☎ 25 9244.

Sports

Swimming pools (covered and open air), Atatürk Sports Centre, Ali Çetinkaya Bulv., B2.

Tennis courts, Kültür Parki, B2.

Sailing, Ege Yat Kulübü, in Karşiyaka (take a boat across from the *iskelesi* departure points along Atatürk Bulv.), A3, B2.

Useful addresses

Airlines

Air France, Atatürk Cad. 156, B2, ☎ 25 5375.

British Airways, Sehit Fethibey Cad. 120, A2, ☎ 14 1788.

Lufthansa, Kizilay Cad. 1/A, A2, ☎ 21 8736.
Pan Am, Vasif Cinar Bulv., A2, ☎ 21 4262.
Swissair, Cumhuriyet Meydani, 11/2, A2, ☎ 21 4757
THY, Büyük Efes Oteli, A2a, ☎ 14 1226 (information), 14 1220 or 25 8280 (reservations).

Banks

International Bank of Commerce (Iktisat Bankasi Türk A.Ş), Cumhuriyet Meydani, apt. n° 11, Alsancak, B2, ☎ 22 5995 to 97 and 22 6246 to 48.
Ottoman Bank, Fevzipaşa Bulv. 1, AB3, ☎ 25 8640.
Türkiye Emlak Bankasi, Izmir Subesi, B2, ☎ 25 8850.

Car rental

Avis, Sehit Nevres Bey Bulv. 19/A, AB2, ☎ 21 5595.
Hertz, Sehit Fethi Bey Cad. 10/E, A2, ☎ 12 5788.
Inter Rent, Cumhuriyet Bulv. 151/B, A2, ☎ 21 4236.

Consulates

Great Britain, Mahmut Esat Bozkurt Cad. 49, A2, ☎ 21 1795.
United States, Atatürk Cad. 92/3, A2, ☎ 13 2135.

Other

Automobile Club, Atatürk Cad. 370, B1, ☎ 21 7149.
Central Post Office, Atatürk Cad., A2.
Hospitals, Devlet Hastahanesi, A3 (off map), ☎ 11 5117; Eşrefpaşa Hastanesi, A3, ☎ 13 7459.
Tourist Information Office, Gazi Osman Paşa Bulv., Büyük Efes Oteli, A1 ☎ 14 2147.

NORTH OF IZMIR

── *FOÇA**

Telephone code: 5431
35 mi/56 km north of Izmir, 205 mi/330 km south of Çanakkale.

Phocaea was founded in the first millennium BC, at the northern point of the Gulf of Izmir; it developed rapidly thanks to two good ports, Nausthatmos and Lamptera. The Phocaeans were skilled navigators and their seafaring exploits led them into the Adriatic, Black and western Mediterranean seas. They established powerful colonies in central Italy, Spain and Gaul including Marsalla (Marseille), which they founded in 600 BC.

Nothing remains of Foça's historical past apart from traces of a 17th-century wall. The town owes its popularity to the beauty of its natural setting* and to the Club Méditerranée, which has constructed white houses along a slope of sweet-smelling greenery facing the sea. The sandy beaches of Foça itself, as well as those on the islets that you can easily reach by boat, also account for its popularity.

Yeni Foça (New Foça) is a modern village about 6 mi/10 km to the north. Its most interesting feature is its long sandy beach. The road to it, that alternately runs along the seafront then rises high above it, is lovely, offering views of wild creeks and beaches.

Access

By bus: There are daily links with Izmir (contact the Tourist Information Office).

By car: Take the Izmir-Çanakkale road and, coming from Izmir, turn to the left. You'll reach Foça after 17 mi/27 km. Yeni Foça is 6 mi/10 m farther on.

By plane: Izmir's international airport is about 31 mi/50 km to the southeast (see p. 138).

(see p. 138)

Accommodation

▲▲▲ **Club Méditerranée,** a tastefully planned vacation village in a particularly pleasant setting with 250 whitewashed concrete bungalows. It is best to reserve before you leave. Contact your travel agent or Club Méditerranée. In Great Britain: 106 Brompton Rd, London SW3, ☎ (01) 581 1161; in the United States: 3 E. 54th St., New York, NY 10022, ☎ (212) 750 1687.

▲▲ **Hanadan,** Büyükdeniz Sahil Cad. I, ☎ 1515. 27 rooms.

There are many small boarding houses in the old town and new hotels are being built in Yeni Foça.

Festivals

The Festival of Folklore Music and Water Sports is held in July (contact the Tourist Information Office for a complete program).

Food

The old town has a choice of restaurants.

Useful address

Tourist Information Office, Atatürk Mahallesi, Foça Girişi, ☎ 1222.

▬ *BERGAMA**** *(Pergamum)*

Telephone code: 5411

54 mi/87 km north-east of Foça, 64 mi/103 km north of Izmir and 151 mi/243 km south-east of Çanakkale.

The ancient city of Pergamum was founded in the eighth century BC, on a hill overlooking the Caicos River plain. We know more of its history, however, from the third century BC onward, when Lysimachus took over the western and central parts of Anatolia after Alexander's death.

As Lysimachus himself was nearing death, Philetaerus, one of his generals, rose against him, won over the king of Syria and made Pergamum an independent state. He founded a dynasty which ruled for 150 years. His nephew and successor, Eumenes I (264-241 BC), extended his power to the Aeolian coast, between the Troad and Ionia, and gradually pulled away from the Syrians. Attalus I (Eumenes' adopted son) ruled from 241 to 197 BC and proclaimed himself king after victories over the Galatians and Seleucids. Through his efforts the kingdom reached as far as the Taurus Mountains, while economic and diplomatic relations with Rome were improved. His son and successor, Eumenes II (197-159 BC), strengthened links with Rome, increased his territory and covered his capital with monuments. Pergamum became one of the leading intellectual, artistic and commercial centres of the day. After the peace of Apemeia, the next king, Attalus II, again increased Pergamum's dominion by founding the port of Allateia on the Mediterranean coast (later to become Antalya). Diplomatic relations with Rome became ever closer – so much so that in 133 BC, Attalus III, who never married and had no children, left the kingdom of Pergamum to Rome in his will.

This meant that after 150 years of sovereignty, the kingdom of Pergamum, now part of the Roman Empire, was reduced to being just another city. It was, however, allowed the privilege of becoming the first capital of the Roman province of Asia. During this period the town prospered and developed, and new monuments were built. At about the same time, one of the greatest figures in medicine, Galen of Pergamum, was appointed Court Doctor by Emperor Marcus Aurelius and the Asclepion became one of the leading medical centres in the world.

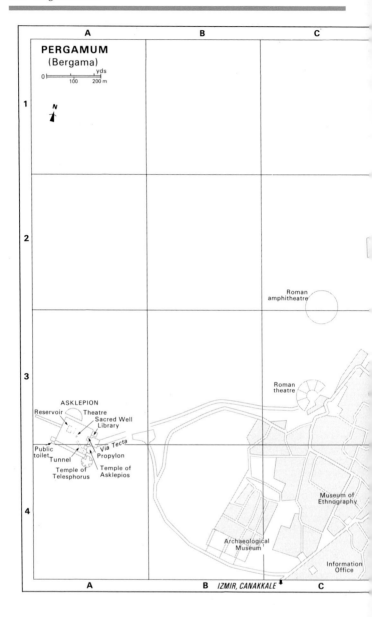

PERGAMUM
(Bergama)

ASKLEPION
Reservoir — Theatre
Sacred Well
Library
Public toilet
Tunnel — Propylon
Via Tecta
Temple of Telesphorus
Temple of Asklepios

Roman amphitheatre

Roman theatre

Museum of Ethnography

Archaeological Museum

Information Office

IZMIR, CANAKKALE

The decline of Pergamum coincides with that of Rome, from the third century AD onward. The town continued its decline under the Byzantines, despite an active Christian community centered around the Church of St John, one of the seven famous churches in Western Anatolia. Considerable damage was wrought on the town during Arab invasions. In the 12th century, it passed into the hands of the Seljuk Turks and then, in the 14th century, it became part of the Ottoman Empire.

The archaeological site in Pergamum includes three parts: the Asclepion, the Acropolis and the town itself. A visit to the first two will give you an overall view of the city and its ancient splendour during the Hellenistic golden age.

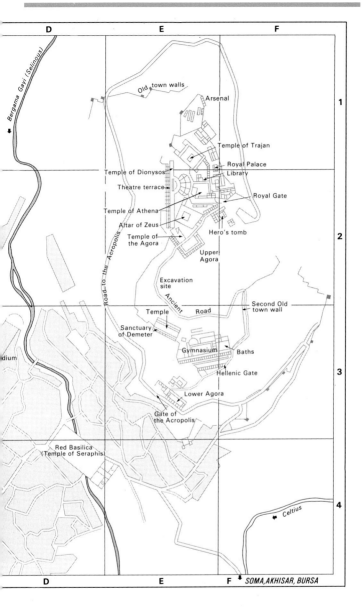

The town, constructed primarily by the Romans, is remarkable for the vast size of its buildings.

What to see

Acropolis***

Open daily 9am-noon, 1-7pm.

You reach the Acropolis by an asphalt road about 3.5 mi/6 km from the town centre. The fortifications were built around Pergamum in the Hellenistic era and were expanded twice, first by the Romans and later by the Byzantines.

The restored northern portico of the Asclepion evokes Pergamum's former glory in Hellenistic times.

The **Temple of Athena** stands within the first walls to the west, behind the Royal Gate. It was built in the third century BC by Philetaerus in honour of Athena Polias, goddess of the town. Her *temenos*, or sacred room, occupied the right side of the edifice. When Attalus I conquered the Galatians, he added an inscription in the sanctuary which read, *'Nikephoros'*, or She Who Grants Victory. The building covered an area of about 3229 sq ft/300 sq m and was once surrounded by Doric columns.

The famous **library** is still being restored; you can only distinguish it by a chaos of stone blocks behind the north portico of the Temple of Athena. It was built under Eumenes II in the second century BC and possessed 200,000 scrolls and documents – a considerable number for the time.

These were classified according to subject matter and placed on shelves about 20 in/50 cm from the ground to protect them from the damp. Readers could either take them home or consult them on the spot in the reading room, which was dominated by a statue of Athena. In 47 BC a fire destroyed Alexandria's famous library and Anthony, anxious to secure the favours of the divine Cleopatra, made her a gift of Pergamum's priceless treasure.

The **Temple of Trajan** (now being restored) is on a raised terrace about 66 ft/20 m above the Temple of Athena. It was constructed between AD 98 and 117 in honour of the Roman emperors Trajan and Hadrian. A monumental flight of steps led up to the temple which was a peripheral structure (with one row of columns all round) facing south. There were six Corinthian columns on the front and nine on the sides.

Steps led from the terrace of the Temple of Athena to what is probably the most remarkable piece of architecture on the Acropolis, the **theatre****. It was built between the third and second centuries BC on the south-west slope of the hill at such a dramatic angle that it is considered to be the steepest theatre in the world. The view over the valley is spectacular. The architects had to dig into the hillside and reduce the span of the theatre to a much tighter semicircle than was the norm in Hellenistic times. It covered an area of 46,285 sq ft/4300 sq m and comprised 80 rows of terraced steps that could hold 15,000 spectators. There were three separate sections, and in the middle of the first was a royal box for statesmen and foreign guests. The stage itself was made of wood and had to be put up and then taken down for each performance, according to the rules of classical Greek theatre. Once dismantled, the terrace afforded access to the Temple of Dionysius. During Roman times a marble stage was built.

The small **Temple of Dionysius,** near the stage at the foot of the theatre, was constructed under Eumenes II and restored by Caracalla (211-217). It was reached by a flight of 25 steps and had six columns.

South of the theatre, along the ancient Pergamum road, you reach another terrace that once held the **Altar of Zeus,** built under Eumenes II. Apart from the foundations, very little remains. There was once a podium decorated with reliefs on its sides. Built on the podium was a U-shaped portico with Ionic columns, open to the west. The sacrificial altar stood in the middle.

Below the terrace of the Altar of Zeus lie scattered remains of the **Upper Agora.** You can still distinguish a path that divided the square in half along the east-west axis.

On leaving the Upper Agora, follow the main road to another terrace, the **Temple of Demeter***, built to the goddess of fertility in the second century BC during the reign of Attalus I. This Ionic temple is regarded as the oldest edifice on the Acropolis. You can still see columns of the propylons (monumental gateways) and, to the right of the courtyard, the seats used by priestesses during ceremonies. There was an altar just in front of the sanctuary itself and the *temenos* was lined on three sides by porticoes.

Continuing along the ancient road to the east, you come to the **gymnasiums.** The first, for young men, overlooked the plain and had a wide terrace lined on three sides by porticoes and buildings. You can still make out the ablutions area to the west and a small auditorium to the north, above which was the middle gymnasium for boys ten to fifteen years old. On another terrace below was a third gymnasium, probably for children between ages six and ten.

Follow the same ancient road around to the right to reach the **House of Attalus,** an example of a wealthy Pergamene residence. It was built in the Hellenistic period with evenly cut blocks of stone and restored under the Romans using a first-century BC technique incorporating rubble, lime and mortar. Just in front of the entrance is a bust of Hermes, now decapitated. In the western wing of the house there was a large sitting room. Rooms in the northern wing were once decorated with mosaics and frescoes. Fragments can be seen in the rooms that have been restored.

Below the House of Attalus, beside the road that leads to the Acropolis, is the **Lower Agora,** a vast rectangle of 19,375 sq ft/1800 sq m. Remains of tombs and catapult ammunition (found in the ancient citadel of the Acropolis) lie scattered about the square. The agora was once surrounded by porticoes, which in turn opened onto workshops and stores. A church featuring three naves was built here in the early Christian era.

Asclepion**

Open daily 8am-6pm.

Medical centres, or asclepions, deriving their name from Aesculapius, the Greek god of healing, were well-known establishments throughout the Mediterranean. The one at Pergamum was built in the Hellenistic era and was considerably modified and enlarged under the Romans.

It is generally accepted that Archias, son of Prince Aristachminos of Pergamum, was responsible for bringing the worship of Aesculapius to Pergamum. Having miraculously recovered his health at the healing sanctuary in Epidaurus, which had been famous since the fifth century BC, he brought back a small group of priests and, as a gesture of gratitude, built a temple to the god. Apart from the temple itself, the Asclepion was a medical complex including centres for treatment and convalescence, a medical school, a meeting place for philosophers and scholars, a library, and even a theatre for the entertainment of patients and townspeople alike.

Treatment itself began with autosuggestion; sleep and dream analysis played an important role. It was believed that the gods themselves could give patients indications of the kind of treatment to follow. After this preliminary session, the patients drank the waters, had thermal or mud baths, sunbathed, bathed in seawater and were rubbed and massaged. They also took medicines made from plant extracts and used special ointment compresses. Music, plays and games formed part of the cure. The patients made offerings and sacrifices to the god, first to obtain a rapid cure and secondly, to express their gratitude if their request was met.

The first gateway to the Asclepion, known as the **Viran Gate,** is to the west of the town on the **Sacred Way** that linked the Roman part of the town with the Asclepion. The street was made of large stone slabs and was lined with porticoes that opened onto shops.

The Sacred Way leads to a **small square** surrounded on three sides by Corinthian porticoes and on the fourth by a propylon. The northern portico was restored and is still in good shape.

The **propylon** constituted the main entrance to the Asclepion and was formed by four Corinthian columns surmounted by a pediment. It was built under Antoninus Pius in AD 142 by Claudius Charax, one of the doctors of the Asclepion. From there a dozen steps led into the sanctuary, in the middle of which was the altar dedicated to Aesculapius.

The **library** to the north of the propylon was set up in the first quarter of the second century AD by a rich citizen named Flavian Melitena. The floor was paved with coloured marble and the ceiling lined with sculpted wood. Small hollows were carved out of the walls to store parchment scrolls. The word parchment comes from *pergamen*, which was a writing surface prepared from animal skin. There's a large, semicircular alcove in the wall facing the door that used to hold the statue of Hadrian, now in the town museum.

The **theatre**[*] is to the west of the library, behind the north portico (where 20 of its 45 columns remain). Its terraced steps were built into the southern slope of a hill, in a semicircle, like all Hellenistic theatres. It was once generously decorated with white marble and could seat 4000 spectators. There was also a gallery in the middle of the auditorium that could seat 16 dignitaries or foreign visitors. Beneath this was a pedestal about 3.3 ft/1 m tall which was probably for the statue of Dionysius that you can see in the museum. The theatre has been restored and is used for festivals.

The main courtyard of the Asclepion had three **porticoes,** to the north, west, and south, under which patients could take shelter from the sun or rain. The northern one has been restored.

Inside the **main courtyard** there was a spring where patients could drink sacred water – reputed to have healing powers – and a pool where they could bathe and rub themselves with mud.

In the south-west corner of the main courtyard, where the roof was once held by four Corinthian-style pillars, there are ruins of **public toilets.** Those for men were richly decorated and had 40 seats whereas those for women were much simpler and had only 17. The elaborate water system made them the most advanced sanitary installations of the time.

The **Temple of Aesculapius**[**], a circular construction 66 ft/20 m high with a 79 ft/24 m diameter, stands to the south of the small square beyond the propylon. It was built in AD 142 and dedicated to Aesculapius. Access to the temple was through a monumental doorway that opened onto a vast staircase. Six Corinthian-style pillars held up the cupola which was decorated with mosaics and had an opening in the middle to let in light. Seven statue alcoves were carved into the walls in an alternating curved and rectangular design. The temple was converted into a church under the Byzantines.

After having drunk sacred water from the sacred spring, patients walked through the **Sacred Tunnel,** a marble corridor, to reach the Temple of Telesphorus. The passage is 262 ft/80 m long, 9 ft/2.7 m wide and 10 ft/3 m high but is no longer covered in marble. However, you can still see openings in the vault to let in light and air. Still visible too are the water channels that were dug out of the rock and covered with large stone slabs. Water from the sacred spring flowed through them to the temple.

The **Temple of Telesphorus** is just to the south of the Temple of Aesculapius and is even larger (197 ft/60 m in diameter). It was built in honour of the son of Telesphorus, another god of medicine, who was also god of convalescence and of dream interpretation. After spending time in the temple, patients took the stairs down to treatment pools excavated into the rock below.

The town

The **Basilica*** (known as Kizil Avlu, the Red Courtyard) is on the road into town from the Acropolis. Its colossal red brick walls are the remains of the Basilica of St John of Pergamum, built on the site of the ancient Temple of Serapis, which dated from Roman times. According to legend, the well in the middle of the courtyard was connected to the Acropolis by a series of tunnels.

Archaeological and Ethnological Museum*

Open Tues-Sun 9am-noon, 1:30-5pm.

The archaeological section of the museum has a large collection of statues, pottery, fragments of reliefs and mosaics, and various objects dating from prehistoric, Hellenistic, Roman and Byzantine eras. In the ethnological section you can see clothes, embroidery, household items and furniture from the region.

Access

By bus: There are regular services from Izmir to Bergama's Santral Garaj (station) on Hükümet Cad.

By car: There is a good road from Izmir. After about 62 mi/100 km, take the Bergama road to the right and continue for 4 mi/7 km.

Accommodation

▲▲▲ **Tusan Bergama Moteli,** 7 mi/4.4 km south-west of town, Bergama Izmir Yolu, Çati Mevkii, ☎ 1173. 42 rooms. This is the nicest place to stay in Bergama, with lovely gardens.

▲ **Balay Oteli,** Hükümet Cad. This modest hotel is located in the centre of town.

▲ **Park Oteli,** Park Otel Sokak 6, ☎ 1246. Conveniently located near the bus station.

Festival

The **International Fair** is held in July (contact the Tourist Information Office for a complete program).

Shopping

Bergama has very good quality **carpets,** although they are generally expensive. There are also some **antique shops** in the modern section of the city.

Tourist Information Office, on entering the town from Izmir, is opposite the Archaeological Museum, Izmir Cad., Asklepion Yol Kavşagi, ☎ 1862.

TROY* *(Truva)*

Telephone code: 1961.

138 mi/223 km north-west of Bergama, 20 mi/32 km south-west of Canakkale and 193 mi/312 km north of Izmir.

The site of Troy was discovered in the 19th century by Heinrich Schliemann (1822-1890), a passionate admirer of Homer. His excavations (52 ft/16 m) revealed nine superimposed layers dating from the fourth millennium BC to the Roman era. The ruins themselves may disappoint visitors, but Troy is interesting for its legendary history. The site covers the nine historical periods corresponding to the nine different civilizations that lived here.

Troy I (3200-2600 BC): This was the first settlement, inhabited by people who most probably came from Anatolia. They built a protective stone wall around the town and their houses were made of clay with reed roofs. They were familiar with the techniques of copper- and pottery-making.

Troy II (2600-2200 BC): A period of great development followed the town's initial destruction. It was rebuilt on a larger scale according to an overall plan. The potters' wheel had been discovered, and gold, silver and bronze were used. The entire town was then wiped out by an enormous fire, the cause of which is unknown.

Troy III, IV and V (2200-1900 BC): There is little change from the former period although more stone was used for building purposes.

Troy VI (1900-1300 BC): Invaders destroyed the existing civilization and introduced a new culture. The city expanded and houses tended to be larger. Horses were used. Toward the end of this period, the inhabitants began to cremate their dead. Troy VI was devastated just before 1300 BC by a violent earthquake.

Troy VII (1300-700 BC): Almost immediately after the town had been rebuilt it was destroyed again, by the famous Trojan War that lasted nearly 10 years. The cause of the war was mainly political, economic and commercial rivalry between the Greeks and Trojans, rather than the misadventures of beautiful Helen sung by Homer. Toward 1200 BC, invaders from the Balkans settled in Troy, but the town seems to have been uninhabited from about 1100 to 700 BC.

Troy VIII (700-350 BC): The town came under Hellenistic influence. A period of prosperity in the seventh and sixth centuries BC was followed by one of slow decline.

Troy IX (350 BC-AD 400): Alexander the Great's visit to the city in 334 marked a period of renewal. Troy then came under Seljuk control, followed by that of the Romans. In the third century it became the seat of the diocese and remained so until the arrival of the Turks in 1306. From the 14th century on it was gradually abandoned.

It's not easy to find your way around unless you follow the arrow markers placed throughout the site.

You first come to a gate in the middle of the **ramparts** of Troy VI. Not far away is a rectangular lookout tower where besieged inhabitants dug a well during the Trojan War. Then you come to the ruins of two **houses** that date from Troy VI. Their roof supports can still be seen: the first of these, to the left, consists of two stone pillars; the second, of the twelve remaining column bases. On top of the hill are stone blocks and bases belonging to the ancient **Temple of Athena.**

Farther on are the *megarons,* or proto-historic dwellings dating from Troy I; these are among the oldest known to date. Cross the ramparts of Troy II and IV to reach the two-storey Pillar House which dates from Troy VI. After this you reach the south-west gate of the second town with its wide, paved **chariot ramp.**

Interesting monuments outside the walls include a **temenos** with two wells, a **Roman theatre** with some of its mosaics preserved in glass cases, the **Roman bouleterion**[*], or Senate, and a wooden model of the famous Trojan Horse.

Access

By car: The road to Troy is a 3.7 mi/6 km branch off the main Izmir-Canakkale road.

Accommodation

There are no hotels or restaurants in Troy itself; all accommodation listed is in nearby Canakkale.

Hotels

▲▲▲ **Anafartalar,** Kayserili A. Paşa Cad, ☎ 4454. 69 rooms. Near the ferry docks with an attractive view and rooftop restaurant.

▲▲▲ **Tusan Truva Motel,** P.K.8 Intepe, ☎ 1461. 64 rooms. Located just outside Canakkale on the road to Troy in the middle of a pine forest.

▲▲ **Bakir Oteli,** Yali Cad. 12, ☎ 4088. 35 rooms. This is a modern hotel with a view of the straits.

▲▲ **Truva,** Yaliboyu, ☎ 1024. 66 rooms. Very comfortable, located just outside the town centre.

▲ **Yaldiz,** Kizilay Sok. 20, ☎ 1793. 20 rooms. Near the ferry docks on a quiet street, this is a clean, modern hotel.

Student accommodation

Intepe Youth and Scout Camp, Güzel Yali Mevkii, ☎ 1626.

Festival

The Troy Festival is held from August 10-18.

Food

For a pleasant meal, try one of the many restaurants on the seafront, overlooking the Dardanelles. In summer, tables are set outside along the sidewalks.

Useful address

Tourist Information Office, Iskele Meydani 67, Canakkale, ☎ 1187 or 2371.

EAST OF IZMIR

▬ SARDIS[*]

56 mi/91 km east of Izmir and 313 mi/505 km west of Ankara.

Sardis, capital of the ancient kingdom of Lydia, stood on the banks of the river Pactolus, which was prized for its gold-bearing sands. Croesus (560-546 BC) was its most famous king, renowned for the rich offerings he made to the temples of Delphi, Ephesus and Didyma. In 133 BC the town fell to the Romans, who later endowed it with one of the seven churches of the Apocalypse and set up a bishopric. However, at the beginning of the 15th century, Sardis was completely destroyed by Tamerlane's troops.

The ruins of Sardis (open daily 9am-7pm) are mostly located in two areas: to the east of the village are the **Gymnasium** and the **Synagogue,** and to the south is the **Temple of Artemis.**

The Synagogue is a long building lined with porticoes that was built in the fourth century AD and comprised a forecourt and a main room. You can still see some of the beautiful mosaics that covered the floors and walls.

The Gymnasium was built by the Romans over an area of approximately 242,190 sq ft/22,500 sq m.

The Temple of Artemis was built in the third century BC. Magnificent Ionic capitals and some fine sculptures have been preserved. Under the Romans it was dedicated to the emperor Antoninus Pius and his wife Faustina, considered to be the earthly representatives of Zeus and Artemis.

Access

By bus: There are regular departures from Izmir to Sart, the nearest village. The trip takes 1.5 hours.

By car: Sardis is just off the main road between Izmir and Ankara.

APHRODISIAS***

92 mi/149 km east of Ephesus, 138 mi/223 km south-east of Izmir and 77 mi/124 km south-west of Pamukkale.

The site is open daily, 8:30am-5:30pm. The museum is generally closed at meal times. Excavation work is still under way and parts of the site may be closed to the public.

In 1959 the Turkish government decided to resurrect the city of Aphrodite half-buried in Geyre, a small hamlet overshadowed by Baba Daği at an altitude of 1640 ft/500 m. Walls about 2 mi/3.5 km long were discovered surrounding what proved to be an exquisitely preserved city rising up among olive trees and wild grass.

The site was first inhabited in the third millennium BC. The worship of Aphrodite, universal goddess of love and mother of fertility, began in the seventh century BC. However, the city was not famous until Roman times, when it was considered a free town and developed into a religious, literary and artistic centre. The celebrated white and blue-grey marble from a nearby quarry produced material for highly skilled works of sculpture. The agora, temple, baths and stadium date from this period.

The worship of Aphrodite did not die out the moment the town converted to Christianity. But when the Byzantines took over, they wiped out all traces of what they considered licentious rites. They christened the town Stravopolis (town of the cross), made the temple a church and founded a diocese.

Aphrodisias declined between the 11th and 14th centuries when the town was first taken by the Seljuks and later sacked. In the 18th century the Turks built the village Geyre, derived from Caria, the name of the site when it was the main town in the ancient province of Caria.

What to see

The **museum*** (near the entrance to the site) is a good introduction and has an excellent collection of sculptures and archaeological items.

The columns of the **propylon.** or monumental gateway, were set upright in 1963.

The **stadium**** (to the north-west of the site) is probably the best preserved of antiquity and is the largest in Asia Minor, measuring 820 ft/250 m long and 112 ft/34 m wide. Originally designed for athletic games, gladiator contests were introduced at a later date by the Romans. The 22 terraced rows and a porticoed standing gallery could hold 25,000 spectators.

The **Temple of Aphrodite** (heading south) was built in the first century BC and was converted into a church by the Byzantines in the fifth century AD. Of its 42 Ionic columns, 12 admirably fluted ones remain as a testimony to the finesse of the work as a whole. There was a statue of Aphrodite in the middle that was 10 ft/3 m tall. When the temple was converted into a church, the walls of the *naos* (inner cell) were destroyed and rebuilt outside the lateral colonnades, in such a way as to form three naves.

The **Odeon**** (to the east of the temple) was excavated in 1962. It has been beautifully and miraculously preserved, as earthquakes are common in the region. The upper terraces have disappeared, but the lower ones, of which the ends have been sculpted into feline paws, together with the orchestra section of white marble and the finely decorated stage, make the whole a small masterpiece of elegance and refinement. The statues and mosaics that once adorned the stage and orchestra have disappeared. The Odeon was originally connected to the agora by an open corridor lined with statues of local dignitaries.

The **Baths of Hadrian** (in the south) include five large galleries, a *palaestra* (wrestling school) surrounded by colonnades, various pools, a *caldarium* (hot bath), a *tepidarium* (warm room) and a *sudatorium* (perspiring room). You can still see some of the beautiful marble tiling.

The **theatre*** (east of the baths) was built into the Acropolis. It too has weathered particularly well and its terraced rows for 10,000 spectators remain almost intact.

Access

You'll have to take a taxi or dolmuş from one of the nearby towns (Nazilli or Karacasu), unless you have a car. If this is the case, take the road to Geyre off the Aydin-Denizli road, 40 mi/65 km from Aydin.

Accommodation and food

See Denizli, p. 153.

▬ PAMUKKALE - HIERAPOLIS***

Telephone codes: (Denizli) 621; (Pamukkale) 6218.

11 mi/17 km north of Denizli, 69 mi/112 km north-west of Aphrodisias, 168 mi/271 km south-east of Izmir, 135 mi/217 km east of Kuşadasi and 186 mi/300 km north-west of Antalya, via Burdur.

Pamukkale, which means cotton castle in Turkish, is a remarkable natural site that should not be missed. This castle has been fashioned naturally by the hot water, rich in calcium carbonate, that gushes out of the mountain at a temperature of 127°F/53°C and flows toward the plain. The flow of this calcareous water down the mountain has sculpted a gigantic series of cup-like turquoise pools, the sides of which are ribbed with startlingly white stalagmites. The sun bathes this natural wonder in the most glorious colours: pink and gold in the early morning, bright white at noon and mauve at the end of the day. You will not be able to resist paddling from pool to pool nor sitting for a moment on a snow-white ledge, bathing your feet in the warm water.

The water has been renowned for its therapeutic powers since antiquity and has always been recommended for people suffering from rheumatism or from circulatory and respiratory disorders. There is also a spa on the top of the plateau that has been in use since Roman times. Here, small canals run the length of the streets and the hotels have thermal swimming pools.

On the plateau stand the **ruins of ancient Hierapolis,** founded by Eumenes II, King of Pergamum in 190 BC. In 129 BC, Hierapolis came under Roman control and was later destroyed by earthquakes and rebuilt several times. The city was at its most prosperous in the second and third centuries, when it became an important thermal centre.

Christianity came to Hierapolis early; St Philip, one of the 12 Apostles, came here to spread the gospel. When he died, the first church was built over his tomb. Up until the sixth century AD, Hierapolis was a religious centre and had numerous monuments. The 10,000 or so inhabitants lived in a fortified city that included churches, thermal baths, hydrotherapy and massage centres, a theatre, a library and a market decorated with fountains and statues.

Later, the town developed as a result of the local cotton trade, only to be destroyed in 1354 by a violent earthquake. A large part of the town still lies unexcavated beneath mounds of rubble.

What to see

The **Baths** have been well-restored and now house the archaeological museum, which displays sculptures and items of architectural interest from excavations at the site.

The **Nymphaeum** is not far from the spring that fills the new baths. It was originally built as a monumental fountain in the second century AD and was restored during the fourth.

The **Theatre**** was built into the hillside during the reign of the Roman emperor Hadrian. The steps are in relatively good condition and the stage is decorated with beautiful reliefs.

The **Temple of Apollo** is still under excavation. Apollo was the chief deity of Hierapolis and his temple is the most well-known religious monument in the city. So far, Hellenistic traces from the third century AD have been found.

The **Necropolis** stretches beyond the monumental, triple-arched victory gate to the north of the city, extending more than 1.2 mi/2 km. It is one of the largest and best preserved in all of Asia Minor. Thousands of tombs, sarcophagi and funerary monuments of all shapes and sizes lie scattered over this vast tract of land overrun by wild grasses.

Access

By bus: There are regular Izmir-Denizli, Bodrum-Denizli services. From Denizli take another bus or dolmuş to Pamukkale.

By car: Leave Denizli by the 320 to the east and take the Pamukkale exit to the north.

By train: The Izmir-Denizli journey takes six hours.

Accommodation

Pamukkale

Hotels are often full in summer. A little farther out, however, toward Kur-Tur, there is sometimes room in guesthouses.

▲▲▲▲ **Motel Koru,** ☎ 1020. 90 rooms. Swimming pool and a beautiful view.

▲▲▲▲ **Tusan Moteli,** ☎ 1010. 47 rooms. Inside a small fortress that dates from the 11th or 12th century, with a swimming pool, panoramic view and good restaurant.

▲▲ **Pamukkale Motel,** ☎ 1024. 31 rooms. Mainly renowned for its swimming pool, which features fragments of marbled columns.

▲ **Mistur Hotel,** ☎ 1013. 34 rooms. This is well-located and has camping facilities.

Denizli

▲▲ **Altuntur,** Kaymakei Cad. 1, ☎ 1 6176. 64 rooms. Good restaurant.

▲▲ **Halley,** Cumhuriyet Cad., ☎ 1 9544. 59 rooms. Located one block from the station.

▲ **Etemaga,** Istasyon Cad. 34, ☎ 1 4568. 40 rooms.

Campground

Kirikulu Sue Kamp, in Karahayit village, 3 mi/5 km north of Pamukkale.

Food

In Pamukkale there are restaurants only in the larger hotels.

Useful addresses

International Bank of Commerce (Iktisat Bankasi Türk A.Ş), for currency exchange, Oğuzhan Cad. 10, Denizli, ☎ (621) 113 56/74.

Tourist Information Offices:

Pamukkale: opposite Tusan Moteli, ☎ (6218) 1077.

Denizli: next to the railway station, ☎ (621) 1 3393.

SOUTH OF IZMIR

▬ KUŞADASI**

Telephone code: 6361.

58 mi/94 km south of Izmir and 121 mi/195 km north of Bodrum.

Located in the heart of ancient Ionia, Kuşadasi, meaning Bird Island in Turkish, was once a quiet little fishing village overlooking one of the most beautiful bays of the Aegean Sea. It has rapidly developed into one of the most popular seaside resorts of the coast.

Although Kuşadasi was most probably founded on the ancient site of Neopolis, there are no ruins and the town has very little of historical interest. On the other hand, because of its beautiful location and its excellent hotels, it is an ideal base for excursions to the many archaeological sites in the region, including Ephesus, Priene, Miletus, Didyma, and even the Greek island of Samos.

What to see

The islet of **Güvercin Adasi***, Pigeon Island has a 14th- or 15th-century fortress. It is said that the Barbarossa brothers, infamous Turkish pirates, used it as a hideout in the 16th century while buccaneering in the Mediterranean.

The former **Mehmed Paşa caravanserai*** opposite the port has been converted into a hotel.

Access

By boat: There are regular sea links with Istanbul, Izmir and the island of Samos.

By bus: There are regular bus services to Izmir and Bodrum.

By car: The road from Izmir is very good and there are beautiful views on the stretch between Selçuk and Kuşadasi.

Accommodation

The most comfortable hotels are, with the exception of the Kervansaray, generally in one of the many clubs or vacation resorts that have sprung up on the outskirts of Kuşadasi over the last few years.

▲▲▲▲ **Kervansaray**, ☎ 2457. 25 rooms. In a former Ottoman caravanserai in town, tastefully decorated in keeping with the style of the time.

▲▲▲ **Club Akdeniz**, 4.3 mi/7 km outside of the town, ☎ 1521. 416 rooms. Facing a fine sand beach. The rooms are in small two-storey buildings scattered over a 37.5 acre/15 ha park (although it is called a club, no organized activities are planned).

▲▲▲ **Club Kuştur**, 2.4 mi/4 km outside of the town. 450 rooms in 41 comfortable bungalows set among trees and flowers in a garden of exotic plants. Cabaret shows or games in the evening.

▲▲▲ **Hotel Club**, 12 mi/20 km outside of the town, ☎ 6366. 90 rooms. The hotel was completed in 1987. 1.2 mi/2 km from the village of Davutlar in the Güzelcamli National Park. Very pleasant setting.

▲▲▲ **Hotel Imbat**, 1.8 mi/3 km outside of the town, ☎ 2000. 140 rooms. Built on a cliff above a small private beach. The hotel restaurant has a panoramic view.

▲▲▲ **Hotel Marti**, 1.8 mi/3 km outside of the town, overlooking the Kadinlar beach, ☎ 3650. 59 rooms.

▲▲▲ **Omer Village**, 3.7 mi/6 km outside of the town, ☎ 1017. 110 rooms. Facing a palm-lined beach of fine sand.

▲▲ **Akmar,** Istiklal Cad. 13, ☎ 1501. 46 rooms. Located in Kuşadasi on the seafront.

▲▲ **Çiğdem,** 50 rooms. In a quiet part of town about 550 yds/500 m from the centre and 220 yds/200 m from the beach.

▲ **Pamuk Kuşadasi,** ☎ 3191. A small, centrally located hotel. Good value.

Kuşadasi also has a great many guesthouses.

Campgrounds

There are two campgrounds in pleasant surroundings between Selçuk and Kuşadasi: **BP Mocamp,** ☎ 1106, and **Önder,** ☎ 2413.

Food

There's a choice of restaurants in the port opposite Pigeon Island. For a very pleasant dinner in the former caravanserai, you must reserve a table (☎ 2457).

Useful addresses

International Bank of Commerce (Iktisat Bankasi Türk A.Ş) for currency exchange, Barbaros Hayrettin Paşa Bulv. 8, ☎ 1 4075 or 1 2530.

Marina, open all year round, 1200 moorings.

Tourist Information Office, Iskele Meydani, ☎ 1103.

▰▰▰ SELÇUK*

Telephone code: 5451.

11 mi/18 km north-east of Kuşadasi and 46 mi/74 km south of Izmir.

Ephesus was an important centre in both the Hellenistic and Roman eras. St John, who lived and preached there for a number of years, was buried on a nearby hill. He was known as the Holy Theologian *(Haghios Theologos),* a name that was remembered throughout the centuries. When in 1426 the Ottoman sultan, Murad II, annexed the small hill town, he gave it the Turkish version of the name of Ayasoluk. Much later, in 1914, Ayasoluk became Selçuk.

Around the eighth century the Ephesians had to leave their town because the port was silting up. They settled on the hill to the north, abandoning ancient Ephesus to marshland.

What to see

The **Gate of Persecution** (or Byzantine Gate), built in the seventh century with stone from former edifices, leads into the Basilica of St John.

Basilica of St John*. On his death, St John was buried on Selçuk hill and his grave was marked with a commemorative stone. Then, in the fifth century, a church was built there by Theodosius II. In the middle of the following century, the Roman emperor Justinian, and his wife Theodora, decided to replace the small church with a large sanctuary in the shape of a cross. It measured 36 ft/110 m by 131 ft/40 m and had six domes. The remains of this impressive construction are what you can see today. During the Middle Ages it was an important pilgrimage centre before being converted into a mosque by the Seljuks at the beginning of the 14th century. Not long afterward it was destroyed by an earthquake.

The **Isa Bey Camii*** (at the foot of the south-west slope of the hill) was built in 1375 under the auspices of Isa Bey, who ruled the Seljuk principality of Aydin. It is thought to be the first asymmetric mosque in Islam, measuring 187 ft/57 m by 167 ft/51 m, and was built to a large degree with stones from other buildings. The most interesting features are the sculpture work on the doorway and the tiles inside. You can also see Turkish-Islamic tombstones in the courtyard.

The **Selçuk citadel** that crowns the hill was built in the Byzantine era. Since then it has been modified several times and was restored about 15 years ago.

Archaeological Museum** *(open Tues-Sun 8am-6pm)*. The museum is a pleasant modern building with a fine collection of artifacts taken from the excavations that have been going on for more than a century in and around Ephesus. There are statues of Artemis with numerous breasts, taken from the Prytaneum; statues and busts of Eros and statuettes of Priapus, god of virility. You can also see fragments of mausoleums, sarcophagi and frescoes, mosaic tiles, relief decoration on capitals, as well as household objects, tools and coins.

Environs of Selçuk

The **House of the Virgin*** (Meryemana) is about 5 mi/8 km from Selçuk on Mount Aladag. 'The house of the Virgin was square and made of stone . . . rounded or octagonal behind . . . the front part was separated from the rest by light wickerwork partitions.' Thus spoke Anna Katharina Emmerich, a visionary from the Augustine convent of Dulmen, near Düsseldorf. The Virgin, she said, died in Ephesus and her house was on a hill, at the end of a mule track, facing the island of Samos in the Aegean Sea. Thanks to these revelations an expedition discovered the foundations of the house where Mary is believed to have spent the last years of her life and that, on her death, was converted into a chapel.

The first pilgrimage to Meryemana took place in 1896, five years after the discovery of the House of the Virgin. Since then pilgrims and tourists have visited it continuously, including Pope Paul VI in 1967, when he consecrated it as a place of pilgrimage. Pope John Paul II also went to meditate there in 1979. The chapel you see today has been restored. Its floor plan is cruciform in shape with a rectangular narthex leading into the main sanctuary. The small room to the right is said to have been that of the Virgin.

The **Grotto of the Seven Sleepers** is on the eastern slope of Mount Pion about 0.6 mi/1 km from the Magnesia Gate in Ephesus. During excavations carried out in the ruins of a church, a dozen sepulchres were found. A legend, told by both Christians and Muslims, says that seven young Ephesians fled the persecutions of Emperor Decius (AD 250-253) and took refuge in a cave. There they fell asleep and didn't wake up until 200 years later, during the reign of Theodosius II. When they died they were buried in the same cave and the church was built over them.

Access

By bus: The Izmir-Kuşadasi bus stops here.

By car: Selçuk is on the main Izmir-Antalya road, the E87.

Accommodation

▲▲ **Hotel Ak,** Kuşadasi Cad., 14, ☎ 2161. 20 rooms.

▲ **Motel Kala Han,** Atatürk Cad., 49, ☎ 154. 18 rooms.

▲ **Tusan Efes,** Efes Yolu, 38, ☎ 1060, 12 rooms. Located ten minutes from the ruins of Ephesus.

Selçuk also has accommodation in family guesthouses although there is more to choose from in Kuşadasi (see p. 154).

Food

There are restaurants on the main street, such as **Yeni Hitit,** which is well organized and has quick service.

Useful address

Tourist Information Office, Atatürk Mahallesi, Efes Müzesi Karşisi 23, opposite the museum, ☎ 1328 or 1945.

The ruins of Ephesus, the largest commercial centre in antiquity, offer the visitor a fascinating glimpse into the past.

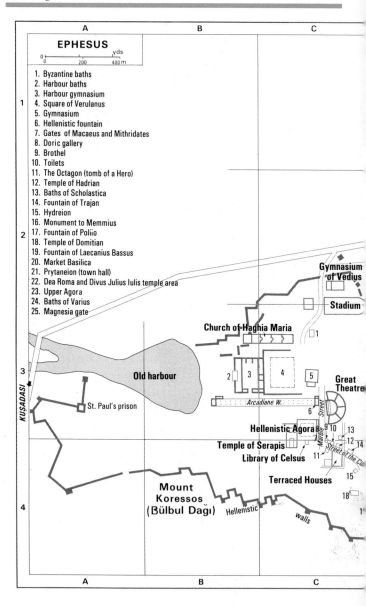

EPHESUS

scale: 0 — 200 — 400 m / 0 — yds

1. Byzantine baths
2. Harbour baths
3. Harbour gymnasium
4. Square of Verulanus
5. Gymnasium
6. Hellenistic fountain
7. Gates of Macaeus and Mithridates
8. Doric gallery
9. Brothel
10. Toilets
11. The Octagon (tomb of a Hero)
12. Temple of Hadrian
13. Baths of Scholastica
14. Fountain of Trajan
15. Hydreion
16. Monument to Memmius
17. Fountain of Poliio
18. Temple of Domitian
19. Fountain of Laecanius Bassus
20. Market Basilica
21. Prytaneion (town hall)
22. Dea Roma and Divus Julius Iulis temple area
23. Upper Agora
24. Baths of Varius
25. Magnesia gate

Gymnasium of Vedius

Stadium

Church of Haghia Maria

Old harbour

St. Paul's prison

Great Theatre

Arcadiane W.

Middle Street

Hellenistic Agora

Temple of Serapis

Library of Celsus

Street of the Cur

Terraced Houses

Mount Koressos (Bülbül Dağı)   Hellenistic   Walls

KUŞADASI

--- **EPHESUS***** (Efes)

2 mi/3 km west of Selçuk, 48 mi/77 km south of Izmir and 11 mi/18 km north-east of Kuşadasi.

As early as the second millennium BC there was a small town in the 'meadows of Asia,' as this region was known to Homer. The community was centered around a temple to Cybele, the mother-goddess of Anatolia. Because of its advantageous position on a trade route, its sheltered port and fertile soil, the town developed rapidly.

Little by little, however, alluvial deposits from the Cayster River (known today

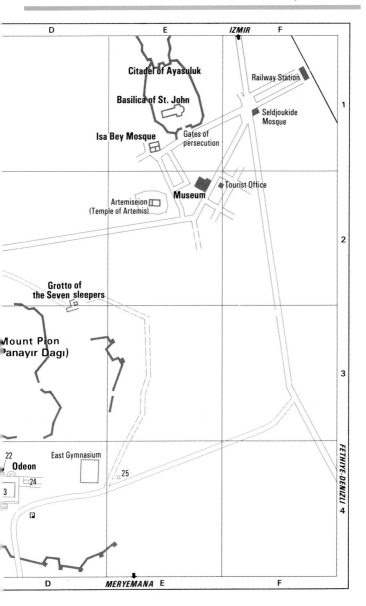

as Küçük Menderes, 'little meander') silted up the port, made a swamp of the plain and increased the distance between the town and the sea by several miles, which meant that the population had to move. But the inhabitants refused to leave the town and their goddess, so they settled on the eastern slope of Mt Pion, about 1312 yds/1200 m from the temple.

Toward the middle of the 10th century BC, the Ionians, led by Androcles, landed in the Latmos Gulf. They gradually absorbed and influenced the surrounding civilization; Cybele became Hellenized as Diana and later Artemis. The town prospered, regaining its importance as a flourishing commercial centre.

Pilgrimage sites

Every year, thousands of Catholics come to pray at the house of the Virgin Mary, near Ephesus, and to gather at the ruins of St John's Basilica, one of Christendom's earliest holy places. St Paul was born at Tarsus, near Adana, and converted his first believers there. While still in Turkey, he wrote his Epistles to the Ephesians and Galatians and was an active evangelist throughout the region. St John, to whom Jesus had entrusted his mother, wrote his Gospel in the Izmir region where he had his vision of the Apocalypse.

St Nicholas, a familiar figure to Protestants, was born in Patara. He became Bishop of Myra (now Demre), where he performed miracles and where his tomb can be visited. In the year 325 he took part in the Ecumenical Council at Nicaea (today's Iznik) well before he became known as the European Santa Claus.

Many Muslims consider Konya a sacred city. The founder of the order of the Whirling Dervishes lived here and the city has managed to keep its religious character. Its most famous monument, the Mausoleum of Mevlâna, spiritual leader of the Mevlevî Dervishes, is located in a former monastery.

In the sixth century BC, Ephesus was taken by Croesus, King of Lydia, and later came under the control of Cyrus, King of the Persians. These changes did not prevent the town from prospering; on the contrary, the Temple of Artemis, begun by Croesus, was embellished with new marble columns and elegant sculptures by successive rulers.

In 356 BC Herostatus the Mad, who wished to win eternal fame, did so by setting fire to the temple. According to legend, Artemis could not defend her house because she was away at the birth of Alexander the Great, who was born the same night. In 334 BC Alexander freed Ephesus from the rule of the Persians, and when he died, Lysimachus, his general, decided to make it into Anatolia's most important port. He built a new town near the sea and forced the Ephesians, who were still against the idea of moving from their temple, to move in. He even destroyed two neighbouring ports, Lebedos and Colophon, forcing their populations to move and in so doing add to the prosperity of the new settlement. Ephesus revived, thanks to the busy new port, and became the largest commercial centre of antiquity.

In the second century BC, Ephesus came under the control of the kings of Pergamum and was later left to the Romans in 133. The Roman period was Ephesus's most prosperous, to the extent that the town was to be considered one of the most important in the world, second only to Alexandria. It flourished architecturally under Roman emperors who built a profusion of magnificent monuments. Most of the ruins date from this period.

Paul of Tarsus came to live in Ephesus in 53 BC. He condemned idolatry and the cult of Artemis and set up a Christian community. Under his leadership Ephesus became the third largest centre of Christianity after Jerusalem and Antioch. St John also went there to live, accompanied by Mary, and wrote his Gospel.

Decline set in during the third century AD. In 263 the Goths burned the Temple of Artemis as they sacked and pillaged the town. Gradually all the pagan centres were abandoned for monuments built to the glory of the Christian God, and Ephesus became an important diocese.

What to see

The site is open daily until 6pm.

There are two entrances. The most practical way of visiting the site, if you go there by taxi, is to arrange with your driver to be dropped off at the Magnesia Gate at the top and after the visit to meet the taxi at the other entrance on the Kuşadasi road. Try to avoid walking around the site in the middle of the day; it gets very hot and there's not much shade.

The remains of the illustrious city have been particularly well preserved and it is easy to imagine what daily life there was like for its inhabitants.

The restored two-storey façade of the Library of Celsus.

It is advisable to begin the visit from the top so that by walking down the **Street of the Curetes** and the **Marble Street,** you always have a view of the whole city (it is easier to walk down anyway because the slope is quite steep).

You enter through the **Magnesia Gate,** just opposite the East Gymnasium. The gate once had three arches, the main one in the middle for horses and chariots, and smaller ones on either side for pedestrians.

The **Upper Agora**[*] was used for administrative purposes and was where important questions regarding the city were debated. It was a vast complex of buildings spread over an area of about 129,168 sq ft/12,000 sq m. The ruins you see today date from the reigns of Augustus and Claudius in the first century AD.

The **Baths of Varius** are in the north-east corner of the agora, at the foot of Mt Pion. The remains are those of a typical Roman bath built in the first century AD comprising a *frigidarium* (cool room). *tepidarium* (warm room) and *caldarium* (hot bath).

North of the agora two remaining colonnades mark the site of the **Market Basilica** built under Emperor Augustus. Notice the columns with their alternating Ionic and Corinthinian capitals. The basilica was once a vast construction with three naves.

Continuing northward you come to the **Odeon**[*] a little theatre with about eight well-preserved rows with a seating capacity of 1400. Two doors led into the theatre, one at either side of the proscenium. There were statues decorating the front of the stage facing the audience. The theatre was used not only for plays and concerts but also for town council meetings. During excavations, fragments of an inscription were found that ascribed the construction of the Odeon to Publius Vedus Antoninus (who was partly responsible for the rebuilding of Ephesus), and his wife, Flavia Papiana, in the second century AD. As there are no gutters in the orchestra section for draining rainwater, part of the theatre may well have been covered, probably by a wooden roof; however, no traces have been found.

The **Prytaneion,** or town hall, to the west of the Odeon, was first built in the third century BC and then rebuilt four centuries later under Augustus. Most of what remains dates from Augustus, although you can still see the earlier altar dedicated to Hestia (Artemis) Boulaea, guardian of the Prytaneion, on which an eternal flame burned as a symbol of the life of the city. It was the sacred centre of Ephesus and was used for important religious ceremonies and meetings of the town magistrates. Two statues of Artemis found in front of the building are now exhibited in the Ephesus museum.

The **Temple of Domitian** (656 ft/200 m south-west of the Odeon) was constructed between AD 81 and 96 on an enormous rectangular terrace that covered an area of almost 2 sq mi/5 sq km. A colossal statue of Emperor Domitian once stood inside. You can see parts of it, namely the head and left arm, in the Izmir museum.

The **Street of the Curetes**** is a wide avenue that sweeps from the Prytaneion down the hill to the Library of Celsus. The 'Curetes' were priests who guarded the flame to Hestia Boulaea. Their marble street was lined with buildings and adorned with statues of public figures. Along it you can still see remains of the city's water system.

To the left of the Street of the Curetes, on leaving the square of Domitian, you come to a **Triumphal Arch.** Its pillars are decorated with reliefs of Herakles wearing the skin of the Nemean lion. Because these sculptures predate the rest of the Triumphal Arch, it is believed that the pillars were taken from a building outside Ephesus.

The **Fountain of Trajan** (farther down to the right) was once a two-storey monument about 39 ft/12 m high. A colossal statue of Emperor Trajan has disappeared from the central niche in the back wall, except for his foot, which you can still see resting on a terrestrial globe. The fountain pool (215 sq ft/20 sq m) was surrounded by statues, some of which are exhibited in the Ephesus Museum.

The **Baths of Scholastica** (in the street going up to the right after the fountain), together with the public toilets and the brothel (a little farther down), formed a large group of buildings constructed toward the end of the first and the beginning of the second century. The bathing installations were revised on the instigation of a lady named Christian Scholastica, whose decapitated statue can be seen in the entrance. Three rooms lead on from here, the *frigidarium* (cool room) with an oval pool, the *tepidarium* (warm room) in which bathers could rest, and the *caldarium* (hot bath), where you can still see remains of the heating system in the walls. The floors above the baths had rooms where up to 1000 people could read or relax.

The **Temple of Hadrian**** stands on the Street of the Curetes beside the Baths. It was built in honour of the Emperor Hadrian in the first half of the second century and has since been restored. Part of the front colonnade and certain friezes inside have been replaced by copies, but you can see the originals in the Ephesus Museum. There is a bust of Tyche, goddess of fortune and protectress of the town, on the keystone of the arch. Notice also the young woman on the semicircular tympanum of the doorway that leads into the *cella* (chapel). She is depicted as a symbol of abundance and fertility emerging bare-breasted from acanthus leaves.

Ruins of **terraced houses**** can be seen in front of the Temple of Hadrian, on the hillside overlooking the Street of the Curetes. The house fronts facing the avenue were used as shops. Two double- or triple-storeyed houses were built on each terrace, with the ground floor of the upper house partly resting on the flat roof of the lower one. Some of these mansions were excavated only in 1970 and contain perfectly preserved mosaics and frescoes. They are closed to the public.

The **brothel** (to the right, on the corner of the Street of the Curetes and the Marble Street) was built in the second century AD and restored in the fourth after an earthquake. The main entrance opened onto the Marble Street. Directions to the house are given farther north along the road and include drawings of a heart, a woman's face and a foot pointing south!

The **Library of Celsus**** located where the Street of the Curetes ends and the Marble Street begins, was built by Liberius Julius Aquila in memory of his father, Celsus, governor general of the Roman province of Asia. The Goths set fire to it in the middle of the second century. The marble frontage survived but thousands of works were lost. The façade was later converted into a fountain which crumbled in the fifth century during an earthquake. Yet, 85% of the library was recovered during excavations carried out by Austrian archaeologists, who managed (at the end of the 1970s) to reconstruct the two-storey façade. The four statues of women, representing the virtues of Celsus, are reproductions of originals that are now in the Vienna Fine Arts Museum. Because Celsus helped the town, he was given the privilege of being buried in the town centre, between the library and the entrance to the Lower Agora. You reach his grave chamber through a narrow passage outside the northern wall.

To the right of the library courtyard a triple arched **monumental gate** leads into the Hellenistic Agora. According to inscriptions on the attic, it was built early in the Christian era by Mazeus and Mithridates, two slaves freed by Emperor Agrippa. They built it in honour of the emperor, of his son-in-law Augustus, and of the latter's wife and daughter, Livia and Julia.

Having passed through the propylon you enter the **Hellenistic Agora.** This marketplace was a vast square with sides 361 ft/110 m long. It was surrounded by commercial galleries and adorned with busts and statues of eminent people. There was a **clepsydra** in the middle of the square, a sort of water-clock that measured the time allocated to orators for their speeches.

The **Marble Street**** is the main street that runs right through the town from the western end of the Street of the Curates, past the theatre, to the Gymnasium of Vedius farther north. The theatre was first built in the Hellenistic era; it was restored and repaired toward the fifth century AD and is one of the best-preserved roads of antiquity. On the left of the road as you walk down toward the theatre, there's a sort of raised platform that was used only by pedestrians (as opposed to horses and chariots).

The **theatre**** dates from the Hellenistic period (third century BC) and was remodeled and enlarged in the first and second centuries AD. The stage originally had three levels; the first two were completed under Nero (54-68) and the third under Trajan (98-117). The theatre could hold 24,000 spectators who came and went through arched passageways at each side of the *cavea* (auditorium). This was built into the western slope of Mt Pion at a height of 98 ft/30 m and comprised 66 terraced rows divided into three sections. There was once a standing gallery above the top rows. The stage façade, which was adorned with columns and statues, measured 476 ft/145 m wide and 59 ft/18 m high. On each of the three stage floors were boxes for artists and stage properties.

The grand **Arcadian Way** (36 ft/11 m wide and 1739 ft/530 m long) was the main street to the harbour. It dates from Hellenistic times and was partly restored under Emperor Arcadius (AD 395-408). On either side of the street there was a row of galleries that opened onto shops. Two enormous gateways like triumphal arches stood at either end of the street, while halfway down, four columns once held the busts of the four Evangelists. Today all that remains are the pedestals.

The Arcadian Way led northward between the theatre and a **gymnasium** until it reached the Temple of Artemis. To the west of the gymnasium there was an enormous square, surrounded on three sides by galleries, that was used for open-air exercises and sporting events. Continuing westward you come to a monumental gateway leading into the **harbour baths** which were built in the second century AD and renovated under Constantine (327-361).

North of the harbour baths are the ruins of the **Church of the Virgin Mary** or the Double Church, considered the oldest church built to honour Christ's mother. The Ecumenical Councils of 431 and 449 were held here. Fifteen centuries later, on July 26, 1967, Pope Paul VI reinforced Ephesus's Christian history by declaring the church a place of pilgrimage.

Environs of Ephesus

See the section on Selçuk (p. 155) for the **Grotto of the Seven Sleepers** (about 2 mi/3 km from Selçuk) and the **House of the Virgin Mary** (Mereyemana, 5 mi/8 km from Selçuk).

Access

By bus: There are regular buses from Izmir to Ephesus.

By car: Take the E87 south from Izmir and turn west at Selçuk to reach Ephesus.

By taxi and dolmuş: You can find these in Selçuk, Izmir or Kuşadasi.

Accommodation

For hotels, see Selçuk (p. 156) or Kuşadasi (p. 154).

Festival

The **International Festival** is held in the theatre every year in May, featuring folkdancing, music and theatre.

Food

Several restaurants are located near the two entrances to the archaeological site.

▬▬ PRIENE**

36 mi/58 km south of Ephesus, 26 mi/42 km south of Kuşadasi, 16 mi/25 km north of Miletus, 33 mi/53 km north of Didyma and 84 mi/136 km south of Izmir.

Priene was one of the most beautiful towns of the ancient world thanks to the skilful town planning of Hippodamus, the great architect of Miletus, who laid out attractive buildings and terraced residential areas according to a geometric grid. The city was originally built on a peninsula and had two harbours, but the silt deposits of the Meander River (Menderes) closed the ports and gradually pushed the town farther inland. The ruins you see today are about 9 mi/15 km from the sea on a mountain ridge overlooking the river valley.

The city may well have been founded before the first millennium BC by Carians who lived in the area before the arrival of the Ionians. The first city built on the site was destroyed by the Persians at the beginning of the fifth century BC as punishment for a revolt by Ionian cities. The new town was built around 350 BC, when Alexander the Great, then master of Asia Minor, came to consecrate the Temple of Athena. Priene was later controlled by the kingdom of Pergamum and later still by Rome, which added it to its Asian province in 136 BC.

What to see

Parts of the **city walls** are well preserved. They stretch for almost 1.5 mi/2.5 km and are 20 ft/6 m high and 6.6 ft/2 m thick. Four gates lead from the walls into the city.

You have the best views of the **streets** from the acropolis or the peak of the citadel. They were laid out in a checkered pattern during the fourth century BC, according to the plans of Hippodamus of Miletus. The main streets are

16-23 ft/5-7 m wide. Terraces were also carefully designed along a north-south axis, linked together by flights of steps. Each house had a bath (water distribution was generous) and usually comprised a rectangular courtyard with a sitting room on one side and private rooms on the other.

The **Temple of Athena** (south of the main street) was built in 375 BC by Pytheos, the architect responsible for the Mausoleum of Halicarnassus, and completed with funds provided by Alexander the Great. It was one of the finest examples of Ionic architecture in Asia Minor but unfortunately all that remains today are the foundations and a few columns. It must have measured 98 ft/30 m by 66 ft/20 m with six columns on the façade and eleven on the main sides. A 23 ft/7 m statue of the goddess adorned the entrance. An altar to the east of the temple, designed like Pergamum's altar to Zeus, was reached by a monumental staircase.

The **Theatre*** is considered one of the best preserved of the ancient Greek world. The stage, which had an upper floor, formed part of a rectangular building. In front of it, between the audience rows and the orchestra, are pedestals that once supported statues. These have remained in their original position in spite of the remodeling that took place under the Romans when the stage was widened by 6.6 ft/2 m and the seating for local dignitaries was moved back.

The **Agora,** or marketplace, was located right in the heart of the town. It was lined with shops and surrounded on three sides by colonnades. A street that ran the whole length of the town from east to west led to it. There was a temple in the middle of the square where official ceremonies were held.

The **Bouleterion*** for city council meetings (to the north-east of the Agora) was built according to a quadrangular plan with marble steps on three sides. It could hold an audience of 640. Members of the council sat on the terraces while special benches were reserved for magistrates and visitors. Offerings were made at the beginning and end of each session on the sacrificial altar in the middle of the building. The roof was supported by four columns, decorated like the walls with Doric motifs.

The **Temple of Demeter,** built over the acropolis can be seen to the north. The *temenos* measured 148 ft/45 m by 56 ft/17 m and was reached through an entrance on the eastern side of the building. The southern side had a series of rooms used by priestesses while the western side had a little ditch for collecting sacrificial animal blood.

Not much remains of the large **Stadium** (627 ft/191 m by 66 ft/20 m) to the south of Priene.

Access

By private car, with a tour group, or by catching a dolmuş from Kuşadasi or Selçuk.

MILETUS**

16 mi/25 km south of Priene, 39 mi/63 km south of Kuşadasi and 95 mi/153 km south of Izmir.

Miletus is located near the small village of Balat, just beyond the Meander River (Büyük Menderes) valley. The river's alluvial deposits silted up the port in the same way as they did at Priene, forcing the town inland.

The Carians are believed to have been the first inhabitants here, followed by settlers from Crete and Greece. The city they founded was on a peninsula, which at that time jutted out more than 1 mi/2 km into the Gulf of Latmos. There were two ports that contributed to the town's wealth, making it the largest commercial centre of the 12 members of the League of Ionian Cities. Renown and prosperity increased in the sixth century BC, when the temple at Didyma was annexed by Miletus. It attracted large numbers of pilgrims and proved a considerable source of income.

In 494 BC the Ionian cities revolted unsuccessfully againt their Persian occupiers and Darius had Miletus completely destroyed. It was rebuilt but did not thrive again until after 334 BC, when Alexander the Great conquered the Persians and freed the cities.

At the beginning of the third century BC, control of Ionia passed into Roman hands, but Miletus remained relatively untouched as it was declared a free city. Caesar, Anthony and later St Paul spent time there, and a bishopric was also established.

What to see

The **Theatre**** rises impressively from a hillside about 98 ft/30 m above the plain. It was built in the second century AD and is one of the most beautiful examples of Graeco-Roman theatres. The first terraced rows of the auditorium, which could hold 20,000 spectators, and the arched passage-ways below, have been well-preserved. The façade measured 459 ft/140 m and the 112 ft/34 m—long stage was decorated with friezes and Roman-style statues. In the middle of the row nearest the stage you can still see the imperial box flanked by two columns.

The **Bouleterion** (for city council meetings), not far from the **Southern Agora,** was built like a theatre with a semicircular auditorium for 1000 people. The wooden roof rested on walls lined with decorative Ionic half columns.

Of the **Nymphaeum,** opposite the Bouleterion, only three arched alcoves and rubble from former aqueducts remain. The large fountain has long since disappeared. It was decorated with nymph reliefs and once stood in the middle of a three-tiered ring in front of the alcoves.

A row of Doric columns is all that remains of the **Northern Agora** built in the sixth and fifth centuries BC and remodeled in the second century AD. The Southern Agora (in the middle of the city below the Bouleterion) dates from the third century BC but was considerably reshaped in the second century AD. It was surrounded by Doric and Corinthian columns.

The **Baths of Faustine*** are still in good shape. The building was first a gymnasium in the Hellenistic era but was later converted into baths by Faustine, wife of Emperor Marcus Aurelius. Mosaics and statues adorned the rooms and pools. Statues of Apollo and the Muses were discovered in the main chamber; the lion fountain and the statue of the god Meander are still in their original position, in the *frigidarium* (cool room).

South of the Southern Agora stands the **Ilyas Bey Mosque,** built in 1404 by Emir Ilyas Bey. There is impressive work on the front of the mosque and on the doorway with side columns. Inside, the stone *mihrab* (prayer niche) has been finely sculpted.

To the south was the **Sacred Gate** that opened onto the road leading to the Temple of Apollo in Didyma.

Access

By private car, with a tour group, or by catching a dolmuş from Kuşadasi or Selçuk.

▬▬ DIDYMA*

Telephone code: (Izmir) 51.

12 mi/19 km south of Miletus, 45 mi/72 km south of Kuşadasi, 33 mi/53 km south of Priene and 101 mi/163 km south-west of Istanbul.

Unlike Priene and Miletus, Didyma was not a town but a religious monument dedicated to Apollo. It rivaled those of Claros and Delphi for many years.

The oracle at Didyma probably came into being during the seventh century BC, but Miletus annexed the temple there in about 540 BC. When the Ionian cities rebelled in 494 BC, Darius retaliated by ordering the destruction of Miletus and, with it, the temple at Didyma. It lay forgotten until the victory of Alexander the Great over the Persians in 334 BC. Toward 300 BC the Miletians decided to rebuild it, but the work was continually interrupted over a period of 200 years and the temple was never finished. In spite of this, however, visits and consultations with the oracle continued.

On arrival in Miletus, pilgrims to the temple were taken by sea to the port of Panarmos about 9 mi/14 km away. From there a 4 mi/6 km sacred way led to the temple. It was lined with statues of sphynxes, lions and priests of the oracle, and ended on an esplanade, where the pilgrims spread their offerings. When the Meander River's alluvial deposits filled up the port at Panarmos in the first century AD, Emperor Trajan ordered a 9 mi/15 km road to be built from Miletus to link up with the sacred way to the temple.

With the advent of Christianity the temple declined. It was used as a fortress by invading Goths in AD 262. Under the Byzantines in AD 385, a Christian church was built inside, ordered by Emperor Theodosius, who decreed that consultation of pagan oracles would be punished by death.

What to see

Although the Temple of Apollo* was never completed and was partly destroyed in an earthquake, what remains is impressive. Only three of the 108 columns forming the double colonnade around it can be seen today, but the wonderful Roman reliefs on the bases of what were the eight central columns on the eastern side are a testimony to its former splendour. Part of the frieze on the outer colonnade comprised gigantic heads of Medusa, a good example of which can be seen at the entrance to the site.

A person wishing to consult the oracle had first to cleanse himself with water from the sacred well, then sacrifice an animal on the altar. After this he was shown into a room (about 52 ft/16 m by 82 ft/25 m) that was lined with three rows of four columns each. There he gave a priest the question, in writing, that he hoped to put to the oracle. The priest took the question to the *naiskos*, a small building with four Doric columns, where the priestess presided in the midst of statues of Apollo. She sat on a tripod over an opening out of which spewed vapours that sent her into a state of temporary delirium. The priest had to interpret the oracle's reply and then go into a room that had two columns, where he wrote out the answer that he finally handed to the questioner.

Altinkum Plaji*, 'golden sand,' one of Turkey's most beautiful beaches, is located 2.4 mi/4 km south of Didyma.

Access

By car, with a tour group or by catching a dolmuş from Kuşadasi or Selçuk.

Accommodation

Altinkum Plaji (2.4 mi/4 km away) has a good choice of hotels and guest-houses. See also 'Accommodation' in Kuşadasi p. 154.

Food

There are restaurants on the site not far from the ruins and seafood cafés on the beachfront in Altinkum.

How to speak Turkish-English

The names of cities, rivers and kings of Anatolia have become part of the English language and are used as common expressions today.

The Gordian Knot: At Gordium, Alexander the Great cut the now-legendary knot that attached the yoke to the shaft of the King of Phrygia's chariot.

The Midas Touch: This comes from famous King Midas, who had the ability to change everything he touched into gold.

To meander: This derives from the name of a winding river in Anatolia known today as the Menderes.

Mausoleum: The tomb of King Mausolus at Halicarnassus (Bodrum) was one of the Seven Wonders of the Ancient World.

Kiosk: The Turkish word köşk (1608) originally meant an open summerhouse or garden pavilion.

▅▅▅ *BODRUM* (Halicarnassus)

Telephone code: 6141.

164 mi/264 km south of Izmir, 108 mi/174 km south of Kuşadasi, 119 mi/191 km south of Ephesus, 121 mi/195 km north-west of Marmaris, 177 mi/285 km north-west of Fethiye and 559 mi/900 km south of Istanbul.

In around 1000 BC, Dorians from Troezene in the Peloponnese set foot in south-west Asia Minor, in the area around present-day Bodrum peninsula. A few centuries later, Halicarnassus (now Bodrum) became a member of the Dorian league of cities that included places on today's Turkish mainland, on Greek islands and on the island of Rhodes, such as Cnidos, Cos, Kamiros, Lindos and Ialyssos. However, because of its alliance with the Ionians of Caria, the town was later expelled from the league.

In the middle of the sixth century BC, the whole region was taken by the Persians, who had conquered the kingdom of Lydia. A tyrant named Lygdamis governed Halicarnassus during the reign of Xerxes (510-465 BC). He was succeeded by his daughter, Artemisia I, who was named admiral of the fleet of Halicarnassus and supported Xerxes in his battle against Athens.

In 377 BC, Mausolus, ruler of Caria, threw off Persian control and formed an independent kingdom setting up Halicarnassus as his capital. On his death in 353, his wife and sister Artemisia II, succeeded him and built a magnificent funerary monument in his honour. It became one of the Seven Wonders of the Ancient World and is the origin of the word mausoleum.

The city was conquered by Alexander the Great in 334 BC and was ruled respectively by Philip V of Macedonia, the Seljuks and the Byzantines, before being annexed in AD 1300 by the Emirate of Menteshe. At the beginning of the 15th century, Halicarnassus was occupied by the Knights Hospitaller of St John who were crusaders from Rhodes. They built a fortress on the end of the peninsula. However, when Süleyman the Magnificent took control of Rhodes in 1522, he confiscated all the Knights' possessions and Bodrum became part of the Ottoman Empire.

Today the Castle of St Peter rises impressively above twin bays dotted with small white houses, forming what is known as Turkey's St Tropez. The sea, the village and the port are bathed in an atmosphere of relaxation and leisure. Bodrum's squares and narrow streets are lively late into the night and you'll have no problem finding stores, restaurants, art galleries and workshops open.

What to see

The **Castle of St Peter**** *(summer: open daily, 8:30am-noon, 3pm-7pm; winter: open daily, 8:30am-noon, 1pm-5:30pm)* was founded in 1402 by the Knights of the Order of St John. These soldiers of the Cross founded a community and system of government on the island of Rhodes and then built the Castle of St Peter on the mainland – regrettably, they built it with stone taken from the ruins of the mausoleum. The castle you can visit today is surrounded by three terraced ramparts with two triple-storey towers. A staircase leads up to the covered walkway that goes around the fortress. Inside, there is an intriguing **Museum of Underwater Archaeology,** where you can see parts of a Phoenician galley, amphorae, cups, vases, copper ingots, Greek statues and glass and metal artifacts.

The Mausoleum* *(Open Tues-Sun 8am-noon, 3pm-7pm)* is on the road to Ortakent just before you leave Bodrum. Apart from a large hole and a few remains of the base, there is not much left of what was formerly one of the Seven Wonders of the Ancient World, the magnificent funerary monument to King Mausolus. It was begun during the king's reign in the fourth century BC and completed, after his death, by Queen Artemisia. Its rectangular foundations were about 66 ft/20 m long and the monument itself was 164 ft/50 m high. The sepulchral chamber was surrounded by 36 Ionic columns that supported a roof shaped like a stepped pyramid. On the top was a chariot with statues of Mausolus and Artemisia. Beautiful marble

The Castle of St Peter stands guard over the bay of Bodrum, ancient Halicarnassus.

reliefs depicting Hellenic wars with Amazons and centaurs adorned the four sides of the pedestal. The whole structure was probably destroyed at the beginning of the 15th century by an earthquake.

The small **museum** at the entrance to the site houses a model of the mausoleum, along with various pieces of the original structure. Parts of the statues and chariot that were discovered by an Englishman in the middle of last century are exhibited at the British Museum in London.

As you leave Bodrum, you will see the remains of an ancient **theatre** to the right of the road on Göktepe hill. It was built in the second century AD on a site overlooking the bay. All that's left now are a few terraced rows of seats.

From Bodrum, you can take a boat excursion to Knidos and Datça. The cheapest leave from Cumhuriyet Beach.

Access

By boat: Turkish Maritime Lines run boats between Istanbul and Mersin that stop at several ports, including Bodrum, en route. From May 1 to October 31, there's a daily 1.5-hour ferry service between Bodrum and Cos Island. There are also boats to Rhodes, Samos and Lesbos (check with the **Tourist Information Office**). A new service has started between Bodrum and Datça.

By bus: In the summer there are daily connections with Istanbul (16 hours) via Izmir.

By car: There's a good new asphalt road between Izmir and Bodrum.

By plane: Either take a dolmuş from Dalaman Airport near Muğla (62 mi/100 km), which connects Bodrum to Istanbul and Ankara; or take a dolmuş or bus from Izmir Airport via Izmir to Bodrum.

Accommodation

It is difficult to find a pleasant hotel in Bodrum that is also quiet. The least noisy part of town is in the little port facing the sea but because this is a protected area new hotels cannot be built. The best accommodation is located outside the town at one of the following hotels:

▲▲▲▲ **Torba Tatil,** a resort village in Torba, 4 mi/6 km from Bodrum, ☎ 2343. 35 rooms. This club was built recently in the traditional style of the Aegean coastal villages.

▲▲▲▲ **TMT Motel,** 1.2 mi/2 km from Bodrum, in Akçebük, ☎ 1440. 171 rooms. An extremely well-planned series of small cottages in a garden beside the sea. You can enjoy peace and quiet as well as a wide range of water sports.

▲▲▲ **Halikarnas,** Cumhuriyet Cad., 128, ☎ 1073. 28 rooms. Located on the eastern bay, this hotel has a disco.

▲▲▲ **Milta,** a resort village 4 mi/7 km from Bodrum, ☎ 2343. Located in a charming cove surrounded by rolling green hills.

▲▲ **Baraz,** Cumhuriyet Cad., 62, ☎ 1857. 24 rooms. Well located with a terrace for drinks or a meal.

▲▲ **Gözen,** Cumhuriyet Cad., 18, ☎ 1602. 24 rooms. Nice and clean.

There are many other hotels in the centre of Bodrum but they're not sheltered from the music that floats up from the street into the early hours. There are, however, some modest guesthouses of 10 to 15 rooms that are quiet, particularly those heading out of town toward the TMT Motel. New motels are being built on the outskirts of town.

Food

Most of Bodrum's restaurants are along Cumhuriyet Cad., or in streets perpendicular to it. Prices are usually high but the setting is pleasant. A former caravanserai has been converted into a restaurant called **Haci Molla** near the Tourist Information Office.

Useful addresses

International Bank of Commerce (Iktisat Bankasi Türk A.Ş), for currency exchange, Dr. Akim Bey Cad., 6, ☎ 2831.

Marina, *open all year round,* ☎ 1860. Room for 300 boats.

Tourist Information Office, in the harbour, Eylül Meydani, 12, ☎ 1091.

▬ *MARMARIS*

Telephone code: 6121.

112 mi/180 km south-east of Bodrum, 43 mi/70 km south of Muğla and 174 mi/280 km south-east of Izmir.

The Aegean and Mediterranean seas meet at Marmaris, a seaside resort and yachting harbour that has been a popular vacation centre for a number of years.

What to see

Of ancient Physkos, a prosperous port in the fourth century BC, nothing remains. From Marmaris's more recent history there are the small ruins of a **medieval fortress** and a caravanserai to visit.

Marmaris is mainly an extremely pleasant seaside resort and departure point for boat excursions, especially to Rhodes (in the tourist season there's a daily trip to and from the island by ferry – expect long waits at customs).

Environs of Marmaris

There are a number of places of historical or simply picturesque interest to visit around Marmaris:

Amos (at the entrance to the Bay of Marmaris) has theatre and temple ruins among rocks and pine trees.

At Idyma (21 mi/33 km north of Marmaris), you can walk around ancient tombs and explore an acropolis with medieval walls.

Datça[*] (46 mi/74 km west of Marmaris) is a picturesque little village on the edge of a pine forest with beautiful beaches. From the winding road there is a wonderful panorama of the coast.

The remains of the ancient city of **Knidus**[**] (59 mi/95 km west of Marmaris) are on the tip of a peninsula about 12 mi/20 km west of Datça. Because the road is rough, try catching a boat there from Datça. Knidus was once a powerful Carian city, a flourishing port and a renowned cultural and artistic centre. The pride of the town was the famous nude statue of Aphrodite (alas never found) by the sculptor Praxiteles. Today you can see the acropolis, the theatre that held 4500 spectators and the two gateways to the ruins of the temples of Dionysius and Apollo.

Access

By boat: **Turkish Maritime Lines** has boats that stop here on the Istanbul-Mersin route. There are daily 2-hour crossings between Rhodes and Marmaris.

By bus: Regular services from Izmir. In summer there are others from Istanbul and Ankara.

By car: The quickest route from Izmir is via Aydin and Muğla rather than Söke and Milas.

By plane: The airport is near Muğla, 43 mi/70 km away.

Accommodation

Hotels

Hotels are often fully booked in summer; you should therefore reserve a room in advance.

▲▲▲▲ **Datça Club,** 46 mi/74 km from Marmaris, ☎ 1170. 108 rooms. A charming site with beautiful beaches.

▲▲▲▲ **Marti Motel,** 6 mi/9 km from Marmaris on the Datça road, ☎ 4910. 280 rooms. Good location on a lovely bay.

▲▲▲▲ **Turban Motel,** 4 mi/7 km from Marmaris, ☎ 1843. 246 rooms. Resort village in a pine forest beside a sandy beach.

▲▲▲ **Hawaï,** Cildir Meydani, ☎ 4003. 56 rooms. Overlooking the sea.

▲▲▲ **Lidya,** Siteler Mahallesi, 130., ☎ 2940. 220 rooms. Located around the bay; rooms have a sea view or overlook the gardens.

▲▲▲ **Otel 47,** Atatürk Cad., 10, ☎ 1700. 51 rooms. This comfortable hotel is one of the newest in Marmaris.

▲▲ **Marmaris,** Atatürk Cad., 30, ☎ 1308. 30 rooms. Located on the waterfront, with a beautiful view of the bay.

▲ **Atlantik,** Atatürk Cad., 11, ☎ 1218. 42 rooms. Lovely sea view, but tends to be noisy.

Most of the **guest houses** are along Siteler and Atatürk Cad.

Campground

Engür Camping, 9 mi/15 km south of Marmaris *(open from May 1 to October 10).*

Food

Restaurants are mainly concentrated in the area around the Tourist Information Office.

◆◆ **Bamboo,** Atatürk Cad., 9, ☎ 1339.

◆◆ **Mangol,** Keremalti Mahallesi, Haci Sabri Sok, ☎ 1784.

◆◆ **Tilla,** Atatürk Cad., ☎ 1843.

◆ **Kara Seniz,** ☎ 2837.

◆ **Liman,** ☎ 1373.

Useful addresses

International Bank of Commerce (Iktisat Bankasi Türk A.Ş.), for currency exchange, Barbaros Cad., 9, ☎ 1 4838.

Tourist Information Office, in the harbour, Iskele Meydani 39, ☎ 1035.

CENTRAL ANATOLIA

The heart of Turkey is an immense plateau broken up by rivers and cliffs. In the middle of this tableland is a vast salt lake, Tuz Gölu, which occasionally runs dry in summer. Besides Ankara, the capital, the major towns are Kayseri and Nevşehir in the centre, and Konya in the south.

The region was first inhabited during the Palaeolithic period. With Çatal Höyuk (south-east of Konya), the centre of Anatolia became one of the cradles of urban civilization. Here, relics dating from the seventh century BC have provided evidence of humanity at an advanced stage of development as early as the beginning of the Neolithic period. Later, during the second millennium BC, the entire area was ruled by Hittites from their capital, Hattuşaş, on the high northern plateau. Traces of their reign can be seen in the Ankara Museum, which holds the most beautiful collection of Hittite artifacts extant.

Throughout history this region has been a true corridor between Asia and Europe, trodden by migrants, hordes of invaders and long caravans of merchants of the most diverse origins. In turn, Phrygians, Galatians, Romans, Byzantines, Seljuks and Ottomans all swept in and took control.

The extraordinary central region known in Roman times as Cappadocia has been a refuge for the persecuted as well as a haven of contemplation and meditation for recluses.

ANKARA

286 mi/460 km south-east of Istanbul, 362 mi/583 km northeast of Izmir, 302 mi/486 km north-west of Adana, 189 mi/305 km north-west of Ürgüp and 621 mi/1000 km north/east of Antalya.

In the third century BC, the Tectosages, a powerful Gallic tribe, split off from the main horde that was pressing into Greece and crossed into Asia. They built their camp at the gates of Byzantium and were called upon by Nicomedes I, King of Bithynia, to support him against the kings of Pergamum. In return

The rock formations of Göreme, many of which have been hollowed out to create chapels and dwellings.

they were granted Cappadocia and eastern Phrygia, which they named Galatia in memory of their homeland. Ancyra was the capital.

Galatia became a Roman province under Augustus, who provided Ancyra with a hippodrome, thermal baths, and temples, one of which bears his name. This is a white marble monument erected in the year AD 10 to Rome and Augustus. Forty years later, influenced by the teachings of Paul of Tarsus, the Galatians converted to Christianity and Ancyra became one of the first Christian towns of the East.

The area became famous for woven goods made from goats' hair. This was recorded as early as the beginning of the first century AD by Strabo, a native of Cappadocia. He writes of the people living near the Halys River who reared goats and wove their silky hair into magnificent fabrics. He is referring to Angora goats and mohair.

The town prospered under the Byzantines before succumbing to successive attacks by Persians, Arabs, Turks and Crusaders. In 1127, Ancyra was annexed by Seljuk tribes and took the name Engüriye, which Westerners translated as Angora. In 1304, the town came under Mongol control and was incorporated into the Ottoman Empire in 1414. In spite of its being on the caravan route to the eastern provinces, Angora did not always enjoy economic stability. Instead, it experienced alternating periods of prosperity and decline. Under Murad III, who was Sultan of Turkey from 1574 to 1595, a trade agreement was signed in 1590 that opened up the Ottoman Empire's weaving industry to English merchants. But there were two arduous wars during this reign – the first against Persia, the second against the Hapsburgs – which put a strain on the state finances and led to heavy inflation. The situation degenerated until Murad IV came to power in the 17th century.

However, a decline set in again during the 18th century, and by the 19th century, Angora had become one of the poorest centres in the country. At the beginning of the 20th century, it was a dull market town lost in the middle of the Anatolian steppe, with barely 30,000 inhabitants.

Nevertheless, the situation was to change. On October 30, 1918, at the end of World War I, the Ottoman Empire was dissolved by the victorious nations. All that remained was the Angora province where the young Turkish officer, Mustafa Kemal, emerged as a leader by opposing the partition of his country. On April 23, 1920, he proclaimed the 'first Grand National Assembly of Turkey'. He made Angora the capital and founded the new Republic of Turkey in 1923. Given the name Atatürk, or 'father of the Turks,' he was to say: 'The nation is ready and resolved to advance unhalting and undaunted on the path of civilization.'

In the middle of the arid steppe, dams were built, trees were planted, parks and gardens were opened. Today, still somewhat austere in spite of its greenery, the new Ankara, Yenişehir, a modern, spacious town, rises from the foot of the ancient citadel.

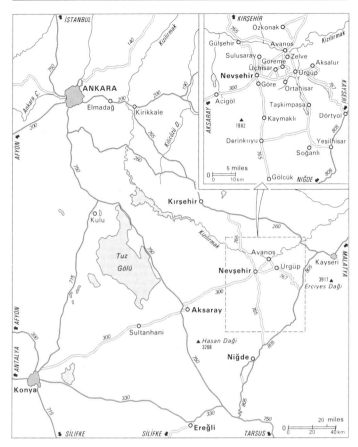

CENTRAL ANATOLIA

PRACTICAL INFORMATION

Telephone code: 4.
Map coordinates refer to the map pp. 176-177.

When to go

The weather is dry and sunny throughout the year. Even at the height of summer, days are never excessively hot and evenings are cool.

Access

By bus: Practical, inexpensive buses run from the central bus station to all the main towns in the country. The *Otogar*, B1, or bus terminal, is located one block north-west of the railway station.

By car: Ankara is on the E5 between Istanbul and Adana, which is a good, though heavily used road. As always in Turkey, be particularly careful when driving because Turkish drivers may ignore speed limits and common traffic regulations.
Ankara-Istanbul: 286 mi/460 km.
Ankara-Izmir: 362 mi/583 km.
Ankara-Adana: 302 mi/486 km.

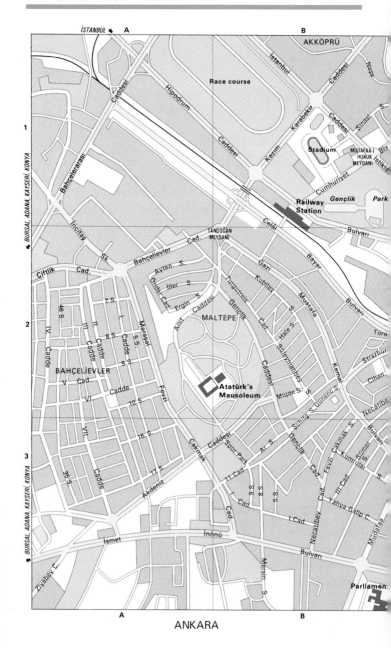

ANKARA

Ankara-Ürgüp: 190 mi/305 km.
Ankara-Antalya: 621 mi/1000 km.

By plane: Both domestic and international flights are provided by Turkish Airlines. There are regular (hourly) flights between Ankara and Istanbul, but it is advisable to reserve in advance. The Turkish Airlines Air Terminal is located in the railway station, B1. You can take an airport bus from here to the airport, 19 mi/30 km north-east of the city. For information,

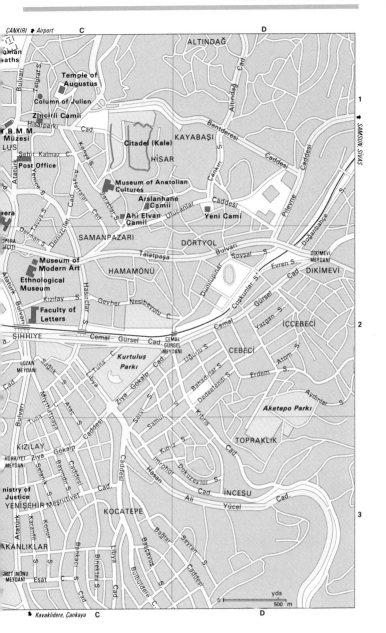

ŞANKIRI ✈ Airport   C   D

ALTINDAĞ

Temple of Augustus
Column of Julien
Zincirli Camii
Hisarparkı
B.M.M. Müzesi
LUS
Post Office
Şehit Kalmaz
Citadel (Kale)   KAYABAŞI
HİSAR
Museum of Anatolian Cultures
Arslanhane Camii
Ahi Elvan Camii   Ulucanlar   Yeni Cami

SAMANPAZARI   DÖRTYOL
Talatpaşa   Soysal
Museum of Modern Art   HAMAMÖNÜ
Ethnological Museum
Kızılay
Faculty of Letters   Gevher Nesiberoğlu

SİHHİYE   Cemal Gürsel   Cad.   CEMAL GÜRSEL MEYDANI   CEBECİ
LOZAN MEYDANI   Kurtuluş Parkı
KIZILAY   İCCEBECİ
HÜRRİYET MEYDANI   Ziya Gökalp   Erdem
Aketepo Parkı
ministry of Justice
YENİŞEHİR   TOPRAKLIK
KOCATEPE
İNCESU
AKANLIKLAR
SMET İNÖNÜ MEYDANI

DİKİMEVİ MEYDANI
DİKİMEVİ

✈ Kavaklıdere, Çankaya   C   D

yds
0   500 m

☎ 312 4910; for reservations, ☎ 312 6200; for ticket sales, ☎ 312 4900.
By train: There are good rail connections between Ankara and Istanbul on the daily *Doğu Express* and better still, sleeping cars on the night train, the *Anadalu Express*. Express trains run between Ankara and Izmir three times a week (12-hour trip) and there are other connections with Adana, Kayseri, Erzurum, and Van.

Old proverbs
adapted from the Turkish by Necmi Gürmen

'To make a poor man happy, God makes him lose his donkey, then lets him find it.'

'A horse belongs to the man who knows how to ride it; a sword to the man who knows how to gird it.'

'When the village is in sight, you don't need a guide.'

'He who dares not strike his donkey, beats his donkey's saddle.'

'One day the ageing wolf will fall prey to curs.'

'There comes a time when we lose our souls, but never our habits.'

'He who holds a honey jar in his hands, licks his chops.'

'When you do business 'at home', the prices are never the same as at market.'

Accommodation

The capital is well equipped for visitors, but, because the distances can be great, it is advisable to reserve in advance or check available space as soon as you arrive at the airport, train or bus terminal.

▲▲▲▲▲ **Büyük Ankara Oteli,** Atatürk Bulv. 183, C3, ☎ 134 4920. 185 rooms. Located on a hill, this hotel offers a splendid view over Ankara and the surroundings.

▲▲▲▲ **Ankara Dedeman,** Büklüm 51, near the Parliament, C3, ☎ 117 6200. 250 rooms. Air-conditioned rooms and a swimming pool.

▲▲▲▲ **Best Otel,** Atatürk Bulv., 195, Kavaklidere north, C3, ☎ 167 0880. 50 rooms. Located near the Büyuk Ankara Oteli, in the southern section of the city.

▲▲▲▲ **Büyük Surmeli,** Cihan Sok. 6, Sihhiye, BC2, ☎ 230 5240. 250 rooms. Centrally located in the new town.

▲▲▲ **Bulvar Palas,** Atatürk Bulv. 141, near the Parliament, C3, ☎ 134 2180. 180 rooms. The hotel restaurant serves delicious Turkish specialities.

▲▲▲ **Etap Mola,** Atatürk Bulv. 80, C3, ☎ 133 9065. 57 rooms. Good location, in Kizilay.

▲▲▲ **Kent,** Mithatpasa Cad. 4, Kizilay, C2, ☎ 131 211. 120 rooms. Centrally located with an excellent restaurant.

▲▲▲ **Keykan,** Fevzi Cakmak Sok. 12, B3, ☎ 230 2195. 50 rooms.

▲▲ **Stad,** Istiklâl Cad. 20, BC1, ☎ 310 4848. 217 rooms. Located to the north of the city centre, in Ulus.

▲ **Anit,** Gazi Mustafa Kemal Bulv., B2, ☎ 229 2385. 92 rooms. Conveniently located near the Tourist Information Office.

▲ **Güleryüz,** Sanayi Cad. 37, C1, ☎ 229 2385. Located in Ulus.

You can find many inexpensive hotels in the Ulus area,   .

Student accommodation
Cumhuriyet student hostel, Cebeci, D2, ☎ 319 3634.

Campground
Susuzköy Mocamp, 12 mi/20 km from Ankara on the Istanbul road, ☎ 43 1366. Capacity: 400.

Food

Most of Ankara's restaurants are concentrated in Ulus, Kizilay and Yenişehir. There are others in the Youth Park around the lake and on Atatürk Bulv. Here are some suggestions:

♦♦♦ **Milka**, at the Büyük Hotel on Atatürk Bulv., 185, Kavaklidere, C3, ☎ 18 6677. This is a more expensive restaurant with a garden and ornamental pool.

♦♦ **Limam Lokantasi**, Izmir Cad., 11, Kizilay, B3, ☎ 230 2725. Centrally located, for fish specialities.

♦♦ **Piknik**, Tuna Cad. 1, Kizilay, C2-3, ☎ 17 1761. Inexpensive, quick service. Outdoor dining during warm weather.

♦ **Ciftlik**, on Ulus Square, C1. An inexpensive restaurant with traditional kebaps.

♦ **Fiesta Kafeterya**, Ishani Cad., 3, Kizilay, C2. One of Ankara's many good, but inexpensive restaurants.

Getting around

Exploring on foot is pleasant, but remember that the town is spread out over a great distance. You'll have no problem finding buses and taxis.

Shopping

You won't find a covered bazaar here as in Istanbul, but there are shopping centres in Ulus, Kizilay and Kavaklidere. For carpets, try **Bergama Hali**, a shop located on Atatürk Bulv. 15/A, Kavaklidere, C3 (off map), or **Mihri Hali**, Güven Sok. 107/7 32, Kizilay. Interesting leather shops include: **Antilop**, Atatürk Bulv. 107/7, Kizilay, C2-3; and **Hazas**, Cimah Cad. 29/D, Cankaya, CD3 (off map). You can find traditional Turkish crafts (kilims, jewelry and embroidery) at the store run by the Ministry of Tourism, Gazi Mustafa Kemal Bulv. 33, B2, ☎ 29 2930.

Useful addresses

Airlines

Air France, Emek Ishani 1304/13, Kizilay, C2, ☎ 25 3992.

Pan Am, Atatürk Bulv 53, C1.

Sabena, Bayindir Sok., 11/12, C3.

Turkish Airlines, Gazi Mustafa Kemal Bulv. 33, B2, ☎ 312 6200.

Banks

Bank Mellet, Ziya Gökalp Bulv. 6, Kizilay, C2-3

Citibank, Atatürk Bulv. 107/B; Kavaklidere, C3 (off map), ☎ 33 0745.

International Bank of Commerce, Atatürk Bulv. 169, Kavaklidere, C3 (off map), ☎ 117 9980.

Ottoman Bank, Atatürk Bulv. 46, C1, ☎ 24 1275.

Turkiye Emlâk Bankasi, Ankara Şubesi, ☎ 311 4428.

Visa and American Express credit cards are widely accepted in Ankara.

Car rental

Avis, Tunus Cad. 10/5 Bakanliklar, C3, ☎ 125 1725; Esenboga Airport, ☎ 12 2820.

Europcar, Küçük Esat Cad. 25/C Bakanliklar, C3, ☎ 18 3430; Esenboga Airport, ☎ 12 2820.

Gökaltay, Atatürk Bulv. 183/9, C3 (off map), ☎ 17 9800.

Hertz, Atatürk Bulv. 169/F, C3, ☎ 118 8440; also at Esenboga Airport.

Inter Rent, Cinnah Cad. 61, Çankaya, D3 (off map), ☎ 38 9900.

Embassies

Canada, Nenehatun Cad. 75, Gaziosmanpasa, C3 (off map), ☎ 127 5803.

Great Britain, Sehit Ersan Cad. 46/A, Çankaya, ☎ 127 4310.

United States, Atatürk Bulv. 110, C3 (off map) ☎ 126 5470.

Other

Bus station, Hipodrom Cad., near the railway station, B1.

Post office, Atatürk Bulv. 59, C1.

Railway station, Talât Pasa Bulv., Yenişehir, B1, ☎ 311 0620.
Touring Automobile Club, Adakale Sok. 4/11, Kizilay, C2-3, ☎ 31 7648.
Tourist Information Office, Ministry of Culture and Tourism Building, Gazi
Mustafa Kemal Bulv. 33, B2, ☎ 229 2930; also at the Esenboga Airport.

GETTING TO KNOW ANKARA

Map coordinates refer to the map pp. 176-177.

Most visitors spend half a day seeing the town and may stay a night.
Although Ankara may not at first strike you as a particularly attractive capital,
it does, however, possess a great many archaeological treasures. Also,
because it is a relatively recently planned centre with wide avenues and new
buildings, it has become the Turkish symbol of modernity.

Museum of Anatolian Cultures*** C1

Open Tues-Sun, 8:30am-12:30pm, 1:30-5pm.

The best way to begin a visit to Ankara is to go to the Hittite Museum, which
exhibits exceptionally interesting collections. The museum was installed in a
former *bedesten*, a covered bazaar, that was built between 1467 and 1471
under the auspices of Mahmud Paşa, Prime Minister to Mehmed the
Conqueror. Other sections of the museum are housed in the adjoining
Kurşunlu Han, a former caravanserai. You can see photographs of the
building, in the hall of the main museum, retracing the different stages of
restoration. The result is extremely impressive.

The collections are displayed in chronological order, starting from the main
entrance, with the oldest on the right-hand side and the most recent on the
left.

Palaeolithic period (30,000 BC – early Stone Age): The collection features
stone implements, awls, fragments of animal skeletons (hyena and hippo-
potamus) and human remains from various sites, particularly the Karain cave
near Antalya.

Neolithic period (7000-5500 BC – late Stone Age): There is a reconstruction of a **sanctuary*** from Çatal Höyük with wall paintings dating from the
seventh century BC, taken from the original site (on the plain to the
south-east of Konya). Obsidian tools are displayed along with seals, metal
ornaments, terra-cotta figurines, and plaster relief heads of bulls, considered sacred in ancient Anatolia. The site at Çatal Höyük may be the first
known urban settlement.

Statuettes dating from 5500 BC have been taken from excavations at
Hacilar, not far from Burdur. These are mainly figurines in different positions,
including fertility and mother goddesses.

Chalcolithic period (5500-3000 BC): This is a transitional period between
the Stone and Metal ages when metals were not only prized in their natural
state as ornaments but melted down and manufactured for use as tools.
Also, for the first time in history, towns were surrounded by ramparts, at the
site at Hacilar.

Jar-shaped tombs contain weapons, ornaments and pottery. The ceramic
collection features both plain and patterned pieces, the latter with geometric
designs. Some of the pots are monochrome, others painted in several
colours. The displays include clay animal figurines, sickles, seashell
necklaces and bone implements.

Early Bronze Age (3000-2000 BC): Objects found in tombs from this
period confirm that from the third millennium BC onward, the Anatolians
made extensive use of bronze, silver, gold and lead.

There are effigies of fertility goddesses embellished with gold on the head
and stomach. The site at Alaçahöyük has provided jewelry, stag figures
decorated with silver, and finely wrought solar disks inlaid with gold.

Alişar III section

At the end of the Early Bronze Age, a type of pottery known as 'Alişar III

Ware', was developed. It mainly features richly decorated vessels with elaborate geometric designs.

The major sites are Alişar and Kültepe (former Kanesh). Other objects were found along with the pottery, mainly alabaster statuettes of lions and human figures.

Assyrian Trading Colony period (1950-1750 BC): This period in Anatolia was marked by the arrival of Assyrian merchants who were attracted to the area purely for commercial reasons. In exchange for the clothes, scents and tins that they brought, they obtained gold and silver.

They set up nine trading centres, the capital of which was near Kültepe, not far from Kayseri. This site is an extremely rich source of information on the economic, judicial and literary aspects of life at that time. The documents are mostly cuneiform tablets. Apart from these archives there are stamp seals, animal-shaped goblets, libation vases, lead statuettes, ivory figurines and marble idols.

Hittite period (1750-1200 BC): In about 1700 BC the Hittites came from the Caucasus, expelled the Egyptians (whereupon the Assyrian merchants were forced to leave Anatolia), and gradually built up their kingdom.

They made Hattuşaş (present day Boğazköy) their capital. Hieroglyphic and cuneiform tablets found at this site provide information on the history of their reign. Other items were found there, including monumental bas-reliefs and statues. On a smaller scale they made highly developed cylinder and stamp seals with cuneiform inscriptions for their kings, together with bull-shaped *rhyta* (drinking cups) and large pottery vases. Some of these items were also found at Alaçahöyük and Kültepe.

Around 1200 BC, invaders from the West known as Sea Peoples attacked and destroyed Hattuşaş along with the other Hittite cities, eliminating the Hittite kingdom.

Phrygian period (1200-650 BC): The Phrygians, the most powerful of the Western invaders, set themselves up around Gordium and Midas. Most of the items displayed come from the large tumulus in Gordium and include household goods made of bronze, a cauldron, a recently restored inlaid screen and a beautiful table.

The Phrygian state was in turn conquered by Cimmerians from the Ukraine.

Urartian period (1000-600 BC): While the Hittites were succumbing to Phrygians, Achaeans, Dorians and Ionians in Western Anatolia, an Asian kingdom was established in Eastern Anatolia around Lake Van by Urartians, expert metalcraftsmen. Items in the collection testify to this, including bronze and silver tableware, pottery, jewelry and a cauldron with a stand.

The Urartians were conquered by the Assyrians in the seventh century BC.

Classical period (characterized by the Lydians in the fifth and fourth centuries BC): The main items displayed from this period are bronze statuettes, gold jewelry and coins.

In about 650 BC the Lydians took control of territories belonging to Aeolians, Ionians and Dorians, and set up their capital at Sardis, where coins first came into use. The last of the Lydian kings was Croesus who saw his kingdom fall to the Persians.

In the **central hall** of the museum is a collection of Hittite sculpture with **bas-reliefs*** from Alaçahöyük and high-reliefs from Arslantepe near Malatya.

Ethnological Museum* C2

Open Tues-Sun, 8:30am-12:30pm, 1:30-5:30pm.

The museum is to the left of Atatürk Bulvari, between the old and the new town. The remains of Atatürk were kept here for 15 years, from 1938 to 1953, when the mausoleum where he now lies was built. As you approach the museum, which was built at Atatürk's request, you will notice his equestrian statue that dates from 1927. Along with modernizing his country, he wished his people to feel that they belonged to a unique nation with centuries-old traditions. There are fine collections of traditional Turkish

'My Anatolia' by Yaşar Kemal[*]

Why is it that the same geographical region recurs in all your work? You always portray the Çukurova plain around Adana that stretches between the Taurus Mountains and the Mediterranean Sea including the Seyhan and Ceyhan river basins.

Of all Turkish writers I'm probably asked that question the most and on the whole it leaves me somewhat perplexed. Why me more than anyone else? I've replied differently at different times. After all, what author doesn't have his own geographical area? Some writers entirely invent one, others base theirs on the place where they spent their childhood. I was born and grew up in Çukurova, ancient Cilicia, and lived there up to the age of 26. This region has become inextricably linked to my whole existence. I've based my world and that of my books on it. And yet, like Tolstoy, Dostoyevski, Stendhal and Faulkner, I have not made a case study of it. My boundaries *don't* just stop at Çukurova: I've also got seas. I've written about the Sea of Marmara and its people. I'm also working on Istanbul, endeavouring to create a whole universe around the town. I've already written three novels about it and I'm continuing.

What are you most attached to in Anatolia? A landscape, an atmosphere, an oddity?

Anatolia is an extremely complex and varied 'bit of earth'. A novelist can easily create a world from it. Anyone who truly tunes in to Anatolia will encounter a host of striking images and be able to produce other extremely rich ones. 'Getting under Anatolia's skin' allows the artist to reach an almost limitless level of creativity. Here landscapes, remains of past civilizations, traditions and customs all mingle and complement one another. Anatolia is an alchemy of atmospheres. Ürgüp, Göreme, Çavuşin, Ihlara and Mount Erciyeş are living poems, tokens to the climate and character of the region. When I think of the multitude of human types, of the traditions, creations, historical adventures, languages and the way all these have melted into the great wealth of Anatolian culture, I remember various cults from ages past that we've now lost, such as those of bulls and quails. Yet even today the unfathomable depths of Anatolia's history and customs continue to spread in secret. I feel that archaeologists in their research should take this into account.

What site in Anatolia would you like to show a friend and for what reasons?

I would like to show them the shores of Lake Van. Nowhere else on earth would you find so wild, so harsh and, at the same time, so gentle a landscape. You can say the same for its people and its obscure, thrilling history. Lake Van was put there like a well, surrounded by Mounts Suphan, Nemrut and Esruk. So many people who enriched humanity throughout the ages, such as the Urartians, Hurrites and Assyrians, came from there. The lake shores were the melting pot of Mesopotamian civilizations. Light is slowly being thrown on their past, and we understand the present better.

Mount Ararat and Lake Van are the jewels of the earth, while Göreme, Van, Urfa and the Harran region are rich in legend. At Urfa, for example, ancient biblical Edessa, you will hear the story of Joseph, attributed to Abraham and Nimrod. The famous catapult is still in the castle at Urfa. Abraham, who was abandoned by his mother in a basket down the Euphrates, was saved from the water by a doe that nursed him. The cave where he grew up in Urfa is now a place of worship. And again near Urfa on the Harran plain, Adam first ploughed the land.

What town, village and museum would you most recommend and why?

The Museum of Anatolian Cultures, in Ankara would be one of my choices.

costumes, embroidery, carpets, weapons, furniture and ceramics. You can also see a *mimber* (pulpit), carved wooden doors and a model sitting room.

The Old Town[*]

After visiting the Ethnological Museum, tour the old town, which spreads over the two hills forming the northern limits of the city. One of these has

One must also see Istanbul, ignoring its state of abandonment, its dirt and pollution, its traffic jams and poverty. Istanbul was first built to blend in with its natural surroundings, resulting in a magnificently harmonious city. The combination of the landscape and the work of the builders was one of the miracles of human achievement. Istanbul reached the height of architectural perfection with its mosques, minarets, Byzantine churches and *yali* . . . but now look at today's miserable constructions. They are unbelievable examples of the poverty of modern architecture. Nevertheless, Istanbul's foundations are so strong that in spite of all our efforts we haven't been able to destroy them yet. Before annihilating the town we should first be able to visit it. We should be busy with films, photos and paintings to fill a special Istanbul museum for posterity. Istanbul, wonder of the world, is disappearing fast.

On another note, what about typical Anatolian dishes?

Well, I would stick to those from my home region, Adana: *mercimek köfte* (lentil fritters), *kisir* (cracked wheat, onion, peppers and parsley), *içli köfte* (savoury meatballs), *kabak çiçeği dolmasi* (stuffed courgette or zucchini flowers) and Adana *kebap*.

What do you think is the best way of getting to know an Anatolian?

You should first be familiar with his history. The Anatolian countryman was in constant revolt from the 13th to the 19th century. The first rebellion, led by Baba Ishak, was held in check by mercenaries hired by the sultan in Byzantium and who committed terrible massacres.

After that, uprisings took place continuously and each time the servants of the Sublime Porte, the sovereign's 'lost soldiers,' incited the peasants. They occasionally came to an agreement with the authorities who appointed them vizir or minister, or else they escaped. But it's the peasants who have always suffered. These uprisings or *celâli* were all very similar and continued over several centuries, producing great poets such as Pir Sultan Abdal, Köroğlu and Dadaloğlu.

Today, in spite of all his problems, the peasant has the temperament of an open-minded man. A simple 'Hello!' is enough to enter into conversation with him and get to know him. Hospitality is the rule in Anatolia. The most important person is the one with the most guests. If you don't have any you are considered unlucky. This is illustrated by the countless poems, tales and epics on the sacred character of giving refuge. Even if a murderer seeks shelter in the house of his enemy, he should generally be pardoned. Because a guest is considered to have been sent by God, if he seeks shelter in another's house he cannot be handed over, whatever his crime. Anatolia past and present is full of this tradition: you only have to open the *Iliad*. Ottoman history also has numerous examples. If a bey, or lord, in revolt against the sultan takes refuge in another bey's house, his host will not give him up. Respecting this code of honour has cost the head of many a lord.

Today there's an easy, well-known way of becoming friends with a country-man: it's simply to be his guest, to sit at his table and share what there is. An Anatolian saying that is still valid today goes: 'A single coffee gives rights for forty years.' Yet I feel it won't hold out for long, because hospitality, like all traditions and human values, is dying out. As for creating other ties with the region, Anatolia has long fostered religions of love and formed sects based on friendship, and because of this will always be a place of love and friendship. As in most places and with most people, these are the best paths to follow for a real understanding of Anatolia and her people.

Translated from the Turkish by Altan Gokalp.

* See p. 75 and 'Suggested Reading' p. 249.

been invaded by an ever-growing population of Anatolia's poor who move in from the country in hope of work. Theirs is a shanty town of hastily erected, though not necessarily squalid, dwellings known as *gecekondu*, literally 'houses built overnight.' The citadel was built on the other hill, which was the centre of the Ottoman part of town. Here you can still see old clay houses in picturesque little streets.

The Citadel*, C1, has two sets of walls. The outer walls, almost 1 mi/1.5 km long, were built in the ninth century with stone from ancient monuments in the lower town. There are about 15 towers and bastions that are now in a somewhat ruined state. The inner walls stretch for a little more than 0.6 mi/1 km around the summit of the rocky hill and date from the seventh century. Like the other walls, they were built with stone from ancient monuments. About forty towers placed along the walls form a kind of rectangular castle with a large interior courtyard. You enter through a wide gateway, to the right of which stands Şark Kulesi, the main tower, and you find yourself in the middle of an old village with narrow streets and old coloured houses* of wood and clay. There is also a mosque here, Alaeddin Camii, with a 12th-century mimber (pulpit). The fortress built on the top of the hill in the northern part of the village overlooks the whole town and the surrounding desert.

Not far from the Citadel and the Hittite Museum is the town's oldest and most important mosque, the Aslanhane Camii, C1. It is particularly well-preserved and dates from the early 13th century when it was built in honour of Emir Şeref Addin. His türbe, built over Roman foundations in 1350, can be seen a little farther up the hill beyond the mosque. The mosque's prayer room has a magnificent wooden ceiling supported by tall columns crowned with capitals. The mihrab (prayer niche) is decorated with beautiful tile mosaics; the mimber dates from 689 of the Hegira (Gregorian Calendar year 1290) and is made of carved walnut.

There are two other fine mosques near the Aslanhane Camii, the Ahi Elvan Camii, C1, built at the end of the 14th century, and the Cenabi Ahmed Paşa Camii, D1, on Ulucanlar Caddesi. The latter is attributed to Sinan, the famous 16th-century architect, and has a red porphyry cupola and a white marble mihrab and mimber.

The remains of the Roman town also lie at the foot of the Citadel around the hill to the left of the three mosques. The most important monument from this period is the Temple of Augustus*, C1 (open daily 8:30am-6pm), as it features an engraved text in Latin and Greek, a kind of testament summarizing the main political events and achievements of Emperor Augustus' reign. The Latin part can be seen on the right and left-hand walls inside the vestibule; the Greek text is on the right-hand wall outside. The temple was converted into a church in the fourth century and abandoned at the beginning of the 15th century, when a small mosque, Haci Bayram, was built on the eastern side.

The Roman Baths, C1 (open daily 8:30am-5:30pm), are behind the Tourist Hotel on Çankiri Caddesi. They date from the third century BC. You can still make out some of the rooms, including a frigidarium (cool room), caldarium (hot room), tepidarium (warm room) and apodyterium (dressing room). The water system and hot air channels are also visible.

The most recent monument of Roman Ancyra is the Column of Julian on Hükümet Meydani*, C1, erected in honour of Emperor Julian who passed through the town in AD 362. It is 48 ft/14.5 m high, has a Byzantine capital and is embellished with horizontal fluting.

Museum of Modern Art C2

Open Tues-Sat 8:30am-noon, 1:30-5pm.

This is next door to the Ethnological Museum and was the town hall until 1976. It houses a good retrospective of modern Turkish painting and sculpture. Some of the rooms are used for temporary exhibitions.

The New Town

The new town begins south of the railway bridge that crosses Atatürk Bulvari, C2-3. This boulevard is Ankara's main artery that runs the length of the town from north to south and is lined with luxury shops, large hotels and administrative buildings. At the southern end of the boulevard is a wooded hill known as Çankaya, where you can visit the Presidential Mansion.

Atatürk's Mausoleum**, AB2 (open daily, 8am-noon, 1-5pm), was built on a hill overlooking the Maltepe district between 1944 and 1953. You walk up to the monument along an avenue lined with 24 stone Hittite lions that leads to a vast courtyard with two museums. These house Mustafa Kemal's private library, documents, stamps and coins, the books and works of art that were dedicated to him, his cars, and various presents he received during his political career. All in all, it's a lively collection of memorabilia from his life and work. The mausoleum itself stands on a raised area reached by 33 steps. It's a grandiose yet sober construction reminiscent of a classical temple, surrounded by a portico with square pillars. The speech made by Ismet Inönü on Atatürk's death has been inscribed on the walls at the entrance, along with extracts from two of Atatürk's speeches addressed to the Senate and Turkey's youth. The interior of the monument is lined with marble while the ceiling features gold mosaics. The sarcophagus itself is a monolithic block of marble that weighs 40 tons. Atatürk is in fact buried in a vault below. Ismet Inönü, the second president of the republic, is buried in a tomb outside the mausoleum beneath the western colonnade.

CAPPADOCIA★★★

Cappadocia is a high plateau in Central Anatolia at an altitude of 3280 ft/1000 m about 186 mi/300 km south-east of Ankara. The plateau was formed during the Palaeozoic era; it was later raised by the folding of the mountains in the Tertiary period that created the chains of the Taurus Mountains in the south and Anti-Taurus in the north. Caught between this pair of natural pincers, the plateau cracked and fissured, and several volcanoes erupted, such as Erciyes Daği (ancient Mount Argaeus, 12,851 ft/3917 m) overlooking Kayseri, and Hasan Daği, (10,722 ft/3268 m), between Aksaray and Niğde.

The plateau's powdery surface is largely due to a soft stone called tuff, formed by the agglomeration of ash and mud that erupted from the two volcanoes. What characterizes Cappadocia more than anything, however, is the erosion caused by wind and water that for centuries have rushed violently through a natural corridor from the heights of Anatolia to the sea, carving out an extremely unusual lunar-like landscape as they pass. You will come across strange rocky needles in the middle of canyons and ravines and on cliff faces that look as if they've been sculpted by man. They sometimes stretch for miles, standing tightly against one another like giant statues. Some of the cones are capped by a block of hard rock that has resisted erosion, acting as a kind of hat protecting the softer stone beneath.

The first Western explorer to Cappadocia, Paul Lucas, who crossed it on horseback in 1705, was fascinated by the extraordinary landscape and the population that lived in its natural rock caves: 'I saw the inhabitants with hoods and bonnets like those of Orthodox priests, and women with babes in arms who looked like living images of the Virgin Mary.'

The unique magical atmosphere of the area created by its geological formations has been enhanced by dwellings carved out of the rock since the third century AD. Some of the hollowed-out rocks are large enough to contain one or more rooms with windows right up to the top. Sometimes whole rock faces have been carved and modified to such an extent that they look like enormous urban tower blocks set with openings of all shapes and sizes for doors and windows.

An entire troglodytic world came into being when monastic groups fled religious persecution, and when Byzantines took refuge from repeated Arab attacks. They left paintings on cave walls throughout the area, which not only contributed greatly to Christian art in the East, but also proved a rich source of historical information.

PRACTICAL INFORMATION

Avanos is 172 mi/277 km south-east of Ankara and 8 mi/13 km north-west of Ürgüp.

Kayseri is 204 mi/328 km south-east of Ankara, 209 mi/336 km north-east of Konya, 47 mi/75 km east of Avanos and 54 mi/87 km east of Ürgüp.

Nevşehir is 175 mi/281 km south-east of Ankara, 140 mi/226 km north-east of Konya, 68 mi/110 km from Kayseri, 8 mi/13 km from Avanos and 14 mi/23 km from Ürgüp.

Ürgüp is 189 mi/304 km from Ankara and 155 mi/249 km from Konya.

There is no real centre in Cappadocia today; however, four towns, Avanos, Kayseri, Nevşehir and Ürgüp, serve as stopovers when visiting the area. Nevşehir is the largest but the least attractive; Avanos has more character; Kayseri is an important carpet-manufacturing centre and has many mausoleums; and Ürgüp is becoming the centre for tour groups.

When to go

Avoid visiting Cappadocia in winter as heavy snowfalls can make driving impossible. Summers are hot and dry. The best time to plan your trip is in the spring or fall.

Access

By bus: Cappadocia has regular bus links with a number of towns including Adana, Ankara, Istanbul, Izmir, Kayseri and Konya.

By car: This is the most direct means of transport to Cappadocia. The roads from Konya and Ankara are good and you will see some spectacular scenery. Because even the area's smallest villages are becoming increasingly popular, more and more roads are being asphalted.

By plane: Kayseri has the nearest airport – from here you have connecting flights to Ankara on THY airlines (see p. 179). There is a bus service from Kayseri to Avanos, Nevşehir and Ürgüp.

By train: There is a daily express train between Ankara and Kayseri. Avoid the train from Konya to Kayseri; the bus is faster.

Accommodation

For accommodation you would do best to stay in one of the four main towns. This is especially true if you don't have a car, because you will have better access to transportation for visiting the region.

Avanos

▲ **Venessa,** Orta Mah., ☎ (4861) 1201. 76 rooms. This modern hotel is located near the bridge over the Kizilirmak.

There are a number of small, new and inexpensive guesthouses not far from this hotel.

Kayseri

▲▲ **Hattat,** Istanbul Cad., 1, ☎ (351) 1 9331. 70 rooms. Considered the best hotel in town.

▲▲ **Turan,** Turan Cad., 8, ☎ (351) 1 1968. 70 rooms. This hotel has a Turkish bath.

▲ **Terminal,** Istanbul Cad., 76, ☎ (351) 1 5864. 20 rooms. Conveniently located next to the bus terminal.

Nevşehir

▲▲ **Göreme**, Bankelar Cad., 16, ☎ (4851) 1706. 72 rooms. Comfortable hotel on the main street.

▲▲ **Orsan Kapadokya**, Kayseri Cad., ☎ (4851) 1035. 80 rooms. Pleasant hotel with swimming pool.

▲ **Lale**, Belediye Yani, ☎ (4851) 1797. 28 rooms. Located a few blocks from the centre.

▲ **Hotel Kaymak**, Eski Sanayi Meydani II, ☎ (4851) 5427. Clean hotel near the bus station.

Ürgüp

▲▲▲▲ **Turban Ürgüp**, leaving Ürgüp on the road to Nevşehir, ☎ (4868) 1490. 235 rooms. A well-planned hotel built in traditional Cappadocian village style, with a swimming pool.

▲▲▲ **Büyük**, Kayseri Cad., ☎ (4868) 1060. 48 rooms. Near the town square, with pleasant service.

▲▲ **Boydaş**, Karayazi Köyu, ☎ (4868) 1259. 120 rooms. Modern with balconies and a discotheque. Popular with tour groups.

▲▲ **Tepe**, Teslimiye Tepesi, ☎ (4868) 1154. 51 rooms. Located on the road to Kayseri with an exceptional view.

Like other towns in Cappadocia, Ürgüp has a wide choice of guest-houses.

Because Cappadocia's tourist industry is flourishing, hotels and guest-houses are being built or restored throughout the region. Apart from the four towns just mentioned, you can stay in Ortahisar, Üçhisar, or Göreme. Tourist Information Offices can help you find somewhere to stay.

Campground

Pariskamp, Ortahisar, near the turnoff to Göreme, ☎ (4868) 1435.

Festivals

June: Konya Rose Festival.

August: Avanos Festival (three days between Aug. 16 and 23).

September: Ahi Eran Festival in Kirşehir.

October: Folk Poets' Contest and horse races.

Food

There are few sophisticated restaurants in Cappadocia but you do have a choice of simple fare. Those in Göreme and Üçhisar have striking settings.

Getting around

There are buses, *dolmuş* and taxis in nearly all the villages. You can also rent mopeds or horses (inquire at Tourist Information Offices).

Useful addresses

International Bank of Commerce (Iktisat Bankasi Türk A.Ş.), for currency exchange, Cumhuriyet Cad., 9, Nevşehir, ☎ 1840.

Tourist Information Offices

Avanos: Orta Mah., near the bridge, next to the Hotel Venessa, ☎ (4861) 1360.

Kayseri: Honat Camii Yani, ☎ (351)1 9295.

Nevşehir: Lale Cad. 22, ☎ (4851)1137.

Ürgüp: Kayseri Cad, 37, ☎ (4868) 1059. The largest in the area.

Farmworkers in the fields in Cappadocia.

▬ ÜRGÜP REGION***

Ürgüp

Ürgüp is an attractive market town in the heart of cave-dwelling Cappadocia. It stands out white against an ivory cliff background on the main road that crosses Cappadocia from Aksaray to Kayseri. Apart from being a practical base for visiting the region, it has interesting shops to explore for local arts and crafts including carpets.

When visiting troglodyte homes, tread with care – some of the floors on certain sites are not very safe.

Mustafapaşa

Heading south of Ürgüp on the road to Soğanli you reach Mustafapaşa, ancient Sinasos, after about 4 mi/6 km. It's a pretty village that was inhabited by Greeks until the Treaty of Lausanne required that they leave in 1923. Some of its old freestone houses have been well preserved. You can recognize them by their traditional verandas supported by columns. There's an unusual stone **church*** to visit, dedicated to St Basil, patron saint of Cappadocia. The original frescoes were covered over with paintings, probably by the Greeks before they left. Just south of Mustafapaşa is Lake Damsa where you can swim.

Taşkinpaşa

This is a small village 12 mi/19 km from Ürgüp, formerly known as Damsa. As you enter you can see the remains of an old *medrese*, with an especially fine portal, and a sculpted *mihrab*. Inside the village are a mosque and *türbe* that date from the Seljuks.

Soğanli**

Continuing south you come to Soğanli, a small village beside a stream about 28 mi/45 km from Ürgüp. Of the numerous cave churches, a dozen can be visited. Because some of them are kept locked, ask the caretaker for the keys.

Karabe Kilise has well-preserved paintings dating from the seventh and eighth centuries that were covered over in the 11th and 12th.

Yilanli Kilise* (Church with a Snake) is so called because of the fresco of a naïvely stylized dragon to the left as you enter. There is also a medallion of Christ in the vault and other paintings of the Last Judgment with Joseph, Abraham and Isaac holding their grandchildren.

Kubbeli Kilise (Domed Church) is unusual in that it was built on three different levels and looks like a small mountain peak. There are frescoes on the vault of the dome.

Sakli Kilise (Hidden Church) is a little church, signposted on the side of the road; it contains no visible frescoes.

After visiting Soğanli, you may like to visit one of Cappadocia's finest underground cities, in which case you need to retrace your steps along the road until you reach the turnoff on your left for Derinkuyu, a town about 14 mi/23 km away.

Derinkuyu**

Open daily 9am-noon, 1:30-6:30pm.

The town is 27 mi/44 km south-west of Ürgüp and is believed to be the largest of Cappadocia's underground cities. Throughout history various invaders surged through the region causing the inhabitants to take refuge underground: the Arabs in the seventh century, the Seljuks in the 11th when they took control of Caesarea, and Tamerlane's Mongols in the 15th. As the armies came and went the Cappadocians built labyrinthine underground cities several storeys deep, which sometimes extended over several miles. At Derinkuyu 24 different levels have been listed but only eight are open to the public. In these you can easily distinguish ventilation ducts (there are 52), water channels from a well 197 ft/60 m deep, emergency exits and various rooms. The first floor was for animals, the second for shops and the rest for habitation and refuge. There's a large cruciform church on the seventh floor. The entire city could shelter about 10,000 people and a connecting tunnel, which hasn't yet been fully excavated, is thought to have linked Derinkuyu with the underground city at Kaymakli 6 mi/10 km away. As the average constant temperature was between 46°-50°F/8°-10°C in summer as in winter, life could continue underground for months at a time without anyone above knowing anything about it.

Kaymakli*

Open daily 8am-noon, 2-5pm.

This strange underground city is 6 mi/10 km north of Derinkuyu and about 25 mi/40 km south-west of Ürgüp. So far excavations have revealed eight levels of rooms linked by a series of corridors and stairs. You can see the vast ventilation shaft that aerated the entire city as well as heavy circular stone blocks that were rolled against the main entrance on each floor in times of danger.

Continue the circuit in a northerly direction to Nevşehir (12 mi/20 km).

Nevşehir

This is the largest town in Cappadocia, built on a hill on top of which stand the ruins of a **Seljuk citadel**. Like Ürgüp, Nevşehir is a convenient base for visiting the area.

Hacibektaş

The town is 28 mi/45 km north of Nevşehir via Gülşehir, and 42 mi/68 km from Ürgüp. It is mainly renowned for the beautifully preserved seminary of the Bektashi order of dervishes founded in the 13th century by the mystic Hacibektash Veli, who was born here. As chaplains, members of the order had considerable influence over the Janissary Corps of the sultan's army. Today you can see the *tekke* (dervish house), the *türbe* (mausoleum) of Hacibektash Veli in the garden and the reconstructed soup kitchen.

For a visit of Avanos, go back toward Gülşehir (about 16 mi/25 km) and take the turnoff to your left just before the town. Avanos is 14 mi/23 km farther on.

Avanos**

Avanos is 8 mi/13 km from Ürgüp, on the banks of the Kizilirmak River (Red River), at an altitude of 3116 ft/950 m. It is an attractive market town of about 11,000 inhabitants. It used to be one of the most important weaving centres in Cappadocia and is still known for its cottage industries. The ancient art of carpet weaving, and the judgment required to create the pattern and colour, have gradually died out over the years. Recently, however, there has been a revival in the tradition, supported by young villagers. Production of onyx has also increased, but Avanos is most famous for its pottery. The potters of Avanos have created new shapes and colours and have learned to adapt them to the tastes of foreign visitors. They are extremely welcoming to anyone who wishes to try his or her hand at the wheel.

Thanks to a conservation program some of the town's old quarters on the right bank of the river have been saved from demolition and restored. Old houses are being transformed into museums or guesthouses. Something else to enjoy is the **market*** on Friday, which has managed to keep its picturesque quality despite its location just opposite a football stadium.

About 4 mi/6 km east of Avanos, not far from where the Ürgüp River flows into the Kizilirmak, you come to the ruins of **Seljuk caravanserai***, known as Sari Han or the yellow caravanserai. The stone inside turns beautiful shades of ochre at sunrise and sunset. Striking too is the finely worked entrance portal. The outer walls were completely restored but some of the stones have since been removed. What remains, however, is an impressive monument standing mysteriously in the middle of a wild desert.

To reach Zelve from Avanos, take the Göreme road south for about 1.8 mi/3 km until you reach the Zelve turnoff to your left. The site is 1.2 mi/2 km farther on.

Zelve***

Depending on the route you take, Zelve is 4-7 mi/7-12 km from Ürgüp in the middle of apricot and olive groves. It is a former troglodyte hamlet at the bottom of a natural amphitheatre guarded by a forest of 'fairy chimneys' (a column of tuff topped by a boulder). Since before the iconoclastic period, Christians and Muslims succeeded each other here right up to 1956 when loose scree and fallen rocks made life too dangerous. The Islamic-Christian coexistence explains the small mosque, monastery and several churches side by side. Among the latter is the **Church with a Stag**, dating from Byzantine times. A cross in relief is still visible on the vault, and traces of ochre-coloured paint date from the ninth and tenth centuries. The apse collapsed in 1937 during an earthquake. The church gets its name from the painting of a stag on the wall opposite the cross, to the right of the cross. The well-preserved **Church of the Fish*** has a lovely fresco in its adjoining chapel. Adjacent to this church is the **Church of the Grape**, where you can see strips of frescoes illustrating bunches of grapes.

When the hamlet was inhabited, the upper levels were used by families, whereas the lower were for animals, as is borne out by the presence of mangers and drinking troughs.

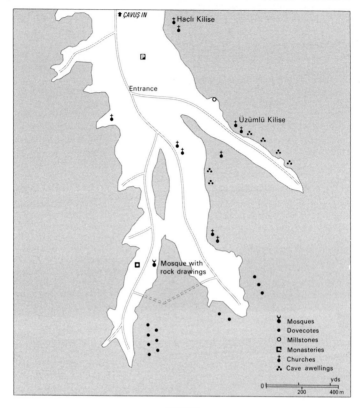

ZELVE

In the midst of **fairy chimneys*****, about 0.5 mi/0.8 km from Zelve, you come to a vineyard in a hollow where the 'vines of the Pasa' stretch out in lines.

To reach Çavuşin, return to the Göreme road; Çavuşin is almost immediately to your left (it is about 6 mi/10 km from Ürgüp). Just before you arrive, you'll notice a church carved into a rocky tower with iron stairs outside for access. It is dedicated to Emperor Nicephorus Phocas and is known as the **Pigeon House of Çavuşin**. Inside, **frescoes*** illustrate scenes from the Gospel in shades of brown, red and green. There's an interesting painting in the northern apse, a sort of family portrait of Nicephorus Phocas with Empress Theophano surrounded by the emperor's father and brother.

Çavuşin**

This is an unusual stone city built into a high rock face riddled with caves and troglodyte dwellings. A narrow path signposted in blue leads up to the **Church of St John the Baptist***, hewn out of the cliff. There are well-preserved sculptures in relief on the vault and ceiling, mainly of trees symbolizing paradise or of Maltese crosses. The paintings on the vault are also in good condition. A fresco on the right-hand wall illustrates the baptism of Christ by St John.

About 1 mi/1.6 km south of the village you come across a completely isolated church in the middle of the Güllu Dere Valley (Valley of Roses). This is the **El Nazar Church*** (the eye of fate). Although much of the church has fallen down, parts of the vaults and walls are covered with fine fresco scenes of Christ's childhood. About 1.2 mi/2 km from the Güllü Dere Valley is another valley known as the Valley of Love. The name derives from the fairy chimneys, which resemble giant phalluses.

Göreme

Göreme Village, known as Avcilar until 1982, is 1.2 mi/2 km from Çavuşin. It is a fascinating place full of cones, rocks and caves that are still in use today. St Hiero is the patron saint of the village. You can visit the onyx workshops for which Göreme is famous.

Göreme Valley***

Open daily 8:30am-5pm.

This lovely valley in the heart of what was once known as Korama holds the greatest concentration of rock monuments in Cappadocia, about 350 churches and chapels. Inside, like an illustrated Bible, the course of Christ's life is depicted in extraordinarily well-preserved frescoes. There are scenes of the Last Supper, the Crucifixion, the Resurrection, and the Ascension. Most of these tiny churches were excavated into the rock in the 10th and 11th centuries and are faithful architectural reproductions of traditional Byzantine churches.

A glass pyramid marks the entrance to the site. Once inside, a network of paths, tunnels and stairways takes you to the main churches.

Tokali Kilise** (Church with the Buckle). This is on the left side of the road, before the site entrance, and is the largest in the valley. The name comes from a golden ring that was once fixed in the middle of the vault in the nave at the back but has since disappeared. The church is composed of two distinct parts. The first is a simple vaulted room decorated with well-known scenes from the life of Christ, including some of the famous miracles such as the Wedding Feast of Canaa, the Miracle of the Loaves and Fishes, and the Healing of a Blind Man. The second part is much larger, comprising five apses to the east and an adjoining chapel to the north. There is a rich collection of fine paintings, including the Crucifixion, an Anastasis (Christ between two angels), an illustration of the Resurrection, scenes from the lives of saints, and other episodes, mainly from the life of St Basil, patron saint of Cappadocia. Steps lead down to the crypt, where tombs were dug out of the rock.

The **Elmali Kilise*** (Church with the Apple) is about 328 ft/100 m to the right once you've entered the site. Although little remains of the façade, the frescoes have weathered particularly well, and you can still see four of the columns that supported the dome. The brightly coloured paintings on the vaults date from the 11th century and represent scenes from the life of Christ, such as the Nativity, Baptism by St John, the resurrection of Lazarus, the Entry into Jerusalem, the Last Supper, the Crucifixion, the Holy Women at the Tomb, and the Ascension. Portraits of saints, prophets and archangels figure on the pendentives.

Barbara Kilise (Church of St Barbara). The stylized paintings of the Iconoclast period have not weathered well, despite restoration. However, you can make out familiar scenes of Christ and the saints, especially St George, St Nicolas, and St Barbara, for whom the church was named.

Yilanli Kilise (Church with the Snake). This is another church that derives its name from a naïve fresco of a dragon, this time being overcome by St George. In another painting, Constantine and Helen are shown standing on either side of the Cross. Above the church is a kitchen and refectory, where you can see a long stone table where the monks had their meals.

Karanlik Kilise (Dark Church). This is rarely open to the public and is kept in almost total darkness, which means that the frescoes have been extremely well preserved. The sole means of lighting is a torch. Although, as in most of the churches, the scenes deal with the life of Christ, they are not shown in chronological order and the overall effect is far more aesthetic than didactic. One cannot admire the lovely frescoes of the Adoration of the Magi, the Last Supper, the Crucifixion and especially the Betrayal by Judas, without being

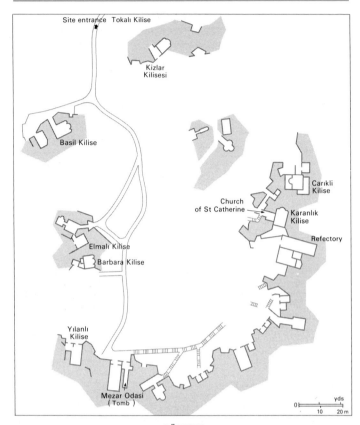

GÖREME

reminded of the mosaics in St Vital in Ravenna. These paintings mark the beginning of a new, more refined art that was to develop throughout the Byzantine world, replacing the former rigid, more symbolic art. Because the church was once part of a monastery complex, there is also a refectory with a double apse where you can see a table, benches and shelves hewn out of the rock.

Çarikli Kilise[*] (Church with Sandals). The church is so named because of a footprint below the fresco of the Ascension in the southern transept, said to be that of Christ. The name could also have something to do with the fact that all the people in the frescoes are wearing sandals. The walls are adorned with brightly coloured paintings of the Evangelists, the Nativity, the Baptism of Christ, the Transfiguration and the Resurrection of Lazarus.

There are a great many other churches hidden among the rocky outcrops and hollows of the valley, but to explore them you need time and a guide. Some of them don't have names and are simply numbered. In 1987, 26 new churches were listed.

A path leads off to some of these churches from above the parking lot at Göreme. One of them is **Meryem Ana Kilise** (Church of the Virgin Mary), so called because most of the frescoes are dedicated to her. Unfortunately, because of the risk of rocks collapsing, UNESCO workers, who have been doing restoration work in the area, have forbidden access to the church. You can, however, enjoy the magnificent view of the Kiliglar Valley with its orchards, vegetable gardens and armies of fairy chimneys.

The **Chapel of St Eustathius** is decorated with frescoes by unknown artists.

There is a frieze of animal motifs typical of the Iconoclastic period and another classical one of saints and scenes from the New Testament.

Just above the Church with the Buckle is a beautiful little chapel, known as n° 20, covered in frescoes.

The village of Üçhisar is just over 2 mi/4 km from Göreme (7 mi/12 km from Ürgüp).

Üçhisar**

A tall rock pinnacle stands in the middle of the village, the counterpart of the one at Ortahisar across the road on the other side of the valley. It's an impressive tower, riddled with caves, which served as a fortress for the population in times of danger. The people could also hide underground during sieges because they had access to well water. The top of the tower offers a panoramic view of the whole region, with its cliffs, ravines and twisted rocks, which take on different hues of pink, soft blues, or yellow depending on the time of day.

For Ortahisar, go back to the main Nevşehir-Ürgüp road, turn left toward Ürgüp and take the second turnoff on your right.

Ortahisar**

This is another rocky crag in the middle of a village, honeycombed by caves and crevices. The view from the fortified terrace that crowns it is tremendous, well worth the hard climb up steps and ladders. Homes in the rock were abandoned some time ago for new ones with terraces in the village, which grew up around the foot of the crag in a network of picturesque alleyways.

From here it is easy to continue on to Kayseri (to the north-east) via Ürgüp or Aksaray (to the south-west) via Nevşehir.

▬▬ KAYSERI*

(54 mi/87 km east of Ürgüp).

Ancient Caesarea, present-day Kayseri, lies at an altitude of 3461 ft/ 1055 m at the foot of Erciyes Dağı. As capital of the Roman province of Cappadocia under Tiberius (AD14-37), the town converted to Christianity at an early date. St Basil was born here in the fourth century, and later became its bishop and the founder of monasticism in the East. Between the seventh and ninth centuries Caesarea was harassed by numerous Arab invasions. In the 10th century it became such a stronghold for a powerful Cappadocian family that one of the members, Nicephorus Phocas, was declared emperor by his troops in 963. Toward the middle of the 11th century, the Seljuks entered Asia Minor and laid claim to the town, which the Mongols later took in 1243. The Mamelukes in turn conquered the area in 1419, and Kayseri was finally integrated into the Ottoman Empire by Sultan Selim in 1515.

Today Kayseri is a lively town with narrow winding streets, elegant minarets and attractive houses with roof terraces. It is an important agricultural centre and specializes in foodstuffs and cottage industries. The famous *pastirma* comes from here: sun-dried beef coated with garlic, peppers and spices. Kayseri's silk carpet industry is the second largest in Turkey.

What to see

The **citadel***, an impressive black fort in the middle of the town, is a fine example of medieval military architecture. Sixth-century foundations were built upon and extended in the 13th century and there have been several restorations since. The walls are a dark volcanic basalt fortified by 19 square towers. From the covered way around them you have a good view of the town with the snowy heights of Erciyes Dağı in the distance.

Fatih Camii is a small mosque within the citadel walls built by Mehmed II Fatih in the 15th century. Below the citadel to the east is the **Huant Hatun Mosque** and adjoining *medrese* (theological school) dating from the

The strangely sculpted landscape of Cappadocia alone is worth a trip to Turkey.

13th century. The mosque itself looks like a caravanserai with its 8 impressive naves and 63 pillars.

South-west of the citadel are the **bazaar**, *bedesten* (covered market) and the enormous Vezir Hani caravanserai of black volcanic rock. Not far from here is **Ulu Cami** (the Great Mosque), which was built under the Danişmend Turks in the first half of the 13th century. Its minaret is embellished with mosaics.

Sahibiye Medrese, a Koranic school open to visitors, faces Kayseri's main square, Cumhuriyet Meydani, and has a fine Seljuk portal with a typical stalactite vault. There's a Roman hypogeum (subterranean tomb) inside the school.

Heading north-west of the main square you reach two other 13th-century

buildings worth visiting, the **Haçi Kilic Camii** (with fine Seljuk doorways) and the **Çifte Medrese** (twin seminaries).

South-east of the citadel, 0.5 mi/0.8 km down Talas Caddesi in the middle of a little square on the right, you come to **Döner Kümbet**[*], the Revolving Tomb. This is probably the most beautiful mausoleum in the whole town, which is high praise considering there are so many of them that Kayseri has come to be known as the city of mausoleums. The tomb is housed in a cylindrical edifice with a polygonal base topped by a conical roof. The whole monument is adorned with extremely delicate, finely worked arabesques and animal figures.

Another mausoleum, **Sirçali Kümbet**, is 650 ft/200 m from here, but unfortunately nothing remains of its 14th-century tile decoration. From here take the avenue to the left that leads to the **Archaeology Museum** *(open Tues-Sun 8am-noon, 1-5:30pm)*. Its collections include finds from the Kayseri region, especially from Kültepe, where remains of the ancient Hittite city of Kanesh were discovered. Cuneiform tablets record commercial transactions between Assyrians and Anatolians dating from the beginning of the second millennium BC. There are also displays of Hittite, Roman and Byzantine sculptures, jewelry, coins, ceramics and an exhibition of local ethnographic artifacts.

Environs of Kayseri

Haidar Bey Kosk, in the suburbs of Kayseri (take a taxi), is the only remaining private Seljuk residence in Turkey. The freestone complex comprises a series of vaulted rooms arranged around an interior courtyard.

Sultan Han, 28 mi/45 km out of Kayseri on the Sivas road, is a beautifully preserved and restored Seljuk caravanserai.

▬▬ AKSARAY

58 mi/93 km south-west of Ürgüp, 112 mi/180 km south-west of Kayseri and 43 mi/70 km south-west of Nevşehir.

Cappadocia can be seen as a triangle contained within the area between Kayseri to the east, Niğde to the south and Aksaray to the west. Aksaray itself is an oasis centre with some noteworthy monuments. Among them are **Ulu Camii,** a mosque from the Seljuk period with a beautiful *mimber* (pulpit) and **Kadiroğlu Medrese,** a former Koranic school that dates from the same period and was restored in the 16th century. The **Zinciriye Medrese,** another religious school, dates from the middle of the 19th century.

Ağzi Kara Han *(open daily, 8am-8pm)* is a caravanserai 8 mi/13 km to the east of Aksaray that was built between 1231 and 1239. It is the third largest in Turkey, after Sultan Han and the Kayseri caravanserai. There is a covered section for winter use and an open one for summer. A traditional mosque stands in the middle. Caravanserais were built at strategic points along trade routes, where merchants could find shelter, spend the night, rest their horses and exchange goods. They also served as refuges against thieves. Those who sought protection paid a tax to the sultan and in return were housed and fed for three days. These fortresses were also used as arsenals and military camps.

There's another caravanserai, **Sultanhani***, 30 mi/48 km to the west of Aksaray *(open daily 7am-7pm)*. It was built in 1229, but burned down at the end of the 13th century; it was completely restored about 20 years ago. In the middle of the open section is a mosque on four pillars, surrounded by colonnades. The different rooms of the caravanserai included sleeping quarters, kitchens and shops. The stables and storage rooms were to the right of the courtyard.

KONYA

Telephone code: 331.

155 mi/250 km south of Ankara, 155 mi/250 km south-west of Ürgüp and 217 mi/350 km north-east of Antalya.

The city derived its first name, Iconion (image), from an ancient sculpture of Medusa that had been carved into its ramparts. The Romans changed it to Iconium, the Seljuks to Coniem and finally the name Konya, from the Turks, has stayed. As former capital of the most powerful Seljuk state, set in the middle of a fertile plain, Konya is a far cry from ancient Christian Cappadocia, with its extraordinary rock dwellings and lunar landscapes.

The town's origins are very old, dating back to an early human settlement in the third millennium BC. Hittite influence in the area during the second millennium BC has been recorded and the Phrygians founded the first large settlement on the site in the first millennium BC. The town then came under Lydian and later Persian control. Seleucid kings took over, followed by the kings of Pergamum. In 133 BC the town became part of the Roman Empire. During his evangelistic wanderings in Asia Minor, St Paul visited Iconium but was imprisoned, beaten and finally expelled.

Iconium passed into Byzantine hands and became a bishopric. During this time, in the seventh, eighth and ninth centuries AD, the town suffered repeated Arab attacks. In 1069, the Seljuk Turks took control and a few years later, under the new name of Konya, the town became the capital of the Seljuk sultanate of Rum. The Seljuks ruled until the 13th century, during which time the sultanate of Rum flourished, due mainly to the success and development of Muslim art. Thanks to the imagination of its architects and the skill of its artists who cut, hollowed, sculpted and carved stone and marble, Konya was endowed with remarkable edifices. Some of them, such as the Alaeddin and Sahip Ata Mosques, the Karatay *Medrese* and Ince Minare Museum bear witness to this today.

With the arrival of the Mongols in the second half of the 13th century the Seljuk sultanate began its long decline, and by the middle of the 15th century, Konya had become a part of the Osmanli states.

However, it wasn't until the end of the 19th century and the arrival of the railway, that Konya finally emerged as a regional centre of 300,000 inhabitants prospering among orchards and market gardens. There are a number of natural springs in the area that come up from the base of the Taurus Mountains, which no doubt help account for the fact that the Konya plain is Turkey's major breadbasket.

Konya is renowned for Mevlâna Celâleddin Rumi, the founder of the Order of the Whirling Dervishes. Although the dervish orders were dissolved by Atatürk, the spirit of the Mevlevi still influences the town.

What to see

Map coordinates refer to the map p. 201.

Mevlâna Museum**, B2

Open Tues-Sun 9:30am-6:30pm.

The former *tekke* (dervish house or convent) of the Whirling Dervishes has been a museum since 1925. You can recognize it from afar because its tall, partly tiled minaret rises high above the town as does its turquoise dome. The first Order of the Whirling Dervishes was founded in Konya although the dervish philosophy itself originated in Central Asia through the beliefs of wise men who scorned riches and ambition. These beliefs spread and different sects of dervishes (from the Persian word *darwish* meaning 'poor') were formed.

Mevlâna Celâleddin Rumi (1207-1273), a young mystic poet, met a dervish named Şemsi in Konya who stirred his interest in Sufi mysticism. As a result he founded a new religious order known as the Whirling Dervishes because of the spinning in their dance, the *sema*. The new religion was based on good, charity, humanity, love, and union with God. This latter was made possible through the *sema*, symbolizing the movements of the earth as well as those of the soul. For the young mystic, poetry, music and dance were indispensible for the perfection of the soul. Poetry awoke the spirit, music nourished it and dance led to divine ecstasy. Rumi himself wrote the *Mesnevi*, a Persian poem of 25,000 verses.

During the *sema*, the dervishes in their long tunics and tall red felt hats spin to the sound of flutes and dulcimers. They dance barefoot and can spin for hours in ecstatic communion. With their arms outstretched, their bodies form the shape of a cross. Their right arms are held slightly higher than their left with their palms facing upward to receive blessings from God that are then restored to the earth by the left hand turned toward the ground. The dervishes have no fear of death: they await it with joy because it is then that they will be united with God. This belief is expressed by what they wear: the red hat stands for the stele that will be placed on the tomb, the black cape represents the tomb itself and the white tunic the funeral shroud.

The museum has displays of carpets and turbans but is above all a place of pilgrimage for Muslims all over the world who come to pray at the Mevlâna's tomb.

In the funerary section, in a large room facing the mausoleum, are the sarcophagi of the Mevlâna's family as well as those of some of his followers and friends. Slightly apart is the Master's **tomb**, a marble sarcophagus covered by a heavy cloth of richly embroidered gold brocade. Exhibits in the same section include dervish clothes, gifts from sultans and handwritten documents.

The **mosque** and **sema room** were built under Süleyman the Magnificent. In the *sema* room, where the dervishes performed their ritual dances, there are displays of musical instruments, carpets and beautiful crystal lamps. The mosque itself houses a fine collection of prayer carpets and illuminated Korans*.

There are other museum exhibits in former dervish cells to the left of the courtyard as you enter the complex. These include two ancient kilims, one from the 13th century, the other from the 15th. To the right of the courtyard are the former kitchens and the refectory (presently closed), where future dervishes carried out their novitiate for 1001 days.

This was no easy matter for the novices because their timetable over the 1001 days had to be scrupulously respected: 40 days of looking after animals, 40 days of sweeping out the rooms of the poor, 40 days of drawing water, 40 days of bed making, 40 days of sawing wood, 40 days of cooking, 40 days of going to the market, and so on. If a novice missed a single day he had to begin all over again. Finally, on day 1001, he could put on the dervish costume, be initiated to the *sema* and contemplate God.

Alâaddin Camii* A1

The mosque was originally built on a hill inside a fortified citadel. Only a few sections of the citadel walls remain, protected by a concrete shelter, and the mosque you see today stands in the middle of a park right in the town centre. Four successive sultans took part in the building, which was finally completed under Alâaddin Keykubad I in 1220.

The wooden roof of the prayer room is supported by 42 antique columns with capitals. There are two masterpieces here: the finely carved wood *mimber* and the marble *mihrab*, although the latter was damaged during the last century. The two *türbe* in the courtyard are typical of Seljuk mosques. In general, a mosque's adjacent *türbe* consisted of a small circular or polygonal room topped by a conical or pyramidal roof. The room contained the cenotaph, or empty tomb monument of the founder of the mosque, while his real tomb was in a crypt below the *türbe*. In the case of the Alâaddin mosque, one of the *türbe* contains the remains of Sultan Keykubad I's ancestors and the other has eight cenotaphs, five of which belong to Seljuk sultans.

Büyük Karatay Medrese* A2

Open Tues-Sun 9am-5:30pm.

This religious school for Koranic teachings constructed by Emir Celâleddin Karatay in 1251 is another typically Seljuk building. The entrance is through a white marble portal that has been richly and harmoniously sculpted. The main dome inside is exquisitely covered in tiles (mainly blue, some black and gold). Around the bottom of the dome in the *iwân* (a room with three vaulted sides, typical of *medreses*), is a strip of enamel tiles covered with a hymn to victory. The hymn is written in Kufic script (Arabic writing that originated in Kufa, Iraq).

Inside the *medrese* is an interesting **Museum of Ceramics and Tiles****. The displays are mainly of enamel fragments that adorned *türbe*, mosques, palaces, vases, dishes and plates throughout Seljuk and Ottoman history. One of the rooms contains the *türbe* of Celâleddin Karatay.

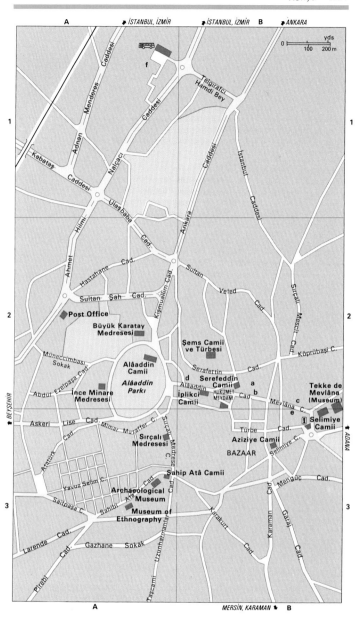

KONYA

Museum of Ethnography* A3

Open Tues-Sun 9:30am-6pm.

The collection features crocheted fabrics, clothes, embroidered table mats, silver jewelry, carpets, household utensils, decorative artifacts, weapons, keys and illuminated Korans.

Whirling dervishes

Her face pressed against an ornamental grille, Selma scrutinizes the ceremonial hall with its sculpted wooden pilasters below. All around are the faithful, gathered behind delicate railings. In the centre, a wide empty space gives onto the *mihrab* – a stretch of curving wall, arching upward toward Mecca.

Suddenly the silence becomes more intense and the dervishes appear. They're wearing white robes covered with black capes and have tall felt toques on their heads. The sheik enters last. Together they bow to the *mihrab* while a slow chant begins. An adolescent sings a very old love poem to the glory of the Prophet then the flute player improvises a strong clear melody punctuated by the beat of kettledrums.

The sheik strikes the ground and the dervishes move forward. They circle slowly around the large room three times in honour of the three paths that lead to God: the paths of science, of intuition and of love. Then, letting their black capes – symbol of the grave – fall to the ground, they stand luminescent and white like immaculate souls. Slowly, very slowly, they begin to turn, with their right hands lifted toward heaven for a blessing and their left hands turned toward the earth to share the blessing with the world.

This is when the sheik joins the dance and the rhythm accelerates. He represents the sun by the radiance of his knowledge while the spinning dervishes are the planets rotating around him in communion with the Law of the Universe. They spin faster and faster to the pure sound of the *ney*, a reed flute, which evokes divine mysteries to those who know how to listen. Their whole being is abandoned to the dance, their souls stretched toward mystical ecstasy and union with Supreme Reality.

Kenizé Mourad
On Behalf of the Dead Princess
(De la part de la princesse morte), Robert Laffont, 1987.

Archaeological Museum A3

Open Tues-Sun 9:30am-6pm.

Greek and Roman finds from excavations in the Konya region are displayed here. The most noteworthy item is a sarcophagus from the third century AD found at Sidemara, present-day Ambar, decorated with bas-reliefs illustrating the 12 labours of Hercules (Herakles). Apart from other sarcophagi there are also Phrygian stelae and Greek vases.

Aziziye Camii B3

This mosque in the bazaar district has twin minarets. The first mosque on the site was built in the 17th century, and the one you see today, an example of Baroque influence on Ottoman architecture, dates from 1872.

Ince Minare Medrese A2

Open Tues-Sun 9am-5:30pm.

This theological school located on the western slope of Alâaddin Hill was built in the second half of the 13th century for the teaching of the *hadith* (the study of the words and acts of Mohammed). Two-thirds of the slender brick and green tile minaret that gives the school its name fell after being struck by a lightning bolt in 1901. The entry portal has been richly sculpted with bands of Koranic epigraphs. Today the seminary houses a **Sculpture Museum** with collections of wood and stone carvings dating from the Seljuks.

Sahip Ata Camii A3

This is a Seljuk mosque from the 13th century. Although part of the building has been destroyed, you can still see the elaborate portal and the blue tile decoration on both the fluted minaret and the *mihrab*.

Selimiye Camii B3

This was built by the Ottoman sultan Selim II between 1566 and 1574. In style it is said to resemble works by the architect Sinan (it bears a likeness to the Fatih mosque in Istanbul). The six-columned portico, the *mihrab* and *mimber* have been embellished with carved marble.

Sirçali Medrese A3

Open Tues-Sun 9:30am-6pm.

The former theological school, now converted to a museum of funerary monuments, was founded in 1242. The founder's *türbe* can be seen to the right of the finely worked entry doorway. The walls of the *iwân* on the other side of the courtyard are covered in outstanding enamel tilework. Seljuk stelae, Ottoman funerary monuments and Hittite jars are some of the items displayed in the collection.

When to go

Konya is at its most pleasant in spring and autumn. However, even in July and August temperatures are never excessive and evenings are always cool.

Access

By bus: Regular services link Konya with Adana, Ankara, Antalya (via Silifke), Istanbul and İzmir. Buses are generally quicker than trains.

By car: The roads from Ankara and Ürgüp are very good. However, those from Antalya, Izmir, or Istanbul via Adapazari and Afyon, are generally fairly rough allowing only an average speed of 30 mph/50 kph.

By plane: The nearest airport is at Ankara. From there you can always take a regular bus to Konya.

By train: Trains run from Ankara, Istanbul and Izmir but the trips are slow.

Accommodation

At the moment there are no luxury hotels in Konya. The town is mainly frequented as a place of pilgrimage by Muslims and the rare performances for tourists by the Whirling Dervishes in December have in no way detracted from the holy atmosphere of the city.

▲▲ **Konya,** Mevlâna Alani, B2c ☎ 2 1003. 29 rooms. Quiet hotel near the Tourist Information Office.

▲▲ **Özkaymark,** Otogar Karsisi Parking, A1f, ☎ 3 3770. 90 rooms. Conveniently located near the bus station.

▲▲ **Selcuk,** Alâaddin Cad., Badakik 50, B2d, ☎ 1 1259. 52 rooms. Relatively comfortable, in a good location near Alâaddin Park.

▲ **Başak Palas,** Hükümet Mey., 3, B2a, ☎ 1 1338. 40 rooms. Near Şerefeddin Camii.

▲ **Dergah,** Mevlâna Cad., 19, B3e, ☎ 1 1197. 43 rooms.

▲ **Sahin,** Hükümet Alani, 6, B2b, ☎ 1 3350. 47 rooms.

Festivals

May (first week): Culture and Folklore Festival.

July 7: Rose Festival.

August: Konya Fair.

December 10-17: Dances by the Whirling Dervishes.

Food

There is not a wide choice of elegant tourist restaurants in Konya.

♦♦ **Konya Kaziou,** Karabekin Cad., 20, A3 (off map), ☎ 1 9105. One of Konya's best restaurants, specializing in good Turkish cuisine (no alcohol).

There are other little restaurants in Alâaddin Park, B3, that are particularly pleasant in the evening.

A national hero and philosophic humorist

Nasreddin Hoca (pronounced Hodja) probably lived at the end of the 13th or beginning of the 14th century, during the reign of the Seljuk sultans of Konya. He must have lived through the Mongol invasion of Asia Minor and witnessed the ensuing devastation. It appears that he was on good terms with the Mongol governors, although legend prefers the image of Hoca as a mediator at the court of Tamerlane, who conquered Anatolia a century later.

What is believed to be Hoca's tomb is in what is now a district of Akşehir, near Konya, home of the Whirling Dervishes. Little is left of the mausoleum, just one wall, a gaping hole with a wire fence and an enormous padlock.

Many witty stories are attributed to Hoca, all true, of course. Hoca's view of the world and his opinions on the essential or even metaphysical questions of life are frank, natural and often disarmingly candid. Straightforward common sense is one of the secrets of his Oriental wisdom and solace. His witticisms have become popular sayings and are quoted in everyday conversations in Turkey. Here are some examples:

Heaven helps the man who helps himself!

One day, while Hoca was repairing the roof of his house, an old beggar came by and called up to him, 'Come down! Come down, Hoca! I've got something to ask you.'

'Can't you see that I'm working? This is no time to bother me. What do you want?' replied Hoca, annoyed by the interruption.

'Come down, come down, Hoca! I haven't got any money . . . not a penny left. Look at me . . . I'm hungry Hoca. Please, just one small coin. Only one and my family will be happy.'

'Alright, come up then,' called Hoca condescendingly, 'come up to me here, on the roof.'

'Oh! You are a good man, Hoca. I knew it,' sighed the old man as he slowly climbed the ladder.

Once he was on the roof, Hoca gave him a self-satisfied look and announced: 'Now that you're here, let God give you your one little coin!'

Cogito ergo sum

A man was selling a parrot at the market for a very high price. Nasreddin Hoca told the merchant that he was asking far too much for the bird.

'Ah, but it talks!' explained the vendor.

A week later Nasreddin went back to the market determined to sell a turkey that he had under his arm. He was asking such an exorbitant price that the astonished villagers exclaimed that the bird could never be worth so much.

'Ah, but it thinks!' he retorted.

Old wine

'I'm told, Hoca, that you have some wine that's forty years old. Could you give me a little?'

'If I were in the habit of giving my wine to everyone who asked, it wouldn't be forty years old!'

Shopping

You can find beautiful antique carpets in Konya, especially in Mevlâna Cad., B2-3 A former hamam (Turkish bath) in this street, near the Tourist Information Office, has been tastefully converted into a carpet shop.

Earthenware, wickerwork, and wooden spoons decorated with inscriptions are for sale in the bazaar and along Istanbul Cad., B1.

Useful addresses

Banks

Ottoman Bank, Alaeddin Cad., 16, B2, ☎ 2 0443.

Türkiye Nmlak Bankasi, Konya Subesi, for currency exchange, ☎ 2 3550.

Other

Bus station, just 1.2 mi/2 km from the centre of town on the road to Afyon.

Post Office, Hükümet Meydani, B1-2.

Tourist Information Office, Mevlâna Cad., 21, B2, ☎ 1 1074. Next to the Mevlâna Museum.

THE MEDITERRANEAN COAST

B etween a dive into the clear water of a wild creek or sunbathing on dazzling white sand, you'll be able to explore the remains of about 6000 years of history along a turquoise coast over 600 mi/1000 km long.

Countless remains of the Mediterranean's multimillennium past are dotted along the rugged coastline. A Roman temple emerging from a pine forest, tiers and columns of a Greek theatre rising out of oleanders, a carved sarcophagus or the remains of a Byzantine church appearing from among bushes – these are some of the sights you'll inevitably encounter along a coast that has so far managed to preserve its natural beauty.

The coast is a paradise for archaeology fans and sea lovers alike. Swimmers have long stretches of sandy beaches, and sailors an endless choice of islands, deserted creeks, and inlets that are often inaccessible by land.

The winding road through ancient Lycia between Fethiye and Antalya crosses mountainous areas where sheer cliffs plunge straight into the sea. The going is slow but the views are marvelous.

Ancient Pamphylia, known as the land of all tribes, once occupied the area around the Gulf of Antalya. It was the home of

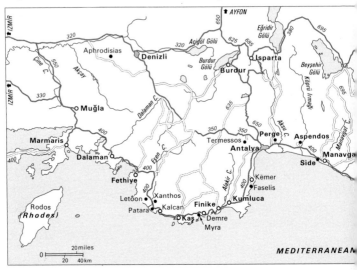

MEDITERRANEAN COAST

many famous ancient sites, such as Aspendos, Perge, Phaselis and Side. To the west of Antalya the mountains come right down to the sea in many places and as a result the beaches tend to be pebbly. East of Antalya, however, as the Taurus Mountains slope gently down to the plain, sandy beaches stretch on for miles.

Most of the coast road from Antalya to Adana, the centre of ancient Lycia, follows the mountainside about 330 ft/100 m above the sea, and takes you through yet more spectacular scenery.

ANTALYA**

Telephone code: 31.
234 mi/376 km south-west of Konya, 186 mi/300 km east of Fethiye and 345 mi/555 km west of Adana.

In any conversation about Turkey, the warmth and hospitality of the people inevitably comes up and will be confirmed by anyone who has been lucky enough to visit the country for even the shortest of stays. To foreign visitors arriving in Antalya, the town seems to be one of Anatolia's friendliest. The geographical setting is impressive too. Whether you arrive by land or sea you'll be struck first by the huge ring of mountains surrounding the gulf, and then by the brightness of the light on the white house fronts.

Antalya has a wonderfully mild climate. Tourist brochures promise 300 days of sunshine a year if not more – and they're not exaggerating. These favourable temperatures encourage the growth of all sorts of plants and shrubs throughout the town so the air is scented by orange, lemon, banana and avocado flowers all year round. In the heat of the day you can find a cool spot among lilies, roses and exotic plants in Karaali Park, just south of the cliff overlooking the bay. There are banks of flowers in the streets, and shady palm trees along residential avenues. You can see the water needed for all this greenery flowing through channels in the streets fresh from the Taurus Mountains.

In the interests of tourism the little fishing harbour below the cliff has added attractive mooring space for pleasure craft. The shady terraced restaurants here are frequented by visitors who drop in from the sea or from the town above via flights of steps and winding alleys.

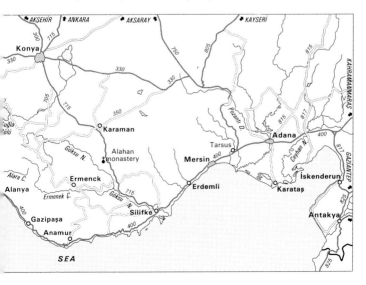

In spite of Antalya's growing population and urban development, a serious effort has been made to preserve the old houses in the fishing quarter on the seafront. Some of them are being restored and converted into guest houses. Similarly, the old town, with its famous fluted minaret, steep narrow streets and small square courtyards, has managed to keep its character and charm.

Although ancient Attaleia was founded in 158 BC by a Pergamene king, Attalus II, excavations in the region suggest that the origins of the town date back to a much earlier period. Soon after its founding the town took advantage of its strong position as a port on the edge of a fertile plain and grew from a modest naval base into a flourishing trade centre and one of the Mediterranean's largest towns. Under different names (Attaleia, Attalia, Adalia, Adalya and even Satalia at the time of the Crusades), and different masters (Romans, Byzantines, Seljuks and finally Ottoman sultans at the end of the 14th century), the town was never abandoned and never lost its determination to survive.

Nothing much remains of Antalya's ancient fortifications apart from Hadrian's Gate, Hidirlik Tower, some ramparts near the shore and a few other towers (one of which is now a clock tower).

What to see

Map coordinates refer to the map p. 209.

Antalya Museum** A2 (off map)

Open Tues-Sun 8:30am-noon, 1:30-5:30pm.

The museum is 1.6 mi/2.5 km west of the town centre on the Kemer Road. Its excellent collections include ancient artifacts found in archaeological sites around Antalya, and an ethnographic section. The exhibits are displayed in chronological order through a series of 15 rooms. Space has been made in the museum for a children's play area with old toys and a small workshop. There is also a patio for refreshments.

Prehistoric section: Cooking utensils, various objects and animal fossils found in Karain Cave and in other sites in the region.

Protohistoric section: Tools and funerary items, and objects dating from the end of the Neolithic and Chalcolithic periods to the beginning of the Bronze Age.

Classical section: Terra-cotta figurines and utensils from the Mycenaean to the Hellenistic periods. Roman sculptures. Study of techniques used in the manufacture and decoration of ceramics.

Sculpture section: Two rows of gods, goddesses and mythological figures facing each other. These are all Roman copies of Greek originals found at Perge.

'Small objects' section: Oil lamps, glass objects, bronze sculptures, marble and terra-cotta statuettes.

Imperial sculpture section: Busts of emperors, empresses and dignitaries typical of Roman statuary found at Perge. Among them are: Faustine, Hadrian, Septimius Severus and Trajan. A beautifully sculpted group of black and white marble called the *Dancer and the Three Graces*.

Sarcophagi section: The most outstanding here are those of Domitian and Hercules. Stelae and funerary urns found in the region.

Mosaics and icons section: Byzantine mosaics found near Xanthos. Examples of local sculpture, together with the sculptor's instruments, are displayed around the central mosaic section. In an adjoining room there are icons dating from the 18th and 19th centuries.

Coin section: Gold, silver and copper coins from Hellenistic times to the present. A study of minting traditions over 2500 years old in Anatolia.

Turco-Islamic section: Items from the Seljuks and Ottomans including enameled earthenware, pottery, jewelry, talismans, carpets, books and Korans.

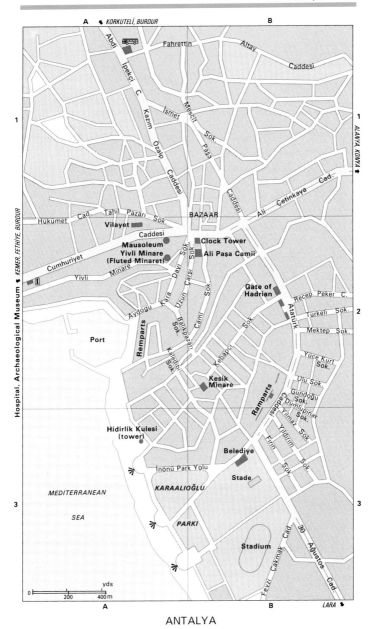

ANTALYA

Ethnographic section: Reconstruction of a tent and different house rooms. Carpets, traditional costumes, weapons and battle dress, musical instruments.

The Gate of Hadrian* B2

This impressive marble arch, framed by two towers, stands on the eastern side of what were once Roman walls. According to the Latin inscription, the gate was built in honour of Emperor Hadrian who visited the town in AD 130.

Ramparts* AB2

These walls were built in the Hellenistic era when the upper town was fortified. They were reinforced under the Byzantines, then repaired and modified by the Seljuks.

Vivli Minare* A2

This is a slender, graceful minaret in the middle of town with a fluted shaft and blue enamel decoration. Built in the early 13th century under Sultan Alâaddin Keykubad I, it is the oldest remaining Seljuk monument. The mosque beside it, Alâaddin Camii, was built nearly a century and a half later.

Hidirlik Kulesi A3

This tower, located on the seafront in the south-east corner of the ramparts, was built by the Romans. Its rounded upper part, with traces of a former balcony, suggests that it may once have been used as a lighthouse or observation tower.

Kesik Minare B2

The first edifice here was a Roman temple that was converted into a basilica in the fourth century. The Byzantines took it over, carrying out restorations in the fifth, seventh and twelfth centuries. Finally, when the Seljuks came to power, it was converted into a mosque. In 1896 part of the minaret burned down during a fire.

Beaches

As the seafront consists mainly of steep rocks (about 164 ft/50 m high) reaching right down to the water, it is very difficult to actually get to the sea and swim. Some of the hotels have built stone steps down to the shore with landing stages built into the rock, but the real swimming beaches are out of town.

Konyaalti Beach, stretching for 2-3 mi/4-5 km from the southern end of the town westward to Mount Bey, is a wide pebble beach. **Lara Beach,** however, on the other side of town, about 7 mi/12 km away, has fine sand.

On the way to Lara Beach you pass Gencliki Park (about 5 mi/8 km east of Antalya) where you can see the **Düden Waterfalls***, the most impressive falls in the Antalya region. Water comes gushing out of the Taurus Mountains, crosses the plain and then hurtles over cliffs into the sea.

Access

By boat: Boats sailing the Istanbul-Izmir-Mersin route stop at Antalya.

By bus: Regular links with Ankara, Istanbul and the main towns in the area. The bus station is on Kâzim Özalp Cad., A1.

By car: The coast road is being improved.

By plane: Turkish Airlines operates regular flights to and from Istanbul (daily in summer), Ankara (several times a week) and Izmir.

Accommodation

Antalya has a choice of modern hotels right in the centre although the most pleasant are a little out of town on the seafront, mainly along Lara Cad.

▲▲▲▲ **Adalya,** a centrally located hotel in the old harbour, A2, ☎ 1 8066. 28 rooms. Taken over by the Turban chain and luxuriously restored.

▲▲▲▲ **Seza,** 6 mi/10 km, out of town on Lara Cad., ☎ 2 8377. 150 rooms. A comfortable new seaside establishment in a large, well-kept garden. There is a separate commercial water sports centre for wind surfing, water skiing and canoeing.

▲▲▲▲ **Talya,** Fevzi Çakmak Cad., B3, ☎ 1 5600. 150 rooms. An extremely luxurious hotel not far from Karaali Park with every amenity imaginable including a casino.

▲▲▲ **Start,** Ali Çetinkaya Cad., B1, ☎ 1 1192. 56 rooms. Slightly outside the centre, usually recommended to businessmen.

▲▲ **Antalya,** Lara Yolu 84, B1 (off map), ☎ 2 3600. 12 rooms. A small motel set in a park near the Düden Waterfalls.

▲▲ **Bilgehan,** Kazim Özalp Cad., 194, A1, ☎ 2 5324. 88 rooms. Very central.

▲▲ **Perge,** Karaali Yat Limami, B3, ☎ 2 3600. 21 rooms. A modest centrally located hotel very near Karaali Park.

▲ **Büyük,** Cumhuriyet Cad., 57, A2, ☎ 1 1913. 42 rooms. Right in the centre overlooking the harbour.

▲ **Yalcin,** Husnukarakas Cad., 1253, B1, ☎ 1 4190. 23 rooms. Near the Start Hotel.

Guesthouses

A number of guesthouses in the old town are being renovated under the auspices of the Ministry of Culture and Tourism.

Ak Asya Pansiyon, Yeni Kapi Fi Sok., 5, B2, ☎ 1 1404. 16 rooms.

Altun Pansiyon, Kaleici Meydani, 10, AB2, ☎ 1 6624. 15 rooms.

Turel Pansiyon, Caylayan Mahallesi, 2055, B3 (off map), ☎ 2 0453. 13 rooms.

Festivals

The **Music and Film Festival** takes place in late May/early June. Some of the performances are held in the theatre at Aspendos.

The **Film and Art Festival** is held in autumn (early September). The closing ceremony usually takes place in the Aspendos Theatre.

The **International Song Festival** takes place in October.

Food

Many of the hotel restaurants specialize in fish. One of Antalya's most pleasant places to eat or simply have a drink is the **Hisar**, set in the ramparts overlooking the old harbour. You reach it from Cumhuriyet Square and can sit out on the terrace, where the view is splendid.

There are restaurants all along the seafront in the port. If you have a car, there are other restaurants in hotels along the coast on the road to Alanya (such as the **Lara** or **Sera**).

Useful addresses

Banks

International Bank of Commerce (Iktisat Bankasi Türk A.Ş), Cumhuriyet Cad., 70/A, A2, ☎ 1 6792. For currency exchange.

Ottoman Bank, Ali Çetinkaya Cad., 22/A, B1, ☎ 1 1080.

Türkiye Emlâk Bankasi, Antalya Subesi, ☎ 2 2417. For currency exchange.

Other

Tourist Information Office, Cumhuriyet Cad., 91, B1, ☎ 1 1747. There are two other information offices, one on either side of the port. The first is near Customs; the second is at the Ministry of Culture and Tourism in Selçuk Mahallesi near Mermeli Park.

Turkish Airlines, THY, Cumhuriyet Cad., 91, B1, ☎ 1 2830.

EAST OF ANTALYA

▬ *PERGE***

11 mi/18 km north-east of Antalya.

Perge is thought to have been founded by the Achaeans who settled in

Anatolia after the Trojan War. Its name, like that of Pergamum, is of Indo-Germanic origin. *Perg* means 'high place'. Accordingly, the heart of the town would have been the acropolis, a wide platform on the northern hill at an altitude of about 164 ft/50 m. Perge prospered during the Classical period and was famous by the time Alexander the Great passed through in 333 BC. In AD 49 Saint Paul came here to preach and founded a church.

The second and third centuries were Perge's golden age, when wealthy citizens adorned the town with fine monuments. Ramparts 43 ft/13 m high fortified by about 30 towers once surrounded the site. Some of them are still standing.

What to see

The first monument you reach on entering the town is the **theatre**** on a hillside to the west. It's a classical theatre with a capacity of 12,000 comprising a *cavea* (semicircular outdoor auditorium), an orchestra section and a stage building. The *cavea* was formed of about 50 terraced rows of seats and was crowned by an arch-shaped gallery with gateways opening out onto a view of the stadium and the rest of the town. In the third century the semicircular orchestra was surrounded by a balustrade to protect spectators during gladiatorial contests or when wild beasts were in the arena. Part of the stage is well preserved. The stage building had three floors and was 170 ft/52 m long. Of the richly decorated doorways only the two to the south of the stage remain; the central and northern ones have been destroyed.

The **stadium*** stretches for 768 ft/234 m over flat ground facing the theatre. With its racetrack and 11 terraced rows for seating 15,000 spectators, it is the best preserved of ancient Pamphylia. The southern part is completely open, which could mean that a monumental wooden gateway once stood here, although not a trace remains. The northern part is closed off and was separated from the rest of the stadium in the third century by a wall, forming an arena for animal fights and gladiatorial bouts.

Two **monumental gateways** formed the main entrance to the town. On either side are the remains of rounded towers about 49 ft/15 m high. You pass through the outer gate to a courtyard where the impressive Hellenistic Gate, a large triumphal arch comprising three sections, was built in the third century BC.

The **agora*** is a vast quadrangle to the east of the Hellenistic Gate. Its large central courtyard is lined with well-preserved shops where the floors are covered in colourful mosaics. Rising up from the middle is a circular edifice with porticoes, the remains of the temple to Tyche, goddess of the Aksu River.

Perge has two **colonnaded streets**. The first runs along a north-south axis from the victory gate to the Nymphaeum at the foot of the acropolis. The second, running in an east-west direction, crosses the first at right angles about 820 ft/250 m from the Nymphaeum. These streets are about 66 ft/20 m wide and are divided down the middle by a canal 7 ft/2 m wide. They are lined with Ionic colonnades that once opened onto shops behind.

The **nymphaeum,** or fountain, is a 69 ft-/21 m-long building comprising three statue niches. The middle one contains a statue of the river god. Water from here was channeled through the town by the canal in the middle of the colonnaded streets.

The town **baths** were housed in what is now the ruins of a building with window arches, which you will find at the western end of the street that crosses the town on an east-west axis.

Access

By car: Drive east from Antalya for 10 mi/16 km to Aksu, then turn north for 1.2 mi/2 km to Perge.

By dolmuş: You can easily take a dolmuş from Antalya to Perge.

The Roman aqueduct of Aspendos, built in the second century AD, is over 2790 ft/850 m long.

ASPENDOS***

22 mi/36 km east of Perge and 29 mi/47 km east of Antalya.

The exact origins of Aspendos are not fully known. Greek settlers from Argolis may have founded the site in 1190 BC. However, because the name Aspendos is of Anatolian origin, it seems that the Greeks, instead of building a new settlement, came to live in an already existing town. If this is the case, Aspendos could date back as far as the Hittites.

On the death of Alexander the Great, Aspendos came under the control of the Ptolemies (Greek kings of Egypt) before being annexed by the kings of Pergamum. In 133 BC, after the last Pergamene king had willed his kingdom to Rome, Aspendos became part of the Roman Empire. As the town was built on the banks of the navigable Eurymedon River (present-day Köprü-çayi), it quickly developed into an important commercial centre. Apart from orchards, vineyards and olive groves, Aspendos was known for its rich pastures, the best in the region for breeding horses.

The Byzantines changed Aspendos to Erimopolis, but why and for how long, nobody really knows. In the seventh century the illustrious city was pillaged during Arab invasions and was finally taken by Seljuk Turks, along with the rest of the Antalya region. But the city was gradually forsaken and then completely abandoned in the 18th century. Since 1923, however, it has been considered one of the most interesting archaeological sites in the country.

Roman Theatre***

Open daily 8am-7pm.

You can't miss the theatre built on the eastern side of a little hill, because the road leads right up to its entrance, a door in the centre of the stage building. It is without doubt the best-preserved theatre in Anatolia. According to the inscriptions on the walls, two citizens named Crustus Crispinus and Curtius

Auspicatus built it in the second half of the second century AD during the reign of Marcus Aurelius.

The **cavea** (or semicircular auditorium), which could hold up to 20,000 spectators, consists of two sections divided by a horizontal corridor. Ten stairways provided access to the 20 rows of terraced seats in the lower section and 21 other stairways reached the 21 upper rows. The rows made from calcerous rock of a marble-like quality are in particularly good condition. The gallery of 59 arcades along the top of the *cavea* is thought to have been added later to shelter the audience from rain. The city magistrates had boxes above the two side entrances.

The **orchestra** forms the central part of the theatre between the terraced rows and the stage building. You can still see some of its original stone floor as well as parts of the water furrow that once surrounded it. A stone parapet was added at the end of the third century for the safety of spectators during animal fights and gladiatorial contests.

Plays were performed on a wooden **stage** in front of the impressive façade of the stage building that comprises several storeys and stands as high as the auditorium gallery. The building was once covered in marble, and its two floors were embellished with columns and statues. Actors could enter and exit the stage through five doors. A wooden roof jutted out from the building over it, thus perfecting the extraordinarily fine quality of the acoustics. Zeno, the theatre's famous architect, designed it with such care that the slightest murmur on stage could be heard clearly at the top of the *cavea*.

When the Seljuks inherited Aspendos they used the building as a palace and decorated it with black tile motifs for plants and white for birds, all on a turquoise background (these tiles are displayed in the Antalya Museum). This is probably why the theatre is in such good shape today.

Acropolis

Open daily 8am-7pm.

The **agora**** is on the largest hill above the acropolis, partly resting on huge vaulted supports. About a dozen ancient shops that can still be seen on the western side were built on a raised platform reached by a flight of steps. They led to a porticoed gallery that has since disappeared. On the other side of the agora are the foundations of a basilica that also served as a market and a courtroom. The best-preserved sections are at the northern end where you can see a portal and arcades.

The **fountain,** or *nymphaeum,* stands in the northern section of the acropolis. It was built into a long two-tiered wall, each layer bearing five statue niches. Water flowed through a double canal behind the fountain from an aqueduct built on a level with the central niche.

The **bouleterion**** ruins can be seen north-west of the acropolis, behind the fountain. It was a semicircular building where city council meetings were held and it also served as an odeon.

To the north, in the lower part of the town, are impressive remains of an **aqueduct** that not only supplied the town with water but also served as a bridge in winter. The lower section of the aqueduct was used to cross the plain when Lake Karagöl flooded and transformed it into a marsh.

Access

By car: On the main road 29 mi/46 km east of Antalya is the left-hand turnoff to Aspendos. The site is 3 mi/5 km farther on.

▬ SIDE**

Telephone code: 3213.

22 mi/36 km south-east of Aspendos and 46 mi/74 km east of Antalya.

Side is located on a peninsula 3 mi/5 km south-west of Manavgat and has two good sandy beaches. The year it was founded is unknown but the Greeks settled here in the seventh century BC. The town flourished through slave trading and piracy, its two main commercial activities. In AD 67 the Romans took over, expelling the pirates and putting an end to the slave traffic. It is generally considered that the town reached the height of its prosperity between the second century and the middle of the third century AD. After this, a decline set in, followed by a renewed period of prosperity from the fifth to the seventh century, which ended with the arrival of the Arabs, who invaded and burned the town.

No one knows exactly when Side was abandoned, but over the years parts of it were gradually covered by sand dunes. At the beginning of the century, emigrant Turks moved here from Crete and built a village among the ruins.

What to see

The **fountain** is an imposing monument outside the city walls opposite the main gate. It was built in the second century BC as a 164 ft-/50 m-long edifice preceded by a 33 ft-/10 m-wide pool that was decorated with marble reliefs. The **main gate**★ is in ruins, though it is still an impressive stone construction, dating from the first half of the third century BC. It is set in **ramparts** that surround the city bearing Hellenistic, Roman and Byzantine traces. Leading off from a vast square just inside the main gate are two **colonnaded streets** paved with wide stone slabs. Side's water supply flowed through channels dug beneath them. They led onto covered arcades, the city's shopping area, which in turn led to the residential area. Although most of the **houses** have been destroyed, you can still see their marble courtyards and geometric mosaics on the floors of their ancient rooms. Continuing down the most westerly colonnaded street, you come to the **agora** on your left, which was used as a slave market. Its columns formed a series of commercial galleries that were sheltered by a large wooden roof.

Unlike others in Pamphylia, Side's **theatre**★★ was not built on a hillside but on flat ground commanding a central position on the narrowest part of the peninsula. The well-preserved *cavea*, with a diameter of 361 ft/110 m, could hold 20,000 spectators. To obtain the required height, its terraced rows were built over a series of supporting arches. As in other theatres, the auditorium was divided by a wide horizontal corridor. Decorative fragments found here suggest that the rectangular 197 ft-/60 m-long stage building, comprising a basement section and two storeys, may have been as richly adorned as the one in Aspendos. Again, a small wall was later added around the orchestra for wild-beast fights and gladiatorial contests.

Two small rectangular **temples** on the seafront, one probably dedicated to Athena (the main divinity of the town) and the other to Apollo, were erected in the second century AD. Because they both featured white marble Corinthian columns that could be seen from several miles away, they were useful landmarks for sailors. A little to the east of the temples is a platform in a small square with yet another temple with a semicircular *cella* (inner chamber). This is the **Temple of Men,** the Anatolian moon goddess. Originally built on the water's edge, it now stands several yards inland, separated from the sea through the gradual formation of sandbars. The ancient **harbour** and jetty follow the peninsula around to the north-west of the temples.

The **Side Museum**★ *(open daily, 9am-5pm)* is housed in the fifth-century Roman baths on the right-hand side of the main colonnaded street as you head south from the main gate. Most of the finds from excavations in the town itself are displayed here, including a sarcophagus with illustrations of Eros, and part of another one featuring a dog. There are also some fine statues, such as those of Hercules, Zeus and Hermes.

Access

By car: After going 43 mi/70 km east from Antalya on the road to Alanya, turn right for 2.5 mi/4 km to Side.

Accommodation

Hotels

▲▲▲ **Defne,** ☎ 1880. 110 rooms. On the beach, with sports facilities.

▲▲ **Cennet,** ☎ 1167. 103 rooms. Pleasant location on the beach.

▲▲ **Motel Turtel,** 3 mi/5 km from Side on the seafront, ☎ 2225. 50 rooms. Small two-storeyed, air-conditioned houses set in a large park.

▲▲ **Sidelya,** on the beach not far from the town. ☎ 4258. 61 rooms. 16 bungalows with a total of 42 apartments.

▲ **Karaelmas,** ☎ 350. 68 rooms. Centrally located on the seafront.

Guesthouses

Side has a wide selection of *pansiyons*, especially near the bus station.

Food

The old harbour is the place to look for good seafood.

Useful address

Tourist Information Office, at the entrance to the village before the main parking lot, ☎ (3213)1265.

▬▬ ALANYA

Telephone code: 3231.

41 mi/66 km south-east of Side, 82 mi/132 km south-east of Antalya and 264 mi/425 km west of Adana.

Set attractively among orange groves and lemon trees at the foot of the Taurus Mountains, Alanya is well worth a short visit. You will certainly enjoy strolling through the narrow streets near the Red Tower or along the ramparts for the fine view, visiting the caves, or swimming from one of the beaches.

Thanks to its sheltered harbour and its more or less invincible position, Alanya played an important role during the Hellenistic age and was used later as a refuge by pirates. However it was the Seljuk sultan, Alâaddin Keykubad I, who contributed most to the town by building a palace and a naval dockyard. After the Seljuks, the Karamanians took control of the town until 1471, when the Ottomans came to power.

What to see

The old part of the town is surrounded by **ramparts** built during the reign of Alâaddin Keykubad I. The walls zigzag impressively around the promontory, enclosing remains of a former palace, inner fortress and Byzantine church.

The **Kizil Kule***, or Red Tower *(open Tues-Sun 9am-noon, 2-7pm),* an octagonal bastion with five floors, was built in 1225 to guard the entry to the naval dockyards and the fort. Today it houses an ethnographic museum. It owes its name to the red stone and brick of the walls. The tower was once topped by a conical roof, but this has long since disappeared and today you can climb to the top for an excellent view of the town's old houses.

The **naval dockyards and arsenal,** also built by the Seljuks, are protected by ramparts south of the Red Tower. They are composed of five sections.

The **Damlataş Cave** *(open summer 10am-8pm; winter 10am-5:30pm)* is on the seafront to the north-west of the citadel. It is well-known not only for its stalagmites and stalactites, but also for its beneficial effect on those who suffer from asthma and bronchitis.

Access

By boat: Boats sailing the Istanbul-Mersin route stop at Alanya.

By bus: There are regular links with Ankara, Antalya, Mersin, and Istanbul.

By car: The Antalya-Adana road is being improved; the best stretch so far is between Antalya and Alanya.

By plane: See Antalya p. 211. Buses run from Antalya Airport to Alanya.

Accommodation

Alanya owes much of its recent development to tourism. Here are some suggestions for accommodation in and around the town:

▲▲▲▲ **Alantur,** Çamyolu Koyu, 4 mi/6 km east of Alanya, ☎ 1224. 99 rooms. Open from the beginning of April to the end of October. Water sports facilities, sea view and garden.

▲▲▲ **Panorama,** Keykobat Cad. About 0.5 mi/0.8 km east of the town centre, ☎ 1181. 162 rooms. Pleasant hotel with a panoramic restaurant, an Olympic-size swimming pool and a large beach.

▲▲ **Alanya,** Gullerpinar Mahallesi, ☎ 1138. 66 rooms. Centrally located.

▲▲ **Banana,** Cikcikli Koyu, just over a mile (2 km) east of Alanya. ☎ 1568. 142 rooms. Facilities for water sports.

▲ **Yeni International,** Keykobat Cad., 211, ☎ 1195. 35 rooms. Just outside the centre.

Food

There are numerous fish restaurants and cafés between the park and the harbour. Some recommendations along Gazi Paşa Cad. (seafront road): **Akdemiz, Havuzbaşi, Konya, Hahperi** and **Yildiz.**

Useful addresses

Tourist Information Office, Carsi Mahallesi, Kalearkasi Cad., ☎ 1240.
Turkish Airlines, Bostanci Pinari Cad., 16, ☎ 1194.

ANAMUR*

78 mi/125 km south-east of Alanya and 159 mi/256 km south-east of Antalya.

Mamure Kalesi** is an extraordinary fortress just outside Anamur right on the sea shore. It was built in the 13th century of solid ochre-coloured stone.

Anemurium (just outside Anamur) is a small ancient site dating from the third century, where you can see the remains of ramparts, a theatre, baths and an aqueduct.

Access

By bus: Buses connect Anamur with Antalya to the west and Mersin to the east.
By car: Follow the coast road from Antalya to the east.

SILIFKE

Telephone code: 7591.
86 mi/139 km east of Anamur, 100 mi/161 km south-west of Adana and 245 mi/395 km east of Antalya.

The city was founded in Hellenistic times by Seleucus I Nicator (one of Alexander's generals) on the banks of the Göksu River. It is mainly renowned as the town where the German Holy Roman emperor, Frederick Barbarossa, drowned while preparing to embark on a Crusade.

There is little to see apart from the 12th-century **fortress** and the **Archaeological Museum** which is outside the town centre *(open Wed-Mon 9am-5pm).*

Accommodation

The hotels and guest houses in Silifke itself tend to be modest establishments. More comfortable places are in Taşucu about 7 mi/11 km to the west.

▲▲▲ **Tastur**, Tasnen, Taşucu, ☎ 290. 54 rooms. This modern hotel is one of the few in its category in this region.

Festival

The **International Music and Folklore Festival** takes place at the end of May.

Useful address

Tourist Information Office, Atatürk Cad., 1/2, opposite the bridge over the Göksu River. ☎ 1151.

UZUNCARBURÇ**

19 mi/30 km north of Silifke.

The mountain road north of Silifke winds through farmland to a forested plateau at an altitude of 3936 ft/1200 m, where you will find the ancient ruins of Olbia Diocaesarea.

What to see

The **Temple of Zeus Olbius** (third century BC) is antiquity's oldest Corinthian-style religious building. Many of the columns are still standing and the atrium wall is in good condition. The **Temple of Tyche** was constructed in the second half of the first century BC. The five remaining columns are granite monoliths with Corinthian capitals. The vaulted entrance and some of the terraced rows of the **theatre** can still be seen, but the stage building has disappeared. The **Lycian tomb** to the south of the site is a square two-storeyed monument with a pyramidal roof. The town was once surrounded by protective **walls** and **towers.** One of the latter, to the north, measuring about 72 ft/22 m, is still in good condition.

MERSIN

58 mi/94 km north-east of Silifke and 304 mi/489 km east of Antalya.

Mersin is Turkey's major Mediterranean port set on the edge of a fertile coastal plain among orange, lemon and banana groves. It is a modern industrial city with a population of 152,000. There is little of touristic interest in Mersin itself apart from the annual textile and fashion fair held in September.

TARSUS

18 mi/29 km north-east of Mersin.

Tarsus is one of the oldest towns in Asia Minor. Because of the advantages once offered by its large natural harbour (now completely silted up), it has been inhabited for many thousands of years. It figured in Greek mythology, was mentioned as early as 850 BC, and according to Islamic belief, was founded by Seth, Adam's son. It was also one of the Roman Empire's intellectual centres. Tarsus is best known as St Paul's native town and the place where Anthony and Cleopatra first met.

What to see

Cleopatra's Gate (also known as St Paul's Gate) was most certainly an ancient gateway from the sea into the old city. Cleopatra is supposed to have passed through here in a small boat to meet Mark Anthony. **Ulu Cami** is a large 15th-century mosque built on the site of a former cathedral to St Paul. Beside it is a 14th-century minaret. **St Paul's well** is of Roman origin and is said to have belonged to the house where the apostle once lived. **St Peter's Church** was built by Armenians in the 14th century and was converted a century later into the **Kilise Camii** you can see today. **Emperor Justinian's bridge** over the Tarsus (Cydnus) River dates from the sixth century and was restored under early Islamic rulers.

The **Museum** *(open Tues-Sun 8am-5:30pm)* houses collections of glass-ware, sculpture, ceramics and Islamic artifacts in a former *medrese* (theological school).

ADANA

Telephone code: 711.

23 mi/37 km east of Tarsus, 302 mi/487 km south-east of Ankara, 120 mi/193 km north-west of Antakya and 345 mi/556 km east of Antalya.

Adana, Turkey's fourth largest town with over 500,000 inhabitants, is an important industrial and agricultural centre that owes much of its wealth to the textile industry. Although it does not hold much interest for a tourist, it is a useful base for visiting the area.

What to see

Hadrian's Bridge was built in the second century by the emperor and was later repaired by Justinian. **Ulu Cami,** dating from the first half of the 14th century, is recognizable by its black-and-white marble exterior.

The **Ethnography Museum** *(open Tues-Sun 8am-noon, 1-5pm)* is housed in a former church and includes musical instruments, jewelry, weapons, clothes, handwritten documents, Korans, *kilims,* embroidered fabrics and a reconstruction of a turn-of-the-century household interior.

The displays in the **Regional Museum** *(open summer 8am-noon, 1-5pm; winter 8:30am-noon, 1-5:30pm)* include prehistoric finds, Hittite statues and bas-reliefs, tombs, stelae, and statues from Greek and Roman times, Byzantine artifacts and Islamic works of art.

Access

By bus: Buses run regularly from Ankara (13-hour trip) and from Istanbul (24 hours) to Adana's busy, modern station (Otogar).

By car: Turkey's major highway, the E5, passes through Adana.

By plane: Turkish Airlines (THY) provides regular connections from Ankara and Istanbul to Adana's Şakirpaşa Airport. You can take an airport bus into town.

By train: The Taurus Express runs twice a week from Istanbul to Ankara via Adana.

Accommodation

▲▲▲▲ **Büyük Sürmeli,** Kuruköpru Özler Cad., ☎ 23600. 170 rooms. The most comfortable hotel in this region.

▲▲▲ **Adana Sürmeli,** İnönü Cad., 151, ☎ 17321. 116 rooms. Comfortable, with air-conditioned rooms.

▲▲▲ **Inci,** Kurtulus Cad., 40, ☎ 14274. 90 rooms.

▲▲ **Ipek Palas,** İnönü Cad., 103, ☎ 14657. 84 rooms. Facing the harbour.

▲▲ **Koza,** Özler Cad., 103, ☎ 14657. 66 rooms.

▲ **Duygu,** İnönü Cad., 14, ☎ 16741. 36 rooms. Overlooks the waterfront.

There are reasonably priced, modest hotels near the bus terminal, around Havuzlar Caddesi.

Food

Adana's restaurants are mainly located on Atatürk Caddesi, near the harbour.

Useful addresses

Tourist Information Office, Atatürk Cad., 13, ☎ 11323.

Turkish Airlines (THY), Atatürk Parki Karsisi, ☎ 12399.

▬ *ISKENDERUN*

Telephone code: 881.

83 mi/133 km south-east of Adana, 385 mi/620 km south-east of Ankara and 429 mi/690 km east of Antalya.

Very little remains of Iskenderun, formerly Alexandretta, founded by Alexander the Great. However, its setting in the middle of a gulf with the Amanos Mountains behind is impressive. The port handles a lot of Mediterranean traffic and has expanded since the opening of a steelworks about 12 mi/20 km away. There's a beautiful **beach** * about 20 mi/32 km south-west of Iskenderun near Uluçinar, a little fishing village on the mouth of the Arsuz River.

> #### Accommodation
>
> ▲▲▲ **Hatalyi**, Osmangazi Cad., 2, ☎ 1 1551. 60 rooms.
> ▲▲ **Bahadirli**, 12 Eylül Cad., 31, ☎ 1 2932. 42 rooms.
> ▲ **Guney Palas**, Bes Temmuz Cad., 17, ☎ 1 1020. 30 rooms.
> **Kavakli** guesthouse, S. Pamir Cad., ☎ 1 4606. 29 rooms.
>
> #### Useful address

Tourist Information Office, Atatürk Bulv. 49/B, ☎ 1 1640/20.

▬ *ANTAKYA* *

37 mi/60 km south of Iskenderun, 422 mi/680 km south-east of Ankara and 466 mi/750 km east of Antalya.

The present town is but a pale reflection of ancient Antioch, the great Seleucid capital and longstanding rival of Alexandria. It influenced the history of Christianity in that early Christians fled to it for refuge and Saints Peter and Paul preached and wrote here. From 1098 to 1268, it was the capital of a Frankish principality founded by the Crusaders. The town's more recent history was marked by French occupation from 1919 to 1938; the town reverted to Turkey in 1939.

What to see

Part of a Roman aqueduct remains. The two arches of a **bridge** over the ancient Orontes River dating from the third century feature Roman eagles. The **Grotto of St Peter**, a cave where the apostle preached, is 1.2 mi/2 km to the north-west of the city. The Crusaders expanded the church in the 12th and 13th centuries.

The most superb collection of Roman **mosaics** ** from sites in the vicinity and from ancient Antioch's wealthy residences is displayed in the archaeology museum, the **Antakya Hatay Müzesi** *(open Tues-Sun 9am-noon, 1:30-5pm).*

WEST OF ANTALYA

▬ *PHASELIS* **

Telephone code: 3214.

35 mi/57 km west of Antalya.

Ancient Phaselis has been abandoned for centuries to the sound of lapping water and the hum of cicadas. It is well worth a detour. The white ruins near the shore blend harmoniously with the encroaching vegetation against a perfect azure background of sea and sky.

Phaselis was founded in the seventh century BC by settlers from Rhodes. Along with the other south-western Anatolian cities, it came under Persian rule in the fourth century BC and was then controlled by Alexander the Great for a quarter of a century until the Ptolemies of Egypt took over. Between 190 and 160 BC the city was first controlled by Rhodes, then allied to Rome and later freed.

The Byzantines built large protective walls around Phaselis, but the city nevertheless suffered repeated attacks from Arab pirates until 1158, when the Ottomans came to power. Over the years that followed it gradually declined.

What to see

The site is open daily 7am-8pm.

Phaselis is an enchanting peninsula with **three harbours.** The northernmost, and the narrowest, was the busiest, because it was sheltered by a prolongation of the city walls into the sea. Part of the jetty can still be seen today, along with the foundations of an ancient lighthouse.

About 15 terraced rows and the stage remain of the small **theatre*** on the north-west slope of the acropolis.

The **main street***, a wide 984 ft/300 m–long avenue through pine trees, once linked the north-eastern and south-western harbours. It ended in a monumental gateway built in commemoration of Emperor Hadrian's visit to Phaselis. East of the avenue was the theatre; to the west were three agoras dating from different times; and on a small hill to the north were two temples. One was dedicated to Athena Polias, the main divinity of Phaselis, and the other to Hestia and Hermes.

The **aqueduct** once supplied the city with water from neighbouring hills. Some of the arches stretching across to the north of the site are still intact.

The **necropolis** can be visited at the foot of the hills behind the northernmost harbour. Because the terrain is flat, you will see sarcophagi as opposed to traditional Lycian cliff tombs.

Access

By car: Take the road south from Antalya through Kemer. About 7 mi/12 km beyond Kemer, you come to a bend where you take a left-hand turnoff for Phaselis. You'll see the ruins after 0.6 mi/1 km.

Accommodation

▲▲▲ **Iberotel Palmyre,** Kemer, 7 mi/12 km north of Phaselis, ☎ 2512. 900 beds. A modern vacation centre near a forest with direct access to the sea.

DEMRE*** (Myra)

55 mi/88 km south-west of Phaselis, 90 mi/145 km south-west of Antalya and 96 mi/155 km south-east of Fethiye.

Myra is part of Anatolia's rich and distant past. Its fame dates back to well before the ancient historians Pliny and Strabo sang its praises, until at least the fifth century BC. It was one of the most brilliant of the famous Lycian league of cities.

The Persians under Cyrus took control of Myra, along with many other cities in Anatolia, only to relinquish them to Alexander the Great in the fourth century BC. By AD 43 the Romans were in control and two centuries later Myra became an important Christian centre, where St Nicholas was to become bishop. Arab attacks began in the seventh century followed by earthquakes and frequent floods. The city turned into an unhealthy swamp and the once-illustrious Myra gradually sank into oblivion.

What to see

A short distance from the market town of Demre, a path leads through greenhouses to the ancient city of Myra that clings to the rock face above. Some of the **rock tombs***** were hewn out of the cliff as early as the fourth century BC. They are quite difficult to reach because the surface is sometimes slippery, in spite of narrow steps specially carved in places. Some of the tombs are real funerary chambers, copies of Lycian dwellings with stone joists. Some bear inscriptions, others relief illustrations of the deceased, showing him surrounded by family and friends.

The **Roman theatre** is to the right of the tombs. The *cavea*, which was largely carved out of the rock, and the first floor of the stage building are in good condition. Façade decoration consisting of columns, alcoves, bas-reliefs and statues has disappeared. Overlooking the theatre from its lofty pinnacle is the ancient acropolis.

Church of St Nicholas** *(open 9am-7pm)*

Retrace your steps to within about 660 ft/200 m of the centre of Demre and follow the signs. The rather strange architectural jumble you come to is 'Aya Nikola', a church dedicated to St Nicholas, the Baba Nöel of Lycia, the Western Father Christmas.

Nicholas from Patara (an important Lycian port) was consecrated bishop of Myra at the end of the third century. In spite of imprisonment and torture during the reign of Emperor Diocletian, he traveled the region spreading the gospel and speaking out against idolatry. He even destroyed the Temple of Diana.

One night, the story goes, St Nicholas slipped three bags of gold through the windows of three poor girls who would never have had adequate dowries and thus enabled them to marry decently. The three sacks of gold in the legend that has come down to us through the centuries are now the pawnbroker's symbol of three golden balls, and the tradition of giving presents at night has been moved from St Nicholas' day to Christmas.

The foundations you see today date from the first church that was built over the tomb of St Nicholas in the fourth century and destroyed in 1034 during an attack by the Arab fleet. Later, Constantine IX Monomachus and Empress Zoë had the church rebuilt and surrounded by walls. In the 19th century the Russians built a monastery here in honour of Nicholas, their patron saint.

Few of the Byzantine frescoes remain. The bright colours and well-defined outlines of the ones that do have faded over the years. You can, however, see the atrium, the twin narthex, the baptistry and an early Christian tomb with two recumbent statues. This contained the mortal remains of St Nicholas until 1087, when Italian merchants made off with them and displayed the relics in Bari, their hometown.

▬ KAŞ*

Telephone code: 3226.

29 mi/47 km west of Demre, 119 mi/191 km south-west of Antalya and 68 mi/109 km south-east of Fethiye.

It is difficult not to succumb to the charm of this little fishing village huddled against the mountainside, where you can walk among old Greek-style houses with picturesque wooden balconies, and see ancient Lycian sarcophagi lying beneath olive trees.

A path leads westward from the village centre to a Hellenistic **theatre** that was hewn out of the rock without, surprisingly, a stage. There are **tombs** on the hillside behind the theatre and others, including Roman sarcophagi, east of the harbour on the shore and even in the sea.

You can take an interesting trip, by boat, to **Kekova****, about 19 mi/30 km east of Kaş. Kekova Bay and Island must be one of the loveliest spots on the Aegean coast, where the ruins of an ancient city rise out of a wild unspoiled landscape. You can also see a Byzantine basilica and the underwater ruins of a sunken city.

Useful address

Tourist Information Office, Cumhuriyet Meydani 6, ☎ 1238.

PATARA

20 mi/33 km west of Kaş, 139 mi/224 km south-west of Antalya and 47 mi/76 km south-east of Fethiye.

Once Lycia's main port, Patara is now an inland site separated from the shore by encroaching sand dunes. The ruins here include Hadrian's vast granary, some tombs, the ancient city's triumphal arch, which dates from about AD 100 and some Roman baths. From the top of the sand-covered **theatre*** you have a panoramic view of the whole site.

LETÔON

4 mi/6 km north-west of Patara, 143 mi/230 km south-west of Antalya and 43 mi/70 km south-east of Fethiye.

Letôon was one of Lycia's most venerated holy places where three temples were built in honour of the kingdom's main gods, Leto and her two children, Apollo and Artemis. Apart from the ruined temple, there are also the remains of a **theatre*** and a *nymphaeum* (fountain) to visit.

XANTHOS**

4 mi/6 km east of Letôon, 40 mi/64 km south-east of Fethiye and about 6 mi/10 km inland.

The ancient capital of Lycia now drowses on a rocky spur overlooking the valley of Koca Çay and the whole sweep of the coastal plain. Xanthos came under Persian control in the sixth century BC as did all Lycian cities, and later sided against the Greeks in the Peloponnesian War before being taken by Alexander the Great. The city grew rapidly when Anatolia fell into Roman hands and then declined at the same time as the Roman Empire. It was gradually destroyed by Arab attacks that began in the seventh century AD.

What to see

The city and acropolis could be approached from the south through a **gateway** during Hellenistic times. Not far away is an arch dedicated to Emperor Vespasian.

North of the gateway, on the other side of the road, only the base remains of what was once a magnificent funerary edifice, the **Monument of the Nereids**. The upper part, with its sculpted decorations, along with other remains of ancient Xanthos (collected by C. Fellows during his 1842-43 excavations) can be seen at the British Museum in London.

Higher up to the left opposite the parking lot you come to the **theatre**. The vaulted entrances, semicircular orchestra and stage façade all testify to the theatre's Roman origins.

Three small monuments stand side by side to the west of the theatre. The first is the **Pillar of the Harpies,** a funerary monument consisting of a small sepulchre chamber resting on top of a 17 ft/5 m monolithic pillar supported in turn by a stepped base. The bas-relief decorations from the fifth century (now in the British Museum) have been replaced by cement copies. They portray winged monsters with vultures' bodies and women's faces personifying tempests and death. The second monument, a traditional **Lycian sarcophagus** with a hull-shaped lid, dates from the fifth century BC. It rests on top of a pillar of several superimposed blocks. The third is another monument on a high base dating from the first century AD.

The square **agora** to the north of the theatre dates from the second or third century AD. An **inscribed stele** stands near the eastern corner. This monolithic obelisk 13 ft/4 m high, featuring Lycian inscriptions and a few Greek verses, is the funerary monument of a local king dating from long before the agora, from the end of the fifth century BC. The bas-reliefs that adorned the death chamber are displayed in London and Istanbul.

On the other side of the road beyond the parking lot a path leads to the

The rock tombs of Fethiye, small reproductions of Greek temples, are carved into the cliffs above the city.

remains of a large **basilica,** where you can see ornamental mosaic tiles. In a little forest to the north is a **Lycian necropolis** of sarcophagi and rock tombs dating back to an earlier era.

FETHIYE*

Telephone code: 6151.

201 mi/323 km south-east of Kuşadasi and 186 mi/300 km west of Antalya.

Ancient Telmessos is now a welcoming seaside resort tucked behind a pretty harbour, protected from winds and storms by a string of islands. Some of its tombs are among the best preserved of ancient Lycia. There are two types, either rock tombs hewn out of the cliff face above Fethiye, or sarcophagi scattered about the quay and the higher parts of town. Some of the rock tombs resemble Greek temples with pediments, porticoes and cornices. Others are replicas of wooden Lycian dwellings.

Before Pliny and Cicero, Herodotus mentioned the magic of the 'snakemen of Telmessos'. They were snake charmers, hereditary soothsayers famed throughout ancient Anatolia. One of them, Aristand of Telmessos, became

an adviser to Alexander the Great after having predicted his glorious future. In the sixth century BC Telmessos was ruled by the Persians, followed by the Lycians at the beginning of the fourth century, and then by Alexander the Great in 334 BC. The town continued changing hands, coming under the control of the Ptolomies of Egypt, the Seleucids, the kings of Pergamum and then the Romans. In the seventh century AD the Byzantines named the town Anastasiopolis, which was changed to Makri by the early Turks and finally became Fethiye at the end of the 19th century.

What to see

The **Tomb of Amyntas***, not far from the centre, was carved into the cliff face above the town like many other Lycian tombs, but it is definitely one of the most outstanding. It was built in the fourth century BC with a façade like a Greek temple on which two Ionic columns frame a stone door, a replica of a traditional Lycian wooden door. The deceased was laid to rest on a stone bench in the tomb chamber that could be closed by a movable slab of stone. The words 'Amyntas son of Hermapios' are inscribed on the pediment.

On leaving the rock tomb follow Kaya Caddesi to the **fortress** overlooking the bay, built by the Knights of St John, Crusaders from Rhodes.

Although nothing remains of the temple of Apollo or the large theatre near the harbour, Fethiye's new **Museum** *(open Tues-Sun 8am-noon, 1-5pm)* gives you a chance to see other architectural finds from ancient Lycia. Near the entrance is a fourth-century BC, 4.4 ft/1.35 m stele from Letôon (Lycia's religious centre), inscribed with religious texts in three languages: Lycian, Greek and Aramaic. Other gravestones and sarcophagi can be seen in the museum garden.

Environs of Fethiye

The islands in the bay make an interesting day trip, and you can see Byzantine ruins on them. It's also a pleasant place for a swim. Check with the Tourist Information Office for information on boat excursions.

The white ruins of **Kaya,** about 12 mi/20 km south of Fethiye, cling to a hillside among oaks and olive trees. This is a deserted town of crumbling houses; life stopped here in 1923 with the exodus of the town's Greek inhabitants imposed by the Treaty of Lausanne.

Ölüdeniz** ('dead sea'), 7 mi/12 km from Fethiye, is a lagoon separated from the sea by a narrow channel. The calm waters and wild mountain background make this a spectacularly beautiful place.

Access

By bus: Regular services link Fethiye to Antalya, Izmir, Kaş and Marmaris.

By car: There are two possible routes from Antalya. You can take the coast road via Finike and Kaş, in which case the road follows the seafront for most of the way and is winding and steep in places (allow at least 8 hours) or follow the inland route via Korkuteli (the road is often rough).

Accommodation

Fethiye

You may prefer to stay in one of the hotels or guesthouses on the beach in Ölüdeniz (7 mi/12 km away) but if not, here are some suggestions for Fethiye:

▲▲ **Likya,** Karagözler Mahallesi, ☎ 1169. 16 rooms. Faces the sea, with gardens and swimming pool.

▲▲ **Seketur,** Çaliş Gullukbasi, about 3 mi/5 km from Fethiye centre, ☎ 1705. 35 rooms. Beside the beach.

▲ **Dedeoğlu,** Iskele Meydani, ☎ 4010. 38 rooms. Faces the harbour. Recently renovated.

▲ **Mutlu,** Sahil Yolu Çalis, ☎ 1013. 33 rooms.

Fethiye has many simple, reasonably priced guesthouses, including:

Dostlar Pansiyon, Dolgu Sahasi, ☎ 1775. 12 rooms.

Pinara Kesikkapi, Dolgu Sahasi, ☎ 1874. 11 rooms.

Ucler Pansiyon, Karagözler Mahallesi, ☎ 2931. 16 rooms.

Ölüdeniz

▲▲ **Meri,** ☎ 1430. 75 rooms. Bungalows in a very beautiful setting on a hillside leading down to a private beach unique of its kind. Unfortunately the rooms are not sufficiently soundproofed.

Guesthouses: These are both numerous and inexpensive.

Campgrounds: Deniz Kamping Motel and **Osman Cavus Kamping** both face the beach.

Food

There is a wide selection of restaurants on the waterfront. For an even nicer setting, go to Çaliş (3 mi/5 km away) or even Ölüdeniz, where you can find reasonably priced restaurants on the beach.

Useful address

Tourist Information Office, Iskele Meydani, 1, ☎ 1527.

NORTH OF ANTALYA

TERMESSOS

21 mi/34 km north-west of Antalya.

The ancient site of Termessos is in the middle of a national park on Mt Gulluk, which covers an area of 16,750 ac/6700 ha. Well-preserved ruins rise mysteriously out of a wild rugged landscape at an altitude of 5248 ft/1600 m.

Scholars generally agree that Termessos was founded by early Anatolian peoples; exactly when is not clear. They made their first historical mark in 334 BC when Alexander the Great tried, without success, to take their invincible fortress.

In the second and third centuries Termessos became a flourishing ally of Rome, and was adorned with temples, monuments and statues. Christianity spread from Antalya to Termessos, where a bishopric was set up under the Byzantines following the schism in the Roman Empire. Decline then set in and the town was gradually abandoned during the fifth century.

What to see

The path from the main entrance to the site leads to all the essential monuments.

The **gymnasium*** is a large, columned courtyard 164 ft/50 m–long by 26 ft/8 m–wide that leads to a series of rooms. The front wall is fairly well preserved. On the façade you can see statue niches where portraits of town dignitaries once stood. The building to the right, still adorned with columns, is where the athletes had baths.

The **theatre****, the best-preserved building on the site, was constructed under Augustus between 27 and 14 BC. The 27 tiered rows are almost intact and could hold about 4200 spectators. As in most Roman theatres, the rows are accessed by vertical stairways and separated by a horizontal corridor. The stage and orchestra are in ruins.

The **agora,** the ancient town centre, is a large trapezoidal space to the west of the theatre. There were once *stoa* (porticoes) on three sides; only the southern part was open. Below the agora is a construction with five connecting cisterns protected by dome-like lids.

The square edifice just south of the agora is the **odeon***. Not much remains of its walls that were once covered in coloured mosaics. The building was used for concerts and sometimes served as a *bouleterion,* or municipal building, for city council meetings.

West of the agora are the remains of a **Corinthian Temple** with six columns. Beside them is the **Stoa of Attalus,** built by the Pergamene king, Attalus II, to thank Termessos for its military assistance.

The ruins of several **Temples of Artemis** lie south of the odeon on the edge of a deep precipice. From here the view across the Antalya plain is tremendous.

There are a lot of **tombs** to be seen, mainly to the west and south. Some of them are rock tombs, others funerary chambers, and still others stone sarcophagi that have for the most part been knocked over and broken.

Access

By car: Leave Antalya on the road to Isparta; after 7 mi/11 km take the Korkuteli road to the left. After about 9 mi/14 km you will come to the turnoff to Termessos National Park. From here it is approximately 6 mi/9 km to the ruins.

EASTERN TURKEY

E astern Turkey's high plateaus and crisscrossed mountains have been formed by the meeting of two massive moutain ranges, the Pontics chain to the north and the Taurus to the south.

The landscapes you will see here are very different from those of coastal Turkey. Their harshness and austerity give the impression that this is a forgotten part of the country, an intensely silent, barren steppe. Yet the aridity is occasionally broken by pastures, forests, streams and lakes. It is a wild, expansive region that has played an important role in Turkey's history.

Abraham passed through here on the long road to the land of Canaan, and Noah's Ark is believed to have touched ground on Mount Ararat. The Urartians built a powerful kingdom in the rocky heights above Lake Van, and the royal sanctuary of Antiochus I has long been protected by stone gods in the heart of the Anti-Taurus mountains.Turkey's more recent past is evoked by the ruins of Armenian churches and Ottoman cities.

Three major roads cross Eastern Turkey: the northern route links Ankara to the Iranian border by way of Sivas, Erzincan, Erzurum and Ağri; the middle one runs from the capital through Kayseri, Malatya and Elaziğ to Lake Van; and the third is a continuation of the Mediterranean road that crosses the former Mesopotamian plain past the Syrian and Iraqi borders.

Communications and hotel facilities are not as well-developed as in the rest of the country partly because of terrain and altitude. This means that not many tourists travel in the east and those who do are bound to meet with some kind of adventure. Any misadventures will be largely made up for by the generosity and hospitality of the people and by the breathtaking beauty of natural sites.

Because of Eastern Turkey's geography, it is difficult to suggest itineraries from a convenient, central town. Erzurum is the capital of East Anatolia, but for the moment road and rail communications between it and the rest of the region are not easy. The following chapter describes specific places to visit in the north, south, and central region, around Lake Van.

Mother and child in the small village of Harran, ancient Carrhae, in Eastern Turkey.

▬ TRABZON**

Telephone code: 031.

200 mi/322 km north-west of Erzurum, 227 mi/366 km east of Samsun and 496 mi/798 km east of Ankara.

Ancient Trapezus was founded toward the end of the seventh century BC by Greek colonists from Milesia. Because of its position on the trade route between the Black Sea and Persia, it rapidly developed into a major commercial centre. This prosperity continued into the first century BC when, in spite of being occupied by Lucullus' troops during the war between the kingdom of Pontus and the Romans, Trapezus managed to keep its status as a free city. Later Byzantium took control and evangelized the population, during which time Emperor Justinian reinforced the ramparts. On April 13, 1204, Crusaders attacked Constantinople, dealing a severe blow to the already declining Byzantine Empire. Two of Emperor Andronicus I's grandsons, princes Alexius and David Comnenus, fled to Trebezond (as it was then known) and founded their own Greek empire on the Black Sea. From then on the city became the centre of Byzantine art. During the 14th and the beginning of the 15th century, the empire was weakened by battles with Genovese merchants intent on capturing the Black Sea trade. In 1461 the Byzantine territory of Trebezond fell to Mehmed II, conqueror of Constantinople, who converted all the churches into mosques.

What to see

Aya Sofya** is on a hillside overlooking the sea, 1.9 mi/3 km from the town centre. It was the jewel of Trebezond, a white- and ochre-coloured Byzantine church with a red tiled roof. Under the Comneni it was a basilica with three naves; in the 13th century it was modified by Emperor Manuel I, who gave it a cruciform plan and a dome. The three projecting porches date from the same period. A frieze on the pediment of the south porch illustrates the story of Adam and Eve. The walls inside are covered with magnificent 13th-century frescoes of saints and apostles as well as moving scenes from the Old and New Testaments.

The **Basilica of St Anne,** from the eighth century AD, is the oldest church in Trabzon. It consists of three distinct naves separated by columns with Ionic capitals. Above the door are traces of an inscription and some bas-relief work.

Fatih Camii, or **Ortahisar Cami** (so called because of its position in the heart of the Byzantine citadel), is the former Church of the Golden-headed Virgin *(Panaghia Chrysokephalos).* Before becoming a church it was an old Byzantine basilica that was transformed in the 13th century. The name 'golden-headed' derives from the fact that the cupola was once decorated on the outside with copper plating.

Environs of Trabzon

Sumela Monastery*** is about 31 mi/50 km from Trabzon. Leave Trabzon on the main Erzurum road; when you reach Maçka take the left-hand turnoff onto a smaller road to Sumela marked Meryem Ana.

The famous monastery, a powerful example of Byzantine architecture, is balanced dramatically between earth and sky on a sheer cliff face in the Pontics Mountains. You follow a steep path through forests and glades that ends in steps up to the entrance at 3936 ft/1200 m. According to legend, the Virgin Mary appeared to two Athenian monks and asked them to found a monastery in an isolated valley in the Pontics Mountains. In 385 a few cells and a little chapel were built into the rock. When the two saints died on the same day in 412, the monastery became a place of pilgrimage and one of the most important monastic centres in the east. Its influence was strong even during the Ottoman period. On several occasions fires broke out and the monastery was rebuilt.

Sumela was temporarily abandoned during World War I and then permanently so in 1923 as a result of the Greco-Turkish conflict. Today you can see the remains of the library and kitchens as well as some lovely paintings in the

Church of the Assumption of the Virgin****** which was built under a natural arch in the rock. Apart from a few fragments from the 15th and 16th centuries, most of the paintings date from the 18th. There's a magnificent *Last Judgment* on the rock wall, together with scenes from the lives of Christ and Mary.

The cells and refectory in the 14th-century convent building have not been well-preserved. Nevertheless, it is impossible to remain unmoved by the extraordinary wild beauty of the setting.

Access

By boat: There are sea links between Trabzon and Istanbul (check departure times at a Tourist Information Office).

By bus: Regular connections with Ankara, Erzurum and Samsun.

By car: From Ankara you can either drive through Samsun and then follow the coast road or go through Erzincan; about 32 mi/52 km before Erzurum take the Trabzon turnoff to the left onto a road that is currently being improved. You can also reach Trabzon from the east from Artvin. This is a beautiful route that follows the shore most of the way.

By plane: Regular flights to Ankara and Istanbul.

Accommodation

▲▲ **Özgür,** Kibris Sehitler Cad., 29, ☎ 1 1319. 45 rooms. Near the Tourist Information Office.

▲▲ **Usta,** Telgrafhane Sok., 3, ☎ 1 2195. 72 rooms. Comfortable; considered the best hotel in Trabzon.

▲ **Horon,** Sira Mağazalar, 125, ☎ 1 1199. 42 rooms. Conveniently located near the main square, Taksim Meydani.

Useful addresses

Automobile Club, Comlekci Yokusu, Liman Cikis Kapisi Karşisi, ☎ 1 7156.

THY (Turkish Airlines), Kemarkaya Mahallesi, Meydani Parki Karşisi, ☎ 1 3446.

Tourist Information Office, Taksim Cad., Atatürk Alani, 31, ☎ 1 4659.

ERZURUM*

Telephone code: 011.

120 mi/193 km east of Erzincan, 131 mi/211 km south-west of Kars, 200 mi/322 km south-east of Trabzon, 244 mi/393 km north-east of Van and 553 mi/890 km east of Ankara.

Erzurum was a former caravan stop on the trade route from the Black Sea to Persia and is now the capital of Eastern Anatolia. Located at an altitude of 6396 ft/1950 m on a winding plain ringed by mountains, it is the coldest town in the country during winter.

The province was first inhabited by Cimmerians in the eighth century BC, then by Scythians, who in turn were ousted by Persians in the sixth century BC. Control of the town passed through different hands: Alexander the Great conquered the area when he swept east and was followed by Sumerians, Romans and then Byzantines in AD 395. The Arabs succeeded them, ruling for four centuries, then, in the middle of the 11th century, Seljuk Turks came to power. Erzurum was finally integrated into the Osmanli Empire in 1515.

The name Erzurum derives from Arz-er-Rum, the 'land of Rome' as the Arabs termed it during the Byzantine period. More recently, the town was the venue for an important historical meeting. On July 22, 1919, Mustafa Kemal held a congress here defining and defending modern Turkey's boundaries.

What to see

The **Ulu Cami*** (Great Mosque), founded in 1179, is the oldest mosque in Erzurum. It is noteworthy for its seven parallel naves, a *mihrab* with a dome, and a courtyard lined with porticoes.

The **Çifte Minare Medrese,** or **Hatuniye Medrese** (Twin Minaret Seminary or Hatun Seminary, *open from 9am-5pm*). This was a renowned medical school founded in 1253 by Huant Hatun, daughter of Alaeddin Keykubad I. Its name derives from two fluted minarets with attractive blue tile decoration. The seminary itself is a rectangular building of grey tuff stone surmounted by a cupola with a pyramidal top. In the southern end of the complex is the impressive **Hatuniye Türbesi** (tomb of Hatun), built in 1255 for Mahperi Hatun, Alaeddin Keykubad's daughter. The style of the mausoleum with its beautiful external decoration is Seljuk.

The **Emir Sultan Türbesi** (Mausoleum of Emir Sultan) was built in the 12th century and restored in 1950. Notice the richly decorated façade, the ornamental niches and the relief decoration of human and animal heads. The two smaller 13th-century tombs beside it probably belong to Emir Sultan's sons.

The theological school, **Yakutiye Medrese,** was constructed in about 1308 and is now used by the army. Its domes and minarets are finely sculpted and the portal is bordered by a sculpted band of twin-headed eagles and palm leaves.

The **Lâla Mustafa Paşa Camii** was built by Sinan in 1563 under the auspices of Lâla Mustafa Paşa, governor of Erzurum.

Environs of Erzurum

Palandöken **ski resort** is approximately 4 mi/6 km south of Erzurum on a road that winds through spectacular mountain scenery.

Access

By bus: There are regular services to Erzurum from Ankara, Kars and Trabzon.

By car: The road is generally good from Ankara and Kars. Part of the Trabzon-Erzurum stretch is being improved.

By plane: Daily flights from Ankara, Istanbul and Izmir (the last two through Ankara).

By train: Daily flights from Kars and Istanbul.

Accommodation

▲▲ **Büyük Erzurum,** Ali Ravi Cad., 5, ☎ 16528. 50 rooms. A new hotel, with a restaurant.

▲▲ **Oral,** Terminal Cad., 3, ☎ 19740. 90 rooms. Comfortable, but sometimes noisy. Located outside of the town centre.

▲▲ **Sefer,** Istasyon Cad., ☎ 13615. 36 rooms. Modern and convenient.

▲ **Buhura,** Kazim Karabekir Cad., ☎ 15096. 44 rooms.

▲ **Efes,** Tahtacilar Cad., 30, ☎ 17081. 46 rooms.

▲ **Kral,** Erzincankapi, 18, ☎ 17783. 48 rooms. Centrally located.

▲ **Polat,** Kazim Karabekir Cad., ☎ 11623. 60 rooms.

Useful addresses

Railway station, Istasyon Cad., ☎ 14798.
THY (Turkish Airlines), 50 Yil Cad., SSK Rant Tesisleri 24, ☎ 18530.
Tourist Information Office, Cemal Gürsel Cad., 9, ☎ 15697.

▄▄▄ *KARS**

Telephone code: 0211.

131 mi/211 km north-east of Erzurum, 288 mi/464 km north of Van via Horasan, and 275 mi/442 km east of Trabzon.

Kars is a grey garrison town in the middle of an austere plateau only

28 mi/45 km from the Russian border. The Armenians first founded it as the capital of their kingdom. It was then taken over by the Seljuk sultanate under Alp Arslan in 1068, a move that was contested by the Georgians in 1205, who annexed it to their own kingdom. The Ottomans reclaimed it in 1515 and built a fortress. Kars then became the subject of numerous battles between Turks and Russians over control of the territory. Finally, with the 1920 Treaty of Moscow, Kars was proclaimed Turkish.

The town still looks like a provincial 19th-century Russian centre, with its grid street plan, basalt edifices and carved façades. It is a mandatory stop for anyone wishing to see Ani (27 mi/44 km), the former Bagratid capital on the Russian border, because the paperwork needed for the visit must be obtained in Kars.

What to see

The **Church of the Apostles**** was built during the Armenian Bagratid dynasty between AD 930 and 937 and then converted into a mosque on the arrival of the Seljuks. It's a domed edifice with a high drum section decorated with 12 arcades in which there are faint relief carvings of the apostles. The church now houses a **museum** containing ancient archaeological finds and ethnographic displays.

The **citadel*** rises to the north of the town on a hill. It was built in the 12th century and greatly modified over the years by successive rulers: Turks, Seljuks, Ottomans and Russians. There are two sets of walls, one of which is flanked by towers marking the boundary of the lower town. During the 18th century there were about 3000 houses and a great many mosques and oratories in this old part of town. The ruins of various Muslim monuments still stand.

Taş Köprü is a fine stone bridge with three pointed arches built by the Ottomans in 1579. It spans the Kars Çayi River that separates the upper and lower towns.

Yusuf Paşa Camii is an attractive Ottoman mosque that was constructed in 1664 under Seyid Yusuf Paşa.

Access

By bus: Regular services to and from Erzurum and Van.

By car: The road is scenic and narrow. Drive with great care.

By train: Twice weekly train connections (slow) from Ankara and Istanbul.

Accommodation

▲ **Temel Palas,** Halit Paşa Cad., 41/A, ☎ 1376. 20 rooms.

▲ **Yilmaz,** Kucukkazimbey Cad., 114, ☎ 1074. 36 rooms. Near the bus terminal.

Useful addresses

Security headquarters, Karadağ Cad. (at the top of the avenue). This is where you get permission to visit Ani.

Tourist Information Office, Lise Cad., 9, ☎ 2300/2912.

*ANI***

27 mi/44 km east of Kars and 163 mi/263 km north-east of Erzurum.

Founded in the ninth century by Ashot Msaker, Ani was the Armenian capital of the Bagratids in the middle of the 10th century before falling into the hands of the Byzantines, Turks, Georgians and Mongols. These latter managed to ruin the town's rich livelihood, which originated from trade with merchant caravans that stopped on their way to and from the East. By the 14th century the decline was such that Ani's inhabitants had begun to emigrate and, soon after, the town was abandoned.

The ruins of the town are spread over a vast triangular plateau bordered on the east and west by two deep canyons that converge in the south.

What to see

To visit the site you must obtain permission from the Security Service in Kars. Remember that because of Ani's proximity to the Russian border, photography is not allowed.

The town is enclosed first by two natural canyons, then by **ramparts**** consisting of a double set of walls dating from the 10th century. The towers on the inside walls are in good condition, but not the outer ones. You enter through Alp Arslan Kapı gate, which is decorated with a bas-relief of a lion. Walk 656 ft/200 m farther to the right where two dungeons stand sentry to another gate, the Çifte Badan Kapı, also known as the Kars Gate. About 984 ft/300 m farther on you come to Hidrellez Kapı, or the 'gate of the beginning of summer', adorned with a checkered pattern dating from Georgian times. Beyond this, at about 0.5 mi/0.8 km from the main gate, is Dere Kapı or 'small valley gate'.

The **cathedral****, constructed at the end of the 10th century, was taken by the Turks in 1064 and transformed into a mosque, then was reconverted into a cathedral by the Georgians at the end of the 12th century. With its rectangular floor plan and alcoves in the transept, it constitutes a remarkable example of Armenian architecture. Despite its damaged cupola, it is relatively well preserved. Particularly noteworthy are the decoration on the exterior walls and its finely crafted columns.

Saint Saviour Church. This is a vast circular edifice, inside of which are fragments of frescoes from the end of the 13th century.

Saint Gregory of Honentz Church. This large cruciform-shape basilica contains paintings of scenes from the New Testament and the life of St Gregory the Illuminator, founder of the Armenian church. Equally noteworthy are the reliefs of animals.

The **Georgian Church** is about 328 ft/100 m to the right of the main gate. It dates from the beginning of the 13th century and though in ruins, still has fine bas-reliefs, including the Annunciation and Visitation.

The **Church of Saint Gregory** was founded in the year 1000. It's a vast circular edifice near the edge of the plateau.

The **Church of the Holy Apostles** is in ruins. Adjoining it you can see a 13th century building that was probably nonreligious in origin but has some interesting decoration. There are ornamental reliefs on the dome and a finely carved Iranian style portal with numerous inscriptions.

▬▬ DOĞUBAYAZIT**

Telephone code: 0278.

59 mi/95 km east of Ağrı, 177 mi/285 km east of Erzurum and 204 mi/328 km north of Van.

Doğubayazit lies at an altitude of 5248 ft/1600 m on a plain beneath the slopes of Mount Ararat. It is one of Turkey's easternmost towns, the last main stop before Iran, which is only 22 mi/35 km away.

What to see

The **Palace of Ishak Paşa** *(open Tues-Sun 8am-6pm)* is nearly 4 mi/6 km south of Doğubayazit on a rocky hillside. Built as a summer residence for a governor of the region at the end of the 17th century, it is a remarkable architectural mixture of Persian, Ottoman and Seljuk styles. The fine entry portal recalls other Seljuk works. Inside the complex you can visit a mosque (with a decorated dome and a minaret, which has a panoramic view of the area), the harem, a reception room, baths and the kitchen.

Facing the palace on another hillside are the ruins of a **Seljuk fortress.** There is an enormous relief on the walls bearing a Urartian inscription in cuneiform lettering.

Ağri Daği*, or Mount Ararat, the mountain where Noah's Ark is supposed to have ended up after the deluge, reaches 16,942 ft/5165 m at its highest point and is always covered in snow.

Biblical Turkey

Abraham is believed to have been born in the region of Urfa, and at Harran (sometimes known as Charan in the Old Testament), women still press around the well where Abraham's servant is said to have met Rebecca, the future wife of Abraham's son, Isaac.

Mount Ararat (16,942 ft/5165 m), which borders on Iran and the USSR, is another important biblical site: 'But God remembered Noah, and all the beasts, and all the cattle that were with him in the ark; and God made a wind blow over the earth, and the waters subsided; the fountains of the deep and the windows of the heavens were closed, the rain from the heavens was restrained, and the waters receded from the earth continually. At the end of 150 days the waters were abated; and the ark came to rest in the seventh month, on the seventeenth day of the month, upon the mountains of Ararat' (Genesis 8, 1-4).

Numerous expeditions have searched here for the wreck of Noah's Ark but, so far, all have been in vain.

Access

By bus: Regular departures from Ağri, Erzurum and Kars.

By car: Find out about the condition of the road from the nearest Tourist Information Office before setting out for Doğubayazit.

Accommodation

▲▲ **Isfahan,** Emniyet Cad., 26, ☎ 1139. 56 rooms. Modern hotel, with a good restaurant.

▲ **Sim-Er Moteli,** Tes, PK 13, ☎ 1601. 38 rooms. Another modern hotel, located 3 mi/5 km east of the town, on the road to Iran.

Doğubayazit also has a choice of cheaper and more basic accommodation.

▬▬ *VAN***

Telephone code: 0611.

204 mi/328 km south of Doğubayazit, 104 mi/168 km east of Bitlis, 244 mi/393 km south-east of Erzurum and 250 mi/402 km east of Diyarbakir.

The ancient city of Van was built at an altitude of more than 5576 ft/1700 m on the shores of a large lake near the border between present-day Turkey and Iran. The city itself lay at the foot of a huge rock that was crowned by a citadel.

According to legend, Van was founded in the early ninth century BC by Semiramis, Queen of Babylon, and was enlarged later by a local prince. Toward the middle of the ninth century BC the king of Urartu, Sarduri I, took control of the region and established his Urartian capital in Van, changing the name to Tushpa. In the eighth century BC, Sargon II of Assyria annexed Urartu, and in the seventh century, the Armenians came to settle beside the lake. Not long afterward, in the sixth century BC, Tushpa was taken by a people called the Medes (from an ancient kingdom north-west of Persia), and then by the Persians a century later.

By the end of the second century BC Tigranes the Great, King of Armenia, had built an empire that extended as far as Syria. It was to experience a turbulent succession of dynasties until the 11th century AD. In 1021 Seljuk warriors plundered through Vaspurakan (as the Armenian state had come to be known), and after their victory at Manzikert north of Lake Van in 1071, settled on the plateau. Toward the end of the 14th century, the knights of Tamerlane the Mongol devastated the area, and in 1534 Van became part of the Ottoman Empire.

The ancient city of Van survived until the beginning of the 20th century, when on May 20, 1915, Russian troops entered the town and destroyed it completely. The site was under Russian occupation until Armistice day, December 18, 1917. A new town of Van has since grown up, 1.9 mi/3 km from the lake shore. Although it doesn't offer very much in the way of historical interest, it is a good base for visiting neighbouring sites.

What to see

The **Van Museum** *(open Tues-Sun 9am-noon, 1-6:30pm)* is not far from Bayram Oteli. The museum houses very fine archaeological and ethnographic collections, including displays of Urartian sculptures, jewelry and artifacts from the eighth and seventh centuries BC. Upstairs you can see cuneiform inscriptions, Muslim works of art, Kufic inscriptions and an ethnographic section of carpets and rugs.

The **old town** is 1.9 mi/3 km from the new on the lake shore below the Rock of Van. Its mausoleums and mosques date from Seljuk and Ottoman times; the most interesting are Ulu Cami and Hüsrev.

On top of the Rock of Van is a **citadel** with crenellated walls and brick towers, the ancient acropolis of Urartian Tushpa (9th century BC). It extends for 1.2 mi/2 km about 230 ft/70 m above Lake Van. A steep stairway of more than 1000 steps leads up to the site where in the rock itself you can see *khorkor,* Urartian funerary chambers with cuneiform inscriptions. A large vaulted niche on the northern slope of the hill harbours a stone block inscribed in Babylonian, Median and Persian to the glory of Xerxes, first king of Persia, proclaiming him the Great King, King of Kings, King of multi-lingual provinces.

Environs of Van

Lake Van[**] (Van Gölü). The lake fills a volcanic basin 5642 ft/1720 m above sea level, covering an area of 1467 sq mi/3800 sq km. The background of mountain peaks dropping steeply to jagged shores creates a unique impression of wilderness, intensified by the extreme silence that reigns. The water itself has a high concentration of mineral salts, and very limited aquatic life with no fish except in the river mouths.

Akhtamar Island[*] (also known as Akdamar) is the largest of a group of islands in Lake Van. It is just 1.2 mi/2 km from Gevaş, a village on the southern road around the lake between Van and Bitlis. The crossing takes 20 minutes.

Saints Thaddaeus and Bartholomew journeyed through Armenia's mountains in the first century spreading the Gospel. In 303 King Tiridates III converted to Christianity and made it the state religion. Monks settled on Akhtamar Island in the 8th century. In the 10th century, Gagik Artzruni, King of Armenia (908-936), founded an independent Armenian state around Van which he named Vaspurakan. He decided to build a palace that was to be richer and more beautiful than those of the Caliphs of Baghdad; the site he chose was Akhtamar Island. All that remains of the palace is the **Church of the Holy Cross,** a famous monument that prefigures Roman art in the West.

The architect Manuel built the church between 915 and 917, adopting a Byzantine cruciform floor plan, but to the tall drum he added a conical dome. The outside walls are decorated with wonderful friezes of animals, human faces, saints and prophets. King Gagik is depicted on the main façade offering a model of his church to God. The inside of the church was once covered in paintings, but only faded fragments remain, illustrating scenes from the Old and New Testaments. Several monastic buildings can be seen on the grounds outside the church. They were part of a centre for patriarchs of the Armenian church in the 10th century.

The ruins of an ancient fortified city dating back to the Urartians, can be visited on the hill at **Çavuştepe**[*], 22 mi/35 km south of Van. The ruins stand inside two citadels perched on neighbouring ridges and include a palace and a street about 492 ft-/150 m-long and 23 ft-/7 m-wide that leads between walls to ancient storerooms, where some 30 jars are displayed in rows. Especially interesting are the foundations of a temple built in honour of the god Irmushini with a cuneiform inscription bearing the name of King Sarduri III (eighth century BC).

At **Güzelsu**, 36 mi/58 km east of Van, you can see an impressive Kurdish fortress, also known as the Castle of Hoşap, that was built high on a crag in the 17th century and now overlooks a small village. The carved portal between the castle and the village is especially beautiful.

Access

By boat: There are regular services across Lake Van between Van and Tatvan. Check departure times at the local Tourist Information Office or at main ones throughout Turkey.

By bus: Regular links with Diyarbakir, Kars and Tatvan.

By car: As usual in this region, drive with care; not all the main roads are asphalted yet.

By plane: Regular connections with Ankara. Flights for Istanbul and Izmir stop in Ankara.

Accommodation

▲▲▲ **Akdamar,** Kazim Karabekir Cad., 56, ☎ 1 8100. 69 rooms. Very comfortable; the best hotel in town with good food.

▲▲▲ **Büyük Urartu,** Hastane Sk., 60. 75 rooms. Comfortable.

▲▲ **Büyük Asur,** Cumhuriyet Cad., 126, ☎ 1 8792. 46 rooms. Comfortable, with a restaurant.

▲▲ **Tekin,** Küçük Cami Civari, ☎ 1 3010. 52 rooms.

▲ **Beskardes,** Cumhuriyet Cad., 54, ☎ 1 1116. 48 rooms. Modest and inexpensive.

▲ **Caldiran,** Sihke Cad., ☎ 1 2718. 48 rooms.

▲ **Güzel Paris,** Hükümetkonagi Arkasi. ☎ 1 3739. 56 rooms.

Shopping

Van has wonderful carpets and kilims from Eastern Turkey. Among the shops recommended are two on Cumhuriyet Cad., **Galerie Akdamar** and **Galerie Hosap.**

Useful addresses

THY (Turkish Airlines), Cumhuriyet Cad., 196, ☎ 1 1241.

Tourist Information Office, Cumhuriyet Cad., 127, ☎ 1 2018.

▰▰▰ *DIYARBAKIR*******

Telephone code: 8311.

250 mi/402 km west of Van, 58 mi/94 km north-west of Mardin and 117 mi/189 km north-east of Urfa.

Diyarbakir is lost in a vast barren plateau that is oppressively hot in summer. It lies beside the banks of the Tigris River at an altitude of 1968 ft/600 m. The town appears to be an excellent example of medieval military architecture with dungeons, towers, gates and bastions dotted about its 3 mi/5 km of dark basalt walls that earned it the name Diyarbakir the Black. But in fact, the town is very oriental, lively and warm, coloured by the shimmering bright costumes worn by the town's Kurdish population.

Amida, as Diyarbakir was known in antiquity, was annexed by the Roman Empire on the signing of a treaty in AD 297. A fortress was built first, followed by ramparts constructed for the town's protection under Emperor Constantine in 349. The Arabs took Amida in 638 after conquering Byzantine troops on the banks of the Yarmak River. The town later became part of the Umayyad and Abbasid caliphates. Although Amida managed to free itself, it fell successively to other victors: Marvanids, Artukids, Mongols, and then to Tamerlane at the end of the 14th century. Finally, in 1515,

Turkish troops occupied the town and Diyarbakir, as it was then named, was incorporated into the Ottoman Empire.

What to see

Ever since the **ramparts**** were first built, the walls have been constantly demolished, restored, and modified by successive authorities in the town who have usually managed to recycle the old stone. The result is a plethora of different styles and inscriptions, with Byzantine pilasters, Seljuk reliefs, Greek and Latin engravings and Kufic inscriptions.

The immense stone ring that encircles the town for more than 3 mi/5 km with 16 dungeons and five monumental gates is imposing and impressive. If you prefer a shorter visit to the ramparts, concentrate on the most interesting walls near the three main gates. These are Harput Kapisi to the north, Urfa Kapisi to the west and Mardin Kapisi to the south. Try also to see two fine bastions, **Evli Beden** and **Yedi Kardeş** between the Urfa and Mardin gates.

Urfa Kapisi*, known as Bâb ar Rum in the Middle Ages, originally had three openings, two of which were walled in at the end of the 12th century. Again, there were two towers. An eagle in relief above the gate is shown spreading its wings over a bull.

Harput Kapisi, known in the Middle Ages as Bâb el Armen (the Armenian Gate or Gate of Deliverance) stands on the site of a former Roman gate. There are towers on either side and acanthus leaves as decoration on the capitals.

Mardin Kapisi, known as Bâb at Tell (Hill Gate) in the Middle Ages, was built between two semicylindrical towers that were frequently modified. Here again, two of the three openings in the gate were walled in.

The vast courtyard of **Ulu Cami**** contains two ablutions fountains. One has a roof supported by eight small columns while the other is a much less elaborate monument, just a square pool. To the left is the prayer room with a central nave and *mihrab*. The galleries along the east and west wings of the mosque are unique in that the columns from antiquity have Corinthian capitals. The builders made use of an assortment of materials from much older monuments, which enhances the architecture's originality.

North-west of the courtyard a portico leads into the **Mesudiye Medrese**, a basalt building like most in Diyarbakir. The *medrese's* square courtyard is lined on three sides by porticoes and on the fourth by an *iwân*.

The **citadel** was constructed in the fourth century AD on an artificial mound. It contains a small 12th-century **mosque** with a square-based minaret surmounted by a cylindrical shaft.

Just opposite Ulu Cami is the former **caravanserai** of Grand Vizir Haşan Paşa which was built at the end of the 16th century and now serves as an exhibition hall for merchants.

The **Zincirli Medrese** was built at the end of the 12th century according to a traditional Seljuk Koranic school plan consisting of a central courtyard with an *iwân* flanked by long rooms and student cells. It has been converted into an **Archaeological Museum*** featuring Assyrian, Sassanid, Roman, Byzantine, Seljuk and Ottoman collections.

Behram Paşa Camii, built in 1572, has a fine portal with stalactite decoration on the archivolt.

Kasim Bey Camii (1512) is famous for its minaret which stands some distance from the mosque on a base of four columns.

About 5 mi/8 km south of Diyarbaklr is an ancient basalt bridge with 10 arches that was built across the Tigris by the Romans.

Access

By car: There are good asphalt roads from Elazığ, Mardin, Urfa and Van.

By plane: Regular flights from Ankara (daily in summer) and Istanbul (twice a week).

By train: Regular but slow connections with Istanbul (via Ankara), Izmir and Van.

Accommodation

▲▲ **Demir**, Izzet Paşa Cad., 8, ☎ 1 2315. 39 rooms. Very pleasant terrace restaurant.

▲▲ **Büyük**, İnönü Cad., 4, ☎ 1 582. 72 rooms.

▲▲ **Turistik**, Ziya Gökalp Bulv., 7, ☎ 1 2662. 54 rooms. Older, but large and well-maintained rooms.

▲ **Amit**, Gazi Cad., ☎ 1 2059. 44 rooms.

▲ **Aslan**, Kibris Cad., 23, ☎ 1 3971. 40 rooms.

▲ **Dicle**, Kibris Cad., 3, ☎ 2 3066. 30 rooms.

Shopping

Diyarbakir specializes in pottery and silver work.

Useful addresses

THY (Turkish Airlines), Izzet Paşa Cad., ☎ 1 0101.

Tourist Information Office, Lise Cad., 24/A, ☎ 1 2173/1 7840/1 0099.

Train station, Çemiloğlu Cad., ☎ 1 1027.

▄▄▄ *MARDIN***

Telephone code: 8411.

58 mi/94 km south of Diyarbakir and 121 mi/195 km east of Urfa.

Known in antiquity as Marida, Mardin rises from a hillside at an altitude of 4264 ft/1300 m above the Mesopotamian plain.

What to see

Sultan Isa Medrese* dates from year 787 of the Hegira (Georgian calendar year 1385) – the flight of Mohammed from Mecca. The seminary has a richly decorated portal, a mosque, and inner courtyards lined with arcades.

Ulu Cami* (Great Mosque) was built by the Seljuks in the 11th century and modified in the 15th. Its minaret was repaired more recently, in the 1800s. The prayer room is composed of three parallel naves separated by two lines of six pillars. Finally, the *mihrab* is covered by a dome.

The **citadel** is partly in ruins but from it you have a magnificent **view**** of the lower town and the Mesopotamian plains beyond.

Atatürk dam: the fifth largest in the world

To guarantee its economic development, Turkey has decided to create a larger independent energy supply by building up a powerful hydroelectric infrastructure.

Accordingly, construction of the Atatürk Dam has begun on the high plateau of Anatolia. When completed, the dam will be the fifth largest in the world in terms of infrastructure work, civil engineering and water capacity.

The plant should begin operating in 1992, when the eight turbines will begin generating a total of 2400 MW. The earthwork will require moving more than 3001 million cu ft/85 million cu m of ground and the retention capacity itself will be 1,711,718 cu ft/48,470 million cu m. The project is located on the Euphrates, not far from the town of Urfa and should irrigate the 3861 sq mi/10,000 sq km of the vast lower Euphrates region, comprising the plains of Urfa, Siverek-Hilvan and Mardin. The ultimate goal of the Turkish government is to make this region the breadbasket of the Middle East.

The splendid necropolis and sanctuary of Nemrut Daği, constructed by a little known Commage-nean ruler in 30 BC.

Access

By bus: Regular service from Diyarbakir and Urfa.
By car: The roads are in good condition from Diyarbakir and Urfa (E24).

Accommodation

▲ **Bayraktar,** Cumhuriyet Meydani, ☎ 1338. 40 rooms. Located on the main street, with a terrace restaurant.

Shopping

Mardin specializes in woven goods and jewelry.

Tourist Information Office, Halk Kutuphanesi, ☎ 1664.

___ URFA* (Şanliurfa)

Telephone code: 8711.

121 mi/195 km west of Mardin, 117 mi/189 km south-west of Diyarbakir, 90 mi/145 km east of Gaziantep and 224 mi/360 km east of Adana.

Urfa's origins go back to the second millennium BC when it was the capital of a Hurrite state that extended through northern Mesopotamia, Syria and Asia

Minor. It was known variously as Orhoe, Orhai and Osrhoene. In the fourth century BC, after Alexander's kingdom had been divided, the region fell to the Seleucids who renamed the town Edessa, making it the seat of their province. As an important centre on the route through the 'Fertile Crescent' between the Mediterranean shores and Upper Mesopotamia, Edessa was often the cause of confrontations between rival armies, and consequently frequently changed masters, falling into the hands of the Byzantines, Persians, Arabs, Seljuk Turks and Crusaders. The town, now called Urfa, finally became part of the Ottoman Empire in 1637 under Murad IV.

Unfortunately little of its rich past remains to visit, but you can certainly spend a day and a half here on your way south to Sumatar and Harran or north to Nemrut Daği.

What to see

The remains of a Crusader **citadel*** can be seen to the south of the town. In addition to a few wall sections and towers there are some ruins from antiquity; the most striking are two columns that are said to have belonged to King Nimrod's winter palace. One of them bears a Syriac inscription.

The ancient **Spring of Rohas,** also known as **Callirhoe Fountain,** flows up from the foot of the citadel. According to legend, Abraham stopped here on his long migration from Ur to Canaan. Religious buildings, mainly theological schools and mosques, stand along the edge of the pool.

At the **Archaeological Museum** you can see collections of Hittite reliefs, neo-Hittite and Assyrian artifacts from excavations in Sultantepe and an ethnographic section.

Environs of Urfa

Eski Sumatar* is about 17 mi/28 km south of Urfa off the Akçakale road. Head first for Sumatar where you should ask directions to the sanctuary, an impressive pagan centre dating from the second century AD. The Sabaeans, a pagan people, worshipped moon and sun gods and five other celestial bodies. Despite the spread of Christianity and the advent of Islam, their cult continued to thrive. You can see the remains of seven **edifices** arranged in an arc to the north and west of a sacred mound. The ruins of **temples** dedicated to different planets spread over an area of about 1 sq mi/2-3 sq km. It's a good idea to use a local guide because the ruins are not all easy to find.

Harran, 29 mi/47 km south of Urfa, is not far from the Syrian border. According to inscriptions, the town has existed since 2000 BC, and by 1400 BC was already an important centre. This is partly due to its strategic position on the road to Ninevah and Carchemish across the Euphrates, and partly to its religious importance as the largest sanctuary to the moon god, Sin, one of the deities worshipped by Assyrians and Babylonians.

Harran is also mentioned in Genesis as the place where Abraham and his family sojourned for several years before moving on to the land of Canaan. Interestingly too, the town is none other than Carrhae, as the Romans called it, the scene of two important historical events. First, the Roman army led by Crassus was defeated here in 53 BC by Parthians, a Persian people from south of the Caspian Sea. Second, Caracalla is said to have been assassinated here as he passed through the city gates after having made a sacrifice to the moon-god in AD 217.

Harran was destroyed by the Mongols in the 13th century. Today it is a strange little village beside a fortress where the inhabitants live a semi-nomadic life like their Syrian neighbours in clay houses shaped like beehives or ant hills. Within the **citadel** walls you can see three polygonal towers.

The **Great Mosque** (Ulu Cami) was probably built on the site of the pagan temple in the eighth century by Marwan II, enlarged a century later, and then restored by Saladin toward the end of the 12th century. There's a tall square minaret in the courtyard and some of the broken columns are made of pink marble from the Tek Tek Mountains.

Access

By bus: Regular service from Diyarbakir, Gaziantep and Mardin.
By car: All the roads in the region are currently being improved.

Accommodation

▲▲▲ **Harran,** Atatürk Bulv., ☎ 2860. 54 rooms. Air-conditioned rooms and a terrace restaurant.

▲▲ **Turban Urfa,** Köprübasi Cad., 74, ☎ 3520. 55 rooms. Restaurant, bar and some air-conditioned rooms.

Useful address

Tourist Information Office, Vilayet Arkasi, Topçu Meydani, ☎ 1165.

▬▬ *NEMRUT DAĞI****

Telephone code: (Adiyaman) 8781.
22 mi/35 km north of Kâhta, 53 mi/86 km north-east of Adiyaman and 99 mi/160 km north of Urfa.

When Alexander's empire was divided up, the Seleucids created the province of Commagene in the Anti-Taurus Mountains between the Cilicia and Euphrates rivers. A governor declared it an independent state, and Mithridates Callinicus I formed a dynasty at the beginning of the first century BC. His son, Antiochos I, became king of Commagene in 62 BC and developed his domain as a strategic crossroads for traffic from Syria and

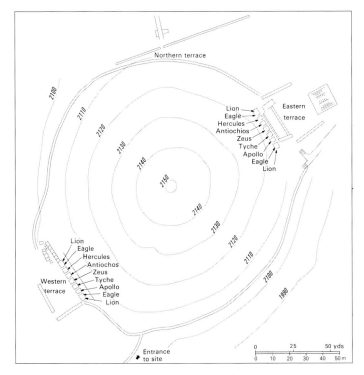

NEMRUT DAĞI

Mesopotamia, between the Romans to the west and the Parthians to the east.

In the year 30 BC Antiochos decided to build a sanctuary that would ensure his immortality. He had an immense temple and necropolis built, embellishing them with statues of gods. The site he chose on Nemrut Daği at an altitude of more than 6560 ft/2000 m was the nearest peak to the 'celestial throne of Zeus'. Inscriptions on some of the monuments record his family lineage in great detail. His father belonged to a Persian dynasty and his mother, Laodicia, was of royal Seleucid descent. The art and sculptures on Nemrut Daği reflect this Greco-Persian alliance.

What to see

The famous **sanctuary***** on the summit of Nemrut Daği overlooks a desolate steppe. It comprises an enormous conical tumulus of crushed stone piled 164 ft/50 m high in an artificial mound 492 ft/150 m in diameter. Flanking the tumulus are three terraces of giant statues.

The site was first discovered in 1881 but it was not fully explored until 1953. However, attempts to solve the mystery of the pyramid have been unsuccessful. Despite modern archaeological methods no one has yet been able to find the funerary chamber itself, nor the entrance to the corridor leading to it. To this day the tomb of Antiochos I remains untouched.

On the **Western terrace,** five colossal statues stand at the foot of the tumulus guarded on either side by both a lion and an eagle. The seated statues are headless. Strewn on the ground before them lie the heads that were knocked off by lightning or earthquakes. From left to right the figures represent: Apollo; a Commagene lady as Tyche, goddess of Fortune; Zeus; Antiochos; and Hercules. The geneology of King Antiochos is illustrated in bas-reliefs showing Macedonian ancestors on one side and Persian on the other.

The **northern terrace,** a former processional way, is in a state of ruin. The ubiquitous lion and eagle once guarded the entrance.

The **eastern terrace** is very like the western side, although the heads and reliefs are in worse condition. The bodies, however, are well preserved.

Environs of Nemrut Daği

The village of **Eski Kâhta** (about 25 mi/40 km west of Nemrut Daği) is located near the ancient site of Arsameia-on-the-Nymphaios. The funerary sanctuary of Mithridates I of Commagene built by his son Antiochos was discovered here, together with a royal inscription, a relief of Heracles greeting Mithridates, a head of Laodicia and various Commagene gods.

Before reaching Karakuş on the road south from Eski Kâhta you'll come to a small bridge across the Cendere River. According to the inscription, it was built in honour of Septimius Severus and his family. About 7 mi/12 km south of Eski Kâhta, on a hill called Karakuş ('black bird') the **Karakus Tumulus** was discovered where the royal Commagene family buried their womenfolk. Guarding the sanctuary are three Doric columns topped by a lion, an eagle and a bull (first century AD).

When to go

A visit to Nemrut Daği is best between mid-June and mid-September. Most people choose to go there at sunset, leaving Kâhta at about 2pm and coming back at night. If, however, you wish to see the sunrise, you will have to leave at about 3am and be prepared for freezing cold regardless of the weather. Whenever you decide to climb, even in summer, you should come well equipped with warm clothing and good walking shoes.

Access

Take a bus or taxi from Adiyaman to Kâhta village 25 mi/41 km to the east. From Kâhta, taxis or minibuses run the 43 mi/70 km or so up to the site. From the parking area to the sanctuary count on a steep 30-minute walk up a stony path.

Accommodation

▲▲ **Arsemia**, Atatürk Bulv. 146, Adiyaman, ☎ 2112. 15 rooms. Just east of the town, with a restaurant.

▲▲ **Nemrut Tur**, Kâhta, on the highway west of town, ☎ 1863. 28 rooms. Terrace restaurant and swimming pool.

▲ **Kommagene Pansiyon**, PK4, Kâhta, ☎ 1092. 15 rooms. Simple but pleasant converted house.

Useful address

Tourist Information Office, Adiyaman, Atatürk Bulv., 41, ☎ 1008.

GAZIANTEP

Telephone code: 851.

93 mi/150 km west of Urfa, 118 mi/190 km north-east of Antakya, 130 mi/210 km east of Adana and 427 mi/687 km south-east of Ankara.

Gaziantep is a modern town known in Turkey as the pistachio-nut capital. It spreads out over a large plain guarded by two hills; a Seljuk castle stands on top of one of them.

The site was very likely inhabited as early as the fourth millennium BC, but the region took on an important role much later in history during the second and first millennia BC, when the Syro-Hittite principalities were established.

What to see

The **fortress*** was founded in the sixth century by Emperor Justinian and rebuilt in the 11th and 12th centuries under the Seljuks. Its massive enclosure is still reinforced by about ten bastions.

The **Archaeological Museum** *(open Tues-Sun 9am-noon, 1:30-5pm)* is housed in a former Seljuk *medrese*. The displays include Hittite and Neo-Hittite reliefs, stamps and seals from different periods, Roman sculptures and an ethnographic section.

Access

By car: The roads from Adana and Urfa are in good condition.

By train: Service from Adana and Malatya.

Accommodation

▲▲ **Kaleli**, Hürriyet Cad., ☎ 13417. 70 rooms. Comfortable, with a rooftop restaurant.

▲ **Büyük**, Suburcu Cad., 20, ☎ 15222. 38 rooms.

▲ **Türk**, Hürriyet Cad., 27, ☎ 19480. 58 rooms. Modest but comfortable.

There is a wide choice of restaurants on Hürriyet Cad., and Istasyon Cad.

Useful addresses

THY (Turkish Airlines), Atatürk Bulv., 3816, ☎ 15435.

Touring Automobile Club, Ali Fuat Cebesoy Bulv., 5, ☎ 25224.

Tourist Information Office, Atatürk Bulv., 121, ☎ 21858.

Train station, Istasyon Cad., ☎ 20719.

▬ USEFUL VOCABULARY

Turkish is a phonetic language and each letter is almost always pronounced the same way regardless of the word it is found in. Any Anglicization of the pronounciation rules of the language will lead you astray: you'll find yourself swallowing vowels and syllables that should be heard. So pay special attention to giving equal importance to each sound.

There are no articles, genders, or prepositions, but there are suffixes. The main grammatical difficulty lies in the rule for vowel harmony. For the sake of euphony, suffixes vary according to the main vowel of the root noun or verb they follow. For instance, *şeker* (sugar) becomes *şeker-li* (with sugar) whereas *tuz* (salt) becomes *tuz-lu* (with salt).

The Latin alphabet replaced Arabic letters in 1928. There are 29 letters in Turkish, of which k, v and ks are the phonetic equivalent of our q, w and x, while the six extra letters are: ç, ğ, ı, ö, ü and ş.

You should know the pronunciation of the following 12 letters:

c	English 'j' as in jam.
ç	'ch' as in chime or cheese.
e	'eh' as in tell or effort.
g	pronounced hard as in gold or gamble.
ğ	always follows a vowel, serving only to lengthen it in the case of a, ı, o and u but pronounced like a 'y' as in yellow after e, i, o and u.
ı	(an undotted i), is a short 'uh' sound like the end of baker or paper.
j	the French 'j', pronounced 'zh' as in treasure or leisure.
ö	'ur' as in church.
r	rolled.
ş	'sh' as in sheep or shine.
u	'oo' as in soon or clue.
ü	'ew' as in new.

Common words and phrases

Good morning	*Günaydin*
Good day	*Günaydin, Iyi günler*
Good evening	*Iyi akşamlar*
Good night	*Iyi geceler*
Good-bye	*Hoşça kalin*
How are you?	*Nasilsiniz?*
I'm fine, thank you	*Iyim, teşekkür ederim*
Please	*Lütfen*
Thank you	*Teşekkür ederim*
Bon appétit	*Afiyet olsum*
To your health	*Şerefinize*
You're welcome, not at all	*Bir şey değil*
If God so wishes	*Maşallah*
Excuse me	*Affedersiniz*
There is/There isn't any	*Var/Yok*
Yes/No	*Evet/Hayir*
I don't understand	*Anlamiyorum*

Time and days of the week

When?	*Ne zaman?*
Yesterday	*Dün*
Today	*Bugün*
Tomorrow	*Yarin*
Morning	*Sabah*
Afternoon	*Oğleden sonra*
Evening	*Akşam*
Night	*Gece*
One hour	*Bir saat*
One o'clock	*Saat bir*
What time is it?	*Saat kaç?*
At what time?	*Saat kaçta?*

Monday	*Pazartesi*
Tuesday	*Sali*
Wednesday	*Çarşamba*
Thursday	*Perşembe*
Friday	*Cuma*
Saturday	*Cumartesi*
Sunday	*Pazar*

Getting around

Airport	*Havaalani*
Boat	*Vapur*
Bus	*Otobüs*
Bus station	*Otogar*
Car	*Araba*
Entrance	*Giriş*
Exit	*Çikiş*
Harbour/Port	*Liman*
Is it far?	*Uzak mi?*
Luggage	*Bagaj*
Plane	*Uçak*
Reservations	*Rezervasyon*
Return (round-trip)	*Gidiş-dönüş*
Single	*Gidiş*
Taxi	*Taksi*
Ticket	*Bilet*
Tourist office	*Turizm burosu*
Town centre	*Şehir merkezi*
Train	*Tren*
Train station	*Gar; Istasyon*
Where is . . . ?	*nerede . . . ?*

At the hotel

A good hotel	*Iyi bir otel*
A room	*Bir oda*
Two people	*Iki kişi*
A single room/double room	*Bir kişilik oda, iki kişilik oda*
A room with a bathroom	*Canyolu bir oda*
What price is it?	*Fiati nedir?*
Hot water/cold water	*Sicak su/soğuk su*
Bed	*Yatak*
An extra bed	*Have bir yatak*
Key	*Anahtar*
Breakfast	*Kahvalti*
Butter	*Tereyağ*
Coffee	*Kahve*
Tea	*Çay*
Milk	*Süt*
Sugar	*Seker*
Bill (check)	*Hesap*

At the restaurant

Beer	*Bira*
Bill (check)	*Hesap*
Bread	*Ekmek*
To drink	*Içmek*
To eat	*Yemek*
Fork	*Çatal*
Fruit juice	*Meyva suyu*
Glass	*Bardak*
Ice	*Buz*
Knife	*Biçak*
Menu	*Menu, yemek listesi*
Mineral water (carbonated)	*Maden sodasi*

Mineral water (non-carbonated)	*Maden suyu*
Pepper	*Kara biber*
Plate	*Tabak*
Restaurant	*Lokanta, restoran*
Salt	*Tuz*
Spoon	*Kaşik*
Vinegar	*Sirke*
Water	*Su*
Wine/red, white	*Şarap/kirmirzi, beyaz*

For further vocabulary look under the food section on page 24.

Driving

Brakes	*Frenler*
It doesn't work	*Islemiyor*
Oil	*Motor yaği*
Oil change, greasing (lubrication)	*Yağ değistirme*
Petrol (gasoline)	*Benzin*
Petrol station (gas station)	*Benzin istasyonu*
Spark plugs	*Bujiler*
Tyre (tire)	*Lastik*

Post Office

Airmail	*Uçakla*
Engaged (busy)	*Meşgul*
Letter	*Mektup*
Parcel	*Paket*
Stamp	*Pul*
Telegram	*Telgraf*
Telephone	*Telefon*
Where is the Post Office?	*Postane nerede?*

Shopping

Bookshop	*Kitabevi*
Cent	*Kuruş*
Copper	*Bakir*
Gold	*Altin*
How much is this?	*Bu ne kadar?*
Is it old?	*Eski mi?*
It's lovely/very beautiful	*Çok güzel*
It's too expensive	*Çok pahali*
Leather	*Deri*
Newspaper	*Gazette*
Silver	*Gumus*
Turkish pound	*Lira*

Numbers

One	*Bir*
Two	*Iki*
Three	*Üç*
Four	*Dört*
Five	*Beş*
Six	*Alti*
Seven	*Yedi*
Eight	*Sekiz*
Nine	*Dokuz*
Ten	*On*
Eleven	*On bir*
Twelve	*On iki*
Thirteen	*On üç*
Twenty	*Yirmi*
Twenty-two	*Yirmi iki*
Twenty-three	*Yirmi üç*

Thirty	*Otuz*
Forty	*Kirk*
Fifty	*Elli*
Sixty	*Altmiş*
Seventy	*Yetmiş*
Eighty	*Seksen*
Ninety	*Doksan*
One hundred	*Yüz*
Two hundred	*Iki yüz*
Three hundred	*Üç yüz*
One thousand	*Bin*
Two thousand	*Iki bin*
Ten thousand	*On bin*
One million	*Milyon*

Miscellaneous

I'm ill	*Hastayim*
Chemist (pharmacist)	*Eczaci*
Dentist	*Disci*
Doctor	*Doktor*
Hospital	*Hastane*
Avenue, avenue of	*Cadde, caddesi*
Square, square of	*Meydan, meydani*
Street, street of	*Sokak, sokaği*
Beach	*Plaj*
Bosphorus	*Boğaziçi*
Golden Horn	*Halic*
Lake	*Gol*
Sea	*Deniz*

▬ SUGGESTED READING

Art, architecture and culture

Aksit, I. *The Civilisation of Western Anatolia* (Aksit Culture and Tourism Publications, 1986).
Algar, A.E. *Complete Book of Turkish Cooking* (Kegan Paul International, 1988).
Atasoy and Raby. *Pottery of Ottoman Turkey: 'Iznik'* (Thames & Hudson, 1989).
Bernadout, R. *Turkish Rugs: Exhibition Catalogue* (Bernadout, 1975).
Goodwin, G. *Ottoman Turkey – Islamic Architecture* (Scorpion Publications, 1977).
—. *History of Ottoman Architecture* (Thames & Hudson, 1987).
Levey, M. *The World of Ottoman Art* (Thames & Hudson, 1975).
Mango, C. *Byzantine Architecture* (Faber, 1986).
—. *Art of the Byzantine Empire 312-1453* (University of Toronto Press, 1986).
Michaud, R. and Michaud, S. *Turkey* (Thames & Hudson, 1987).
Orga, I. *Portrait of a Turkish Family* (Eland Books, 1988).
Piotrovskii, B. *Urartu, The Kingdom of Van and Its Art* (Evelyn, Adams & Mackay, 1967).
Runciman, S. *Byzantine Style and Civilisation* (Penguin, 1975).

Background and travel guides

Bean, G. *Aegean Turkey* (John Murray, 1989).
—. *Lycian Turkey* (John Murray, 1989).
—. *Turkey Beyond the Maeander* (John Murray, 1989).
—. *Turkey's Southern Shore* (John Murray, 1989).
Boyd-Sumner, H. and Freely, J. *Strolling Through Istanbul* (Kegan Paul International, 1987).
Crawshaw, G. *Turkey the Beautiful* (Comet, 1988).

Erim, K. *Aphrodisias: City of Venus Aphrodite* (Muller, 1985).
Farson, D. *Traveller in Turkey* (Routledge, 1985).
Freely, J. *Western Shores of Turkey* (John Murray, 1988).
Gurney, O. *The Hittites* (Penguin, 1980).
Heikell, R. *Turkish Waters Pilot* (Imray, 1989).
Holmes, P. *Turkey: A Timeless Bridge* (Stork Press, 1988).
James, J. *Saddle Tramp from Ottoman Hills to Offas Dyke* (Pelham Books, 1989).
Sewell, B. *South from Ephesus: Travels in Aegean Turkey* (Century, 1988).
Stark, F. *Ionia: A Quest* (Century, 1988).
— . *Lycian Shore* (Century, 1989).
Tachau, F. *Turkey* (Praeger, 1984).
Taylor, J. *Imperial Istanbul: Iznik, Bursa, Edirne* (Weidenfeld, 1989).

History

Addison, J. et al. *Suleyman and the Ottoman Empire* (Greenhaven, 1980).
Atil, E. *The Age of Sultan Suleiman the Magnificent* (Abrams, 1987).
— . *The Illustrated History of Suleiman the Magnificent* (Abrams, 1986).
Cook, M.A., ed. *The History of the Ottoman Empire to 1730* (Cambridge University Press, 1976).
Itskowitz, N. *Ottoman Empire and Islamic Tradition* (University of Chicago Press, 1980).
Kinross, L. *The Ottoman Centuries* (Morrow Quill, 1977).
Landau, ed. *Ataturk and the Modernization of Turkey* (Westview Press, 1984).
Lloyd, S. *Ancient Turkey: A Traveller's History of Anatolia* (British Museum Publications, 1989).
— . *Early Highland Peoples of Anatolia* (Thames & Hudson, 1967).
Mango, C. *Byzantium and Its Image: History and Culture of the Byzantium Empire and its Heritage* (Variorum Reprints, 1984).
Mellaart, J. *Earliest Civilizations of the Near East* (Thames & Hudson, 1965).
Norwich, J. *Byzantium: The Early Centuries* (Viking, 1988).
Ostrogorsky, G. *History of the Byzantine State* (Simon & Schuster, 1970).
Peters, F.E. *The Harvest of Hellenism* (Simon & Schuster, 1970).
Runciman, S. *History of the Crusades* (Cambridge University Press, 1951-54).
Shaw, S.J., ed. *History of the Ottoman Empire and Modern Turkey*. Two volumes: Vol I *Empire of the Gazis: The Rise and Decline of the Ottoman Empire, 1280-1808* (Cambridge University Press, 1977); Vol II *Reform, Revolution and Republic: The Rise of Modern Turkey 1808-1975* (Cambridge University Press, 1977).
Stanford, W.B. and Finopoulos, E.J., eds. *Travels of Lord Charlemont in Greece and Turkey, 1749* (Trigraph, 1984).
Watson, C. *Crusading Through Turkey* (K.A.F. Brewin, 1986).

Literature

Kemal, Y. *The Birds Have Also Gone* (Collins, 1987).
— . *Iron Earth, Copper Sky* (Collins, 1989).
— . *Lords of Akchasaz: Murder in the Ironsmith's Market* (Collins, 1979).
— . *The Undying Grass* (Collins, 1989).
— . *The Wind from the Plain* (Collins, 1989).
Vidal, G. *Julian* (Signet, 1962).

Museums

Davis, F. *The Palace of Topkapi* (Scribners, 1970).
Rogers, J.M., ed. *Topkapi Palace Museum*. Three volumes: Vol I *Albums and Illustrated Manuscripts* (Thames & Hudson, 1986); Vol II *Costumes, Embroideries and Other Textiles* (Thames & Hudson, 1986); Vol III *The Treasury* (Thames & Hudson, 1987).

GLOSSARY

Achmeonidae: Persian dynasty that occupied Turkey from the sixth century BC until the arrival of Alexander the Great in 333 BC.

Acropolis: Upper part of a Greek city comprising a citadel and temples.

Aesculapius: God of medicine, son of Apollo.

Ağa: Former titles for heads of the sultan's militia or of the Ottoman Army. Today it is used for village notables or landowners.

Anastasis: A Greek word inscribed on paintings and sculptures signifying the Resurrection of Christ.

Apodyterium: Dressing room in Roman baths.

Artemis (Diane): Goddess of hunting and fertility, daughter of Zeus and Leto.

Athena: Goddess of wisdom, skills and warfare, daughter of Zeus.

Basileus: Title of the Byzantine sovereign from the seventh century onward ('king' in Greek).

Bayram: Used since the formation of the Turkish Republic to denote both religious and national festivals.

Bedesten: Originally a covered market, today a trading centre.

Bey: A lord, squire.

Bouleterion: Greek council chamber or senate.

Caldarium: Hot rooms in Roman baths.

Cami or Camii: Mosque.

Capital: The part of a column crowning the shaft.

Caravanserai (Turkish: *kervansaray*): An inn and commercial building for merchants and travelers, usually surrounding a large courtyard.

Cavea: Auditorium of tiered seats in a Greek theatre.

Corinthinian: Order of Greek architecture characterized by acanthus-leaf decoration on the capitals.

Cumhuriyet: Republic.

Cuneiform: Ancient lettering used in Asia Minor and Mesopotamia formed with wedge-shaped stamps and studs.

Demeter (Ceres): Goddess of the earth and fertility.

Dervish: Religious follower of a Muslim brotherhood that holds mystical séances, during which the participants communicate with God.

Divan: A collection of Ottoman poems and literature; also used as a term for Ottoman administration and government.

Firman: Edict or decree ordered by the sultan of Constantinople.

Frigidarium: Cold room in Roman baths.

Hadith: Recital and transmission of the words and deeds of the Prophet.

Han (or *hani*): See caravanserai.

Harem: Private apartments (more often, the name given to buildings reserved for women).

Hegira: The forced flight of Mohammed from Mecca to Medina in AD 622. This is year 1 in the Muslim calendar.

Hestia (Vesta): Daughter of Cronos and Rhea, goddess of the hearth, protectress of house and home.

Imam: In general, one who guides a believer to God. More specifically, the prayer leader in a mosque.

Imaret: A series of buildings surrounding certain mosques, usually serving as a refuge for the poor.

Iwan: A typical Muslim style of architecture (both civil and religious) comprising a four-sided area closed on three sides, with the fourth opening onto a courtyard or another room at a slightly lower level.

Janissaries (Turkish: *yeni çeri*): Originally the elite corps of Ottoman infantry appointed by Sultan Orhan Gazi (1324-59). They became the palace soldier guard in later years. The corps was abolished in 1826.

Kalfa: A woman companion in a *seraglio*, or harem, or a woman servant who has served for many years in a household.

Konak: House belonging to a dignitary or notable.

Köşkü: Kiosk, princely summer house or pavilion.

Kouros: Ancient statue of a young male nude.

Kufic script: Arabic writing originating in Kufa, Iraq.

Külliye: A group of buildings that may include a *medrese* or *imaret*.

Leto: Mother of Artemis and Apollo.

Medrese: Religious Muslim establishment of higher education.

Medusa: One of the three Gorgons (with Euryale and Stheno), a monster with serpent hair.

Megaron: Main room of a Mycenaean palace.

Mescrit: Small mosque.

Mihrab: Prayer niche in a mosque indicating the direction of Mecca.

Mimber: Pulpit in a mosque. Most are made of wood, sometimes inlaid with ivory or mother-of-pearl.

Minaret: Tower slightly to the side of a mosque from which the *meuzzin* chants the call to prayer.

Naïskos: Chapel or small temple.

Narghile: Pipe with a long tube attached to a vase of perfumed water through which smoke is drawn before being inhaled.

Narthex: Vestibule preceding the nave in Roman and Byzantine churches.

Nymphaeum: Monumental fountain erected in honour of the Nymphs.

Odeon or **Odeum:** Small theatre or concert hall, often covered.

Ottomans: Turkish dynasty founded by Osman at the end of the 13th century that lasted until the founding of the Turkish Republic in 1923.

Panagia: 'The all holy' – a name commonly attributed to the Virgin Mary.

Pantocrator: An epithet given to Christ meaning 'master of all things'.

Paracclesion: Chapel adjoining a church.

Paşa (pasha): Title for a provincial governor or high-ranking army official.

Propylaeum or **propylon:** Monumental entrance comprising a columned porch and one or more gateways.

Prytaneum or **prytaneion:** Municipal building similar to a town hall.

Saray: Palace.

Satrap: Governor of a satrapy (province) during the Achmeonidae era.

Seleucids: The Hellenic dynasty of Seleucia that ruled from the fourth to the second century BC, when the Romans conquered Asia Minor (189 BC).

Seljuks: Victorious Turkish tribe that settled in Asia Minor in the 11th century and was ousted by the Ottomans at the end of the 13th century.

Shaft: Part of a column between the base and the pedestal.

Stoa: Greek portico.

Sublime Porte: Originally the entrance to the tent or palace, where audiences were given or political meetings held. The term later stood for the palace, the court, the government, and finally, the Ottoman Empire.

Tekke: Dervish monastery.

Temenos: Inner sanctuary of a temple.

Tepidarium: Warm room between the frigidarium and caldarium in Roman baths.

Tethys: Legendary mother of Rivers, daughter of Uranus and Gaia.

Theotokos: An epithet given to the Virgin Mary meaning 'mother of God'.

Türbe: Islamic funerary monument.

Tyche: Goddess of fortune.

■■■ *INDEX*